THE SPEAR OF DESTINY

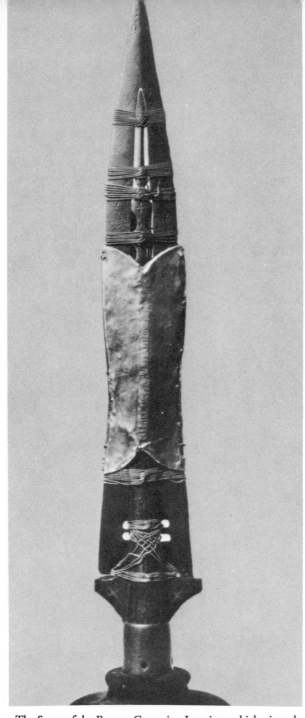

The Spear of the Roman Centurion Longinus which pierced
the side of Christ.

TREVOR RAVENSCROFT

The Spear
of Destiny

THE OCCULT POWER BEHIND
THE SPEAR WHICH PIERCED
THE SIDE OF CHRIST

WEISERBOOKS

Boston, MA/York Beach, ME

First American paperback edition 1982 by
Red Wheel/Weiser, LLC
York Beach, ME
With offices at:
368 Congress Street
Boston, MA 02210
www.redwheelweiser.com

First published in Great Britain, 1973
First American edition, 1973

Library of Congress Catalog Card Number: 82-60165
ISBN 0-87728-547-0

Printed in Canada
TCP

08 07 06 05 04 03
18 17 16 15 14 13

"If the women would not take it for flattery, I would add further unknown words to this story for you, I would continue the adventure for you. But if anyone requests me to do so, let him not consider it a book. I do not know a single letter of the alphabet. Plenty of people get their material that way, but this adventure steers without books. Rather than have anybody think it is a book, I would sit naked without a towel, the way I sit in the bath—if I did not forget the fig leaf."

Parsival: Wolfram von Eschenbach.

CONTENTS

vii

Part III

THE BLOOD AND THE ASHES

Illustrations will be found following page 170.

THE MOULD OF A LEGEND

"But one of the soldiers with a spear pierced his side, and forth-with came there out blood and water.

"And he that saw it bare record, and his record is true: and he knoweth that he saith true, that ye might believe.

"For these things were done that the scripture should be ful-filled, 'a bone of Him shall not be broken'.

"And again another scripture saith, 'They shall look on Him whom they have pierced'."

Saint John 19, 34–37

In the final chapters of the Gospel of Saint John it is told how a soldier pierced the side of Christ with a Spear. The name of this soldier was Gaius Cassius and he attended the crucifixion as the official Roman representative for the Pro-Consul, Pontius Pilate. Cataracts in both eyes prevented this veteran officer from battle service with his Legion and instead he reported on the religious and political scene in Jerusalem.

For two years Gaius Cassius had followed the activities of a certain Jesus of Nazareth who claimed to be the Messiah and looked like undermining the authority of the Roman occupa-tion of Israel.

The Roman centurion watched the Legionaries carry out the execution of Jesus Christ and like them, too, he was impressed by the courage, dignity and bearing of the Nazarene on the Cross.

Isaiah had prophesied of the Messiah, "A bone of Him shall

not be broken." Annas, the aged advisor to the Sanhedrin, and Caiaphas, the High Priest, were intent on mutilating the body of Christ to prove to the masses of the people that Jesus was not the Messiah, but merely a heretic and potential usurper of their own power.

The hours were passing and this presented the excuse they needed. For Annas was an authority on the Law, and the Jewish Law decreed that no man should be executed on the Sabbath Day. Straightway, they petitioned Pontius Pilate for the authority to break the limbs of the crucified men so that they should die before dusk on that Friday afternoon (5th April, 33 A.D.).

A party from the Temple Guard was sent out for this purpose to the mount on Golgotha, which means the Place of the Skull. At their head, the Captain carried the Spear of Herod Antipas, King of the Jews, which was the symbol of the authority to perform the act; or else the Roman soldiers would not have permitted him to lift a finger to the men when he reached the place of execution.

Phineas, the ancient Prophet, had caused this Spear to be forged to symbolise the magical powers inherent in the blood of God's Chosen People. Already old as a talisman of power, it had been raised in the hand of Joshua when he signalled his soldiers to shout the great shout which crumbled the walls of Jericho. The very same Spear was hurled at the young David by King Saul in a fit of jealousy.

Herod The Great had held this insignia of power over life and death when he ordered the massacre of the innocent babes throughout Judea in his attempt to slay the Christ child who would grow up to be called the "King of the Jews". Now the Spear was carried on behalf of the son of Herod The Great, as a symbol of authority to break the bones of Jesus Christ.

When the party from the Temple Guard arrived at the scene of crucifixion the Roman soldiers turned their backs in disgust. Only Gaius Cassius remained to witness how these vassals of the High Priests clubbed and crushed the skulls and limbs of Gestas and Dismas nailed to Crosses on either side of Jesus Christ. The Roman centurion was so repelled by the sight of the dreadful mutilation of the bodies of the two thieves and so touched by Christ's humble and fearless submission to the cruel nailing that he decided to protect the body of the Nazarene.

Charging his horse towards the high central Cross, the Roman centurion thrust a Spear into the right side of Jesus Christ, piercing the chest between the fourth and fifth ribs. Such a manner of piercing was the custom of Roman soldiers on the field of battle when they sought to prove that a wounded enemy was dead; for the blood no longer flows from a lifeless body. Yet "forthwith came there out blood and water", and, in this moment of the miraculous flowing of the redemptive blood of the Saviour, the failing sight of Gaius Cassius was completely restored.

It is not known whether this veteran officer grasped the talisman of power from the hands of the Israelite Captain to perform this deed, or whether he carried out this spontaneous act of mercy with his own Spear. There is no historical proof to indicate with which weapon it was that he unwittingly fulfilled the prophecy of Ezekiel: "They shall look upon Him whom they have pierced."

In the Temple where Caiaphas and Annas awaited news of the mutilation of the body of the Messiah, the Veil of the Holy of Holies was rent from top to bottom to expose the Black Cube of the Old Covenant which now split along its edges to open out into the form of the Cross. The imageless cult of Jehovah was ended; the religion of the "Open Heavens" had begun.

The Spear, like a catalyst of revelation, furnished the living proof of the resurrection for the physical wound from its tapering point was mysteriously sealed upon the risen Christ when he appeared to the spiritual vision of his gathered Apostles. Only the doubting Thomas, trusting solely to the outer appearances of physical sight, failed to perceive the God-Man who passed through closed doors to appear to him.

"Then saith He to Thomas, 'Reach higher thy finger, and behold my hands; and reach hither thy hand, and thrust it into my side: and be not faithless but believing.' "

Because the earthly wounds from the Spear and the nailing

appeared upon the Phantom Body of the risen Christ, the first Christians believed that had his bones been shattered on the Cross, the Resurrection as we know it could never have been accomplished; for this was the meaning they attributed to the mysterious words of Isaiah: "A bone of Him shall not be broken."

Gaius Cassius, who had performed a martial deed out of the compassionate motive to protect the body of Jesus Christ, became known as Longinus The Spearman. A convert to Christianity, he came to be revered as a great hero and saint by the first Christian community in Jerusalem, and a prime witness of the shedding of the Blood of the New Covenant for which the Spear became the symbol.

It was said that for a moment in Time he had held the destiny of the whole of mankind in his hands. The Spear with which he had pierced the side of Christ became one of the great treasures of Christendom and a unique legend attached itself to this weapon in which one of the nails from the Cross was later placed.

The legend grew around it, gaining strength with the passing of the centuries, that whoever possessed it and understood the powers it served, held the destiny of the world in his hands for good or evil.

This legend, which has persisted throughout two millennia of Christendom, has seen its most dreadful fulfilment in the twentieth century.

INTRODUCTION

IN THE BEGINNING
WAS THE MEMORY

The man who would have written this book but for his untimely death was a certain Dr. Walter Johannes Stein, a
Vienna-born scientist and Doctor of Philosophy, who acted
during World War II as confidential adviser to Sir Winston
Churchill regarding the minds and motivation of Adolf Hitler
and the leading members of the Nazi Party.

Very considerable pressure was brought to bear to dissuade
Dr. Stein from revealing what is now presented as the content
of this book, but in the final issue he was not influenced in any
way by such external persuasion, not even in this instance by
Sir Winston Churchill himself who was insistent that the
occultism of the Nazi Party should not under any circumstances be revealed to the general public.

The failure of the Nuremberg Trials to identify the nature of
the evil at work behind the outer façade of National Socialism
convinced him that another three decades must pass before a
large enough readership would be present to comprehend the
initiation rites and black magic practices of the inner core of
the Nazi leadership.

He sadly witnessed the extent to which the Allied Prosecutors
at these trials for crimes against humanity lacked the moral
imagination to perceive the apocalyptic countenance of the
civilisation that had arisen in Germany between the two world
wars—a civilisation based upon a magical *Weltanschauung* which

xiii

had substituted the Swastika for the Cross. He understood why a unanimous agreement had been made among the Judges to treat the accused as though they were an integral part of the accepted Humanist and Cartesian system of the Western world. To have admitted even for an instant what their defeated enemies were really like, to have lifted the veil to reveal the real motives for such an astonishing reversal of values, might have opened millions of people to the risk of a terrible corruption.

It was apparent to Dr. Stein that a decision had been made on the highest political level to explain the most atrocious crimes in the history of mankind as the result of mental aberration and the systematic perversion of instincts. It was thought expedient to speak in dry psycho-analytical terms when considering the motives for incarcerating millions of human beings in Gas Ovens rather than to reveal that such practices were an integral part of a dedicated service to evil powers.

The publication of Aldous Huxley's *The Doors of Perception* heralded the kind of change in public opinion which Dr. Stein had long anticipated, for it attacked the prevailing scepticism regarding the validity of occultism and the existence of higher levels of consciousness and further dimensions of time within reach of the human mind. Huxley's brilliant commentary on his own experience of transcendent consciousness under Mescalin illuminated the anatomy of inner space and projected the idea that man himself is a bridge between two worlds, the earthly and the supersensible. It also publicised the then little known fact that the brain, nervous system and sense organs function as a protective barrier against what would otherwise be an overwhelming intrusion of the 'Total Mind', acting like a reducing valve to ration out that 'measly trickle of the kind of consciousness which will help us to stay alive on the surface of this particular planet."

Although he did not live to see the emergence of the "Psychedelic Age", Dr. Stein predicted that an indiscriminate use of mind-expanding drugs would sweep across the U.S.A. and Europe, providing millions of young people with a perilous and illicit path to revelation for which the vast majority would be totally unprepared. He believed that such a craving to experience transcendent awareness through the media of drugs would be the inevitable reaction to the petrified religious dogmatism and materialistic complacency of the established order in the West, which even the cataclysmic events of the Hitler war had failed to shift.

He intended to launch the content of *The Spear* into the contemporary scene in which a vast public are convinced that their customary condition of reduced awareness is not the only awareness. In the summer of 1957, three days after he had made the decision to start work upon the book, he collapsed in the study of his London home and died in hospital soon afterwards.

I first met Dr. Stein after discovering a book he had written called *Das Neunte Jahrhundert*, which is, in my opinion, the definitive work, on the historical background to the Grail Romances of the medieval age. In this work, he had demonstrated how the legendary quest for the Holy Grail veiled a unique Western path to transcendent consciousness. I was fascinated to discover how he had identified many of the supposedly legendary characters in these Grail Romances as real living historical personalities of the period. It was clear to me that the book had not been written out of the customary form of historical speculation or only through reference to extant medieval chronicles. I came very quickly to the conclusion that the wealth of historical material had been gathered through some quite new technique of historical research involving the use of occult faculties and the practice of mind expansion. I was determined to investigate further and paid a visit without prior arrangement to his Kensington home.

I can remember vividly sitting in the lounge of his rambling house wondering what sort of man the author of this remarkable tome on the Grail would turn out to be. The room, in which I sat waiting for him to conclude an interview in his consulting rooms upstairs, seemed more like a museum storehouse than a living room. It was bursting at the seams as though it could not comfortably contain all the books and paintings which filled it. I guessed that the place had been originally occupied as a makeshift wartime home into which had been crammed paintings, books, art treasures and antiques which had once seen a richer setting.

Bookshelves were tortuously arranged to allow hanging space for paintings of every size and description from modern impressionists to medieval and Byzantine works. There were books everywhere, even the landings of the five-storey house and the ornate downstairs "loo" were cluttered with piles of books reaching to the ceilings.

A huge print of Michaelangelo's "Creation of Adam" occupied a whole side wall above bookcases which contained the most comprehensive private collection of esoteric books I have ever seen. In the place of honour above the fireplace was an enlarged print of Rembrandt's "Red Knight of the Grail" carrying the Holy Lance. On the mantelshelf a beautiful gold Ikon was surrounded by clusters of crystals and quartz, and these items elbowed for space among numerous photographs of famous British and European political figures.

A man who looked to be in his mid-fifties came into the room and introduced himself. Dressed formally in City attire, there was no immediate indication that he was not an Englishman, except for the gold-rimmed spectacles hanging by a ribbon from his lapel in a way reminiscent of German professors. Pale blue eyes, very perceptive and aware, looked out from a furrowed brow as he gave me a warm welcome with just a touch of old-world charm in the manner of the handshake.

Behind the cheerful introductory words I sensed a certain directness which encouraged me to state the nature of my business and my reasons for visiting him without prior warning or introduction. He spoke with a soft Austrian accent not without charm, and though his vocabulary was impressive, his pronunciation of certain tongue-twisting English words was almost comical.

I explained that the reason for my visit concerned his book

on the historical background of the Grail in the Ninth Century which I had recently completed reading. I told him that I had come to the conclusion, for reasons which I was prepared to develop if need be, that his book had been written with the aid of some form of transcendent faculty similar to that which had inspired Wolfram von Eschenbach himself to write his famous Grail Romance, *Parsival*.

I quoted to him the verse which has now been reproduced on the title page of *The Spear*:

"I would add further unknown words to this story for you, I would continue this adventure for you. But if anyone requests me to do so, let him not consider it a book. I do not know a single letter of the alphabet. Plenty of people get their material that way, but this adventure steers without books. Rather than have anybody think it a book, I would sit naked without a towel, the way I sit in the bath—if I didn't forget the 'bouquet of twigs'."

I summarised shortly my own interpretation of these lines, pointing out that the 'bouquet of twigs', often translated as 'fig leaf', was the symbol of the Occult Initiate. Unlike his fellow Minnesingers in the thirteenth century, I said, Wolfram von Eschenbach was making it quite clear that he had not gathered his material off his contemporaries, from traditional folklore or through reading the extant Chronicles. And it was for this reason he stressed that he did not know a single letter of the alphabet for he wished to communicate that his so-called Grail romance was no ordinary book but an 'Initiation Document' of the highest order.

There were many indications cunningly placed in his tale, I told my now attentive listener, which revealed the real source of his inspiration. For instance, this most superlative of all the Troubadours mentioned how his own teacher had searched through all the Chronicles in the thirteenth century "to see where there had ever been a people dedicated to purity and worthy of caring for the Grail. He read the Chronicles of the lands in Britain, in France and in Ireland, and in Anschau he found the tale."

I thanked Dr. Stein for pointing out in his own book, *The Ninth Century*, that Anschau, often erroneously stated as Anjou, was not a physical place at all but a state of transcendent consciousness. What Wolfram von Eschenbach was indicating by his reference to the Chronicle of Anschau was that the past events of history were recoverable by means of higher faculties. He was describing how his teacher in the thirteenth century was able to perceive directly the events which took place in the ninth century, a feat he achieved with clairvoyant vision which breached the time sequence of the historical process. In short, the Chronicle of Anschau was a form of Cosmic Chronicle in which past, present and future were united in a higher dimension of time. And in order to read in this eternal chronicle— says Wolfram von Eschenbach—his teacher "had first to learn his abc's without the art of black Magic." In other words, he had to develop the requisite faculties without resorting to the black arts.

I told Dr. Stein that I had come to the conclusion that his astonishingly well informed work on the historical background to the Grail in the Ninth Century had been accomplished with similar faculties and that only later had he sought confirmation of his findings through personal historical research and from extant texts.

He showed no visible reaction to this outspoken and somewhat audacious statement from a complete stranger but simply waited without saying a word as though he expected me to continue. I began to feel the intensity of his gaze which seemed to take in so many unspoken things. To break the painful silence which followed, I started to describe in some detail my own experience of higher levels of consciousness whilst in a Nazi Concentration Camp during the war, and how the nature of this transcendent experience had guided me to a study of the Grail and to research into the history of the Spear of Longinus and the legend of world destiny which had grown around it.

Turning the pages of a copy of his book which I had brought along with me, I opened it at an illustration of the 'Heilige Lance' in the Hapsburg Treasure House which was reputed to be the Spear which a Roman Centurion thrust into the side of Jesus Christ at the Crucifixion. I recounted my visit to the Hofburg in Vienna to see this Spear some six weeks previously, expressing the opinion that the legend associated with this talisman had been inspired by its singular effect as a catalyst of revelation into those very secrets of *Time* out of which he had written his book.

Dr. Stein was now beaming with obvious amusement and delight. "You must stay for lunch," he said, "so that we can continue this discussion." It was the beginning of a friendship which was to last ten years while, under his expert guidance, I learned 'the abc's of the Grail without the art of black magic' in the house which was to become a second home for me.

I kept in close contact with Dr. Stein until he died in 1957, often staying weeks at a time in his Kensington home, yet it was some years before I began to get a comprehensive picture of his extraordinary life.

Disinclined to talk about himself, he was not the sort of person who could be pressed into answering direct questions. During this period I felt like somebody piecing together an intricate jigsaw puzzle without having the slightest idea of the picture which would finally emerge. Some of the pieces did not appear to belong to the life of the same man.

He was born in Vienna in 1891, the second son of a wealthy and influential Austrian barrister who specialised in International Law. Although he graduated in Science at Vienna (Technical) University, he wrote his doctorial dissertation in Philosophy. This work, later published in book form in Germany, related nine higher levels of consciousness to the physical organs and the biochemistry of the body, anticipating the researches of the newly founded Institute of Psycho-Physical Research in Oxford by half a century.

His chief interest for a period concerned the history of art in relation to the evolution of human consciousness. His researches in this sphere led to an active participation in archeology and to the interpretation of the art and architecture of the Ancient World. On an extensive lecture in Asia Minor, he was a guest at the Palace of Kemal Ataturk, Dictator of Turkey, and persuaded the 'Grey Wolf' to restore the Byzantine frescoes in all the former Christian Cathedrals and Churches which had been turned into Mosques after the Islamic conquest of Constantinople a thousand years earlier.

Dr. Stein established his academic reputation in Germany for his extensive work on Medieval History, yet he came to Britain in the capacity of an economist, accompanying King Leopold of the Belgians on his State visit to London in 1936. In this capacity he helped to frame the famous speech delivered by the Belgian King at the Guildhall which first envisaged a European Common Market.

Though he was decorated for gallantry as an officer in the Austrian Army fighting on the Russian front in World War I, he was a British Intelligence agent in World War II, bringing back from the continent the plans for the Nazi invasion of Britain, "Operation Sea Lion".

These separate pieces of the jigsaw simply cropped up unexpectedly in the course of conversation. For example, I was telling him one day about the attempted assassination of General Rommel in North Africa, and mentioned that I had served in the Commandos with Lt.-Colonel Geoffrey Keyes, V.C., who led the raid. I was surprised to learn that Dr. Stein was a personal friend of Geoffrey's father, Admiral Sir Roger Keyes, V.C., who directed Combined Operations in the early part of the war. In this manner I discovered that Sir Winston Churchill had ordered Admiral Keyes to accompany Dr. Stein on a secret wartime visit to Brussels to persuade the Belgian King to open his country to the Allied Armies in order to prevent the outflanking of the French Maginot Line in the event of a German breach of Belgian neutrality.

There was one single thread throughout his life which gave a central meaning to all his diverse activities—a deep and earnest pursuit of Occultism. He became interested in the mystery of the Holy Grail and the Spear of Longinus while still a student at Vienna University. And it was as a direct result of these researches that he came to know Adolf Hitler, at that time a drop-out living in a Vienna dosshouse. For during the four years prior to the outbreak of World War I Hitler had also discovered the legend of world-historic destiny associated with the Spear in the Hapsburg Treasure House, and was even then in his early twenties dreaming of the day he would claim it as a talisman of world conquest.

Very little has hitherto been published about this period in Adolf Hitler's life, the only other reliable witness being a certain August Kubizek with whom the future Führer shared lodgings for a period in 1909 before quitting without even bothering to say goodbye. Kubizek, a former schoolmate of Hitler's in Linz, graduating with distinction at the Vienna Academy of Music, searched for him in Vienna during the following four years but without success.

All of Hitler's biographers have assumed that the years from 1909 to 1913 were the most negative and inconsequential in his life, years in which he was only concerned in eking out a threadbare existence in a flophouse and selling water-colours on street corners. Yet Adolf Hitler himself claimed later in his autobiography, *Mein Kampf*, that these were the most vital formative years of his life in which he learned all that he needed to know to assume the leadership of the Nazi Party.

Dr. Stein was able to confirm that in this particular statement in *Mein Kampf* Adolf Hitler was telling the whole truth, for he himself witnessed at this time how Hitler attained higher levels of consciousness by means of drugs and made a penetrating study of medieval occultism and ritual magic, discussing with him the whole span of the political, historical and philosophical reading through which he formulated what was later to become the Nazi *Weltanschauung*.

Dr. Stein's connection with Adolf Hitler did not end in Vienna. He watched at close quarters the founding of the Nazi Party and Adolf Hitler's association with the three sinister personalities who groomed him for his meteoric rise to power—

Dietrich Eckart, Houston Stewart Chamberlain and Professor Karl Haushofer.

When Reichsführer SS Heinrich Himmler ordered Dr. Stein's arrest in Stuttgart in 1933 in order to press him into service with the SS Occult Bureau, he escaped from Germany and brought with him to Britain the most authoritative knowledge of the occultism of the Nazi Party. To say more in this short introduction would be to anticipate the content of *The Spear*.

PART ONE

TALISMAN OF POWER AND REVELATION

"Life is a well of joy; but where the rabble drinks too, all wells are poisoned.

"I am fond of all that is clean, but I have no wish to see the grinning snouts and thirst of the unclean. They cast their eye into the well: now their revolting smile shines up out of the well. They have poisoned the holy water with their lustfulness; and when they call their dirty dreams pleasure they poison the language too.

"The flame is vexed when their moist hearts come near to the fire; the spirit itself seethes and smokes where the rabble steps near to the fire. In their hands all fruit grows sweetish and overmellow; their glance makes the fruit tree a prey to the wind and withers its crown.

"And some who turned away from life only turned away from the rabble; they did not want to share well and fruit and flame with the rabble.

"And some who went into the wilderness and suffered thirst with the beasts of prey merely did not want to sit around the cistern with the filthy camel drivers.

"And some who came like annihilators and like a hailstorm to all orchards merely wanted to put a foot into the gaping jaws of the rabble and plug up its throat."

Thus Spake Zarathustra: Friedrich Nietzsche.

CHAPTER ONE

TALISMAN OF POWER

"Adolf Hitler stood in front of me and gripped my hands and held them tight. He had never made such a gesture before. I felt from his grasp how deeply he was moved. His eyes were feverish with excitement. The words did not come smoothly from his mouth as they usually did, but rather erupted, hoarse and raucous. Never before and never again have I heard Adolf Hitler speak as he did in that hour.

"I was struck by something strange which I had never noticed before, even when he talked to me in moments of greatest excitement. It was as if another being spoke out of his body and moved him as much as it did me. It was not all a case of a speaker carried away by his own words. On the contrary; I rather felt as though he himself listened with astonishment and emotion to what burst forth from him with elemental force. . . . like floodwaters breaking their dykes, his words burst from him. He conjured up in grandiose inspiring pictures his own future and that of his people. He was talking of a Mandate which, one day, he would receive from the people to lead them from servitude to the heights of freedom—a special mission which would one day be entrusted to him."

Young Hitler—The Story of our Friendship: August Kubizek.

This scene, which illustrates Adolf Hitler's early vision that a world-historic destiny lay before him, took place in his fifteenth year. After listening with burning enthusiasm to Wagner's *Rienzie*, which tells the story of the meteoric rise and fall of a Roman 'Tribune of the People', Hitler had tramped up to the top of the Freinberg overlooking his home town of Linz.

3

Behind him barely able to keep up, walked his only friend, Gustl Kubizek, the son of a poor upholsterer. And there under the brilliant starlight of the summer's night, he had poured forth the prophetic words which were to be fulfilled with such a staggering concreteness.

Four years later when Adolf Hitler and Gustl Kubizek were sharing a bug-ridden bedsitter in a Vienna suburb, it looked as though Hitler's youthful hopes were to prove no more than a tissue of dreams.

He had failed to gain entry into the Vienna Academy of Fine Arts because his sketches were not up to the required standard, and the School of Architecture had also refused him through lack of qualification. And now, unwilling to take a job, he was eking out a starveling existence on his dead mother's savings, which were almost spent, and on a diminutive Orphan's Pension granted in respect of his father's service in the Customs Department, now shortly to be stopped.

"People who knew him in Vienna that year could not understand the contradiction between his well-mannered appearance, his educated speech and self-assured bearing on the one hand, and the starveling existence that he led on the other, and judged him as haughty and pretentious. He was neither. He just did not fit into a bourgeois order. . . . In the midst of a corrupt City, my friend surrounded himself with a wall of unshakeable principles which enabled him to build an inner freedom in spite of all the temptations around him. . . . He went his way untouched by what went on around him. He remained a man alone and guarded in monkish asceticism the 'Holy Flame of Life'."*

Thrown back on his own devices and, unable to make friends, Hitler became day by day a more solitary and embittered figure. His disappointment had been made yet more acute by Gustl Kubizek's astonishing success at the Music Convervatoire. Yet despite his lack of prospects, he had impelled himself into self-directed studies with a grim determination. Nobody

* *Young Hitler—The Story of our Friendship*: August Kubizek.

4

could rightly accuse him of idleness that year, though many believed his efforts were along misguided lines.

Many hours were spent every day in the Hof Library studying Nordic and Teutonic mythology and folklore, and reading broadly in German history, literature and philosophy. But Hitler's main efforts at this time were still concentrated on architecture and he drew up plans for a number of ambitious building projects that would never have the least chance of materialising:

> "The old Imperial City changed on the drawing board of a 19-year-old youth who lived in a dark insanitary bedroom of the Mariahilf suburbs, into a spacious sunlit exuberant City which contained five, eight, and sixteen roomed houses for working-class families."*

During the long summer vacation when Kubizek was back home in Linz, he began to worry about his friend living all alone in a state of perpetual hunger in the tiny ill-appointed room, and he persuaded his mother to send a number of generously large food parcels:

> "I wondered what he would be doing all alone in the room, and I often thought of him. Perhaps he took advantage of the fact that he now had the room to himself to start, once again, on his building plans. He had not long before decided to rebuild the Vienna Hofburg. Many of the ideas were already formulated and only needed putting on paper. It annoyed him that the old Hofburg and the Court stables were built of brick, not a solid enough material for monumental buildings. So these buildings must come down and be rebuilt in stone in a similar style. Adolf wanted to match the wonderful semi-circle of columns of the new Burg with a corresponding one on the other side, and thus magnificently enclose the Heldenplatz. . . . Across the Ring, two mighty Triumphal Arches should bring the wonderful square and the Hof Museum into one design."†

* ibid.   † ibid.

Gustl Kubizek was to go on wondering what Hitler was doing for a very long time. He did not see his friend again until, twenty-four years later, he had become the undisputed Führer of the Third Reich. For while Kubizek was away on holiday that summer, Adolf Hitler made a most important discovery— a discovery which was to change his whole way of life and set him off on the lonely road to total power.

It was while he was working on his drawings outside the Hofburg Museum that Hitler's spirits reached their lowest ebb. All day he had been shivering with cold and fearing the reappearance of the bronchial catarrh which might once again confine him for a long spell in his miserable lodgings. The sky was overcast and the first cold wind of autumn was driving the rain in his face. His sketchbook had become sodden. It was a moment of painful self-knowledge. He saw with a stabbing clarity that all his grandiose architectural plans, into which he had thrown himself body and soul, were utterly worthless. Who would even look at them? Suddenly he saw himself for what he was—a hopeless failure. He tore up his sketch book in disgust, and walked up the steps to the Schatzkammer where he knew he could find warmth and shelter and the possibility to reassess his hopeless situation.

Adolf Hitler had been inside the Hapsburg Treasure House on many previous occasions and regarded all but a very few of the exhibits as a load of meaningless junk. Not even the official Crown of the Hapsburg Emperors was of German origin. The only Insignia the Hapsburgs could find when they became Emperors to the Austro-Hungarian Empire was the ruby and sapphire Crown of Bohemia, which the family had held since the seventeenth century. Yet the beautiful history-laden Crown of the German Emperors, the central piece of the Reichskleinodien, never found recognition in their eyes as a symbol of the Germanic people within their realm. "How could one remain a faithful subject of the House of Hapsburg whose past and present policy was a betrayal of its German origin."*

<hr>

* *Mein Kampf*: Adolf Hitler.

The very sight of the gaudy regalia in the Treasure House increased his aversion to the whole Hapsburg Dynasty. As a fervent German nationalist, Adolf Hitler could never accept their idea regarding the equality of all races. He felt a great and terrible loathing for the seething rabble of mixed races who swarmed into the Treasure House in the summer months to gawp unthinkingly at the symbols of the decadent and tottering Empire which stretched from the Rhine to the Dniester, from Saxony to Montenegro.*

Adolf Hitler stood in the central gangway barely even aware of the Crowns, Sceptres, and jewelled ornaments all around him, so deeply was he locked in his own thoughts about the hopelessness of his personal situation. He claims that he hardly even noticed an official party moving down the exhibits towards him, a group of foreign politicians on a conducted tour under the guidance of some expert from the Museum Archives.

"These foreigners stopped almost immediately in front of where I was standing, while their guide pointed to an ancient Spearhead. At first I didn't even bother to listen to what this expert had to say about it, merely regarding the presence of the party as an intrusion into the privacy of my own despairing thoughts. And then I heard the words which were to change my whole life: *'There is a legend associated with this Spear that whoever claims it, and solves its secrets, holds the destiny of the world in his hands for good or evil'.*"

Awakened by inherent instincts of tyranny and conquest, Adolf Hitler now listened intently as the academic-looking guide explained that this legend of world-historic destiny had arisen around the Spear which a Roman Centurion had thrust into the side of Jesus Christ at the Crucifixion. There was, he said, only an unproven tradition that this was the particular Spear in question.

Apparently it could only be traced back as far as the German

* "This motley of Czechs, Hungarians, Serbs, Croats and Jews—the promiscuous swarm of foreign peoples which had begun to batten down on that old nursery of German Culture." (*Mein Kampf*: Adolf Hitler.)

7

Emperor, Otto The Great; the Nail, secure within its blade, one of hundreds around the Churches and Museums of Europe, had not been added until the thirteenth century. Some of the German Emperors of the Middle Ages had associated the legend with this very Spear, but nobody had given credence to the legend anyway during the last five hundred years or more, except, of course, Napoleon, who had demanded it after the Battle of Austerlitz, before which it had been secretly smuggled out of Nuremberg and hidden in Vienna to keep it out of his tyrannical hands.

The party moved on while a fascinated Hitler walked a few paces closer to look at this object which apparently had so strange a legend.

The solitary iron Spearhead, black with age, rested on a faded red velvet dais within an opened leather case. A long tapering point was supported by a wide base with metal flanges depicting the wings of a dove. Within a central aperture in the blade a hammer-headed nail was secured by a cuff threaded with metal wire. On the side of the lowest portion of the base golden crosses were embossed.

"I knew with immediacy that this was an important moment in my life," said Adolf Hitler when he later recounted his first sight of the Spear. "And yet I could not divine why an out-wardly Christian symbol should make such an impression upon me. I stood there quietly gazing upon it for several minutes quite oblivious to the scene of the Schatzkammer around me. It seemed to carry some hidden inner meaning which evaded me, a meaning which I felt I inwardly knew yet could not bring to consciousness. The words of Richard Wagner's 'Meistersinger' ran through my mind:

> And still I don't succeed.
> I feel it and yet I cannot understand it.
> I can't retain it, nor forget it,
> And if I grasp it, I cannot measure it.

"It was a verse I had formerly believed to be an expression

of the want of others to understand me and the meaning of my destiny, a daily exhortation and a never failing comfort in my darkest and most solitary hours."

And now this pale and sickly-looking youth, who had so quickly forgotten his earlier mood of hopelessness and despair, felt these mystic lines summed up his own incapacity to understand the illusive message that this ancient talisman of power brought to him and yet at the same time withheld from him.

"The Spear appeared to be some sort of magical medium of revelation for it brought the world of ideas into such close and living perspective that human imagination became more real than the world of sense.

"I felt as though I myself had held it in my hands before in some earlier century of history—that I myself had once claimed it as my talisman of power and held the destiny of the world in my hands. Yet how could this be possible? What sort of madness was this that was invading my mind and creating such turmoil in my breast?"

Adolf Hitler was still standing bewitched in front of this ancient weapon when the doors of the Weltliche Schatzkammer were closing and it was time to depart.

CHAPTER TWO

THE SPEAR OF DESTINY

"They may be called Heroes, in as much as they have derived their purpose and their vocation, not from the regular course of things, sanctioned by the existing order; but from a concealed fount, from that inner spirit, still hidden beneath the surface, which impinges on the outer world as on a shell and bursts it to pieces."

Philosophy of History: Georg Wilhelm Friedrich Hegel.

Adolf Hitler knew his way around the shelves of the famous Hof Library as well as any University graduate for he had spent the better part of a year avidly studying in the warmth and the hush of its huge well-appointed reading room.

"Books were his whole world. In Vienna, he used the Hof Library so industriously that I asked him once, in all seriousness, whether he intended to read the whole library, which, of course, earned some rude remarks. One day he took me along to the library and showed me the reading room. I was almost overwhelmed by the enormous masses of books, and I asked him how it was he managed to get what he wanted. He began to explain to me the use of the various catalogues which confused me even more."*

The morning following his discovery of the Spear of Destiny, Adolf Hitler had not come to browse as was his usual custom through a random selection of books to give substance and support to a precarious castle of dreams. On this occasion he

* *Young Hitler*: August Kubizek.

entered the reading room with measured tread and one single-pointed intent—to trace the Reich's Lance in the Schatz-kammer of the Hofburg back through the centuries before it was mentioned openly in history during the reign of the German Emperor, Otto The Great.

It was not long before a capable use of the catalogues and various works of historical reference uncovered a whole number of Spears which had made greater or lesser claims in some period of history to be the Spear which pierced the side of Jesus Christ at the Crucifixion.

Adolf Hitler quickly overcame his consternation at this unexpected turn of events. He was sure that a diligent search would soon reveal which was the actual Spear of Longinus. He had always been passionately fond of history, the only subject at which he had shone at school. He had only contempt for all but one of his former teachers—"They had no sympathy with youth; their one object was to stuff our brains and turn us into erudite apes. If any pupil showed even a small trace of originality, they persecuted him relentlessly."*

Only his history teacher, Dr. Leopold Potsche, a fervent German nationalist, whom Hitler claimed had a profound effect on his formative years, was exempt from his scathing criticism: "There we sat, often aflame with enthusiasm, sometimes even moved to tears. . . . The national fervour which we felt in our own small way was used by him as an instrument of education. It was because I had such a professor that history became my favourite subject."†

The earnest youth, who was later to claim that "A man without a sense of history is a man without ears and eyes",‡ found little difficulty in sorting out the merits of the various Spears,

---

* *Mein Kampf.*   † ibid.

‡ " 'A man who has no sense of history,' declared Hitler, 'is a man who has no ears or eyes.' He himself claimed to have had a passionate interest in history since his schooldays and he displayed considerable familiarity with the course of European history. His conversation was studded with historical references and historical parallels. More than that: Hitler's whole cast of mind was historical, and his sense of mission derived from his sense of history."

purporting to be the weapon of the Roman Centurion Longinus, which were scattered around the palaces, museums,
cathedrals and churches of Europe.

One such Spear (or, at least, part of it, the shaft) was hanging
in the great Hall of the Vatican but the Roman Catholic
Church made no serious claims as to its authenticity. Another
Spear was to be found in Cracow in Poland, but Adolf Hitler
soon discovered it to be an exact replica of the Hofburg Spear
(without the Nail inserted), copied on the orders of Otto III
as a gift to Boleslav The Brave, on the occasion of some Christian pilgrimage. Yet another Spear, about which the claims
had more substance, had been associated with the early
Christian Father, John Chrysostomus. This Spear, which many
believed to be the Spear forged by the ancient Hebrew Prophet
Phineas, had been brought to Paris from Constantinople in the
thirteenth century by King Louis The Saint, on his return from
the Crusades, It was said to have attracted the interest of the
great Dominican Scholastic, Thomas Aquinas.

Adolf Hitler was excited to find one Spear which appeared to
have been associated with a legend of world destiny throughout
its entire history. This Spear, dating back to the Third Century,
had apparently been traced by numerous historians right
through to the tenth century to the reign of the Saxon King
Heinrich I, the "Fowler", where it was last mentioned in his
hands at the famous battle of Unstrut in which the Saxon
Cavalry conquered the marauding Magyars. After this battle,
the Spear mysteriously disappeared from history, for it was
neither present at Heinrich's death at Quedlinburg nor at the
coronation of his equally illustrious son, Otto The Great, the
first recorded possessor of the Reich's Lance in the Treasure
House of the Hofburg.

The Hofburg Spear received its first recorded mention in the
ancient Saxon Chronicle at the battle of Leck (near Vienna)
where Otto gained a resounding victory over the Mongolian
hordes whose formidable horsed archers had carried their
devastations to the very heart of Europe. The next mention of
this Spear, also attributed with legendary powers, was when

Otto knelt in Rome before Pope John XII to be touched with it upon the shoulder as a holy rite to establish his claim as Holy Roman Emperor.

Adolf Hitler, even then so contemptuous of the effeteness of intellectuals and official scholars with long titles, was convinced that his own further researches would bridge the gap and establish that it was the identical Spear which passed unrecorded between father and son, both great Saxon heroes.*

Tracing the path of this Spear through the centuries and assessing the illustrious lives and dynasties of power of the chain of men who had possessed it and claimed to wield its powers, Hitler was excited to find that in century after century the astonishing legend of the Spear had been fulfilled for good or evil.

Mauritius, the Commander of the Theban Legion, had retained the Spear in his grasp in his last dying breath when he was martyred by the Roman tyrant Maximian for refusing to worship the pagan Gods of Rome. The Theban Legion had been ensnared from Egypt on the orders of Diocletian to attend a mass assembly of the Roman Armies at Le Valais (285 A.D.) where a pagan festival of sacrifice was held to renew the waning fervour of the Legions for the pantheon of Roman Gods.

Mauritius, a Manichaean Christian, had protested against Maximian's threat to decimate his Legion for their Christian faith and, as a final gesture of passive resistance, he had knelt down in front of the ranks of his own soldiers to offer himself

---

* Heinrich Himmler, Hitler's Reichsführer S.S., put the finest scholars in Germany who were employed by the Nazi Occult Bureau, to the task of bridging this gap in the history of the Spear. They met with no success. Dr. Walter Stein, by means of a unique method of historical research involving "Mind Expansion", discovered that Heinrich I sent the Spear to the English King Athelstan where it was present at the Battle of Malmesbury at which the Danes were defeated. The Spear was presented to Otto The Great, on the occasion of his marriage to Athelstan's sister, Eadgita. The condition attached to the Spear as dowry was that the garrison towns of Europe should be turned into trading Cities. Otto The Great, became known as "The Town Founder" and through him the new Economy of Europe emerged out of the Dark Ages.

for decapitation in their stead. His last recorded words were: 'In Christo Morimur."

The veterans of the Theban Legion, inspired by this example of passive resistance, elected to die with their leader rather than worship the Roman Gods in whom they no longer believed. Not even the decapitation of every tenth man could change their minds. Altogether 6,666 Legionaries—the most highly disciplined force in Roman military history—divested themselves of their weapons and knelt to bare their necks for slaughter. Maximian made the dreadful decision to massacre the whole legion as an offering of sacrifice to his Gods—the most terrifying single rite of human sacrifice in the history of the ancient world.*

The martyrdom of the Theban Legion had softened the underbelly of the Pagan World and paved the way for the meteoric career of Constantine The Great, and the conversion of the Roman Empire to Christianity.

Constantine The Great, one of the world's most enigmatic figures, claimed he was guided through 'Providence' when holding the Spear of Longinus at the epoch-making battle on the Milvian Bridge outside Rome. This battle settled the rulership of the Roman Empire and lead directly to the proclamation of Christianity as the official religion of Rome.

Later, the wily Constantine wielded the 'serpent' powers of the Spear to defeat the passive resistance of the 'Dove' in order to yoke the new religion in subservience to his own personal ambitions for the perpetuity of the martial spirit of the Rome of Romulus. Grasping the holy talisman of power and revelation to his breast before the assembled Church Fathers at the first ever Ecumenical Council when, as the 'Thirteenth Apostle' dressed in Imperial Purple, he himself had the audacity to promulgate the Dogma of the Trinity and impose

* The bloody spectacle of the martyrdom of the Theban Legion was outstripped a thousand years later by the monstrous Roman Catholic Inquisition of the Cathars and the Albigensian Manichees in Toulouse when 60,000 passive resisters—men, women and children—were burned or put to the sword in a single day. Only the Gas Ovens of Auschwitz and Mauthausen were to match this deed in bestial cruelty and demonic intent.

it on the Church. In his old age, when building the new Rome in Constantinople—a bastion which would withstand all assaults for a thousand years—Constantine carried the Spear in front of him when treading out the boundaries on the site of the new City saying: "I follow in the steps of Him who I see walking ahead of me."

The Spear had played a conspicuous role through the centuries of the gradual decline of the Roman Empire, both in resisting the invasions from the North and East and in converting the Barbarians to the new faith and the Roman cause.

Hitler was impressed with how the Spear had changed hands generation by generation, passing from hand to hand in a chain of claimants who held it with ever-changing motives. Men like Theodosius who tamed the Goths with it (385 A.D.), Alaric The Bold, the savage convert to Christianity who claimed the Spear after he had sacked Rome (410 A.D.), and Aetius, 'the last of the Romans' and the mighty Visigoth Theodoric, who rallied Gaul with the Spear to vanquish the barbaric hordes at Troyes and turn back the ferocious Attila The Hun (452 A.D.).

Justinian, the absolutist and ecclesiastical bigot, who reconquered the territories of the old Roman Empire, and gave his people the famous 'Codex Juris' had placed the confidence of his great destiny on the Spear. He raised the Spear aloft when ordering the closing down of the "Schools of Athens", exiling the great Greek scholars from his realm. It was a fatal decision which denuded medieval Europe of Greek thought, mythology and art and gave it that special quality of darkness and prejudice which was burst asunder a thousand years later in the brilliant light of the Italian Renaissance.

In the eighth and ninth centuries the Spear had continued to be the very pivot of the historical process. For instance, the mystical talisman had become an actual weapon in the hands of the Frankish General Karl Martel* (The Hammer) when he

---

* Hitler at this time regarded Karl Martel as one of his great heroes. Later he came to curse this Frankish leader: "Only in the Roman Empire

led his army to gain a miraculous victory over the massed forces of the Arabs at Poitiers (732 A.D.). Defeat would have meant that the whole of Western Europe would have succumbed to the rule and religion of Islam.

Charlemagne (800 A.D.), the first Holy Roman Emperor, had founded his whole dynasty on the possession of the Spear and its legend of world-historic destiny—a legend which attracted the greatest scholars in all Europe to serve the civilising power of the Frankish cause. Charlemagne had fought 47 campaigns with the assurance of its victorious powers. And, more than this, the Spear had been associated with his phenomenal clairvoyant faculties through which he discovered the burial place of Saint James in Spain and his uncanny powers of anticipating future events, which had given him a halo of saintliness and wisdom. Throughout his life, this fabulous Emperor had lived and slept within reach of his beloved Talisman; only when he accidentally let it fall from his hands, while returning from his final victorious campaign, did his subjects rightly see it as an augury of tragedy and his imminent death.

Hitler became utterly fascinated with the passage of the Spear through the era in which all his childhood heroes had lived. He found to his astonishment and delight that the great German figures who had filled his youthful dreams had held the Spear as the holy aspiration of their ambitions, their talisman of power.

Altogether forty-five Emperors had claimed the Spear of

and in Spain under Arab Domination has culture been a potent factor. Under the Arab, the standard attained was wholly admirable; to Spain flocked the greatest scientists, thinkers, astronomers, and mathematicians of the world, and side by side there flourished a spirit of sweet human tolerance and a sense of purist chivalry. Then with the advent of Christianity, came the barbarians. Had Karl Martel not been victorious at Poitiers—already you see the world had fallen into the hands of the Jews, so gutless a thing was Christianity!—then we should in all probability have been converted to Mohammedanism, that cult which glorifies heroism and which opens the Seventh Heaven to the bold warrior alone. Then the Germanic races would have conquered the world. Christianity alone has prevented them from doing so."—*Hitler's Table Talk*: August 28, 1942.

Destiny as their possession between the coronation in Rome of Charlemagne and the fall of the old German Empire exactly a thousand years later. And what a pageantry of power and gallantry it was! The Spear had passed like the very finger of destiny through the millennium forever creating new patterns of fate which had again and again changed the entire history of Europe.

The five Saxon Emperors who had succeeded the Carolingians in the possession of this talisman of power, men like Otto The Great, had lived illustrious lives of world-historic significance.

However, it was the seven incredible Hohenstauffens of Swabia, including the legendary Frederick Barbarossa and Frederick II, his grandson, who excited Adolf Hitler's imagination most of all.

Here, indeed, were Germans of incomparable greatness! Frederick Barbarossa (1152–90), who had united in his blood the feuding Welfs and Swabians, had the qualities of a monarch Hitler could really admire . . . chivalry, courage, unlimited energy, great joy in battle, love of adventure, startling initiative, and above all a certain harshness which gave him the ability to both frighten and charm at the same time. Frederick Barbarossa, who fancied he could re-establish the Roman Empire without the Roman Legions, had conquered all Italy, proving himself supreme even over the Roman Pontiff himself; defeating Rome and leading the personal assault on the Vatican to drive the Pope into exile. Later he had knelt in Venice with the Spear in his hands as he kissed the feet of the Pope he had once defeated, but only as a ruse to play for time to reconquer Italy. Finally Barbarossa had died when crossing a stream in Sicily, and the Spear fell from his hands at the very moment of his death.*

Even eclipsing the magnificent Barbarossa himself was Frederick II Hohenstauffen (1212–50), who had arisen like a

* Adolf Hitler named his eyrie in the fastness of the Ober Salzburg "Barbarossa". It was also the name he gave to the attack on Russia—"Operation Barbarossa".

brilliant comet into European history and rocked it to its very foundations. A man of charismatic personality, rare genius and legendary occult powers, fluent in six languages, a chivalrous Knight and a lyric poet who inspired his Minnesingers to chant about the Holy Grail. The incomparable Frederick was also a patron of the Arts, a skilful and courageous commander in the field of battle, a statesman of infinite subtlety and an enigmatic soul, part saint and part devil. Nurtured in Sicily (then part of the extensive German Empire) this Prince of Swabian blood spoke Arabic with his Saracen soldiers, kept a large Harem, penned the first scientific thesis (on Hawking), believed in Astrology and practised Alchemy. Prizing the possession of the Spear beyond all things, he made it the focal point of his whole life—especially calling on its powers during his Crusades (in which Francis of Assisi once carried the Spear on an errand of mercy) and throughout his running battles with the Italian States and Papal Armies.*

The most important discovery of all for the young Hitler tracing the history of the Spear of Destiny did not concern either Emperors or their dynasties of power. It was the discovery that the Spear had been the inspiration for the founding of the Teutonic Knights whose chivalrous and courageous deeds, and whose irreversible vows and ascetic disciplines had been the very substance of his childhood dreams.

Adolf Hitler spent three days in his first tentative researches into the history of the Spear of Longinus. Perhaps he felt a tingling in his spine as he strode across the library to pull out from the shelves the works of the great German Philosopher, Georg Wilhelm Frederick Hegel, for it seemed to Hitler that the men who had claimed the Spear throughout history and fulfilled its legend fitted into Hegel's description of World-Historic-Heroes—"*Heroes who carry out the Will of the World Spirit, the very plan of Providence.*"

---

* Adolf Hitler gave orders for his troops to fight a bloody rearguard action while engineers removed the Memorial Stone of Frederick II Hohenstauffen from the field of battle in Italy. The Memorial Stone was brought back to Germany.

"They may be called heroes, in as much as they have derived their purpose and their vocation, not from the regular course of things, sanctioned by the existing order; but from a concealed fount, from that inner Spirit, still hidden beneath the surface, which impinges on the outer world as on a shell and bursts it to pieces. . . . But at the same time they were thinking men, who had an insight into the requirements of the Time—what was ripe for development. This was the very truth of their age, for their world. . . . It was theirs to know this nascent principle, the necessary, directly sequent step in progress, which their world was to take; to make their aim, and to expend their energy in promoting it. World-historic men—the Heroes of the Epoch—must therefore be recognised as its clear-sighted ones: their deeds are the best of their time."

The philosophy of Hegel was a bit beyond the young Hitler who would not have been able to appreciate such subtle distinctions as the concepts of Being and Existence. But one thing about Hegel did appeal to him and that was the fact all sense of morality seemed to dissolve from the philosopher's soul when he contemplated what he called "World-Historic-Heroes.":

"World history occupies a higher ground than one on which morality has properly its position, which is personal character and conscience of individuals. Moral claims which are irrelevant must not be brought into collision with world-historic deeds and their accomplishment. The litany of private virtues—modesty, humility, philanthropy and forbearance—must not be raised against them."

Hegel's idea that such heroes were completely justified in crushing to pieces everything in their path which might stop them from fulfilling their great destiny, appealed enormously to the grandiose sense of mission in Hitler's breast.

All cynicism about himself, all scepticism about the genuineness of his first eerie experience before the ancient Spearhead in the Hofburg now melted away as he read again with bated breath these words of Hegel which seemed to confirm the role

19

played by the long chain of claimants to the Spear of Destiny. His sense of mission was now enkindled to the point of pain. The Spear in the Treasure House held the key to Power! The key to his own world-historic destiny!

Somehow he too must unravel its secrets and harness its powers to his own personal ambitions for the German people. Might he not himself be the immortal Siegfried destined to reawaken men of German blood from the great sleep which followed the Götterdämmerung? The Sun Hero fated to raise the eyes of all Germans to the greatness of their spiritual heritage?

It was late in the afternoon when Hitler entered the Schatzkammer with awe and fear in his heart to take his second look at the 'Heilige Lance'. In the following three years he was to make countless such pilgrimages to this same spot to scrutinise the ancient weapon and wean it of its secrets.

Once again his immediate experience was one of complete bafflement. He could feel something strange and powerful emanating from the iron Spearhead which he could not readily identify. He stood there for a long while perplexed by its inscrutable riddle: "Studying minutely every physical detail of its shape, colour and substance, yet trying to remain open to its message."

"I slowly became aware of a mighty presence around it—the same awesome presence which I had experienced inwardly on those rare occasions in my life when I had sensed that a great destiny awaited me."

And now he began to understand the significance of the Spear and the source of its legend, for he sensed intuitively that it was a vehicle of revelation—"a bridge between the world of sense and the world of the spirit (Geistliche Welt)."

Adolf Hitler later claimed that it was on this occasion while he was standing before the Spear that: "A window in the future was opened up to me through which I saw in a single flash of illumination a future event by which I knew beyond contradiction that the blood in my veins would one day become the vessel of the Folk-Spirit of my people."

Adolf Hitler left the Hofburg Treasure House that evening with the indelible conviction that he himself would one day step forward to claim the Spear of Destiny as his own personal possession and that he would fulfil a world-historic role with it.

The man who would one day become the undisputed Führer of the Third Reich never recounted what it was he saw in that brief moment when the scene of the Schatzkammer melted away and he was transported in a single flash of illumination into the future.

Perhaps it was a vision of himself standing triumphantly outside the Hofburg proclaiming to the massed ranks of Austrian Nazis in the Heldenplatz and the crowds of unhappy and bewildered City folk crowded into the Ring: "Providence has charged me with a mission to reunite the German Peoples . . . with a Mission to restore my homeland to the German Reich. I have believed in this Mission. I have lived for it, and I believe I have now fulfilled it."*

"Coming events cast their shadow before," says Goethe, the famous German poet and transcendentalist. So perhaps the young Hitler's pre-vision that evening twenty-four years before he came to power was of a more sinister nature!"

Whatever triumphant or ghastly scene was opened up to him, it most assuredly changed his whole attitude to life. "I had set forth in this town while still half a boy and I left it a man, grown quiet and grave," said Hitler in *Mein Kampf*. From that moment forward he had no further wish for the comfort of human friendship. That very night he made arrangements to shift from his lodgings which he had shared with August Kubizek. Now he was a man who stood alone—a man with a mighty and dreadful destiny to fulfil.

"Whatever could have made Adolf Hitler leave me without a word or a sign?" cried the plaintive Gustl when he returned from holiday to an empty room in the Stumpergasse."†

* Hitler's speech at the Anschluss after "Operation Otto" had secured Austria for the German Reich. (March 14, 1938.)

† August Kubizek, *Young Hitler—The Story of our Friendship.*

THE TEMPTATION OF ADOLF HITLER

An Aryan God or a Nietzschean Superman?

"Again, the devil taketh him up into an exceeding high mountain, and showeth him all the kingdoms of the world, and the glory of them.

"And saith unto him 'All things will I give thee, if thou wilt fall down and worship me.'

"Then saith Jesus unto him, 'Get thee hence, Satan: for it is written, Thou shalt worship the Lord thy God, and him only shalt thou serve.'

"Then the devil leaveth him, and, behold, angels came and ministered unto him."

Matthew 4, 8–11.

According to the legend associated with the Spear of Longinus, the claimant to this talisman of power has a choice between the service of two opposing Spirits in the fulfilment of his world-historic aims—a Good and an Evil Spirit.

It may appear ludicrous in terms of conventional morality that anyone should be unable to distinguish between the extremes of good and evil. Yet Adolf Hitler, who at this juncture had by no means decided to tread a satanic path, was incapable of distinguishing between them.

He began his researches into the history of the Spear and the significance of its legend with one tremendous disadvantage. He had absorbed as early as his fifteenth year the works of the tragic philosopher, Friedrich Nietzsche, whose powerful dissertation on "The Genealogy of Morals" sought to make a "Revaluation of all Values" in the proof that so-called evil was good, and what was habitually believed to be good was evil!

And to add to his condition of doubt and indecision two other self-chosen mentors contributed to the complexity of his personal situation. The first was that great pessimist Schopenhauer who denied the existence of good and evil and claimed that there was no Supreme Being behind the creation. And the second was the Maestro, Richard Wagner, who worshipped Lucifer cunningly disguised as an exclusively Aryan Christ.

For three long years Adolf Hitler found himself inextricably bound in a web spun by the thinking of these three men of incontestable genius whose work prepared the soil for the emergence of National Socialism. And it is in this sense that the years spent in the poverty and obscurity of the flophouse, while unravelling the secrets of the Spear, can be called years of "Temptation"—the dreadful temptation of Adolf Hitler.

Adolf Hitler was brought up as a Roman Catholic, a denomination which, up to the age of eleven, he had accepted with a deep earnestness and devotion. The few friends of the family who knew Hitler in his early formative years in Linz have spoken of his capacity for warmth of heart and unselfishness, and all were deeply touched by the patience, tenderness and love with which he nursed his dying mother. We know, too, just how deeply his youthful soul entered into such works as Dante's *Divine Comedy* and Goethe's *Faust*. After he had seen the 'Ariel Scene' of *Faust* with its powerful theme of Christian redemption, "he spoke of nothing else for days."*

The first shadow of doubt arose to disturb Hitler's unquestioning 'faith' in the dogmas of Rome when he discovered

* *Young Hitler*, August Kubizek.

Schopenhauer's *The World as Will and Idea*. Apart from a compendium of the works of Friedrich Nietzsche, it was to become Hitler's other 'bible', seldom out of reach and remaining with him until his suicide in the Berlin Bunker in 1945. Schopenhauer had been the first German thinker of any consequence to study and render critical account of the significance of the great religious, mystical and philosophical systems of the Orient.

This pessimistic thinker, who had enflamed Nietzsche's enthusiasm and devotion as a young student, denied that a God could ever incarnate on earth and replaced the concept of an ultimate reality with what he called 'a blind striving of the Will'. According to Schopenhauer conceptual thought could never attain to truth and the only reality open to human beings was the actual physical experience of Willpower.

It all sounds dull enough stuff! And slightly ridiculous, too, when one comes to consider that this prophet of asceticism and human willpower was a renowned gourmet, delighting in the quantity as much as the quality of his food which he washed down with equally generous measures of rare wines. And often as not enjoying an hour-long snooze at the table of his self-indulgence! But Adolf Hitler, unaware of this startling gap between precept and practice, could reel off passages from Schopenhauer like a priest reciting a creed, and the maxims of this armchair ascetic became the most important moulding force in his life, itself a miracle of willpower.*

Like Nietzsche himself, who formulated the basis of his "Will-to-Power" on the same "Will-premiss", Adolf Hitler accepted as gospel Schopenhauer's considered opinion that the act of sacrifice of Jesus Christ at the Crucifixion was "the very personification of the denial of the will to live". The youth, who

---

* "In his Munich days Hitler always carried a heavy riding whip, made of hippopotamus hide. The impression he wanted to convey—and every phrase and gesture in his speeches reflected the same purpose—was one of force and will . . . His strength of personality, far from natural to him, was the product of an exertion of will: from this sprang a harsh, jerky, over-emphatic manner. . . . No word was more frequently on Hitler's lips than 'Will', and his whole career from 1919 to 1945 is a remarkable achievement of willpower." *Hitler: A Study in Tyranny*: Alan Bullock.

would later rally his retreating armies in the frozen wastes of Russia with the words "he who resigns has lost the right to live", was beginning to have scant respect for the passive resistance of Jesus Christ and the early Christians.

Perhaps the most sustained act of willpower in Hitler's life was the manner in which he pursued his earnest researches into the history of the Spear of Destiny in order to unveil the secrets of its legendary occult powers. And it was as a direct result of these researches that he developed the terrifying *Weltanschauung* which was to change the face of history in the twentieth century:

> "Vienna was and remained for me the hardest, though most thorough, school of my life. . . . In this period there took shape within me a world picture and a philosophy which became the granite foundation of all my acts. In addition to what I then created, I have had to learn little; and I have had to alter nothing."
>
> *Mein Kampf*: A. Hitler

How little his biographers have understood the real significance of what Hitler was reading and what lay as motive behind his choice of subjects and the books he avidly consumed at this time.

Professor Alan Bullock, a historian of great integrity, has even listed the actual subjects (or some of them anyway) in which Adolf Hitler was immersing himself at this time, yet the very truth before his eyes was not sufficient to awaken him to the real motives behind Hitler's studies.

After pointing out scathingly, and perhaps somewhat mistakenly, that Hitler sought only to impress other people and was full of fantastic and inconsequential ideas, Bullock writes: "His intellectual interests seemed to follow the same pattern. He spent much time in the public libraries, but his reading was indiscriminate and unsystematic—*Ancient Rome, the Eastern Religions, Yoga, Occultism, Hypnotism, Astrology . . !*"*

* The italics are mine. And so is the exclamation mark!

25

We shall amply demonstrate that it was from these and kindred subjects that Adolf Hitler was to formulate his personal *weltanschauung* which was to change the face of the world three decades later.

The works of Schopenhauer and Nietzsche, which are laced with eulogistic comments regarding oriental thinking, led the youthful Hitler to a keen study of Eastern Religions and Yoga. It is to his credit that he did not slip into the same errors contained in the vast majority of Theosophical books published in the last decade of the nineteenth century and the first decade of our own century. The Theosophists, except in rare instances of individuals of genuine vision and insight, saw little or no difference between ancient and modern man with regard to faculty and consciousness. Hitler shrewdly guarded himself against such an error and adamantly refused to make purely intellectual interpretations of such awe-inspiring works as the *Rig-Veda*, the *Upanishads*, the *Gita*, *Zend-Avesta*, Egyptian *Book of the Dead*, and others.

He refused to accept the widely-held idea that these works, presenting such a penetrating insight into the relationships between Cosmos, Earth and Man, were born of faculties even remotely corresponding to the modern form of intellect. And he realised, too, that the knowledge contained in them was far older than generally supposed, their content only being set down when the faculties from which they originated were already in a state of atrophy. In short, Adolf Hitler was even then beginning to consider the historical process in terms of an ever-changing condition of human consciousness.

Following the rise and fall of the ancient civilisations, he noticed how their very sequence in history traced the perceptible loss of spiritual faculties. And he began to consider whether such an atrophy of spirit-vision could be related to the waning magic of the blood of the races, the two influences together bringing about the gradual emergence and dominion of materialistic thinking. He came to the conclusion that with the passing of time humanity had entered a kind of canyon of sleep, so that former golden ages, in which man had enjoyed a magical relationship with the Universe, had been forgotten, the only evidence of such sublime conditions lying hidden in myths and legends in which nobody any longer believed.

Unlike Roman Catholic Priests ("Malevolent Parasites") and Puritan Pastors ("submissive as dogs who sweat in embarrassment when you talk to them"), Hitler refused to accept the story of the ancient Hebrews as in any way of positive significance in the long history of mankind. And he began at this time to blame the Jews for the emergence of materialism and for the falsification of everything which ancient man had once cherished.*

When Adolf Hitler came to consider the significance of Christ and Christianity, the Spirit of the Anti-Christ, which speaks so powerfully through all of Nietzsche's later writings, now seized his own fertile imagination. There was no need as far as he was concerned to assess the value of Christianity because Nietzsche had already done it to perfection in a masterful analysis of this religion "for slaves, weaklings and the desiccated residue of racial scum!"

> "Here I merely touch on the problem of the genesis of Christianity. The first principle for its solution is: Christianity can be understood only in terms of the soil out of which it has grown. It is not a counter-movement of the Jewish instinct, *it is the very consequence.*†
>
> "The Jews are the strangest people in the history of the world because, confronted with the question to be or not to be, they chose, with uncanny deliberateness, to be at any price; this price

---

* "The Jew has never founded any civilisation, though he has destroyed hundreds. He possesses nothing of his own creation to which he can point. Everything he has stolen. Foreign peoples, foreign workmen built his Temples; it is foreigners who create and work for him. He has no art of his own; bit by bit he has stolen it from other peoples. He does not even know how to preserve the precious things they have created. . . . In the last resort, it is the Aryan who can form states and set them on their path to future greatness. All this the Jew cannot do. And because he cannot do it, therefore all his revolution must be international. They must spread as a pestilence spreads." (Adolf Hitler: Speech in Munich, 1922.)

† Nietzsche's italics.

was the radical falsification of all nature, all naturalness, all reality, of the whole inner world as well as the outer.

"Out of themselves the Jews created a counter-movement to natural conditions: they turned religion, cult, morality, history, psychology, one after the other, into an incurable contradiction of their own natural values.

"We encounter the same phenomena once again in immeasurably large proportions, yet merely as a copy: the Christian Church cannot make the slightest claim to originality when compared to the 'holy people'. This is why the Jews are precisely the most catastrophic people of world history: by their effect they have made mankind so thoroughly false that even today the Christian can feel anti-Jewish without realising that he himself is *the ultimate Jewish consequence.**

"What is formerly just sick is today indecent—it is indecent to be a Christian today. And here begins my nausea. . . . I pronounce my judgement. I condemn Christianity. I raise against the Christian Church the most terrible of all accusations that any accuser uttered. It is to me the highest conceivable corruption With its ideal of anaemia, of 'holiness', draining all blood, all love, all hope for life; the cross is the mark of recognition for the most subterranean conspiracy that ever existed—against health, beauty, whatever has turned out well, courage, spirit, graciousness of soul, against life itself.

"This eternal indictment of Christianity I will write on all walls, wherever there are walls. . . . I call it the one immortal blemish on mankind."

The Anti-Christ: Friedrich Nietzsche.

Hitler was inflamed into his greatest flights of hatred for Christianity—that diabolical yiddish consequence—when he read Nietzsche's contemptuous lash-out of words about the 'taming' of the Tribes of Ancient Germania:

"To call the taming of an animal its 'improvement' sounds almost like a joke in our ears. Whoever knows what goes on in menageries doubts that the beasts are 'improved' there. They are weakened, they are made less harmful, and through the depressive effect of fear, through pain, through wounds, and through hunger

---

* Nietzsche's italics.

they become sickly beasts. It is no different with the tamed man whom the priest has 'improved'. In the early Middle Ages, when the Church was indeed, above all, a menagerie, the most beautiful specimens of the 'blond beast' were hunted down everywhere; and the noble Teutons, for example, were 'improved'.

"But how did such an 'improved' Teuton who had been seduced into a monastery look afterward? Like a caricature of man, like a miscarriage: he had become a sinner, he was stuck in a cage, imprisoned amongst all sorts of terrible concepts. And there he lay, sick, miserable, malevolent against himself: full of hatred against the springs of life, full of suspicion against all that was still strong and happy. In short, a Christian."

Everything which Nietzsche spat out so wrathfully about the ruination of the virility of the proud and unspoiled Germanic Tribes by the poisonous barbs of a Judaism disguised as Christianity, Adolf Hitler found confirmed again and again in the mighty works of his other great hero, Richard Wagner, the Maestro of Bayreuth.

The fantastic genius of Wagner had inspired Hitler's personal interest in mythology and the early history of the German peoples. The stupendous "Nibelungen Ring"—a majestic theme incorporating four operas in sequence—had made the young Hitler glow with pride at his Germanic ancestry and the Aryan blood in his veins.

The "Ring", inspired by the *Nibelungenlied* (literally, the Song of the Nibelungs), a saga written by an unknown poet and troubadour in the late twelfth century, had taken Richard Wagner some twenty-five years to complete. It was these dramatised myths, projected to call for an awakening of the German "Volk", which later became the very essence of the Nazi propaganda upon which Adolf Hitler romped to power. The final opera of the "Ring" entitled *Götterdämmerung* (Twilight of the Gods) dramatises how the greed for gold sends Valhalla itself into oblivion in flames of desolation following the tremendous bloodcurdling battle of Gods and men.

Richard Wagner, an artist of staggering talent and almost miraculous powers of imagination, attempted "to combine the verse of a Shakespeare with the music of a Beethoven". He saw himself as a prophet with a life destiny to awaken the Germans to the grandeur of their ancestry and the superiority of the blood of their race. He compared the greed for gold in his *Götterdämmerung* to the "tragedy of modern capitalism and the spirit of yiddish usury" which he claimed was threatening to destroy the German people.

By tradition the sleep which followed the *Götterdämmerung* was not an eternal sleep. It was prophesied that the Horn of Heimdall, guardian of the threshold between Gods and men, would one day sound its eerie call once more to herald the awakening of the Germanic Race from its deathlike slumbers. And Adolf Hitler was excited to find that the prediction of such an awakening out of an intellectual and materialistic darkness was confirmed by the religious texts, myths and legends of almost every ancient civilisation. Innumerable sources pointed to the twentieth century as the dawn of the great spiritual awakening of mankind.

More conclusive for Adolf Hitler than the enigmatic prophecies of the ancients was the trumpeting of his beloved Nietzsche regarding the coming *Übermensch*—the Superman, the Elite of the Race, the Lord of the Earth. "I teach you the Superman" are almost the opening words of the incredibly brilliant *Thus Spake Zarathustra*:

"I teach you the *Superman*.

"Man is something that shall be overcome. What have you done to overcome him?

"All things so far have created beyond themselves; and do you want to be the ebb of this great flood and even go back to the beasts rather than overcome man?

"What is the ape to man? A laughing stock or a painful embarrassment. You have made your way from worm to man, and much in you is still worm. Once you were apes, and even now, too, man is more ape than ape. . . .

"Behold I teach you the Superman. The Superman is the meaning of the Earth. Let your will say: the Superman shall be the meaning of the Earth. I beseech you, brothers, remain faithful

to the earth, and do not believe those who speak to you of un-
worldly hopes. . . ."

But the Superman will only appear through man's own self
overcoming; for man is a bridge between the beasts and the
Man-God. Man must imbue the blood with the seed of the
virtues of the Superman, sacrifice himself thanklessly to the task
of the earth itself which is to create Superman.

"Man is a rope, tied between beast and Superman, a rope over
an abyss. A dangerous across, a dangerous on-the-way, a dangerous looking-back, a dangerous shuddering and stopping.

"What is great in man is that he is a bridge and not an end:
what can be loved in man is that he is an overture and a going-
under.

"I love those who do not know how to live, except by going
under, for they are those who cross over.

"I love those who are the great despisers because they are the
great reverers and arrows of longing for the other shore.

"I love those who do not first seek behind the stars for a reason
to go under and be a sacrifice, but who sacrifice themselves for
the earth, that the earth may some day be the Superman's."

For Nietzsche, God is dead. And because God is dead, it is
man who must be responsible for his own evolution and the
evolution of all other kingdoms of Earth. The Superman can
only be realised by the indomitable will of man himself.

In a later work, *Will-to-Power*, Nietzsche became more op-
timistic about the possibility of the immediate appearance of
the Superman, suggesting that a Master-Race (Herrenvolk)
was already building itself up, and that men were preparing
themselves to be the forefathers—even the fathers—of the
coming Superman: "May I bear the Superman is the prayer of
the women; may I create Supermen—the deed of the men."

The appearance of the 21-year-old Hitler steadily degenerated
throughout the latter half of 1910 until he looked almost

31

offensively down-at-heel. Proprietors of cafes and soup kitchens which he ravenously frequented, officials at the libraries, ushers in the galleries of the theatres, as well as the uniformed attendants in the Treasure House of the Hofburg, were all beginning to regard him as a suspicious lay-about, a jobless bum.

For the young man who had stood before the Spear of Longinus and pierced through to a flash of pre-vision of his future, the opinions of others regarding his outward appearance and impoverished circumstances were a matter of total indifference. The one thing which concerned "this apparition which rarely occurs among Christians"* was the attainment of some new form of consciousness through which he could perceive the nature of the opposing Spirits of the Spear and discover further the meaning of his own personal destiny.

Although it is widely known that Adolf Hitler studied various systems of Yoga, there is no evidence at all of him squatting on his bed in the flophouse in Meldemannstrasse after the manner of the Hatha Yoga postures of Patanjali! He was quick to realise that the Yoga of posture and the secrets of breath control were devised for the physiology of the Eastern man of yesterday. He saw it as a path for a people in whom the sense of ego was not strong and in whom the power of intellect had made but little inroad; a technique which sought through asceticism and meditation to purify the physical body to such an extent that it became the eye of the soul. "The last thing I want to do is to end up in the skin of a Buddha" said Adolf Hitler.*

Adolf Hitler was confronting the same situation as the younger generation today who seek the gates of perception and a path to mind expansion without the use of drugs. Amidst a superabundance of ancient texts, he could find no sure foothold to begin the direct climb to transcendent consciousness, and no lucid and immediately practical way of initiation which might defeat the dominion of the senses and the cunning of the sense-bound intellect.

* *Hitler's Table Talk.*

He had no doubt at all that the secret of the Spear of Longinus was associated with a mighty blood mystery and some totally new concept of Time. Yet where in history or in the contemporary scene, he asked himself, could a uniquely Western path to transcendent states of consciousness be found?

The answer came from a surprising quarter. Surprising because he had been living with the solution right under his nose. Richard Wagner's Opera *Parsival*, the opera which had been inspired by the mysteries of the Holy Grail!

Parsival, Wagner's last great work, was a uniquely personal dramatisation of the Grail Romance sung by Wolfram von Eschenbach, a thirteenth-century poet and minnesinger. And within the remarkable verses of this romance of the Middle Ages Adolf Hitler believed he had discovered what he was looking for: a prescribed western path to the attainment of transcendent consciousness and new levels of Time experience.

Richard Wagner, in seeking to give a dramatic form to the search for the Holy Grail, had centred the theme for his opera on the struggle between the Grail Knights and their adversaries over the possession of the Holy Spear—the Spear of Longinus which had pierced the side of Christ!

In the hands of the Knight, Sir Parsival, who served the Archangel of the Grail, the Spear was a holy symbol of the blood of Christ—a sacred talisman of healing and redemption. In the grasp of the sinister Klingsor, surrounded by his seductive flower maidens in the fastness of an eyrie in some southern clime, the Spear became a kind of phallic wand in service of black magic powers.

Adolf Hitler was greatly excited by these discoveries which had taken him several quick and vital strides forward, opening up new vistas of research. He now became impatient to see Wagner's *Parsival* but was forced to wait several months until it was presented at the Vienna Opera House.

Sitting high up in the cheap seats in the Gallery, he was transported by the majesty of the music, a similar *leit-motiv* to *Tristan and Isolde* but yet more haunting and ethereal. He came

33

away from the performance a very perplexed man, torn by two extremes of feeling—elation and disgust.

On the one side he was left in no doubt that Richard Wagner was the supreme prophetic figure among Germans. The manner in which Wagner had exalted the "Brotherhood of Knights" sharing a pure and noble blood had stirred him deeply. And the idea that blood itself should contain the very secret of spiritual illumination into the mysteries of the Grail had excited feelings in a depth of his soul which he had never before experienced.

Yet, throughout the changing scenes of the Opera another side of his nature had been inexplicably sickened by the Grail procession and the rituals in the Grail castle, and, indeed, by all the Christian embroidery and Good Friday mystification.

Outside the theatre in the cold night air of the City he suddenly became aware of the cause of his disgust. He had been inwardly nauseated by the Christian vows and compassionate ideals of the Knights. "I could find no cause for admiration," he recounted later, "for the piddling Knights who had dishonoured their 'Aryan Blood' to follow the superstitions of the Jew, Jesus. My sympathy was entirely with Klingsor."

It did not take long for Hitler to unearth the fact that Wagner had himself been inspired to enclose the theme of *Parsival* around the Spear of Longinus as a result of his studies of the "Heilige Lance" in the Treasure House of the Hofburg.

Richard Wagner and Friedrich Nietzsche had made a special journey to Vienna to stand together before this Spear of Revelation. A journey which was to have a sad ending for both.

It was the mutual study of the history of the Spear and the significance of its legend and their strikingly opposite views about it which finally parted these formerly inseparable friends —the master musician and the cynical philosopher. A parting which led them both to experience a bitter and pathetic loneliness, and later a growing hatred and contempt for one another which spilled over into a stormy public controversy to shatter the emerging Pan-Germanic mystic-pagan idealism to its very foundations.

The setting of the last meeting between Nietzsche and Wagner in Bayreuth is well known because the great sceptic and critic penned it with his customary brilliance. It appears that Wagner, totally unaware at that time of Nietzsche's repugnance towards his thoughts about Christ, had expounded his theme for *Parsival*, projecting it through his own freshly gained religious experience of redemption and return to the Christian fold (all this, of course, on the premise that Jesus was not born a Jew but of glorious Aryan stock).

Nietzsche, to whom Christianity was a depravity, "a saying-No to everything", a capitulation to Pauline poison, could hardly master his feelings of disgust and turned his back on Wagner and Bayreuth for ever.

"It was indeed time to say farewell," he wrote (in Nietzsche contra Wagner) after witnessing his only friend grovelling pitifully down the path of renunciation, "a decaying and despairing decadent, helpless and broken, before the Christian Cross."

Nietzsche described how he left Bayreuth, the great home of the Wagner Festspiel, to feel *that shudder which everybody feels after he has passed unconsciously through a tremendous danger.*"

In verse, parodying the style of Goethe's *Faust*, Nietzsche penned his thoughts about Wagner's conversion.

Is this still German?
Out of a German heart, this torrid screeching?
A German body, this self-'.aceration?
German, this priestly affectation,
this incense-smelling, lurid preaching?
German, this plunging, halting reeling
this sugar-sweetish bim-bam pealing?
this nunnish ogling, Ave levening
this whole falsely ecstatic heaven over heavening.

Is this still German?
Consider! Stay! You are perplexed?
That which you hear is Rome—*Rome's faith without the text.*
    Friedrich Nietzsche: *Wagner as the Apostle of Chastity.*

In a more serious vein, an admixture of fury and disappointment, Nietzsche spoke his mind about Wagner's *Parsival*:

> "Is Wagner's *Parsival* his secretly superior laughter at himself?
> Clearly one should wish that; for what would *Parsival* amount to
> if intended as a serious piece? Must we see it (as somebody has
> expressed it against me) as 'the abortion gone mad of a hatred of
> knowledge, spirit, and sensuality?' A curse on the senses and the
> spirit of a single hatred and breath. An apostasy and a reversion
> to sickly christian and obscurantist ideals? And in the end a self-
> abnegation, a self-crossing out on the part of the artist who had
> previously aimed at the very opposite of this. For *Parsival* is a
> work of perfidy, of vindictiveness, of a secret attempt to poison
> the presuppositions of life—a bad work. . . . I despise everyone
> who does not experience *Parsival* as an attempted assassination of
> basic ethics."
>
> *Wagner as the Apostle of Chastity:* Friedrich Nietzsche.

The public slanging match between Nietzsche and Wagner
was by no means a one-sided affair. Richard Wagner kept his
end up with a very persuasive argument in favour of a form of
Christianity which removed the faith from out of the bosom of
Judaism, proving it to be the very opposite of what the beetle-
browed Nietzsche scornfully called "a Jewish consequence".
For Wagner maintained that it had been revealed to him that
Jesus Christ had been born of the purest Aryan stock and that
the Christian God had never been a member of the racially
desecrated Jewish peoples over whom he claimed to be searching for "a final solution" to deliver the Fatherland from their
corrupting influences.*

The idea that the blood of Jesus was Aryan blood, a concept
which in itself shows a total misunderstanding of the universal
nature of Christianity, gave a quite new meaning to the search
for the Holy Grail. It meant that these holy mysteries were to

---

* The phrase "final solution", which prefigured the Gas Ovens of the
Death Camps and the liquidation of some six million European Jews, was
first uttered by the lips of Richard Wagner during his "Christian" conversion.

be considered as exclusively German and that Grail Knighthood was solely a German prerogative.

The fierce hatred and scorn which had developed between Adolf Hitler's two great heroes and sources of inspiration created for him something of a dilemma—especially since their feud began over the nature of the blood of Christ and the significance of the Spear which shed it.

One great problem remained to be solved: Who was right in his views about Jesus Christ? The musician who had fallen on his knees before an Aryan Christ, or the brooding philosopher who had called the Christian God an idiot? The Master of Bayreuth, the great prophet of a new Pan-Germanic Christianity, or the lonely visionary who predicted the coming of the "Superman"?

Adolf Hitler somehow managed to come to a decision by which he had no need to make a final parting with either of his heroic mentors ("who else could have made such a remarkable intellectual somersault"): He simply borrowed from the irradiating talent of Wagner and the dark brooding genius of Nietzsche those elements which he needed to build his own distorted *Weltanschauung*.

Though he retained the earlier structure and breadth of vision contained in Wagner's *Nibelungenring* and made his own pagan interpretation of the Mysteries of the Grail, he sided with Nietzsche's *Genealogy of Morals* to make the "Revaluation of all Values": *The Christian Good was evil; the Christian Evil was good!*

"My own special talent," said Hitler in a speech after he came to power, "is the capacity to simplify complex problems down to basic issues." And thus it came about that Adolf Hitler, reversing the morality of Christendom in one fell blow, stood before the Spear which had pierced the side of Christ and made an irreversible vow to worship evil.

Numerous visits to the Treasure House to behold the Spear had taught Adolf Hitler that this catalyst of revelation could reveal nothing unless he himself had made a fresh stride forward in his own understanding of the hidden meaning of this magic

37

pivot of history. Now he stood before the ancient weapon on its velvet red dais with an inner certainty that the time had come when a great secret would be revealed to him—the Spirit of the Spear itself would be unveiled!

"The air became stifling so that I could barely breathe. The noisy scene of the Treasure House seemed to melt away before my eyes. I stood alone and trembling before the hovering form of the Superman (Übermensch)—a Spirit sublime and fearful, a countenance intrepid and cruel. In holy awe, I offered my soul as a vessel of his Will."*

Adolf Hitler did not record whether like Nietzsche, he felt "that shudder which everybody feels after he has passed unconsciously through a tremendous danger." The dreadful temptation of Adolf Hitler was ended.

Get thee hence, Jesus: for it is written, "Thou shalt worship the Superman, the Elite of the Race, the Lord of all the kingdoms of the earth and the glory of them, and Him only shalt thou serve."

* Adolf Hitler also described the same vision to Rauschning, the Nazi Gauleiter who later defected to the Allies. The description came up in a conversation in which Hitler was discussing the mutation of the German Race.

"The Superman is living amongst us now! He is here!" exclaimed Hitler triumphantly. "Isn't that enough for you? I have seen the New Man. He is intrepid and cruel. I was afraid of him." In uttering these words, Hitler was trembling in a kind of ecstasy. (*Hitler Speaks*: Hermann Rauschning.)

THE FOOTNOTES OF SATAN

"Alas, sweet Spouse, what fate pursues us?
Thy fearful vision betokens a terrible prophecy;
By it, the child in thy womb is overshadowed.
It will love nothing, it will sunder blood relationships.
At length with passioned words
It will breed dissension among citizens
And will rage like fire in the hearts of the righteous."
Echempertus: Ninth-century Chronicler of the Landulf of Capua.

"Over the realm of all Spirits, that live between heaven and
earth, whether good or evil, Klingsor's power dominated them all:
God alone could protect them."

Richard Wagner: *Parsival.*

The four tables beside the front window of Demel's Cafe were
always reserved for *Stammgäste*—habitues—from Vienna's illustrious families. And although Walter Johannes Stein rarely
went to the City's most exclusive cafe, his mother had for years
been both a regular customer and a close friend of the Demel
family.

The young University student avoided the place at the height
of the summer season when Demel was besieged with tourists
who came to taste the world's most celebrated patisserie. At any
other time of the year he would occasionally drop in for a
coffee on his way home from the University. Frau Demel, after
greeting him warmly and enquiring after his family, could
always be relied on to leave him at a table beside the window

where, undisturbed, he could read through his lecture notes or just sit back and gaze idly at the passing scene in the Kohlmarkt outside.

Gourmets claim that the Crème Grenoble and the Sicilienne at Demel's Cafe are the experience of a lifetime, but coffee and nut mousse with curacao and plums, or raspberry ice cream soaked in Malaga wine, were certainly not the reasons why Walter Stein was to remember vividly the oak panelled walls and marble tables of Demel's for the rest of his life. It was through the trays of *Streuselkuchen, Baumkuchen* and *Gugelhupf* in the showcase window that he first saw the arrogant face and mystic blue eyes of Adolf Hitler!

Walter Johannes Stein attended the Vienna University where he was enrolled for a Science Doctorate. Although considered the outstanding science student of his year, especially with regard to his great facility for mathematics, his own personal interests were towards Classical studies and the History of Western Philosophy. The only "Arts" subject within his syllabus was the short course on German Literature which was compulsory to all students because so many different nationalities attended the University from every corner of the rambling Hapsburg Empire.

One of the set books in the Literature course, selected for the rare quality of its "middle high" German prose, was Wolfram von Eschenbach's *Parsival*. Perhaps this Grail Romance out of the Middle Ages would have been no more than an academic language study for Walter Johannes too, had it not been for a strange extra-sensory experience.

He awoke one night to discover that he had been reciting whole tracts of the minnesinger's romantic verses in a sort of pictureless dream!

Consider only for a moment what it would mean to have a similar experience with Chaucer's *Canterbury Tales*. The language of Chaucer's fourteenth-century prose is difficult enough as nearly every schoolboy knows, but, at least, it is a lineal ancestor of modern English. The speech of the German troubadour belongs to a century and a half earlier and is a mixture of dialects far removed from the modern German idiom; beyond this, it has a complex, uniquely personal and elliptical style.

It was characteristic of his unruffled and methodical approach to everything that he lost no time in snatching up a pencil and paper and writing down the words he had been reciting. Silencing his amazement, for he had never read more than the opening pages of the work, he went down to the study to check his untutored recitation against the words of the text. It was an uncanny experience to discover that this mysterious incursion into dream and awakening was word for word perfect with the original prose.

This extra-sensory intrusion into his consciousness happened twice more during the night; three times in all. On each occasion he followed the same procedure and discovered he had not made a single error, only minor spelling mistakes in writing down the ancient idiom.

He noticed that the words of the troubadour seemed to come to life on his lips like "the speaking of tongues" mentioned in the Pauline Epistles, for the experience was beyond intellectual thinking. It dawned on him through the ease with which he could recite it again and again that the faculty arose out of some form of "Higher Memory".

During the following weeks he read *Parsival* through countless times, suppressing all critical judgement, simply enjoying it as a wonderfully structured and cohesive work of art embracing equally much of every aspect of human existence as Dante's *Divine Comedy*. He was determined not to analyse it and dissect it with scientific coldness and detachment until the whole artistic flavour had permeated his inner life of feeling.

Allowing the quaint and enchanting imagery of this age of chivalry to arise within his mind, he began to note the almost imperceptible budding of a vivid picture-making faculty. Without any marked effort, he found he could now recite verbatim almost the whole work. Refusing to allow this remarkable new aspect of his life to interfere with his day-to-day studies for his Science Doctorate, he regarded it as an inner discipline to say nothing to anyone else about it.

Only when the day arrived for the beginning of the Spring Semester did he start to bring the sharp edge of his critical faculties into a concentrated effort to find out what really lay behind this apparently innocent tale sung by a wandering minnesinger to the Germanic peoples in the thirteenth century.

A round of the bookshops and libraries gathered in contemporary assessments and criticisms of all the Grail Romances of the Middle Ages and many works on the historical and literary background of the period.

It was not long before he found himself confronting the same perplexing problems which today still baffle the leading scholars of medieval history and literature. For instance, what is the Grail? Why is it called "holy" in the Arthurian legends but never mentioned as 'holy' by Wolfram von Eschenbach? Is it a cup? A precious Stone? A transcendent experience? How much of *Parsival* is simply a further embroidery of traditional folklore? How did the apparently untutored bard—he claimed he could neither read nor write—so transcend the traditions of his age in his subtle and progressive treatment of the soul life of his hero? And what of the relationships of the sexes in his verses in which the fulfilment of romantic love finds its highest ideal in an almost modern conception of marriage? How was it that the Knights searching for the most sublime heights of religious experience appeared to be free from the rigours of an ascetic way of life and the vows of celibacy of the monastic orders of the period?

Leading experts claimed that the "Adventures" of the Knights were simply enchanting imaginations of chivalrous deeds in the dawn of the "Romantic Age". And that these Adventures had no meaning other than as facets of a kind of novel which sought to project the freshly emerging experience of romantic love (a sort of redemption of the sexual instincts)

42

and the deepening of the life of the soul in the Middle Ages. The general consensus was that there was no historical reality whatsoever behind the hundreds of named personalities mentioned in *Parsival*, but that the general background woven into the minnesinger's tale had been exclusively drawn from the thirteenth century.

The first significant step towards unravelling the historical significance of this Grail Romance came when he accompanied his family to see Wagner's *Parsival* at Christmas in 1911. The Opera made a tremendous impression on him and became an unforgettable experience. No doubt at all that Richard Wagner had oversimplified and even badly damaged the delicate structure of the work and the intricacy of its plot in his all-too-pointed dramatisation; yet the quality of the music was more than compensation, carrying an indescribably powerful message of the redemptive love of Christ.

The important question which the opera posed for him concerned the source of Wagner's inspiration to dramatise *Parsival* around an actual physical spear. Was it pure fantasy or had the Spear which pierced the side of Christ been passed down through the centuries as a sacred reliquary? And if this was so, what medieval Kings or Princes had held this talisman in their possession? The answers to these questions would indicate the historical characters around whom the story of the search for the Grail had been written!

And so it came about that Walter Stein followed in the steps of Adolf Hitler to the Hofburg Library to research the various Spears mentioned as playing some crucial part in the events of the medieval centuries, and ultimately to stand before the Reich's Lance in the Treasure House and identifying it as the Spear of Destiny, the Spear which a Roman Centurion had thrust into the side of Jesus Christ at the Crucifixion.

During the following months Walter Stein started to open separate files on every aspect of his investigations without the least presentiment that he was beginning a lifetime study of the mysteries of the Holy Grail, or that these files would swell into a whole archive of personal research—an aggregate of work which would be hurriedly burned twenty-four years later when Reichsführer SS Heinrich Himmler ordered his arrest in an attempt to enlist his services and confiscate his papers for the Ahnenerbe, the Nazi Occult Bureau.

In the Spring of 1912, when he had completed his first full year of research, he had already come to the conclusion that the Grail Romance of Wolfram von Eschenbach had been written against the historical background of the ninth century and that the host of weird and wonderful names in its pages veiled actual physical-historical characters who had lived during the age of the Carolingian Emperors.

The ninth century had seen the final melting away of the political and legal structure of the Classic World which was replaced by the individual cultures of the emerging nations and the establishment of powerful Royal Houses, some of which were to last for a thousand years.

The ninth century not only witnessed the sunset of Roman and Greek culture, it also marked the dwindling out of those atavistic powers of the blood through which the Germanic Chieftains had ruled their tribes. Everywhere the beginning of intellectual thinking was replacing the ancient blood-consciousness and millions of men and women across the north of the continent were beginning to experience themselves as separate and isolated individuals instead of mere appendages of their tribes.

The most significant example of this transition from tribal identity to individual self-consciousness can be seen in the dethroning and imprisonment of the "long-haired" Merovingians, who had ruled the Franks by dint of ancient blood-rite alone for hundreds of years.

In special public ceremonies, the Merovingian family, all powerful since the days of the great Chieftain Clovis, were shorn of their locks before jeering crowds to demonstrate that the magic of their blood had atrophied and become fruitless.*

* See *The Long-Haired Kings*: J. M. Wallace-Hadrill (Methuen).

On the other hand, the Carolingians, who superseded them, were all illustrious individuals in their own right, statesmen, scholars and generals. Charles Martel had only borne the desultory title of "Mayor of the Palace" when he led the Franks to victory over Abd-ar-Rhaman at Poitiers and turned back the Islamic invasion of both France and the whole of Europe. Pepin The Short, who conquered Aquitaine, suppressed the Lombards in Italy, and drove the Moors from Languedoc, finally deposed the Merovingian Dynasty and won Papal recognition for the Carolingian House. Charlemagne, crowned Holy Roman Emperor by Pope Leo III in Rome in A.D. 800, and probably the greatest single historical figure since Caesar Augustus, built an Empire in the span of a single lifetime and rose to such a pinnacle of power that he even claimed the right to control the election of Popes.

The symbol of the Merovingians had been the ancient Tribal Spear which denoted spiritual leadership under the Tribal God and terrestrial power of life and death over all Frankish kinsfolk.

Charlemagne, however, treasured as his talisman of power the Spear of Longinus. He founded his great dynasty on the strength of its legend in the hope that the Carolingian House would last a thousand years. For Charlemagne, the Holy Spear symbolised the Blood of Christ and through possession of it he claimed to rule an Empire of mixed races by "divine right", the most exalted servant of the God of the New Covenant.

In this same critical medieval century the heroic poetry of the barbarian tribes of the north were forgotten as devotional works were translated from the Latin in a host of new tongues. As a result of the partition of the Carolingian Empire after the death of Charlemagne, the separate kingdoms of France and Germany came into existence. The first document pointing to the gradual preparation of the future diversity of Europe was the disentanglement of the Latin and the Germanic tongues in the Strassburg Oaths, the treaty concluded by the grandsons of Charlemagne.

In Britain, Alfred The Great was translating the Latin works

45

into the English idiom and helping to lay the foundations of an Island Nation; Norway had its first King and the Danes too were united under a single sovereign; the commerce of the City of Utrecht was preparing the way for the emergence of Holland. Even the foundations of modern Russia were laid in this century when Rurik, the Northman, became the first Prince of Novgorod.

The ninth century was also the age of the great Schism between the Eastern and Western Churches; the final separation appearing at the Council concluded in Constantinople in 869. It was while this crucial Church Council was under way that Pope Nicholas I declared Man was no longer to be considered as a trichotomy of Spirit, Soul and Body. From that time forward the Papal See was to deny the very existence of the Individual Human Spirit, declaring man to be but body and soul and relegating the personal spirit to the lowly estate of a mere "intellectual quality" within the soul itself. In this way the spiritual initiative of Western Man was confined to the prison of three-dimensional awareness of the sense world, and the Dogmas of the Roman Church became the only recognised source of revelation.

In this sharp transition in the evolution of human consciousness, when the intellectual soul of Europe germinated and a new sense of individuality was born among the masses, the age of Knighthood and Chivalry flowered.

With an almost startling suddenness, the troubadours and minnesingers appeared amidst the emerging nations to sing the praises of a personal Romantic Love, which blossomed forth between the sexes and gave fresh and tender relationships to a new ideal of Christian marriage.

Though the Church of Rome regarded all sexual experience as sin and demanded total celibacy of the priesthood, Wolfram von Eschenbach, the greatest of all the minnesingers, described how the Knights could marry and have children, and yet still seek and achieve the highest pinnacle of spiritual attainment— the Holy Grail.

·   ·   ·

46

It was in the heat of the late summer of 1912 that the strange coincidence happened which led Walter Stein indirectly to a meeting with Adolf Hitler. He had set out that morning to the old quarter of the City beside the Danube where there was an odd assortment of bookshops which dealt in religious, theo-sophical, alchemical and occult literature and books of a kindred nature.

In one of these shops—a rather dingy place displaying the name of Ernst Pretzsche—he made the discovery which was to cause him to be the prime witness of the role the Spear was to play in changing the face of the whole world in the twentieth century.

From an almost empty shelf high up at the back of the shop, he picked up a book covered on every page with jottings, entries, cross-references, tabulations, memoranda and footnotes which were all written in the same minute flowery script. The book was a tattered leather-bound edition, one of the numerous nineteenth-century reprints of the early German version of Wolfram von Eschenbach's *Parsival*.

He happened to open it on a page describing Parsival's Third Adventure where there appeared a large circle in ink around the lines describing the hero's mother, Herzloyda:

> Owe daz wir nu niht enhan
> ir sippe unz an den eilften span
> des wirt gevelschet lip.

> (This root of all goodness
> from which the shoot of humility flowered)
> Woe! That there have not remained to us
> Her children to the eleventh generation
> So much is false around us.*

---

* No recognised scholar of this medieval Grail Romance has yet found the key to the historical background of the verses. The extract quoted above is cunningly placed in an adventure far removed from other clues about the origin of the poem itself. Jesse Weston's famous English translation also misses the real meaning of the verse, for like the German scholars themselves

A brief note in the side column read: "Parsival lived eleven generations before the poet Wolfram von Eschenbach—in the Ninth Century around 860–870."

The book appeared to be a very exciting find and, if the other comments were equally relevant and valid, a very valuable one too. He paid willingly more than twice what the book was worth to the shop assistant who obviously took him for a gullible student.

It was a sunny morning in late August and Walter Johannes walked through the streets of the Old City in the direction of the Kohlmarkt where he entered Demel's Cafe. He sat at a table beside the showcase window with a view of the activities of the market outside and settled down to a long perusal of his lucky find, wondering what further revelations the flowery script would yield.

It wasn't long before he became aware of the frightening nature of the jottings. He remained sitting there, unaware of the passing of time, while he read through the whole work, studying the commentary relative to each verse. And the more he read the more disturbed he became.

This was no ordinary commentary but the work of somebody who had achieved more than a working knowledge of the black arts! The unknown commentator had found the key to unveiling many of the deepest secrets of the Grail, yet obviously spurned the Christian ideals of the Knights and delighted in the devious machinations of the Anti-Christ.

It suddenly dawned on him that he was reading the footnotes of Satan!

In contrast to a genuine facility to interpret the whole sequence of "Adventures" of *Parsival* as initiation trials on a prescribed path to the heights of transcendent awareness, there were endless crude, vulgar and, in many cases, obscene comments. A theme of racial fanaticism and an almost insane

---

she does not see the true significance of these three lines. Her translation reads: "Woe worth us! That none of their children should live still, to hand us down, in these days when we look on falsehood, their honour and fair women." (Book III, line 281, J. Weston translation.)

worship of Aryan blood lineage and Pan-Germanism ran throughout the commentary, which was pervaded with loathing and contempt for the Jews who were blamed for all the evils in the world and all the suffering of mankind.

For instance, alongside the verses describing the Grail Procession and the Assembly of Knights at the High Mass in the Grail Castle, there appeared an entry written in large letters scrawled across the printed page: "These men betrayed their pure Aryan Blood to the dirty superstitions of the Jew Jesus— superstitions as loathsome and ludicrous as the Yiddish rites of circumcision."

The vast canvas which the commentary developed about the origin, significance and historical background of the Grail Romance far excelled in insight the most authoritative academic summaries of the time. Walter Stein reluctantly conceded it a kind of crude genius, albeit a dark and brooding genius filled with resentment and hatred for the freedom of the individual and the equity of mankind.

Supporting his interpretations of the mysteries of the Grail, the unknown hand had quoted from innumerable sources— Eastern religions, Mysticism, Alchemy, Astrology, Yoga, Mythology, Ancient Greece and Rome, and a very large number of historical works and chronicles of the medieval age. Whoever the commentator was, he was widely read and his quotes were both relevant and illuminating enough to bring to life the enigmatic verses of the minnesinger. This was Romanticism come of age in a most sinister way!

The word Grail was apparently derived from "graduale" which means gradually, step by step, degree by degree. The search for the Grail was deemed to bring about a gradual development of the inner life of the soul from dullness akin to sleep, through doubt, to a positive spiritual awakening. The commentary interpreted the word "Saelde" (in English, Blessedness), by which Wolfram von Eschenbach denoted the attainment of the Grail, as "the awakening of a dullard from an unthinking stupor."

The Grail is described by the minnesinger as a "Precious

Stone" (Lapsis Excellis) and a footnote insisted that the stone was an alchemical symbol for the pineal gland situated beneath the brain—the Third Eye! And the whole purpose of this romance of the Grail, its plot and the sequence in which its sixteen adventures were written, was to open and activate this 'Pineal Eye' to a vision of the hidden secrets of Time and the meaning of human destiny!

Had this dark genius whose hand had written this fascinating commentary also developed the 'Pineal Eye'? Walter Stein asked himself with a shudder. And, if so, what then could the emergence of such a black magician mean for the world at large?

The commentary identified many of the characters of Wagner's opera, *Parsival*, as real living personalities of the ninth century: for instance, the demonically possessed and dying King Anfortas was named as King Charles The Bald, the grandson of Charlemagne; the sorceress Cundrie was considered to have been Ricilda Boese (Bad), the most infamous whore of the period who seduced him. "Parsival" was named as Luitward of Vercelli, the Chancellor to the Frankish Court, and Klingsor was identified as Landulf II of Capua, the most evil figure of the century.

The battle between the Christian Knights and their adversaries was understood to picture the continuing struggle for power between two opposing factions around an actual physical spear—the Reich's Lance in the Hofburg!

The bloodline of the Carolingian Emperors was identified as the magic source of the revelations of the Grail Family: "A bloodline inherent with unique and magical powers which gave vision into supersensible worlds." And as depicted in Wagner's Opera, the aim of Klingsor and his circle of black adepts was to blind the Grail souls through the arts of sexual perversion and rob them of their vision so that they were no longer guided by the Celestial Hierarchies.

Walter Stein was intrigued by this theme because the works of Dionysius, the Areopagite, which described the Celestial Hierarchies and the part which they played in guiding the historical process, had been sent by Emperor Michael from

Constantinople to Charlemagne as a coronation gift in A.D. 800 when he was crowned Holy Roman Emperor. Although Pope Nicholas I had declared these writings as heretical, King Charles The Bald, called the great English scholar, Scotus Erigena, to his court to translate them. And it was Scotus Erigena, the friend and confessor of Luitward, the King's Chancellor, who had been inspired by the Holy Spear to speak thus about the Grail:

> If to celestial heights
> Thou dost thyself uplift
> With shining eyes thou wilt behold
> the Temple of Sophia.

Walter Stein was impressed by the identification of Wagner's monstrous 'Klingsor' as the Landulf of Capua, for he already knew something of the historical facts associated with this ominous personality, and his later researches were to give him a yet clearer picture.

The influence of the Landulf on the events of the ninth century was enormous and there is no doubt that he was the central figure in all the evil of the time. The Emperor Louis II appointed him as "Third man in the kingdom" and heaped upon him so many honours that he even aspired to make Capua into a metropolitan city and enthroned himself as Archbishop.

Though he enticed his Emperor to make war against the Arabs in Southern Italy, it was his own brother who had invited the infidels to invade the Christian lands. The Landulf, who spent many years in Egypt studying Arab astrology and magic, was secretly their ally. It was through his Islamic connections that he later maintained his castle eyrie in the heights of the mountains in Arab-occupied Sicily. There, at Kalot Enbolot (or Carlta Belota) on the site of an ancient mystery Temple, he carried out the horrific and perverse practices which earned him a reputation as the most feared black magician in the world. He was finally excommunicated in A.D. 875 when his alliance with Islam was unveiled and his evil

51

practices inspired by the seductive Iblis touched the borders of historical narrative.

A number of historians, who perceived how the Grail-inspired spiritual renaissance threatened altogether to eclipse the power of Rome, had written about the sinister relationship of the Landulf and a succession of Popes in their joint attempt to obliterate the esoteric Christianity of the Holy Grail. Yet none exceed in insight Richard Wagner's own imaginative picture of the black magician Klingsor serving the Anti-Christ in a conspiracy to pervert the rightful development of Love and Wisdom in this most important of the early centuries of European history.

Richard Wagner understood how the Landulf's magical rites, involving horrible sexual perversions and human sacrifices, had a devastating effect on the secular leaders of Christian Europe. For the great artist and composer visualized just how such magical rituals unleash elemental powers through which demonic spirits can gain entrance to the blood and the consciousness of those individualities against whom they are directed. And it was in this sense that Wagner in his opera portrayed Klingsor wielding the Spear of Longinus like some mighty phallic wand of perversion against the romantic love which was budding for the first time in this age. "The fire enkindled by his magical rites affected the whole human race" says a Chronicler of the period.

Wolfram von Eschenbach with more subtlety has also described the destructive effects of Klingsor's magic in his picture of the wounded Grail King, Anfortas, in whom true love has been perverted by an inescapable sexual fantasy.

The greatest of the medieval minnesingers had depicted how the King of the Grail has been brought to moral ruin by a sexual perversion which has disrupted the blessed union between heart and brain and robbed him of his spirit-vision. The "Wound" of Anfortas consists of an incapacity to bring to fulfilment the true processes of spiritual development. And it is the "Bleeding Spear" with which the bard symbolises those Klingsor powers which arise from the sexual instincts like the devil "Legion" to annihilate the "Higher Self" and block the path to the attainment of the Grail.

In the scene which takes place in the inner sanctuary within the Grail Castle, it is the sight of the Spear with blood dripping from its tapering point which increases sevenfold the pain and anguish of the wounded King and causes endless lamentation among his Knights. In a solemn ritual, the Spear is carried around the Temple and all four walls are touched with it. A sign that the path to the realisation of the Grail has been obliterated and that the Grail Community has been severed from a vision of the celestial hierarchies and confined forever within the world of the senses.*

Walter Stein was turning the pages in search of further footnotes concerning the sinister Landulf when he felt the chill of some uneasy presence intruding into his consciousness. He put it aside as something totally illogical and read on.

On the blank pages at the end of the book, he discovered some quotations from a contemporary Chronicler describing the events in the life of the Landulf. The night before he was

---

* "The Lord of the castle was brought into the hall and placed, as he bade, on a cot facing the central fireplace. He had paid his debt to joy; his life was but a-dying.

"Into the great hall came the radiant Parsival, and he who had sent him there gave a gracious welcome, bidding him to stand no longer but come nearer and sit 'here beside me. If I should let you sit further away, I would be treating you like a stranger.' Thus spake the sorrowful host.

"He, because of his illness, kept blazing fires and wore warm clothing. The jacket of fur and the cloak over it were lined outside with sable skins wide and long. The poorest skin was yet worth praise, for even it was black and grey. On his head he wore a covering overlaid inside and out with the same costly fur. An Arabian border encircled its crown and in its centre was a precious jewel, a glittering Ruby.

"There where sat many a valorous Knight, Sorrow itself was born into their presence. In through the door dashed a squire, bearing a Lance in his hands. The rite sharpened their sorrow. Blood gushed from the point and ran down the shaft into the hand that bore it and on into his sleeve.

"And now there was weeping and wailing throughout the whole wide hall. The people of thirty lands could not have wept so many tears. The squire bore the Lance in his hands all round the four walls until he reached the door again and ran out. Stilled then was the people's mourning. . . ." (*Parsival*: Wolfram von Eschenbach.)

born, it appeared that his mother had a dreadful vision in which it seemed to her that she gave birth to a burning torch which would set fire not only to their kingdom but to the whole world. Her husband, to whom she recounted this dream, was so deeply shocked that he could barely resist murdering the child at the very moment of its birth. Instead he decided to write a poem warning the world about his son and the tyranny which would raise through him:

> Alas, sweet Spouse, what fate pursues us?
> Thy fearful vision betokens a terrible prophecy.
> By it the child within thy womb is overshadowed.
> It will love nothing, it will sunder blood relationships.
> At length with poisoned words it will breed dissension among
>   citizens
> And will rage like burning fire in the breast of the righteous.

"What he foretold in spiritual ecstasy, we were destined to see with our own eyes," continued the Chronicler. "And the fire which was later kindled by his deeds infected the blood of the whole human race."

At this point, Walter Stein looked up from the book and out through the trays in the showcase window into the most arrogant face and demoniacal eyes he had ever seen.

It was the face of a man with a hanging forelock of brown hair, a little, almost comical moustache clipped short on both sides of the upper lip, and a small dark beard covering the chin. The man was staring in at him with a questioning gaze. He was dressed in a sleazy black overcoat, far too large for him, and toes were visible through a crack in his shoes beneath frayed trouser ends. He held in his hands postcard-size water-colours which he was apparently trying to sell to passing tourists in the *Kohlmarkt* outside the cafe.

Of course, he did not know that he was looking into the eyes of the man who would far outstrip the terrible prophecies associated with Klingsor, the man who would inspire a satanic reign of terror and cold-blooded butchery outstripping in savagery and bestial cruelty all previous ages of oppression in the entire history of mankind.

Quickly turning away from the hypnotic eyes of this strange apparition, he made a tremendous effort to concentrate on reading the remaining jottings on the character of the Landulf of Capua: "The Character of the Landulf was clever, habitually cunning and lascivious, inordinately ambitious and vain, a despiser of monks, a robber of mankind. He betrayed his own Prince, broke his promises, and deceived his grandchildren. Wherever he found bonds of unity he set himself to oppose them. He sowed the seeds of disunion everywhere. If this seems to anyone incredible, let him only consider the oppressions through which he betrayed his Overlords, although three times he swore that he would recognise their authority. More than all he desired to capture the souls of innocent men rather than to acknowledge them as his equals or as worthy of veneration." (Echempertus).

When he got up to leave Demel's Cafe late in the afternoon, the impoverished artist was still waiting outside. Stein bought three of the paintings, paying for them with a handful of uncounted coins and, shoving them into his side pocket, hurried off down the street. It was not until he had reached his own home that he realised he had bought a painting of the Spear of Destiny—the "Heilige Lance" resting on its red velvet dais behind a glass case in the Treasure House of the Hapsburgs.

And upon the card was the same signature as the name on the inside cover of the tattered copy of *Parsival*—ADOLF HITLER!

THE ABC OF THE GRAIL WITH BLACK MAGIC

The Drug–induced Vision of Adolf Hitler

"However wise a man may be, he will assuredly be glad to know what are the guiding thoughts in this narrative and what are the moral impulses it would impart.

"He who seeks to gain instruction from this tale must not wonder at the contrary elements brought to light therein. Here he must learn to flee away, there to chase, how to avoid, when to blame and where to praise. In him alone who is expert in all these possibilities will wisdom be confirmed.

"If he sit not overlong, neither errs in his steps, but understands, then only will he reach his goal. He who enters into all kind of falsehood in his disposition is led thereby into hell-fire; he destroys all his good fame as a hailstorm destroys fruit. His fidelity has a tail as short as a cow's, for when she is bitten in the forest by a gadfly, she is hard put to it to ward off the third sting because of the shortness of her tail."

Parsival: Wolfram von Eschenbach.

Many of Adolf Hitler's fellow inmates in the Vienna flophouse have described his lousy and dishevelled condition at this time. All depict him as lazy, moody and so contemptuous of any form of work that he would pawn his books and few personal belongings rather than go out to work to earn a few miserable *hellers*.

Some have given detailed descriptions of their evil-tempered bedfellow when he was confined to his bunk wrapped only in a blanket after his clothes had been forcibly taken off him and sent away for fumigation.

Needless to say, none of these tramps and drop-outs who shared his impoverished surroundings had any idea of the real calibre of the man who would twenty years later become the leader of the German people, nor had they even the remotest idea of the real nature of his studies, his far-reaching ambitions, or his drug-induced breach into the heights of transcendent consciousness. Yet most of the accepted biographies of Adolf Hitler have without exception resorted to the reports and opinions of drop-outs and rogues to illustrate the vital formative years of a personality who later all but conquered the world.

How, indeed, can one expect the flotsam and jetsam from the City flophouse to understand the real measure of a personality as great as Adolf Hitler? "A man without measure," Constantin von Neurath, one of Hitler's former cronies, aptly called his Führer after his release from a war criminal's sentence in Spandau Jail. And von Neurath, one-time leader of the Hitler Youth and Gauleiter of Vienna, meant that Adolf Hitler had transformed the dimension of measure into an unlimited imagination which was the very source of his evil genius.

Walter Stein, who was to understand the working of Adolf Hitler's mind on all levels, and who would one day become the confidential adviser to Sir Winston Churchill regarding the Nazi Führer and his leading henchmen, did not find it an easy matter to track down the impoverished postcard painter. For a couple of weeks he hung around the popular tourist sights which the city-dwellers themselves only very infrequently visited— St. Steven's Church, the Hapsburg Summer Palace, the Opera House, Spanish Riding School, the Ringstrasse, and, of course, Demel's Cafe in the *Kohlmarkt* where he had first seen him.

As a last resort he returned to the bookshop in the old quarter of the city where he had bought Hitler's copy of *Parsival*. It was a long shot but it paid off. The proprietor, Ernst Pretzsche, showed an immediate interest when he mentioned Hitler's name, and asked him into the small office at the back of the shop.

Pretzsche was a malevolent-looking man with a bald pate, a partly hunched back and a toadlike figure. Walter Stein took an instant dislike to him. It appeared that Hitler was a regular visitor to the shop but that Pretzsche hadn't seen him for over three weeks.

"He knows he can always come here for a square meal and a chat," said Pretzsche. "He's too proud to accept gifts of cash. I let him pawn his books and belongings to raise enough to pay for the bare necessities of living. His books are really worth nothing but they provide me with an excuse to give him a few *hellers*."

Reaching over to a small pile of books stacked in the corner of the office, he said, "Look at these. He scrawls like this all over his books. There is hardly a page without writing all over it. I don't normally part with them. My assistant made an error in selling you that book."

Stein recognised the works of Fichte, Schelling, Hegel, Schopenhauer and Nietzsche. There was also a copy of Houston Stewart Chamberlain's *Foundations of the Nineteenth Century*. He noticed various works on Eastern Religion and Yoga. The *Nibelungenlied*, Goethe's *Faust*, and Lessing's *The Education of the Human Race*.

A number of Hitler's paintings were to be seen around the walls and stacked beside his books, and postcard-size watercolours were displayed on the mantelpiece. It was an ample enough demonstration of the extent to which Hitler's patron had been giving him financial assistance.

There were also other significant things to be seen on the walls of Pretzsche's office which did not pass Stein's notice. Such things as prints of Alchemists at work and Astrological symbols and charts which hung side by side with pornographic cartoons, the sort of vile illustrations which were circulating with anti-Semitic literature throughout Vienna at the time.

A group photograph on the office desk showed Pretzsche beside a man whom Stein recognised as the infamous Guido von List, the founder member and leading figure of an Occult Lodge whose activities, when uncovered by the Press, had profoundly shocked the people of Vienna. Up to the time he was unmasked, Guido von List had enjoyed a very large following as a political writer whose books were widely praised for their themes of Pan-Germanic mysticism. When it was revealed that he was the leader of a blood brotherhood which had substituted the Swastika for the Cross in rituals involving sexual perversion and the practice of medieval black magic, List had fled from Vienna in fear of being lynched by an incensed populace with strong Roman Catholic sentiments.

Walter Stein was not in the least surprised to find background associations such as these to the satanic commentary on the Grail. Pretzsche was a loathsome creature. How he managed to consider himself as a fine specimen of German manhood was hard to understand. Sitting in his cramped den, he felt like a fly caught up in a spider's web. The moist black eyes looking out at him from a sallow bloodless face seemed to exude evil, especially so now that he assumed his visitor to be a fellow traveller in the Aryan racial cause.

Evading all questions about his personal background and political sympathies, Stein revealed only that he was a student at the University and the extent of his astonishment at discovering such a penetrating commentary on the historical background of the Grail in Hitler's copy of Wolfram von Eschenbach's romance of the Middle Ages.

"I am considered in some quarters to be a great authority on occultism," Pretzsche told him. "Adolf Hitler is not the only person to whom I give assistance and advice in these matters. You may come and consult me at any time."

The last thing he wanted to do was to have any further dealings with this toadlike creature who was obviously mixed up with groups practising the black arts. He had already discovered all that he needed to know, for Pretzsche had given him Adolf Hitler's address. He could now find him without further

59

help from anyone. Giving an excuse for haste, he hurried away from the shop.

There appeared to be no other alternative but to visit Adolf Hitler at the hostelry in Meldemannstrasse where Pretzsche had reported him to be living. Herr Kanya, the manager of this hostelry, told him that Adolf Hitler was away at Spittal-an-der-Drau where one of his Aunts had recently died and left him a small legacy. He did not know whether he would continue to stay at the hostelry on his return to the City.

The legacy brought about a radical change in Adolf Hitler's outward appearance, and Walter Stein barely recognised him when, ten days later, he discovered him painting outside the Hofburg. To be sure, the hanging forelock of brown hair and the moustache were still in evidence but the beard had been shaved off and a barber had given him a military short back and sides.

He was wearing a dark suit and a clean white shirt, and his feet were now well shod in a pair of shining new boots. It was hard to believe that this was the same man as the starving scarecrow dressed in rags whom he had seen outside Demel's some four weeks before.

Before describing the discussion between Walter Stein and Hitler and their later association, it must be pointed out here and now that there is no written record of these conversations. That is to say, we no longer have a record of the exact dialogue between the two men, only the sequence of events which took place at their spasmodic meetings, the general content of their discussions, and the nature of the relationship which developed between them. At the time that Dr. Stein recounted these conversations to me very fully, I myself had no idea that the task of writing *The Spear* would fall to me. At that juncture I had been busy trying to persuade Dr. Stein himself to write it, which he would most certainly have done but for his untimely death. It was for this reason that I took no verbatim notes or tape recordings of Dr. Stein's actual words, making only general comments in my own diaries.

Apparently Adolf Hitler resented the intrusion when Walter Stein stood behind him and paid some trivial compliment about the large water-colour he was painting of the Ring. And when Stein produced the annotated copy of *Parsival* Hitler was greatly incensed, angrily cursing Pretzsche for daring to sell one of the books he had left in pawn. Perhaps their conversation would have come to an abrupt end had not Stein openly spoken about his own researches into the Spear of Destiny, and the value he placed on Hitler's commentary on the historical background to the Grail in the ninth century. Hitler was somewhat appeased. But it was Stein's statement, shrewdly placed, that the Centurion Longinus was partly Teutonic which made Hitler prick up his ears. In no time at all they were deep in an animated discussion about the talisman of power which was to become the central pivot in the life of Adolf Hitler and the very source of his ambitions to conquer the world.

Adolf Hitler became quite excited, and began to regard the blue-eyed and Aryan-looking University student as a fellow conspirator in the Pan-Germanic cause, when he explained how one of the earliest German Chronicles in Cologne indicated that Longinus was of Germanic extraction. This Chronicle mentions a letter which Gaius Cassius sent from Jerusalem to his home village of Zobingen, near Elwangen, in which the Roman Officer described the decisive part he had taken at the Crucifixion of the Jewish Messiah. And how the Village Elder had sent a reply telling of the important local events which had taken place in his absence.

At the end of an hour long conversation, in which Adolf Hitler displayed an extensive knowledge of the legend associated with the Spear of Longinus, and the manner in which it had been fulfilled through the centuries, the two men walked across the Ring together to visit the Weltliche Schatzkammer to take a look at the ancient weapon.

As they made their way across the Ring towards the Hofburg, Walter Stein spoke of his astonishment in discovering that the Spear had become the very pivot of historical events in the Middle Ages during the vital most formative era in the future

destiny of Europe. Most of all, he told Adolf Hitler, he had
been fascinated by the incredible portents which always
appeared to take place immediately preceding the death of the
holder of the Spear when it was about to change hands. He
spoke of the fateful portents which appeared just before the
death of Charlemagne, which had been recorded in some detail
by Einhard, a contemporary Chronicler of the Frankish Court.

He recounted how, after the last of Charlemagne's forty-
seventh victorious campaigns, when he was returning from
Saxony, a Comet flashed across the sky and the Emperor's
horse suddenly shied and threw him to the ground. The great
Frankish Emperor had fallen so violently that his sword belt
had been torn off him and the Spear, which he was clasping in
his left hand, had been hurled some twenty feet away from him.
At the same time there were earth tremors in the Royal Palace
at Aachen, and the word "Princeps" had mysteriously faded
from the red ochre inscription high up on a central beam in
the Cathedral, which had formerly read "Karolus Princeps".
Charlemagne himself had taken little notice of these portents
which his courtiers had taken to be a prophecy of his imminent
death. In Einhard's own words: "He refused to admit that any
of these events could have any connection with his own personal affairs." Yet the 70-year-old Emperor drew up his last
will and testament just in case these portents were correct.
And they were!

Adolf Hitler had apparently read the Chroniclers of the life
of Charlemagne but was not much interested in the Carolingians. He preferred, he said, the illustrious lives of the great
German Emperors like Otto The Great, and Frederick Barbarossa. He told Walter Stein the story of the Ravens of Barbarossa who accompanied their master everywhere, never
deserting him even in the fury of his many battles in which
they hovered above the Spear which he clutched in his hand.
And how his Courtiers were not surprised when their Emperor
fell from his horse and died while crossing a stream in Sicily
because the Ravens had three days earlier quitted their master
and flown out of sight across the sea.

Of course, Walter Stein had not the slightest presentiment on that sunny September morning in Vienna in 1912 that the most remarkable "coincidences" in the change of ownership of the Spear of Destiny were yet to come, or, indeed, that thirty-three years later he would himself be indirectly responsible for retrieving the Spear from a secret vault beneath Nuremberg Fortress at the very moment when Adolf Hitler would take his own life in the OHL Bunker in besieged Berlin.

Adolf Hitler led the way up the long side staircase into the Treasure House and strode directly down the gangway towards the place where the "Heilige Lance" rested.

Walter Stein had seen the Spear on many previous occasions. He had always found it awe-inspiring to consider the associations of this ancient iron Spearhead with some of the greatest names in the history of Europe. However, that morning, for the first time the Spear evoked in his heart a deep compassion for the sacrificial life of Jesus Christ whose blood had been shed by its tapering point. For several minutes he stood there lost in deep meditation, forgetting entirely that he was in the company of Adolf Hitler and suddenly caring little for the legend of the Spear or the string of historical personalities who had fulfilled it.

The immediate sense experience of the weapon which had once been thrust into the side of Jesus Christ between the fourth and fifth rib was to find himself aware in agonising immediacy of the event which had taken place 1900 years before on a hillock outside Jerusalem when the Son of God suffered crucifixion for the redemption of mankind.

For some moments he was almost overcome by the powerful emotions which filled his breast and flowed like a river of healing warmth through his brain, evoking responses of reverence, humility and love. One message above all seemed to be inspired by the sight of this Spear which held within its central cavity one of the nails which had secured the body of Jesus to the Cross. It was a message of compassion which had been so wonderfully expressed in the motto of the Grail Knights: "*Durch Mitleid wissen.*" A call from the Immortal Self of Man resounding in the darkness of confusion and doubt within the human soul: Through Compassion to Self-Knowledge.

For the very first time in his life he knew the meaning of compassion, joy and spiritual release. He felt somehow renewed as a complete human being, and he knew intuitively that life itself was a gift of grace from celestial powers. A deep longing arose in his heart to understand the aims of human evolution and to discover the meaning of his own individual destiny. It was a chastening experience.

Walter Stein found that he was not the only one moved by the sight of this historic Spearhead. Adolf Hitler stood beside him like a man in a trance, a man over whom some dreadful magic spell had been cast. His face was flushed and his brooding eyes shone with an alien emanation. He was swaying on his feet as though caught up in some totally inexplicable euphoria. The very space around him seemed enlivened with some subtle irradiation, a kind of ghostly ectoplasmic light. His whole physiognomy and stance appeared transformed as if some mighty Spirit now inhabited his very soul, creating within and around him a kind of evil transfiguration of its own nature and power.

The young student recalled the legend of the two opposing Spirits of Good and Evil associated with this Spear of World Destiny. Was he a witness of the incorporation of the Spirit of the Anti-Christ in this deluded human soul? he asked himself. Had this tramp from the dosshouse momentarily become the vessel of that Spirit which the Bible called "Lucifer", the Spirit whom the verses of the Grail poem described as leading the evil hosts which had been cast down into the souls of mankind.

It was difficult to believe the evidence of his own eyes but events were to prove Walter Stein correct. For it was the sight of this same Spirit within the soul of Adolf Hitler which later inspired Houston Stewart Chamberlain, Wagner's son-in-law and the prophet of the Pan-Germanic world, to proclaim him as the German "Messiah".

It was not only the fanatical followers of the Nazi *Weltanschauung*, or people who had been personally affected by the charisma and dynamism of Adolf Hitler, who were to give evidence of this remarkable phenomena of his "Luciferic" possession. Take, for instance, the testimony of a rational and extroverted person like Denis de Rougement:

"Some people believe, from having experienced in his presence a feeling of horror and an impression of supernatural power, that he is the seat of 'Thrones, Dominions and Powers', by which Saint Paul meant those hierarchical spirits which can descend into any ordinary mortal and occupy him like a garrison. . . . Where do the superhuman powers he shows on these occasions come from? It is quite obvious that a force of this kind does not belong to the individual and indeed could not even manifest itself unless the individual were of no importance except as the vehicle of a force for which our psychology has no explanation. . . . What I am saying would be the cheapest form of romantic nonsense were it not that what has been established by this man or rather— through him—is a reality that is one of the wonders of the century."

Of course, Walter Stein could not have foreseen that day in the Treasure House in Vienna in September 1912 that Adolf Hitler would channelise such demonic powers or harness his personal destiny so completely to the Anti-Spirit of the Spear. "At that time when we first stood side by side in front of the Spear of Longinus," Dr. Stein told me thirty-five years later, "it appeared to me that Hitler was in so deep a condition of trance that he was suffering almost complete sense-denudation and a total eclipse of self-consciousness."

In other words, Hitler's soul life was not mature enough at that moment to maintain an awareness of himself and his surroundings when this alien entity entered him. During the following six months during a series of irregular meetings and discussions with Hitler, Walter Stein was to witness a maturing soul development in this enigmatic character through which he became more and more a conscious and responsive tool of the world-shattering purposes of the demonic Spirit which overshadowed him. "I move like a sleep-walker where Providence dictates," said Adolf Hitler at a Press interview. What a tragedy these robust but sceptical observers of the rise of the Third Reich were incapable of comprehending the staggering truth of those words.

When Dr. Stein recounted this dramatic scene in the Hofburg, I asked him what course would have been open to him had he realised the fearful reign of terror and destruction which would be unleashed by the evil powers working through Adolf Hitler. Was there, in fact, any justification for the assassination of such vehicles of evil before that evil had time to strike?

In reply Dr. Stein cited the instance of Friedrich Staps who planned to kill Napoleon while he was inspecting his Guards at Schönbrunn. Staps, a student, stepped forward to hand Napoleon a petition. He was searched and found to be carrying a long sharp knife on his person. When he was questioned he stated fearlessly that he intended to kill the Emperor.

Napoleon questioned Staps himself, with his aide-de-camp acting as interpreter:

"Why did you want to kill me?" he asked.

"Because you brought misfortune to my country."

"Have I harmed you in any way?"

"As much as you have harmed every one in Germany."

"Who incited you to this crime?"

"No one. I armed myself because I was firmly convinced that by killing you I would render the greatest service to my country and to Europe."

"You are mad, or else ill."

"I am neither."

The doctor Corvisart was summoned and stated that in fact the young man was in good health. Napoleon offered to pardon him.

"I do not wish to be pardoned," replied the youth. "I regret I did not succeed."

"But tell me, if I pardoned you, would you be grateful?"

"I would still want to kill you just as much."

Staps died, shouting 'Long live liberty'."*

Staps, the son of a Pastor, was a member of the then elite

* *Napoleon:* Octave Aubry (Hamlyn).

Germanenorden, the circle which conspired to remove the Spear of Destiny out of Nuremberg before the Emperor could get his hands on it in order to harness the talisman to his own ambitions of world conquest.

Dr. Stein expressed the opinion that such attempts to assassinate tyrants were fully justified, always provided that there was no attempt to escape the consequences of the deed. It would have taken great courage to have killed Hitler in his formative years in Vienna, for there would have been the extra stigma of madness! Who would have credited that a drop-out from the flophouse would one day become the greatest tyrant in world history? How easy it is to be wise after the event!

The relationship which developed between Walter Stein and Adolf Hitler could never be described as a friendship. For his part Stein learned that it is possible to know pity and compassion for somebody one actively dislikes and with whom one has absolutely no affinity.

"I admit willingly," said Dr. Stein later, "that I was fascinated by his studies of the Grail. At the same time, I believed, and quite wrongly as it turned out, that I could transform his thinking and stimulate some genuine social feeling within him. There can be no doubt that he had some quite remarkable gifts, but they were not the kind which could integrate him in society, or even earn him his bread and butter."

Adolf Hitler, it appears, regarded Stein as a spirited young student with an excellent mind, which might through sheer force of personality be won over to the pan-Germanic and racist cause. No doubt there was also an element of pride that he was instructing a brilliant student from the University into matters which no orthodox scholar could ever have taught him.

There was always a kind of hidden enmity between them and never any genuine feeling of warmth on Hitler's part. For instance, Adolf Hitler never used Walter Stein's Christian name in the same way that he addressed Kubizek as "Gustl", nor did he ever use the intimate form of "Du". Instead he always greeted Stein with a touch of aggressive sarcasm calling him "Herr Professor" or "Herr Doctor".

The onus was always with Walter Stein to arrange their meetings at Hitler's convenience and, on many occasions, Hitler did not bother to turn up, leaving Stein waiting around for hours or searching for Hitler at his customary haunts—mostly cafes in the city or in the factory area of Vienna Neustadt where Hitler could most easily find an arena to air his political theories.

And to add to this situation, Adolf Hitler was equally unpredictable in his moods. Some days he would be willing to speak very openly about certain aspects of his occult experiences, whilst at other times he confined his conversations to tedious political arguments or uninterrupted diatribes of racial hatred.

"Only very gradually with the passing of months was I able to gain a complete picture of his life and to discover the background to his studies of the Grail and the mystery of the Spear of Longinus. I was careful never to press him," Stein insisted, "simply waiting patiently for him to unburden his experiences little by little."

The substance of these discussions which took place in the late summer, autumn and winter of 1912 and the spring of 1913 have been the source of the descriptions of Adolf Hitler's life and aspirations in the earlier chapters of this book.

For the University student reared in a cultured environment, Adolf Hitler made an embarrassingly crude companion when they sat in cafes together to discuss their mutual interest of the Grail or the Spear. Often as not Walter Stein would have to sit through demonstrations of Hitler's all-consuming egoism which reached to proportions of megalomania, performances of brutal willpower which were mesmerising to watch. These outbursts always occurred when Hitler involved himself with strangers in furious political arguments in which he all but came to blows. Lashing up an unassailable wave of verbal violence in which he screamed and spat abuse, Hitler reduced his opponents to a shocked and resentful silence. And then, as though nothing out of the ordinary had taken place, he would return to his chair at the table with Stein to sip coffee and resume a quiet discussion on the quest for the Grail or the like.

At other times, especially when Hitler was elated, his normal halting awkward style of speaking was transformed into a magical flow of words, delivered with spellbinding effect. On these occasions it was as though Hitler himself was listening to the extraneous intelligence which had temporarily taken over his soul. Later he would sit back exhausted, a solitary figure cast down from the heights of orgiastic ecstasy and utterly stripped of that charismatic quality which moments before had given him such a masterful command of himself and his audience.

The strange transformation which Stein was witnessing in its early beginnings would later be described by others who saw this Luciferic possession take place yet more concretely as Hitler rose step by step to the very pinnacle of power:

> "Listen to Hitler and one suddenly has a vision of one who will lead mankind to glory," Gregor Strasser, a defected Nazi, recounted twenty years later. "A light appears in a dark window. A gentleman with a comic moustache turns into an Archangel. Then the Archangel flies away and there is Hitler sitting down, bathed in sweat with glassy eyes."

When Hitler elaborated on the Grail, which he conceived as a path leading from unthinking dullness, through doubt, to spiritual awakening, the word most frequently on his lips was *"Initiation"*. Many times he reeled off the ascending grades on the way to the achievement of higher levels of consciousness, disclosing the meaning of the heraldry and armorial insignia of the Knights, which he interpreted as representing the various stages they had attained in the quest for the Grail.

The black Raven was the sign of the First Degree, he explained, because the Raven signified the Messenger of the Grail and the finger of fate which led man to it. The Second Degree was symbolised by the Peacock, its many splendoured plumage demonstrating the capacity for the many coloured imaginative or picture building powers.

The Swan was the sign of the Third Degree because the novice who sought to attain it had to sing the Swan Song. That is, he had to die to his own selfish desires and weaknesses to serve the higher aims of his race.

The Fourth Degree had been given the symbol of the Pelican, the bird which wounds its own breast to feed its young. Such an initiate, concluded Hitler, lived for the perpetuation of his own people and dedicated himself to the nurturing of its youth.

The Lion meant that a man had attained the Fifth Degree and unified his consciousness with the Folk-Spirit of his race. He spoke as the vessel of that Folk-Spirit. Such a man had become the Messianic Leader of his people.

And, according to Hitler's unchristian interpretation of the Grail symbolism, the highest degree merited the Emblem of the Eagle, for the Initiate had now developed the loftiest powers and faculties attainable to man. He could now assume a world-historic destiny.

"What has such a path of Initiation got to do with a Jewish Carpenter from Nazareth?" said Hitler. "A self-appointed Rabbi whose teachings of meekness and love ended in the surrender of the will to survive. Nothing! Nor had the Grail disciplines for reawakening the latent powers in the blood anything whatsoever to do with Christianity."

Was there a single incident or passage in the Grail story which could not stand by itself alone without the cunning intrusion of spurious Christian doctrines?

"No!" said Hitler. "The real virtues of the Grail were common to all the best Aryan peoples. Christianity only added the seeds of decadence such as forgiveness, self-abnegation, weakness, false humility, and the very denial of the evolutionary laws of survival of the fittest, the most courageous and talented."

Walter Stein could always expect a diet of this sort of talk whenever they met, but he used the opportunities, when Hitler was most talkative, to ask those questions which would fill in the gaps in his already mounting knowledge of the background to Hitler's researches into the mysteries of the Grail and the legend of the Spear.

Walter Stein was more than curious to know where Ernst Pretzsche, and his association with the infamous Blood Lodge of Guido von List, fitted into the picture, for he was becoming daily more aware that Adolf Hitler had an experienced spiritual mentor somewhere in the background. Yet he was afraid to ask him about this directly because he had noticed that Hitler always shut up like a clam if he thought he was being interrogated. The solution came one November evening when Hitler brought an alchemical chart to their rendezvous, which he announced he had obtained through Ernst Pretzsche some time previously.

Walter Stein recognised this chart as one of the illustrations in the work of Basilius Valentinus, a sixteenth-century alchemist who had depicted in a series of sketches the central themes from Wolfram von Eschenbach's *Parsival*.

This particular picture, which Hitler had brought along with him, depicted the Knights Parsival, Gawain and Feirifis, the three heroes of the tale, standing before the Hermitage of Treverezent, the aged and wise Guardian of the secrets of the Grail. And Hitler told Stein in confidence that Ernst Pretzsche had discovered that in this enchanting fairytale-like illustration, the whole path to transcendent consciousness was hidden. Walter Stein himself had already fathomed out the hidden meaning in it, and later used the illustration in his own book, *The Ninth Century*.

The path to the Grail is seen (see illust. following page 170) to spiral up the side of a miniature mountain above the cave of the bearded hermit in the rock below. A hare, the sign of both Alchemy and of the fleeting thoughts of the uninitiated, runs towards the path. A little way up the mountainside a large fat hen broods on a nest of eggs to signify the warmth and will-power which must be brought to the development of a picture-building imagination, so that thoughts become as substantial as external objects, and take on a new clarity of form and permanence.

Higher up the narrow winding path, a lion blocks the way. The lion signifies the whole realm of the feelings, that is the sympathies and antipathies, pleasures and aversions, which the Grail-searcher must now master and keep on the tightest reign. To conquer the Lion, he must make his feelings as depersonalised and objective as his thinking, so that the power of feeling itself becomes an inspired form of cognition which informs him of realities rather than his own selfish likes and dislikes.

And now the time has come for the Knight to confront the Dragon and slay him. The Dragon symbolises the powers of the unleashed instincts, impulses and desires—the ever-hungry appetites of the Serpent which fight back so powerfully against the strongest and most dedicated willpower when it attempts to master them.

The next symbol is the most strange and mysterious of all and has baffled the keenest minds in pursuit of the Grail—a Dustbin containing a discarded Sun and Moon! This enigmatic symbolism depicts the condition of soul of a man, however outwardly learned, who is still trapped in the three-dimensional "Dustbin" of consciousness—the world of measure, number and weight. That is, the soul who is not yet capable of the "sense-free" thinking which leads to transcendent consciousness.

Above the Dustbin, which imprisons an unhappy looking Sun and Moon, there is a weird-looking Wizard's Kitchen with smoking chimneys. This extraordinary cookhouse perched near the very summit of the mountain represents the subtle alchemical changes which must take place when Spirit, Soul and Body are brought into that interpenetrating inner harmony within which the faculties of mind-expansion may be developed—the trinity of Imaginative Cognition, Inspiration and Intuition with which the aspiring Knight can cross the bridge between two worlds—the Earthly and the Supersensible.

It is at this stage in the search for the Grail that the Knight must enter into the most penetrating self-knowledge. He must discover for himself the true meaning of impartiality, tolerance and equanimity. An impartiality in which all prejudices, especially those of race, must be wiped from the soul; a tolerance inspired by a true respect for the equality of rights of all men; an equanimity born of the deepest trust in God. Master of his thoughts, his feelings and his powers of Will, the aspirant must be able to discriminate instantly between the morally real and the unreal, the eternal and the ephemeral. Above all, he must value the God-granted capacity for Spiritual Freedom in which, unchained from the dogmas of the Church and the dictates of other men, he is led by his own moral intuition alone. Out of such spiritual freedom, his whole life must become a loving dedication to serving humanity in which all personal motives have been raised to the heights of Universal Ideals.

Here, at the very threshold of the Holy Grail, the words of Saint Paul ring forth—"Not I but Christ in me." The Knight now treads the path of humility which leads to the annihilation of egoism in the consecrated fire of the Love of Christ.

Even when Parsival himself has learned by travail and suffering the deepest meaning of the words *"Durch Mitleid wissen"* (Through Compassion to Self Knowledge), he must wait for the God-granted moment when final illumination is given to him. The moment when, reborn in Spirit, he becomes an active participant of Supersensible Worlds.

Above the mountain, the sun and moon are seen released from their three-dimensional enslavement—the final casting off of the materialistic pollutions of the Dustbin! The Sun and the Crescent Moon, rightly orientated in the sky, are the sign of the Grail, the Holy Symbol of Transcendent Consciousness.

The Grail is also symbolised by a Dove winging its way across from the sun towards the "invisible disc" held between the arms of the Crescent Moon. In other alchemical pictures drawn by the same Basilius Valentinus, the Sun is depicted as the human heart and the Moon as the Pineal Gland—the "precious jewel" mentioned in Wolfram von Eschenbach's *Parsival*.

As we have already mentioned, it is the Pineal Gland which, when opened and activated becomes that organ of vision which Eastern Systems call the "Third Eye". And it is with this highest of all spiritual organs that the secrets of Time are unlocked and the "Akashic Record" is revealed. It is also with the same "Pineal Eye" that events which took place in previous lives on earth are perceived as pictures in a form of transcendent memory.

Adolf Hitler's interpretation of the symbolism of the Grail was by no means as articulate as the above explanation, nor had it any Christian connotation whatsoever, but apparently in its own crude but direct way it mastered the salient points of the quest for the Grail. And Adolf Hitler seemed to be very knowledgeable about the Pineal Eye, the Akashic Record and Reincarnation, even claiming to remember a past incarnation in the ninth century. It was clear enough to Stein that, if Hitler was speaking the truth, he had not attained the requisite faculties by treading the morally demanding path to the Grail but by some other secret and probably highly illicit means.

It was only very gradually in a series of further meetings and discussions (many of which were abortive because of his ever-changing moods and shifting attitudes) that he learned the whole incredible story of how Adolf Hitler achieved transcendent consciousness by means of drugs.

Day by day throughout the first half of 1911, Adolf Hitler had concentrated all his energies and his native shrewdness on solving the riddles presented by the strange and remarkable verses of the intriguing Grail Romance about Knights and their ladies in the dawn of the Middle Ages.

He soon discovered that the colourful story of the search for the Grail was so devised that behind the enchanting flow of words of the medieval minnesinger ever deeper levels of truth lay concealed. The moment quickly arrived when he knew he had travelled as far towards the goal as the powers of intellect could take him. To cross the threshold into transcendent awareness, which might reveal the deepest secrets of the Grail, he was confronted with two choices: the Wagnerian path of renunciation before the Cross of an Aryan Christ, or a direct plunge into the practice of the black arts by way of a short cut to the most high knowledge.

The former path appeared to him as "a monstrous capitulation to spiritual nausea", in Friedrich Nietzsche's words, "the bowing down to the highest of all conceivable corruptions". The latter path, as though his personal destiny was itself guided by the hand of Satan, was effortlessly opened up to him when he made the acquaintance of Ernst Pretzsche, the bookseller who had made an extensive study and practice of the art of Black Magic.

Stein could well imagine how impressed Pretzsche must have been on his first sight of Adolf Hitler browsing through the books on his shelves and entering into furious arguments with his customers. No doubt that Pretzsche had not been in the least put off by Hitler's offensively unkempt appearance and his thin hungry face. How delighted he must have been with Hitler's mystic blue eyes, so brooding and yet so ignited with mission, the extraordinary mixture of arrogance and self-confidence, the passionate belief in the future of Germany, the sheer venom which this animated scarecrow could unleash in a single violent outburst against the Jews.

After their first meeting, Adolf Hitler could always reckon on a warm welcome and a square meal in the cramped office at the back of the shop, where he quickly found out that Pretzsche had made a deep study of medieval occultism, alchemy and astrology. The diminutive figure with a hunched back, huge paunch and disproportionately long arms, that gave him a look of a surrealistic toad, had been brought up amidst the patriotic German-speaking community in Mexico City. His father, Wilhelm Pretzsche, ran an Apothecary's business and spent his leisure hours in an extensive study of the customs and ritual magic of the ancient Aztecs, an interest which the son took up as soon as he was old enough to do so. Returning to his homeland in 1892, Ernst Pretzsche became inflamed by the current Wagnerian Pan-Germanic movement and very soon took an active part in circulating anti-Semitic literature throughout Vienna. Through the medium of his bookshop dealing in occultism and kindred subjects, he became known to an extensive circle of adepts, who regarded highly his expert knowledge of ritual magic. It was in this manner too that Pretzsche came to meet Guido von List, the Aleister Crowley-like figure whose Blood Lodge and black magic rituals shocked the German-speaking world in 1909. And, according to Hitler, Pretzsche was himself present when Guido von List attempted to materialise "the Incubus" in a ritual designed to create a "Moon Child".

Pretzsche, like most Germans associated with the Occult, had made a study of Wolfram von Eschenbach's *Parsival*, and he was thus able to direct Adolf Hitler's attention to some of the most significant verses in it. For instance, the riddle of the source of the work itself:

> "Any one who asked me before about the Grail and took me to task for not telling him was very much in the wrong. Kyot (Wolfram von Eschenbach's Occult Master) asked me not to reveal this, for Adventure (Initiation) commanded him to give it no thought until she herself, Adventure, should invite the telling, and then one must speak of it, of course.
>
> "Kyot, the well-known Master, found in Toledo, discarded (set down in heathen writing) the first source of this Adventure. *He had first to learn the ABC's but without the art of Black Magic.*"

Pretzsche then directed Hitler's attention to another section of the text where Kyot is said to have learned his "ABC's" from Flegetanis which means "the reader of the starry script".

The strange reference to learning the "ABC's", Pretzsche now explained to his eager pupil, concerned the development of a faculty through which Initiates were able to unravel the relationships of spiritual existence and by which they acquired the art of "reading" from the "Cosmic Chronicle" of human destiny in which past, present and future were united in one uncoiling ribbon of Time. And this explanation Adolf Hitler was able to understand easily enough, for he had seen a single picture from this imperishable record which was revealed to him when standing before the Spear of Destiny in the Hofburg in promise of his mandate as the Leader of the German people.

What about the fascinating inclusion of those so tantalising words: "without the art of Black Magic?" With this answer Pretzsche was in his element. He was able to tell Hitler that the Akashic Record could be read more simply and quickly but equally effectively through the practice of the black arts!

It was in the small back office of the bookshop in the old quarter of the city that Ernst Pretzsche unveiled for Hitler the secrets hidden behind the astrological and alchemical symbolism of the search for the Grail, which we have already mentioned at some length. It was there too that the sinister hunchback handed to his monstrous pupil the drug which evoked the clairvoyant vision of the Aztecs, the magic Peyotl venerated like a deity. A drug with a similar effect to that which had aided the Essene Communities to behold the descending Logos, the approaching Messiah; the drug which half-a-century later would inspire Aldous Huxley to write his epoch-making book, *The Doors of Perception: Heaven and Hell,* and send the incredulous Timothy Leary off on his first historic mind-expansion trip which brought to birth the psychedelic age.

According to the ancients such drugs "spoke with God's voice", but which, according to the highest ideals of the Holy Grail, constituted the learning of the "ABC's" *with* the art of Black Magic, a drug-induced pilfering from the Cosmic Chronicle which cheated and destroyed the very meaning of human destiny in the Christian world.*

Pretzsche, who had spent the greater part of his life in Mexico, was sufficiently experienced with the reactions to the Mexican root Peyotl to advise his protégé at what point on the path to the Grail he should take the drug-induced short cut to transcendent consciousness.

* The changing significance of the use of drugs to attain higher levels of consciousness is dealt with in a later chapter in Section III: Hitler's greatest adversary: The Spear as Symbol of the Cosmic Christ.

77

He persuaded Hitler to carry through all the earlier disciplines of the search for the Grail such as single-minded concentration, the meditative power to wield thoughts like things, the rigid control of the feeling life, the attempt at mastery of basic desires. All these aspects were vital, according to Pretzsche, because without such a background of mind control and inner discipline, drugs would not in themselves orientate his vision or make him objectively receptive to the realities beheld in the realm of mind expansion. The drug (now known to contain mescalin, the active principle of peyote) would then adequately compensate for that condition of body chemistry otherwise only mysteriously created by the actual attainment of the highest virtues of the Grail, and so lead him directly into a fruitful experience of transcendent consciousness.

Adolf Hitler conducted his search for the Holy Grail from the dosshouse amongst drunks and junkies, thieves and dropouts. He claimed to prefer remaining unknown and unmolested in this wilderness for rogues and beggars to life "on the other side of the ditch amidst the despicable petit-bourgeois",* than working for a living among "the promiscuous rabble of foreign workers who battened down on the ancient nursery of German Culture."*

To support this embittered and isolated attitude to life, Adolf Hitler never tired of quoting his beloved Nietzsche's *Thus Spake Zarathustra*: "And some who turned away from life, only turned away from the rabble, they did not want to share well and flame and fire with the rabble."

The search for the Holy Grail demands three steps in self-mastery and moral strengthening for every step forward on the path to the highest and holiest of all Christian Mysteries. Yet, instead of selflessness, reverence for life, sincerity and receptivity to the needs of others, Adolf Hitler could now just as surely achieve his goal by following the degraded morality and the ferocious struggle for survival of the dosshouse, which he later described as "a hard school which taught me the profoundest lessons of my life".

* *Mein Kampf.*

Unscrupulous opportunism, astuteness, cunning, brutality and an ever-wary perception into the weaknesses of others to be exploited to immediate advantage—such can be the attitude to life of an aspirant to the Holy Grail who decides to substitute drugs in place of Christian morality!

"It is not by the principles of humanity that man lives by or is able to preserve himself above the animal world but solely by means of the most brutal struggle. . . . If you do not fight for life then life will never be won."*

Walter Stein was able to fit together the final pieces of the jigsaw puzzle of the background to Hitler's breakthrough to transcendent consciousness at their last meeting in the spring of 1913.

Hitler was in an unusually talkative and open mood as the result of a recent visit to Richard Wagner's opera *The Meistersinger*. He was planning to leave Vienna for good and to move to live in Munich the following week. For a change, it was Hitler himself who suggested they should take a final outing together up the Danube to Wachau.

The river was in flood after the melting of the winter snow and the countryside was a fresh verdant green, the soft sunshine reflected on the pine trees on the slopes bordering the river's edge. Adolf Hitler and Walter Stein stood together on the bows of the little steamship as it ploughed its way up the Danube.

Only when they were half way to Wachau did Hitler reveal the real purpose of the trip. He was going to say farewell to an old friend called Hans Lodz, a herbalist who retained in his peasant's blood the last traces of the atavistic clairvoyance of the ancient Germanic tribes. He had originally met Lodz, Hitler explained, when sleeping rough in the country two years earlier. The old man had taken him into his cabin and not only shared his meagre fare but also rendered a great service in

* Ibid.

preparing a special potion through which he had achieved his first sustained experience of the Macrocosm and an insight into the mysteries of Reincarnation. The potion he referred to was the preparation of the roots of Peyotl which had been provided by Ernst Pretzsche.

The two men walked up the riverside from Wachau until they came to a dilapidated log cabin belonging to an aged peasant who earned his subsistence as a wood cutter and herbalist. Hans Lodz turned out to be a busy, restless little man with flowing white hair and beard and a face as creased as a gnarled oak. He resembled a mischievous yet malevolent dwarf from the pages of Grimm's *Fairy Tales* or an illustration from a book on ancient Germanic folklore. He was obviously delighted to see Hitler again and set about making them a vegetable broth, taking every opportunity to make them welcome to his humble surroundings.

Here, in the quiet and solitude of the woods, isolated from the noises and distractions of the big city, Hitler had made the first hazardous incursions into mind expansion. Though Adolf Hitler assessed that Peyotl could provide his most direct short cut to transcendent consciousness, he admitted to Stein that he had not cherished the idea of compromising his own Will to a process over which he might have little control. He had more than just an inchoate feeling that the brain, nervous system and the senses were the very means which so effectively confined man to three-dimensional consciousness and sealed off all awareness of that superconscious area of the total mind from which no secret in the Universe is hidden.

Yet Stein was sure that Hitler never realised that he was a pronounced schizophrenic, or that the top of the Mexican Desert Cactus had a profound and often shattering effect on such subjects—sometimes entirely consuming their sense of identity as it whirled and involuted them through their own minds into higher dimensions of time and consciousness. Nor did Hitler divine that his near-starvation diet and his psychotic condition of permanent inner stress had created that kind of body chemistry which gives little or no protection from the devastating impact of this powerful hallucinogen.

We know today that the peyote experience is in every case conditioned by the temperament, mental equipment and general life of habit of the subject. In response to such conditioning, the resultant type of mind expansion can only take two main directions.

On the one hand, the mind can flow outwards into an awakened awareness of the spirit behind the material world itself, bridging the gap between man and nature, so that all transient and earthly phenomena appear as the outer garment which the Deity wears. On the other hand, the mind can be plunged into a moving tapestry of colourful, mobile, visual imagery in higher levels of awareness which are totally cut off from all terrestrial sense experience.

In the former type of reaction in which nature herself is experienced in transcendent awareness, the subject may even retain the ability to think clearly and can communicate with others throughout the period of intensified visual perception. However, in the latter type of experience, the reaction can be so violent and extreme that all awareness of the sense world is obliterated for a period lasting for many hours.

Perhaps it would have been a happier thing for the world at large if Adolf Hitler's personal reaction to peyote had given him such an intensified aesthetic appreciation of nature, for, even at this late stage, it might well have led him to a successful career as an artist.

Although the human soul is, in a very real sense, imprisoned in an apparently material world of length, breadth and thickness, such an isolated, confined and boxed-in awareness also serves as a protection, for without it we would not only be unable to mature to individual self-consciousness, but also be completely incapable of coping with day-to-day activities which help us to survive physically on earth. Peyote breaches the confines of this prison, for it ruptures what Aldous Huxley so brilliantly calls "the reducing valve" which rations us "with our measly trickle of consciousness" and protects us from the formidable impact of transcendent awareness before we are ready to receive it.

The adjustment of this "reducing valve" by higher Powers so that it filters through into the conscious mind a specific content of transcendent awareness is named as "Grace" by Christian theologians—the bestowing of an inner knowing which acts as balsam, guidance and healing to the aspiring soul.

Adolf Hitler, who actively aspired towards Luciferic possession, was to experience the very reverse of "Grace", for the drug-induced awareness now channelled into his consciousness served to guide him towards his sinister and inhuman goals of personal power, tyranny and world conquest; a kind of guarantee of personal damnation as a recompense for his lonely hymn of hate and scorn and contempt for humanity.

Aldous Huxley has described with rare insight the kind of experience of visual imagery that the average person can expect under the influence of a powerful dose of mescalin.

"The typical mescalin experience begins with perceptions of coloured, moving, living geometrical forms. In time, pure Geometry becomes concrete, and the visionary perceives, not patterns but patterned things, such as carpets, carvings, mosaics. These give place to vast and complicated buildings, in the midst of landscapes, which change continuously, passing from richness to more intensely coloured richness, from grandeur to deepening grandeur.

"Heroic figures, of the kind that Blake called 'The Seraphim', may make their appearance, alone, or in multitudes. Fabulous animals move across the scene. Everything is novel and amazing. Almost never does the visionary see anything that reminds him of his own past. He is not remembering scenes, persons, or objects, and he is not investing them; he is looking at a new creation."*

Nobody would describe Adolf Hitler as an ordinary run-of-the-mill person and his reaction to the drug could not in any

* *Aldous Huxley: The Doors of Perception: Heaven and Hell* (Chatto and Windus).

way be described as typical. Already on the threshold of spiritual perception without the aid of drugs, and possessed with deep mediumistic faculties, his peyote-induced visions appear to have been entirely conditioned by his own specific aims and his extraordinary powers of Will to take a far more definitive form.

It is not possible to describe in any detail the definitive content of these trips into psychedelic awareness, for Hitler was not willing to speak to Walter Stein about them at any length. Indeed, the fact that he achieved transcendent consciousness and formulated his *Weltanschauung* in this period through the medium of drugs became the most closely-guarded secret of his life. Yet he described his experiences sufficiently to give Walter Stein some idea of the categories of awareness which the drug evoked for him.

The most terror-filled moment of his first trip must have been what is today described as the crisis point in the use of hallucogens on psychotic subjects when the soul feels itself whirled out of three-dimensional space with the shock and brutal abruptness of a hooked fish. Yet, while he plunged, spiralled and involuted through those shimmering, sounding, pulsating, praeternatural colourscapes, which are characteristic of the mescalin experience, Hitler appears to have retained some portion of his personal identity, for he described how he was aware at this time that he was caught up in the projected pictures of the rhythms and physiological processes of his own body chemistry—living pictures which mirror in colossal perspective such bio-chemical functions as the beating of the heart and the circulation of the blood, the breathing and the metabolism.

It was not this sphere of the unveiling of the living relationships between the Macrocosm and the Microcosm which fascinated Hitler at this stage. The whole object of these dangerous incursions into the uncharted depths of "inner space" was to discover the meaning of his own personal destiny within the historical process.

The search for the meaning of personal destiny and the active attempt to discover former incarnations on earth through the medium of drug-induced awareness has led countless adventurous members of the younger generation of the present psychedelic age into grave error and illusion. For it is in the subtle, elusive, and immeasurably complex strata of the Akashic Record that everything must appear as chaos and confusion when approached without the long and arduous training and disciplines of occult initiation. Such training, which includes the mastery of all aspects of human thinking, feeling and willpower, opens the requisite organs of spiritual cognition and provides the aspirant with the capacity to orientate himself within the otherwise endless maze of supersensible realms.

Adolf Hitler also experienced the chaos and confusion which results from almost totally unprepared and morally unearned precipitation into the oceans of transcendent awareness. Yet, in this respect, he was not as handicapped as the normal run of contemporary psychedelic "trippers" who have neither the single-pointed concentration nor the forces of willpower to find their way and direct their vision in supersensible existence. Here, Adolf Hitler, whose whole career has been described by the most eminent authorities as "the remarkable achievement of human willpower alone", had a very great advantage.

Amidst the endless rich variety of resounding colour-rinsed imagery which assaulted his consciousness from all quarters, he followed his customary habit of concentrating "on the essential and utterly disregarding the inessential" and, in this way, he managed to rescue from the terrifying confusion of movement and form one single theme of awareness which he felt would further his own aims.

He claims to have made his single breach into lucid comprehension in what he called "universal currents of divine thought" which had inspired the minnesinger to write *Parsival* and Richard Wagner to compose his greatest opera round the pivot of the Spear of Destiny.*

---

* "I wish to say that inspiration is a very evasive, a most elusive subject, which is not easily defined and about which we know little. *Few indeed there*

In these ethereal realms where thoughts are yet more concrete than material objects on earth, Adolf Hitler found himself immersed in an unfurling tapestry which, for want of a better word, we can only describe as a mosaic of "celestial mythology"; yet, while he was transported within the flow of these universal currents of thought which pictured the search for the Holy Grail, he realised at the same time that this ribbon of ethereal symbolism actually mirrored historical events of the medieval centuries.

On yet another level of awareness simultaneously experienced, actual memories of one of his former incarnations began partially to emerge. However, these memories of a former life on earth were apparently not part of a continuous memory process. Rather they were more like still, isolated and momentary flashes which did not follow the normal sequence of terrestrial time—pictures of locations in some Mediterranean climate which appeared to be southern Italy or Sicily, pictures of situations in which people appeared in medieval dress and with the weapons and accoutrements of the ninth and tenth centuries.

Adolf Hitler had often spoken of the surviving Indian tradition of Reincarnation which he considered to be negative and unprogressive, for he refused to regard life as a "wheel of suffering" from which mankind should at all costs escape. He considered the ancient Athenian view of rebirth far more realistic. He praised Plato's "Myth of Er" which concludes the Republic and envisages Reincarnation as a readjustment of the balance of justice from life to life.

Lessing's short historical essay *The Education of the Human Race* had made a great impression on him. He could quote long passages from it which he had learned by heart:

be who know how to tap the source from which it flows, and this undoubtedly is the reason why there has been so little written about it. I am myself convinced that *there are Universal Currents of Thought* . . . and that any one who can experience these vibrations is inspired, providing he is conscious of the process and possesses the necessary knowledge and skill to present them." (*Humperdinck's report of conversations with Richard Wagner.*)

"Go thine inscrutable way, Eternal Providence!

"Only let me not despair in Thee, because of this inscrutableness.

"Let me not despair in Thee, even if Thy steps appear to be retreating. It is not true that the shortest line is always straight.

"Thou hast on Thine Eternal Way so much to carry on, so much to do: often hast thou to step aside! And what if it were as good as proved that the vast slow wheel, which brings mankind nearer to his perfection, is only put in motion by smaller, swifter wheels, each of which contributes its own individual entity thereto?

"It is so! The very same way by which the race reaches its perfection, must every individual man—one sooner, another later—have travelled over. Have travelled over in one and the same life? Can he have been in one and the same life a sensuous Jew and a spiritual Christian? Can he in the self-same life overtaken both?

"Surely not that! But why shouldn't every individual man have existed more than once in the world?

"Is this hypothesis so laughable because it is the oldest? Because the human understanding, before the sophistries of the Schools had dissipated and debilitated it, lighted upon it once?

"Why may not even I have already performed those steps of my perfection which bring to man only temporal punishments and rewards?

"Why should I not come back as often as I am capable of acquiring fresh knowledge, fresh experience? Do I bring back so much from once, that there is nothing to repay the trouble of coming back. Is there a reason against it? Or because I forget I have been here already."

Throughout the verses in his tattered leather-bound copy of *Parsival*, Adolf Hitler had been amazed to discover numerous veiled references to Reincarnation, even actual open mention of the previous incarnations on earth of the leading characters of this Grail Saga. Characters like Cundrie, the Sorceress, named as the reborn Herodias, the diabolical mother of the gyrating Salome, who had demanded the head of John the Baptist in payment for her daughter's seductive charms.

It had been a surprise to Hitler that this concept of Reincarnation should have been incorporated in so Christian a document as the Romance of the Holy Grail. Previously he had considered that the religions of Islam and Judaism (including Christianity, "its Jewish consequence") were among the few religious systems which did not include the Law of Karma, or its equivalent, in their teachings.

Adolf Hitler had been desperately eager to discover the grandeur of his own previous lives on earth. Had he not stood before the Spear of Destiny in the Hofburg and felt intuitively that he himself had held it in his hands as his talisman of power and conquest in some earlier century of history—an all-powerful Caesar, perhaps, or one of the really great German Emperors like Barbarossa, a leader of the Teutonic Knights, or even some celebrated Gothic hero like Alaric The Bold?

In this respect Adolf Hitler had been on the brink of a shattering surprise. Drug-induced mind expansion had proved to him that the spiritual biography of his previous incarnations did not include either the all-powerful ruler or the sort of magnificent blond Teuton which he had so eagerly anticipated.

He had quickly discovered that Wolfram von Eschenbach's *Parsival* was not in the ordinary sense of the word a book. He recognised it as an initiation document of the highest order. He had been shrewd enough to perceive that hidden within its verses was a prophetic picture of the contemporary time; a sort of magic mirror which predicts the cataclysmic events of the passing decades of the twentieth century and makes visible the inward and hidden countenance of this critical historic period in which humanity is thrown against the very threshold of the spirit.

In short, Adolf Hitler saw the so-called Grail Romance as a prophetic document for the events to take place a thousand years later. And he believed that all the ninth-century personalities would reappear in physical embodiment in the twentieth century.

It was against this background knowledge of the contemporary significance of the Grail wisdom, and the anticipated rebirth of the Grail figures in our century, that Adolf Hitler was able to identify the drug-induced imagery of his previous incarnation. He now recognised himself as the rebirth of the historical figure behind Richard Wagner's Klingsor, Landulf of Capua and ninth-century Lord of Terra di Labur, that vast territory which stretched from Naples to Calabria, including Capri, and reached across the waters to Sicily.

Instead of some resplendent Germanic hero he had discovered himself to be the physical re-embodiment of the most dreaded personality in the whole history of Christendom. The chalice for the Spirit of the Anti-Christ.

PART TWO

THE MAN WHO WAS SMOOTH BETWEEN THE LEGS

"He clipped him in such a way that he can never more give pleasure to any woman. But that meant suffering for many people."

Parsival: Wolfram von Eschenbach.

CHAPTER SIX

A VOICE FROM THE WOMB: "BEWARE THE FALSE PROPHET"

"Follow Hitler! He will dance, but it is I who have called the tune!

"I have initiated him into the 'Secret Doctrine', opened his centres in vision and given him the means to communicate with the Powers.

"Do not mourn for me: I shall have influenced history more than any other German."

Thus spake Dietrich Eckart as he lay dying from the effects of mustard gas in Munich in December 1923. One of the seven founder members of the Nazi Party, this imposing Bavarian was outwardly known as a poet, a gifted writer and historian, a *bon viveur* and a lover of witty talk. Yet those who saw him apparently immersed in the gay social round of the Munich Bier-kellers never guessed that behind the jovial façade of this veteran Army Officer was hidden a dedicated satanist, the supreme adept of the arts and rituals of Black Magic and the central figure in a powerful and widespread circle of occultists—the Thule Group.

Adolf Hitler first heard about his future mentor through reports of his repulsive activities at the time of the Communist Putsch in Munich which followed the signing of the Armistice.

Kurt Eisner, a Jew and the leader of the lightning *coup d'état* through which the Social Democrats ousted the Bavarian Monarchy and Government, was shot down in the street. His infuriated supporters plastered a huge portrait of Eisner on the wall beside the spot on which he had been assassinated and all passers-by were forced at gun-point to salute it.

Dietrich Eckart, who had himself organised the killing, ordered that flour soaked in the blood of bitches on heat should be thrown in thin paper bags at the portrait and on the ground below it. Dogs from all over the district quickly gathered and the portrait and its sentinels just as quickly disappeared.

"This Dietrich Eckart is a man I can admire," said Adolf Hitler. "He appears to know the real meaning of hatred and how to demonstrate it."

The pre-war Adolf Hitler of Vienna days, the jobless bum and the half crazy layabout who had merely nibbled at the great hidden mysteries, would have been of no interest to an occult initiate of the calibre of Dietrich Eckart.

Eckart was on the look-out for quite another sort of pupil. He claimed to his fellow adepts in the Thule Group that he had personally received a kind of satanic annunciation that he was destined to prepare the vessel of the Anti-Christ, the man inspired by Lucifer to conquer the world and lead the Aryan race to glory.

The Adolf Hitler who emerged from the blood and slaughter of the trenches of the Western Front was no longer a pathetic entity. He had become a figure of an almost superhuman power. And it was this immeasurably matured and tempered Adolf Hitler with the Iron Cross, First Class, on his breast and the glint of demonic pride in his mystic blue eyes that so impressed the waiting Prophet.

Dietrich Eckart had been among the few who had clamoured for the return of the Reichskleinodien, the Crowns and Sceptres and other treasures of the ancient German Empire which included the "Heilige Lance", when the Hapsburg Dynasty had collapsed in 1917. The moment of recognition came when Adolf Hitler spoke of his own researches into the Legend of the Spear of Longinus and claimed that Providence had spared him from the hail of iron so that he might claim it to fulfil a world historic destiny.

"Here is the one for whom I was but the prophet and the

forerunner," Eckart blasphemously declared to his fellow conspirators in the Thule Gesellschaft.

Adolf Hitler welcomed the declaration of war as an opportunity to end his days of hunger and disillusionment in Munich which were but little better than life in the dosshouse in Vienna. Yet joining the Army, which was to give him a full stomach, status, and a chance to prove himself, was no easy matter. As an Austrian citizen he had to apply for special permission to volunteer. After a short delay King Ludwig of Bavaria granted his petition. He described the moment in *Mein Kampf*: "I opened the document with trembling hands; no words of mine can describe the satisfaction I felt. . . . I sank down on my knees and thanked heaven in the fullness of my heart for the favour of having been permitted to live at such a time."

He enrolled in the 1st Company of the 16th Bavarian Reserve Infantry Regiment, better known as the Lizt Regiment after the name of its founder. After a short period of training in Bavaria, he arrived at the front line in time for the heavy fighting against the English in the first battle of Ypres. Although only 600 out of 3,500 men in his regiment survived the slaughter, Adolf Hitler appears to have relished this rude baptism of fire in which he received an Iron Cross, Second Class.

Except for a period in 1916 when a leg wound gave him a brief respite in hospital, he remained at the front throughout the entire war and lived through some of the fiercest engagements including the long and bloody battle on the Somme.

Adolf Hitler served as a Meldeganger, an orderly-cum-runner who carried messages between regimental H.Q. and the forward units. The life of a runner in wartime is not the cushy number many people might think it to be. He must often break cover while his comrades are enjoying shelter from shell fire and machine guns. He is also the sniper's most frequent target. The most dangerous moments for such runners are most often spent quite alone and for this reason the job requires a special type of initiative.

In the world of peace Hitler had been an outcast; at war he felt fulfilled and very much at home. Yet Hitler was not inspired by an excess of patriotism as many people erroneously believe. The more realistic picture is that of Hitler regarding the war as an opportunity above all to test his belief in his own personal destiny, tempting, on every possible occasion, the protection of "Providence" which he believed to be preserving him for a world-historic mission. And he accepted the harshness of his daily life in the trenches as an opportunity to develop those very qualities of willpower he needed to become the vessel of the uncompromising Spirit which overshadowed him and sought to possess his soul.

Only by putting together the small snippets of information passed on by his wartime comrades can we gain a picture of him at this time which illustrates the emergence of an immeasurably strong and deeper personality.

"A peculiar fellow," Hans Mend, a fellow soldier, called him. "He sat in the corner of our mess holding his head in his hands in deep contemplation. Suddenly he would leap up, and running about excitedly, say that in spite of all our efforts victory would be denied us, for the invisible foes of the German people were a greater danger than the biggest cannon of the enemy. On other occasions, he sat with his helmet pulled over his head quite oblivious to our world, buried so deeply within himself that none of us could rouse him."

None of his fellow soldiers could stomach his superhuman powers of will and self-discipline which led him to accept his lot without any show of weakness or complaint. He apparently gave no thought whatsoever for those things which were the eternal topic of conversation for his fellows—leave, food and women. "We all cursed him and found him intolerable. There was this white crow among us that did not go along with us when we damned the war."

Amidst this daily scene of death and desolation, Adolf Hitler deafened his ears to the human frailty of his comrades and stemmed all natural emotions so that he could be born anew with that super-personal strength and resolution he would need to fulfil the mandate which the Gods of German Folklore had ordained for him.

In August, 1918, he was awarded the Iron Cross, First Class, the very highest decoration a common Corporal in the German Army may gain. Only confirmation of the award, but not the exploits for which it was awarded, was recorded in the official history of the Lizt Regiment. He is generally supposed to have received the decoration, equivalent to the British Victoria Cross, for a feat of astonishing bravery in which, armed only with a pistol, he captured, single-handed, a French Officer and fifteen men.

The few letters he wrote home reveal to what extent he was stripping himself of all human weakness and learning to trust in the intrepid Spirit which would one day lead him to a pinnacle of personal power.

Konrad Heiden's close scrutiny of Hitler's wartime letters inspired him to write: "He presents himself as the impassioned warrior. There is not the slightest soft spot in him. He is brave and attaches no value to his life. But there is also clearly expressed, the belief that he owes his life to a miracle, or rather a whole chain of miracles; that the bursting shells had spared him time and again; that while most of his regiment were sacrificed in the bath of blood, he really enjoyed the special protection of Providence."

Hitler's faith in the protection of "Providence" was to be momentarily shattered in the last month of the war when he was caught in a British mustard gas attack. Badly gassed and blinded for several days, he was sent back from France in a hospital train to Pasewalk, a small town north-east of Berlin.

Yet this gassing, like a demonic grace, was to prove a blessing in disguise, for it brought about the most sustained period of spiritual illumination of his whole life. And in this breakthrough into supersensible vision while his eyes burned in the darkness, Adolf Hitler experienced what he later called "the magical relationship between man and the whole Universe."

Adolf Hitler has been quoted by Hermann Rauschning as saying that "the aim of human evolution is to attain a mystic vision

95

of the Universe." The inner conviction behind this much-quoted statement, rightly attributed to Hitler, arose during this period of enforced and totally unanticipated mystic trance in Paswalk. It was a major stride in the process of total possession by a mighty alien entity.

While the effects of the gas were slowly vanishing from Hitler's eyes and throat in Paswalk Hospital, the totally unexpected news arrived that Germany had lost the war.

Professor Alan Bullock says in his *Study in Tyranny* that "the shock of Germany's surrender was the decisive experience in Hitler's life. Everything with which he had identified himself had been defeated and swept away."

This is also what Hitler later wanted people to believe and he wrote to this effect in *Mein Kampf*. But the very reverse was the truth. Hitler was loyal only to his own lust for power and for this reason he was not at all displeased with the sudden surrender. The poverty, humiliation, and chaos of a defeated nation in the aftermath of war offered him his one and only road to political power. There would have been no place for an Adolf Hitler in a victorious Germany and he was shrewd enough to realise it. His future success would come about entirely by exploiting with unequalled political cunning, the very consequence of the nation's defeat and surrender.

When Adolf Hitler arrived back in Munich at the end of November, 1918, he found his adopted city of pre-war days in a state of siege. The Bavarian King had abdicated and the Government had taken to its heels when the Social Democrats occupied Parliament and proclaimed a Republic. Political violence in the streets was an everyday activity, trade of all descriptions had come to a standstill, food prices were soaring while the mass of poor people starved. Veterans, home from the war, moved round in armed bands without leadership or discipline.

Hitler remained in uniform and drew his weekly pay and rations from the central barracks of the Reserve Infantry in

Munich. He did not wish to face the prospect of permanent un-employment back in civilian life in which the sight of the long food queues for the jobless was a daily sight. He himself had nothing to lose by remaining in the Reichswehr and the Iron Cross, First Class, helped to convince his superiors that he was a man worth retaining. He willingly accepted the offer of per-manent guard duty at a POW Camp at Traunstein, near the Austrian border. There, while carrying out simple unexacting duties, Hitler had time to take stock of the national situation and plan his own entry into the political arena. He returned to Munich in January 1919, when the prisoners were sent home and the Camp was closed down.

The first opportunity to get himself noticed came shortly after his return to the City when he undertook espionage duties. When a Soviet Republic was declared on April 6th, following the fall of the Hoffman Government, Adolf Hitler was among a few specially selected soldiers ordered to remain behind in Munich and circulate freely among the Red soldiery support-ing the revolution.

The Communist régime was quickly and brutally overthrown by a Reichswehr force from Berlin, and Hitler, walking down the assembled ranks of the Red soldiers, singled out the ring-leaders who were taken off for instant execution.

Standing beside the firing squads, he watched his selected victims put up against the wall and shot. The potential quali-ties of the little Corporal with the Iron Cross and the punctil-lious salute had at last been noticed and were quickly rewarded. He was assigned to the Political Department of the District Command and put on a course of political education.

The German Army, contrary to its unbending nineteenth-century traditions, was now deeply involved in the whole political scene, especially in Bavaria where the Reichswehr had been instrumental in overthrowing the Communists.

The District Commanders were secretly supporting and equipping "Free-Corps" bands of veterans that appeared all over Germany and using them as an instrument to dominate the political scene and stamp out the socialist revolution.

The officers who led these bloodthirsty bands brazenly claimed that the war had not yet ended and refused to admit defeat. All their efforts were now concentrated on overthrowing the Republican Government which they claimed was responsible for the "bastardly crime, the shameful and deliberate act of treachery" of the surrender.

When Adolf Hitler reported for duty to the Political Department of the VII Army District Command, he discovered that it had been turned into an intelligence centre for the direction of political terrorism throughout the whole of Germany. From Munich conspirators set out on their assigned tasks of political assassination, committing heartless murders like that of Matthias Erzberger, the man who signed the Armistice, and Walter Rathenau, the Jewish Foreign Minister, whose unhappy business it was to carry through the "Dictungs" of the hated Versailles Treaty.

Adolf Hitler was enrolled on the staff of the "Press and Information Bureau" of the Political Department, the very centre of the subterranean activities of espionage and propaganda. He was put on a short course of political instruction and, thriving in this atmosphere of cloak and dagger terrorism, he quickly established himself as the most outstanding pupil.

It was not long before Captain Ernst Röhm, the outstanding personality at the Army District Command, had spotted the pupil with the voice which had a ring of almost magical power and the eyes with the mystical look of a prophet.

Röhm was a professional soldier who returned from the war with a reputation for singular initiative and a record of great bravery. Short, stocky, a man with immense energy and drive, he had quickly proved himself to be the type of Officer whom the troops could respect and follow. Three times wounded, half his nose was shot away and a livid bullet hole disfigured his cheek.

Röhm is said to have wept when "Peace broke out" and frankly admitted that he thought war brought out the best in men. Spurning return to civilian life, he enlisted financial support from rich industrialists and raised a private army of his own to confront the Communist menace on the industrial scene. At one point, he was in command of some 100,000 men who joined his *Einwohnerwehr*, a kind of civilian defence force.

Adolf Hitler became an instant admirer of this dedicated Reichswehr Captain whom he ultimately promoted to Chief of Staff of the Nazi *Sturmabteilung*. There had been a kind of mutual recognition at their first meeting and Röhm later admitted that from the very beginning he sensed the fantastic potential of leadership in Hitler.

Another personality who was equally impressed with Hitler at first sight was a certain Gottfried Feder, an engineer who lectured in Economics at the Political Centre where Hitler was qualifying to become a Bildungsoffizier.

Feder was excited by the power and venom in Hitler's voice, impressed by his innate political cunning, inspired by the extent of his apparent patriotism, and captivated by the almost magical charisma of his personality.

Feder wasted no time in reporting his exciting discovery to his friend, Dietrich Eckart. A sceptical Eckart—he regarded Feder as somewhat of a crank—was astonished to find that the realistic and ruthless Ernst Röhm was equally impressed by the same Corporal Hitler. Röhm brought Hitler along with him to meet Eckart at his favourite haunt, the Brennessel Wine Cellar. And so it came about that the Occult Master met the long-awaited pupil he was to instruct and initiate—the man who would give him cause to boast on his deathbed: "Do not mourn me. I shall have influenced history more than any other German."

One of the great fabrications of the twentieth century is Hitler's description in *Mein Kampf* of the way he first discovered the German Workers' Party and the terrible dilemma he faced in making the decision to quit the security of the Reichswehr to join what he called "an inconsequential collection of non-entities". And yet most of his biographers have accepted this part of his life story as the truth!

Adolf Hitler claims that he himself discovered the German

Workers' Party by chance in the course of his duties which involved investigating new political groups. He recounts in *Mein Kampf* his surprise at receiving a card telling him that he had been accepted as a Member of The German Workers' Party after he had attended one of their meetings. It was presumptuous and out of the question," he writes, and goes on to describe how he went back to attend a committee meeting just to give them his personal reasons for not joining "such an absurd little organisation."

"The tavern in which the meeting was to take place was the 'Alte Rosenbad' in the Herrenstrasse, a very run-down place. . . . I went through the ill-lit dining room in which not a soul was sitting, opened the door to the back room, and there I was faced with the Committee. In the grim light of a tiny gas four people were sitting at a table and they at once greeted me as a new member of the German Workers' Party. The minutes of the last meeting were read and the secretary gave a vote of confidence. Next came the treasury report—all in all the Party possessed seven marks and fifty pfennigs—for which the treasurer received a vote of confidence. This too was entered into the minutes. . . . Terrible, terrible! This was club life of the worst sort. Was I to join such an organisation?

Adolf Hitler paints a picture of himself and his innermost thoughts and feelings at the time at which he claims he was considering whether to throw in his lot with this insignificant political party. He wanted the readers of *Mein Kampf* to visualise him pondering the problem while sitting on his bed in a sparsely appointed barracks where he claims to have shared his meagre rations with the mice who inhabited his quarters, "the little mice which were a constant reminder of my poverty."

"That I was poor and without means seemed to me the most bearable part of it, but it was harder that I was numbered among the nameless, that I was one of the millions whom chance permits to live or summons out of existence without even their closest neighbours condescending to take any notice of it. In addition, there was the difficulty which inevitably arose from my lack of schooling. After two days of agonised pondering and reflection, I finally came to the conviction that I had to take this step."

This is what Hitler wanted the millions who read *Mein Kampf*, which became the Nazi Bible, to believe. "The grossly impudent lie always leaves traces, even after it has been nailed down," Hitler told his henchmen. And even to this day his lies in this regard have not yet been nailed. The real truth was the very reverse.

It was in this period immediately prior to joining the Party that he was experiencing with the greatest intensity that he was no longer a member of the nameless masses but a man who had been specially singled out for a meteoric political career which would lead to the fulfilment of his childhood dreams of a world-historic destiny. And he was well aware also that his hard apprenticeship was ended and that a long-awaited and pre-scribed pattern of destiny had begun to unfold for him, for he could already recognise the people and the opportunities which were to take him along a direct path to the pinnacle of power.

The truth is that Adolf Hitler had been ordered by the Intelligence Branch of the Reichswehr to join and take over the leadership of the German Workers' Party. And he had been informed exactly how the Reichswehr themselves had refounded this Party with the avowed intent of turning it into the most powerful single movement in Germany.* Adolf Hitler had received the guarantee from General von Epp and his assistant Captain Röhm of all the financial support he would need,

* The German Workers' Party, though it had many times changed its official title, had its origin in a movement begun by Anton Drexler, a Munich locksmith, which had counted its followers in hundreds of thousands during World War I. The motive behind it in the first instance had been to encourage patriotic backing of the High Command and to counter the growing internal discontent in which Socialism and Marxism were beginning to flourish. Now once again in September, 1919, the political agents of the Reichswehr were resurrecting it to counter the anti-military and anti-nationalist sentiments of the working classes, and above all to wipe out the contempt the masses felt for the 'Fatherland Idea' and the 'Officer Class' who had lost face in defeat.

with the additional promise of the support of regular troops and veterans to swell the numbers in the Party's germinal stages and to protect its early public meetings from the violent interruptions of the Communists.

There were other important factors about which Adolf Hitler was careful to make no mention in *Mein Kampf* besides the actuality that he rose to political power as a subordinate and representative of the Reichswehr. Above all he kept silent about the fact that the Committee and the forty original members of the New German Workers' Party were all drawn from the most powerful Occult Society in Germany which was also financed by the High Command—The Thule Gesellschaft.

The hidden activities of the Thule Group worked like tentacles of a higher dimension behind all aspects of life in Bavaria, and especially on the political scene where its machinations were responsible for much of the terrorist activity, race hatred, and most of the cold-blooded murders at that time which were almost a daily occurrence.

This powerful Occult circle included among its members and adepts, Judges, Police-Chiefs, Barristers, Lawyers, University Professors and Lecturers, Aristocratic families including former members of the royal entourage of the Wittelsbach Kings, leading Industrialists, Surgeons, Physicians, Scientists, as well as a host of rich and influential bourgeois like the proprietor of the famous "Four Seasons Hotel" in Munich.

For instance, Franz Gurtner, the Bavarian Minister of Justice, was an active member of the Thule Gesellschaft; so was Pohner, the Police President of Munich, and Wilhelm Frick, his Assistant Police-Chief, who was destined to become Minister of the Interior of the Third Reich. Gurtner too received recognition for his early services to Hitler whilst in the Thule Group by his promotion to Nazi Minister of Justice.

Not only civilians belonged to the Thule Group but also officers and ex-officers of the Reichswehr, who were permitted to attend its meetings, functions and even its secret rituals as "Guests". In this way the Army Law was evaded which stated that German Officers, bound by their oath of allegiance, should not join other organisations or movements in which an oath was required of them.

The man chosen by the Reichswehr to infuse new life into the German Workers' Party was none other than Dietrich Eckart, the central figure of the whole Thule Gesellschaft. He joined Anton Drexler's Committee for this purpose after a promise that full Army backing should be given to it.

Eckart was too shrewd to believe that the German Workers' Party could ever become a popular national movement without the emergence of a Leader who could arouse mass enthusiasm and support from the working classes.

Konrad Heiden, a journalist in Munich at this time, reports how Eckart discussed this problem on a purely external level with the habitues of the Brennessel Wine Cellar in the spring of 1919: "We need a man at the head who can stand the sound of a machine gun. The rabble need to get fear in their pants. We can't use an officer because people don't respect them any more. The best man for the job would be a worker who knows how to talk."

Such a manner of speaking was typical of the outer façade which Dietrich Eckart liked to create for himself. In truth, as we described earlier, he was awaiting the appearance of quite another sort of Leader—a Germanic Messiah who, with the wild eloquence and the mystic powers of the Prophet Mahomet, would fuse politics and religion into an unholy crusade against the ideals of the Christian world.

Dietrich Eckart and a small inner core of Thulists had been prepared for the imminent appearance of the German Messiah in a whole series of spiritualistic seances held together with the entourage of the notorious Russian emigres, Generals Skoropadski and Bishupski. These two Russian Generals, who were known throughout Bavaria for their violent anti-Semitic and anti-Bolshevik views, later provided the cash for Hitler to buy the *Völkischer Beobachter*, the newspaper of which Dietrich Eckart became the first Editor-in-Chief.

The astonishing psychic gifts of the medium, a simple and illiterate peasant woman, were discovered by Dr. Nemirovitch-Dantchenko, a devious character who acted as "Press Agent" for the large circle of White Russians who had settled in Bavaria.

In deep trance this simple hulk of a woman emanated from her vagina ectoplasmic heads and shrouds which manifested as in some ghostly birth from the nether world. It was not the emanations which were of importance to the circle of occultists who so wickedly exploited this poor wretch of a woman, but the voices which rang forth as she spoke in almost poetic form from deep unconsciousness in numerous foreign tongues.

Dietrich Eckart was the master of ceremonies at these regular seances but it was another significant character, Alfred Rosenberg, a German refugee from Moscow, who took it upon himself to question the ever-changing spirits which briefly occupied and possessed the medium. And it was Alfred Rosenberg, too, the prophet of the Anti-Christ of the "Protocols of Zion", who dared to call forth the presence of the Beast of the Revelation— the Luciferic Leviathan which had taken over body and soul of Adolf Hitler.

According to Konrad Ritzler, one of the earliest members of the Thule Group and later the literary editor of its secret publications, all those present were terrified by the mighty powers which they had unleashed. The air in the room became stifling and unbearable and the naked body of the medium became translucent in an aura of ectoplasmic light. Rudolf Glauer, the founder of the Thule Gesellschaft, began to run from the room in panic but Eckart grabbed hold of him and threw him down to the floor. Nobody had the presence of mind to write down the strange utterances which poured forth from the medium like some kind of riddle.

Messages of the greatest import and clarity came at those seances in which dead members of the Thule Group were called up from beyond the grave. The most important prophecy concerning the appearance of the long-awaited German Messiah was spoken by Prince von Thurn und Taxis who had been put to death by the Communists in the Luitpold Gymnasium earlier that year (April 30th, 1919).

The Prince, barely thirty when he was shot to death, had also been a member of the "Mystics of Bavaria", a sect founded at the end of the eighteenth century which later had affiliations with the Germanen Order. Steeped in the traditions of the ancient German Emperors, he had actively joined the plotters against the Communist regime. Now looking pale and ghostly, the head of the Prince manifested above an ectoplasmic shroud while, in a perfect imitation of his earthly voice, the medium in deep trance communicated his thoughts in the German tongue which she herself in waking consciousness was unable to speak.

Instrumental with Dietrich Eckart in starting pressure groups in Bavaria for the return of the ancient Germanic Treasures to Nuremberg when the Hapsburg Dynasty ended in 1917, he now identified the man who became the new leader of Germany as the next individual claimant to the Heilige Lance around which was woven the legend of world conquest.

It was the "shade" of the once blonde and beautiful Heila, the Comptesse von Westarp, in her lifetime the Secretary of the Thule Gesellschaft until the Reds murdered her, who gave the midnight conspirators the most unwelcome surprise.

Like some translucent latterday Cassandra, the prophetess of doom, she rose up from the bosom of the limp and slumbering medium to give a warning that the man who was even now preparing to assume the leadership of Thule would prove himself to be a false prophet. Assuming total power over the nation, he would be responsible one day for reducing the whole of Germany to rubble and its people to a defeat and moral degradation hitherto unknown to history.

Needless to say, her announcement that the coming Messiah was "hard by the door" was received with jubilation, but her words of warning from beyond the grave, which were to prove so shatteringly correct, went entirely unheeded.

CHAPTER SEVEN

THE ANTI-CHRIST OF THE PROTOCOLS: A BLUEPRINT TO POWER

"The Beast does not look what he is. He may even have a comic moustache."

The Anti-Christ: Soloviev.

The key to the rise to fame of Alfred Rosenberg, born the son of an impoverished shoemaker, was the possession of a secret manuscript which he smuggled out of Moscow. The promotion of this man, who rose to become the Reichsleiter of the Nazi Party and its official philosopher, came about because he presented Adolf Hitler with a blueprint to total power—*The Protocols of the Wise Men of Zion.*

The Protocols of the Wise Men of Zion purported to be a record of the proceedings of the World Congress of Jewry held in Basel in 1897 at which, it was claimed, plans were laid and resolutions carried towards achieving world domination.

Rosenberg, a romantic of a sinister kind, had a mysterious story to tell about how a copy of the *Protocols* came into his possession. He claimed that a total stranger had presented him with it. "The man, whom I had never seen before, came into my study without knocking, put the book on my desk and vanished without saying a word."

The *Protocols* proved to be an appendix to a work called *The Anti-Christ.* It was written by a degenerate Russian writer called Nilus, a rascally pupil of the great and profound Russian philosopher, Soloviev. On the cover of the typed manuscript were words taken from St. Matthew: "He is near, he is hard by the door."

After the first quick reading of the manuscript, Alfred Rosenberg knew the *Protocols* to be a forged document. He also knew that he was holding in his hands both political and racial dynamite, which, if used to advantage, might even become the key to his own personal success in a hostile world.

Rosenberg, despite his Jewish antecedents, gained entry into the Thule Gesellschaft by showing the *Protocols* to Dietrich Eckart who proved wildly excited on reading the contents. The manuscript caused similar jubilation at a meeting of the Thule Committee which was held to discuss the most effective way to publish the work.

The Thulists decided not to associate the publication of the *Protocols* with their own occult movement, outwardly known for its vicious anti-Semitic feelings. An independent publisher, Ludwig Müller, of Munich, was chosen to put out the first edition of the work.

The Protocols of the Wise Men of Zion had just the anticipated effect among German intellectuals who had been vainly searching for a scapegoat to explain the defeat of the Fatherland in the World War. At last they believed they had found the real explanation of how Germany had been stabbed in the back while her loyal soldiers were still fighting on French soil. The vile and loathsome yiddish conspiracy had at last been unveiled.

Edition after edition rolled off the press but the demand continued to increase. Foreign publishers saw it as a great money spinner and the *Protocols* appeared in almost every country in the world. Everywhere it circulated people began to discuss the existence of an international network of Jewry secretly conspiring to control world capital and cunningly to manipulate even master-mind, world politics with the aim of dominating all life on the planet.*

---

* In England the *Morning Post* published a whole series of articles which gave credence to the *Protocols*. *The Times*, more sceptical, demanded an immediate investigation to find out the truth, if any, of the serious accusations against the Jews.

To give the maximum credibility to the *Protocols* an elaborate deception had been woven to prove that the International Conference of Jewry held in Basel was not really concerned with its stated intention of discussing the possibility of a permanent home for Jewish refugees in Palestine.

"This was only a blind," said the wily Nilus. "The New Zionist Movement had been born for far more sinister motives. Its secret aim was an uncontested domination of the whole world." At the Basel Conference, he said, leading Rabbis from countries throughout Europe and the Americas had come together to make plans to enslave the whole of mankind. They were preparing themselves for the appearance of the Anti-Christ who would be born a Jew. Under the leadership of the Anti-Christ the Jews would fulfil their ultimate aims.

"We shall everywhere arouse ferment, strife, and enmity," says *The Protocols of the Wise Men of Zion.* "We shall unleash a terrible war on the world. . . . We shall bring the people to such a pass that they will voluntarily offer us the leadership through which we shall dominate the whole world."

The explanation of how the *Protocols* fell into non-Jewish hands was yet another cunning lie. Nilus maintained that a Jewish courier carrying the shorthand notes of the proceedings at the Basel Conference had been bribed to divulge them. For a large sum of cash he was supposed to have permitted agents of the Ochrana to make a copy of the notes before he himself delivered them for safe keeping to the archives of the "Rising Sun" Lodge of the Freemasons in Frankfurt. The whole story was an obvious fabrication. Unfortunately, only too many people were only too willing to believe it. The *Protocols* aroused the wave of seething hatred for the Jews upon which Adolf Hitler rose to power.

The fragment of perverted truth hidden within the *Protocols* would have carried the same powers of conviction had it been directed against any other single race, creed or political movement in the world, especially the Nazis. Indeed the "Demon" who speaks out of the *Protocols* provided Adolf Hitler with a blueprint to total power, a blueprint which he followed un-
108

swervingly until he gained the pinnacle of "Absolute Dictator-ship" over the Third Reich.

The hidden theme, which carries an occult power to sway the mind, had been gathered by the Russian Ochrana from all the genuine prophets whose voices warned a dying epoch that it bore the Anti-Christ in its own image and was preparing in the chaos of its own degeneration for the physical emergence of the Beast from the Abyss.

The groundwork of the document was originally written in the form of a satire by a French lawyer called Maurice Joly, who sought to ridicule the political aspirations of Napoleon III. The title of Joly's masterpiece was *Dialogue aus anfers entre Machiaval et Montesquieu, ou la politique de Machiavel au XIX siècle, par un Contemporain* (Dialogue in Hell between Machiavelli and Montesquieu, or the politics of Machiavelli in the Nineteenth Century, by a contemporary).

Though the anonymity of Maurice Joly was soon uncovered by the Emperor's secret police and he was thrown into jail, the work, originally published in Belgium in 1864, continued to be printed on secret presses.

Joly, an Initiate of an ancient Rosicrucian Order, had resurrected the ideas of Machiavelli in a warning forecast of the future path which might be used to dominate the masses. Anticipating mass communication and many facets of the twentieth-century technology with its instant control over political and economic life, he warned mankind against "the genesis of a new type of Caesarism".

> "We shall talk with the people on the streets and squares and teach them to take the view of political questions which at the moment we require. For what the ruler says to the people spreads through the country like wildfire, the voice of the people carries it on all four winds.
>
> " 'We'—the Beast always says 'We' for he is Legion—'shall create unrest, struggle, and hate in the whole of Europe and thence in other continents. We shall at all times be in a position ot call forth the new disturbances at will, or to restore the old order.'
>
> "Unremittingly we shall poison the relations between peoples

and states of all countries. By envy and hatred, by struggle and warfare, even by spreading hunger, destitution and plagues, we shall bring all peoples to such a pass that their only escape will lie in total submission to our domination.

"We shall stultify, seduce, ruin the youth.

"We shall not stick at bribery, treachery, treason, as long as they serve the realisation of our plans. Our watchword is: Force and hypocrisy!

"In our arsenal we carry a boundless ambition, burning avidity, a ruthless thirst for revenge, relentless hatred. From us emanates the spectre of fear, all-embracing terror."

The Demon pretending to speak on behalf of the Jews really gave the basis for the guiding lines of the establishment and supremacy of the Nazi racial theories, later elaborated by Alfred Rosenberg in *Twentieth Century Myth*.

"We are the chosen, we are the only true men. Our minds give off the true power of the spirit; the intelligence of the rest of the world is merely instinctive and animal. They can see, but they cannot foresee; their inventions are purely corporeal. Does it not follow that nature herself has predestined us to dominate the whole world?

"We shall not submit the greatness of our ultimate plan, the context of its particular parts, the consequence of each separate point, the secret meaning of which remains hidden, to the judgement and decision of the many, even of those who share our thoughts. We shall not cast the gleaming thoughts of our leader before the swine, and even in the most intimate circles we shall not permit them to be carped at.

"We shall paint the misdeeds of foreign Governments in the most garish colours and create such an ill-feeling towards them that the peoples would a thousand times rather bear a slavery which guarantees them peace and order than enjoy their much-touted freedom. The peoples will tolerate any servitude we may impose on them, if only to avoid a return to the horrors of wars and insurrection. Our principles and methods will take on their full force when we present them in sharp contrast to the putrid old social order."

The picture of the Anti-Spirit of the age, which had been

revealed so prophetically in Joly's portrait of modern tyranny, was recognised thirty-three years later by the Ochrana, the Tsarist Secret Police. They saw in it a weapon with which to confront the flame of revolution which was springing up amidst the spiritual disintegration of Holy Russia.

In the hands of a whole succession of Secret Police conspirators, the idea began to take shape that the Jews could be blamed for the advent of radical materialism. They saw how the masses could be persuaded to believe that Bolshevism was the working of the Anti-Christ assisted in its growth by the plotting of international Jewry. Forging the *Protocols* might turn the counter-revolution into a spiritual crusade, even arousing the deeply held religious beliefs of the masses in favour of its cause.

The final version of the *Protocols* brought to Munich from Russia by Alfred Rosenberg in November, 1918, came to be written under very strange circumstances. Nilus, a writer of religion and philosophy, was specially picked out by the Ochrana as their front man, through whom the *Protocols* should be published, for two reasons. He had just completed a book called *Small Signs Betoken Great Events—The Anti-Christ is near at Hand*, which General Ratchkovsky, Chief of the Ochrana, considered an excellent work in which the *Protocols* could appear as an "Appendix". And, in so doing, the Ochrana hoped that the Tsar would be so impressed with them that he would retain Nilus as his spiritual advisor instead of a French healer whom they hated and suspected of being a spy.

Both plans failed. The book was published in the Imperial Printing House at Tsarkoye Selo but the Tsar's reaction surprised the Ochrana. He saw the *Protocols* to be a forgery and he also assessed their potential role as a weapon to defeat his enemies. After much consideration he came to a decision. "We cannot use such an unclean weapon in a just cause," he said, ordering all copies of the book to be destroyed. Nilus was despatched from the Royal Circle in disgrace. And the Ochrana later looked on helplessly when Rasputin was welcomed as the new confessor to the Romanovs, the wonder monk who helped to bring about the downfall of a Dynasty.

Although Nilus had incorporated all the salient ideas of Maurice Joly in his *Small Signs Betoken great Events,* it was the truly prophetic thinking of the philosopher and scientist Soloviev which gave the work such a frighteningly authentic ring. Soloviev, a genuine visionary of the purest Russian tradition, was the author of *The Philosophy of the Organic,* a work inspired by a conception of Cosmic Christianity uniting science and religion in a manner which anticipated the writings of Taillard de Chardin by several decades. It was out of this cosmic world conception, partly inspired by the *Book of Revelation* that Soloviev wrote *The Anti-Christ,* the work from which the Ochrana had projected falsely into the *Protocols.*

Soloviev's Anti-Christ is no mythical figure but inhabits the soul of a man of flesh and blood. A man dressed in everyday clothes and outwardly so inconspicuous that he could pass unnoticed in a crowd. And Soloviev saw that the greatest danger would be just this, "the Beast does not look what he is".

He is young and vigorous and his voice rings out with magical powers which, like the seductive tones of the Pied Piper, can seduce great leaders into a terrifying condition of diminished moral responsibility, and at the same time excite the masses to rise up and turn a dying culture into a heap of rubble and ashes. Beneath a banal and disarming exterior— "he may wear a comic moustache"—he is a blood-hungry tyrant, a mighty demagogue.

Soloviev's "Leviathan" does not take over the soul and the body of a Jew like the Anti-Christ of the *Protocols.* On the contrary, he had the insight to see that precisely the most enlightened Jews, retaining the piety of their age-old wisdom, would be among the few people who identified and denounced the Beast. And Soloviev also foresaw that it would be the Jewish race who would be the victims of the dreadful persecution ordered by the Anti-Christ. He includes in his shattering prophecies even such details and descriptions of how the skins of the Jews would be turned into household articles—just as it came to pass in the concentration camps of the Third Reich in which swaggering SS murdered their Jewish slaves and used their skins to make table lamps.

One can imagine with what hidden delight Corporal Adolf Hitler must have read *The Protocols of the Wise Men of Zion* for this cunning falsification mapped out his own predestined path to world conquest in fulfilment of the legend of the Spear of Longinus. It was even anticipated how the Anti-Christ would become manifest after his chosen vessel had recovered from a short spell of blindness!

The date in which these things should come to pass? 1921!

The age of this vehicle of Hades? Thirty-three years old!

Adolf Hitler celebrated his thirty-third birthday in 1921, the year he assumed the uncontested leadership of the National Socialist Party!

To read the words of the "Demon" who speaks out of the *Protocols* is indeed like listening to the history of Adolf Hitler's meteoric rise to power, a prototype plan of how to establish hell on earth with the consent and co-operation of a whole nation.

Thus speaks the Demon from out of The *Protocols*:

> "Outwardly, however, in our 'official' utterances, we shall adopt an opposite procedure, and always do our best to appear honourable and co-operative. A statesman's words do not have to agree with his acts. If we pursue these principles, the Governments and peoples which we have thus prepared will take our I.O.U.'s for cash. One day they will accept us as benefactors and saviours of the human race. If any State dared to resist us, if its neighbours make common cause with it against us, we will unleash a world war. . . .
>
> "By all these methods we shall so wear down the nations that they will be forced to offer us world domination. We shall stretch out our arms like pincers in all directions, and introduce an order of such violence that all peoples will bow to our domination."*

---

* Translation of *The Protocols of the Wise Men of Zion* by Ralph Manheim. Victor Gollancz, 1944.

CHAPTER EIGHT

KAISER WILHELM'S SOOTHSAYER

The Admiral's Son who was chased by Demons

"Houston Stewart Chamberlain was given to seeing demons who, by his own account, drove him relentlessly to seek new fields of study and get on with his prodigious writings. . . . Once, in 1896, when he was returning from Italy, the presence of a demon became so forceful that he got off the train at Gardone, shut himself up in a hotel room for eight days and, abandoning some work in music that he had contemplated wrote feverishly on a biological thesis until he had the germ of the theme that would dominate all his later works: *race and history*. . . . Since he felt himself goaded on by demons, his books were written in the grip of a terrible fever, a veritable trance, a state of self-induced intoxication, so that, as he says in his biography, *Lebenswege*, he was often unable to recognise them as his own work, because they surpassed his expectations."

The Rise and Fall of the Third Reich: William L. Shirer.

The Spear of Longinus played a vital role in the lives of three other men besides Adolf Hitler and Dr. W. J. Stein in the first two decades of the twentieth century. They were: Houston Stewart Chamberlain, a demonically inspired genius who first excited the Kaiser's interest in the legend of world destiny

114

associated with the Spear; Kaiser Wilhelm who attempted by means of a ruse to steal this talisman of world conquest when Germany stood on the brink of a global conflict; and Quartermaster General Helmuth von Moltke, Chief of the Imperial General Staff of the German Army, who cleverly contrived to keep the sacred weapon out of the hands of his deluded and power-hungry Monarch.

Houston Stewart Chamberlain has been described as both the true successor to the genius of Friedrich Nietzsche and "one of the most astonishing talents in the history of the German mind, a mine of information and ideas."*

He was born in 1855, the son of an English Admiral and the nephew of Field Marshal Sir Neville Chamberlain. Brought up by relatives in Paris, where he was schooled under the private tuition of a remarkable Prussian tutor, his lively and eager mind quickly absorbed the glories of militant Prussia and the works of the great German poets and philosophers like Goethe, Fichte, Hegel and Richard Wagner.

At the age of twenty-seven, Chamberlain moved to Germany where he settled in Dresden and very soon became more German than the Germans, literally adopting their nationality, language, mind and soul. In 1899 he published his most important work, *Die Grundlagen des Neunzehnten Jahrhunderts* (The Foundation of the Nineteenth Century) which exploded like a bomb upon the receptive minds of the German nation and made him famous overnight.

With a stupendous erudition which mesmerised the German intellectuals, he contrived to synthesise the opposing doctrines of Richard Wagner and Friedrich Nietzsche. To the delight of the Junker families and the elite of the Officer Corps, he developed and expanded Wagner's doctrine of the Aryan Master Race. According to Chamberlain there was no need for the tragedy of the "Twilight of the Gods" brought about by the pollution of inferior races. With one stroke of the pen, he eradicated the whole idea that a noble race needed to decline and decay with

* Konrad Heiden: *Der Führer.*

the force of a natural law. For it was at this point in the extension of Wagner's thinking that he cunningly incorporated Nietzsche's belief that a "Higher Race" could be bred.

Chamberlain insisted that the birth of a new race need not arise in the first place through blood relationships. He saw it as more an affinity of souls coming together at a historic moment in time. Such a race could come to birth when "the Spirit of World Historic Destiny" brought about an intermingling of peoples who shared a similar character and manner of thinking, even if their physical characteristics were far from similar.

In the genesis of race, Chamberlain stressed that there had to be both some momentous historical event and a high spiritual ideal which was strong enough to give the population the feeling of a homogeneous and equal spiritual participation.

The uniting of German peoples around Wilhelm of Prussia, Otto Bismarck and General Helmuth Karl von Moltke on the soil of the defeated French in 1870–71 was described as such a world-historic moment when a new race was born—the German Master Race.

"In this manner the ground was prepared for the emergence of a new race of 'Supermen'," said Houston Stewart Chamberlain. And now this new race was establishing itself through the omnipotence of the German mind and the Prussian talent for organisation, the ability in the Ruhr to produce the finest heavy industry in the world and a potentially outstanding mastery of technology. And since, said this English prophet, the German intellect leaves nothing whatever to chance, it must not leave the breeding of the new race to chance. "Just as a pearl can be grown through the medium of an artificial stimulant, so the German mind must guide the Aryan peoples to racial supremacy and world domination."

Chamberlain knew he was writing the new Bible for the Pan-Germanic movement but even he was staggered at the fantastic reception of his work. Kaiser Wilhelm invited him to Court and greeted him with the words: "It was God who sent your book to the German people and you personally to me." Chamberlain returned an even more blasphemous compliment to the Kaiser.

He wrote to say that he had placed the Kaiser's picture in his study opposite Leonardo's painting of the head of Jesus Christ. "I walk back and forth across the room between my Emperor and my God," he said. The Kaiser wrote back to say that every member of the Royal Household, the General Staff and the Guard Corps had read the book and were filled with boundless admiration. And this was not surprising since Chamberlain had named them as the elite leaders and the great heroes of the New Race!

Yet the German people as a whole were sceptical of his racist theories and hostile to his wish to see a German world domination. Many more balanced German thinkers, inspired by the high ideals of Goethe and Schiller, men who rejoiced in the concept of spiritual freedom and equity of all mankind, spoke forth angrily against Chamberlain and similar political tyrants like Treitschke who glorified only in war and conquest.

When Kaiser Wilhelm was publicly rebuked by a socialist Reichstag for interfering too outspokenly in the affairs of government, Chamberlain consoled him by saying that public opinion was made for idiots and malicious traitors. The Kaiser replied: "You wield your pen. I, my tongue. I will strike with my broadsword and say 'In spite of hell and high weather'."

The Englishman's friendship with the German Emperor gradually deepened until he was accepted at the Palace at Potsdam as the spiritual mentor of the Royal Household. His position there was more securely established and yet more dangerous than Rasputin's hold over the Romanov Court.

This extraordinary situation, of an Englishman so firmly entrenched at Potsdam, and enjoying the position of sole confident of the German Kaiser, had created an understandable alarm at the headquarters of German Military Intelligence. Weekly reports on his activities were submitted to von Moltke, who was greatly perturbed by the adverse influences he was having on the power-hungry monarch.

General von Moltke was the nephew of Graf Helmuth Karl von Moltke, the friend of Kaiser Friedrich and of Bismarck, and Germany's most illustrious soldier who had commanded the

German Army to a *Blitzkrieg* victory in the Franco-Prussian War in 1870. Though he had a fine record and had done much to revamp and streamline the General Staff on the lines initiated by his famous Uncle, he secretly wished to decline the supreme post of Quartermaster General when the Kaiser pressed it on him. "I am too reflective, too scrupulous, and if you like, too conscientious for the post," he is reported to have said at the time. A man of a deeply philosophic cast of mind, he was more a scholar than a soldier. Kaiser Wilhelm was impressed by his grave and quiet charm and for some unknown reason nicknamed him "der traurige Julius".

Kaiser Wilhelm lived in the hope that some of the genius of Moltke's military forebears had rubbed off on him. This confidence was not shared by his fellow Generals who were concerned that his main private interest outside his army career was the quest for the Holy Grail! They complained that such delving into medieval mysticism was not a normal healthy interest for a Prussian General and feared that he might fail to show the ruthless determination needed of a supreme commander at times of crisis. When a certain Dr. Rudolf Steiner, publicly known as a Goetheanist scholar and a Master of Occult Science, became a regular visitor to the Moltke home, discreet approaches were made to the Kaiser suggesting he should intervene and warn his Chief of Staff that such interests were undermining the confidence of the senior ranks of the German Army.

The Kaiser waved these criticisms aside. He had no objection to General Moltke's researches into the history of the Holy Grail. He had a genuine respect for Moltke, and such criticisms were a little too close to the bone because the Kaiser himself was so deeply involved in the pursuit of Pan-Germanic mysticism. But whereas the Kaiser did not mind Moltke's association with Dr. Steiner, General Moltke was concerned that the Kaiser was so deeply hypnotised by the personality of Chamberlain.

General von Moltke knew a great deal about Chamberlain of which the Kaiser and his entourage at that time had no idea. He knew, for instance, that he wrote most of his works in a condition of trance in which hierarchies of evil spirits manifested themselves before his gaze. And that he never knew when or where his very soul would be seized by demons who drove him on into the feverish continuation of his work, leaving him later like an exhausted shell, frequently in near hysteria or on the point of collapse. Agents of the Abwehr keeping a close watch on Chamberlain had even reported seeing him fleeing from such invisible demons!

What especially troubled General von Moltke was the profound unity of theme and inspiration in all Chamberlain's works which had a quite remarkable coherence. The General, who had a deep knowledge of the mysteries of the Holy Grail, had no doubt at all that Chamberlain was in the hands of demonic intelligences who sought to influence and disrupt the course of European history. Yet he could see no possibility of persuading the Kaiser that the Englishman might bring about the eclipse of the Hohenzollern Dynasty and bring Germany to defeat at the hands of her enemies.

The problem was made more complex because not all Chamberlain's visions were of demonic origin. Sometimes his mediumistic faculties evoked spirits of great figures from ancient history who appeared before him to inspire him with their words. For instance, Chamberlain's whole theory of race was originally based on a vision of the ancient Prophet Phineas who forged a Spear as a symbol of the magic of the blood of the Jewish Race. Ezekiel too had appeared before his mystic vision —the same Ezekiel who had prophesied to the Jews that they would behold the crucified Messiah whose side they had pierced with the Spear.*

---

* Konrad Heiden in his brilliant biography of Adolf Hitler, *Der Führer*, comes astonishingly near to the truth when he writes: "Chamberlain had learned from the great masters of world domination, from the Jewish prophets Ezekiel, Ezra and Nehemiah, who created, as he says, by order of the Persian King, the race-conscious Jewish people. To penetrate other nations, to devour them from within by superior intellect, bred in course of generations, to make themselves the dominant intelligence in foreign nations, and thus to make the world Jewish—this, according to Chamberlain, is the aim of the Jewish Race."

In following the path of the descending generations of the Jewish race, Chamberlain believed it to have been befouled by "round-headed Hittites with predominantly Semitic noses!" The strain of the Amonites, he said, with their pure Aryan characteristics appeared too late to redeem the corrupt strain.

He described Jesus Christ as a tall, blond, magnificent Gallilean of the Amonite type with a very high proportion of non-Semitic blood. "Whoever claimed that Jesus was a Jew was either stupid or telling a lie . . . Jesus was not a Jew. He was an Aryan." And, according to Chamberlain, only the best strains of Indo-Aryan blood, especially the Teutons, had the necessary virtue in them to understand and put into practice Christ's message; certainly not the Jews who had become 'a negative and bastardly race", nor the chaotic mixture of lower races in the Mediterranean basin. The Blood of Christ was shed exclusively for the Aryan Peoples!

This strangely prejudiced conception of a Christianity exclusive to the Aryans was nothing new. Chamberlain was merely restating with greater scholarship and in far bolder terms the racial doctrines of his beloved Richard Wagner.

Chamberlain first met Wagner in 1882 when he journeyed from Geneva to Bayreuth to attend the Festspiel. The composer immediately became the sun of his life and it was the result of Wagner's influence that Chamberlain decided to move to Germany and immerse himself in German history, philosophy, literature and music.

It was Wagner too who first drew his attention to the existence of the Holy Spear which had inspired the greatest Wagnerian opera *Parsival*. Though it was many years before Chamberlain discovered the extent of Wagner's vision into the history of the Grail in the ninth century, and that his operatic characters had been inspired by actual living personalities living in the Dark Ages.

Above all, Wagner had sown the seed of interest in Chamberlain's mind about the legend surrounding the Spear of Longinus, and seven years later he settled in Vienna to make for himself an intensive study of its history and significance for modern times.

For the next twenty years (1889–1909) until he moved to Bayreuth, the English mystic was a regular visitor to the Hofburg where, like Hitler three decades later, he stood for hours on end contemplating the ancient weapon and hoping to discover its hidden secrets.

Chamberlain claimed to have seen in vision both the Time Spirit associated with the Spear and also the Anti-Spirit which was the source of its black magic powers. He delved deeply into the incredible role the Spear had played in influencing the course of European history for two thousand years. And it was the Spear of Longinus as a symbol of the magic powers inherent in the blood which inspired the very racial theories contained in *The Foundation of the Nineteenth Century,* the book which became the inspiration of Adolf Hitler's Third Reich.

With astonishing mediumistic faculties comparable to those of Madame Blavatsky, Chamberlain perceived in a series of trances many of the great historical personalities who claimed the Spear through the centuries with either good or evil motives. It was the description of these visions which elated Kaiser Wilhelm into a frenzy of excitement and heightened his dreams of personal world conquest.

The German Kaiser proved to have an almost insatiable appetite for Chamberlain's successive and vivid visions of the illustrious men throughout history who had harnessed the powers of the Spear to fulfil a world-historic destiny. Such men as Constantine The Great, Justinian, Charles Martel, Charlemagne, and the greatest of all the German Emperors like Henry The Bird Catcher, Otto The Great, Friedrich Barbarossa, and, of course, the astonishing Friedrich Hohenstauffen.

The moment of decision came for the power-crazy monarch with the withered arm when Chamberlain brought him a personal message from beyond the grave. The wily Englishman informed him that the German Emperor Sigismund had appeared to him in a vision and beseeched him to tell Kaiser Wilhelm that it was a crime against God to allow the Holy Spear to remain outside the borders of Germany. The Kaiser quickly put his own historians to work on the life of Sigismund and they soon confirmed that it was indeed the Emperor who had made a royal decree that the Heilige Lance should rest eternally in the Fatherland.

This revelation came to the Kaiser in 1913, after a series of crises had brought Germany to the brink of war. It was altogether too much for the Kaiser to bear. He decided that it was a matter of dire urgency to regain the Spear for Germany in order to harness its powers to the future destiny of the Fatherland and to bring about the breeding and consolidation of the New Race of *Herrenvolk*.

Accordingly the Kaiser set up an elaborate ruse to bring the Spear into his immediate possession. A great deal of publicity was hurriedly given to the staging of an Exhibition of Germanic Art to be held in Berlin. Inviting the aged Emperor Franz Joseph of Austria to attend this exhibition in person on a State Visit, the Kaiser requested the temporary loan of the Reichskleinodien and the holy relics of the German Emperors, so that they too could be exhibited. In this way the Spear itself was not specifically mentioned except as just one item amongst Crowns, Jewels, Sceptres, Swords, etc., included in the ancient Germanic treasures.

The ruse might well have worked. The only contingency in his careful arrangements with which the Kaiser failed to reckon was his own tongue. By nature a bungler and totally incapable of keeping a secret, it was not long before his entire entourage, the officers of the Guard Corps and many members of the General Staff, knew the real reason for the Kaiser's sudden and uncharacteristic interest in Germanic art. It was quite clear that he never intended to return the Holy Spear to the Hapsburg Emperor but wanted it for himself as a talisman of power to wage a victorious world war.

It was at this point that General von Moltke decided to act. The Kaiser's bombastic speeches and his warmongering discussions with the General Staff had been a cause of grave anxiety for him, especially after the Agadir incident. He despatched a note in secret to Emperor Franz Joseph telling him the real motives behind the Kaiser's request for the temporary loan of the Reichskleinodien and warning him that the Spear in the Kaiser's hands would incite him to initiate the world war which all Christian people feared and dreaded.

Kaiser Wilhelm, who had been informed by his Ambassador in Vienna that Emperor Franz Joseph seemed willing enough to loan the ancient treasures of the German Emperors, was greatly surprised to receive an abrupt letter declining the request. He never knew who had foiled his plans.

It had been partly due to the influence of General von Moltke that Germany had not embarked earlier on a world war. As Chief of Staff, he was continually warning the warmongering Kaiser that there were not yet enough trained divisions in the German Army to carry through the Schlieffen Plan to conduct and win a *blitzkrieg* victory on two fronts.

Secretly von Moltke was in sympathy with the balanced policy of peace and progress carried through by the civil government in the face of the Kaiser's Pan-Germanic mania for world domination. He had found it hard to disguise his pleasure when the German people elected an overwhelmingly anti-Prussian and anti-militarist Reichstag in 1912 which consisted of peace-loving Social Democrats.*

When, on the 28th June, 1914, the Heir Apparent to the

---

* Konrad Heiden has summed up the contrast between these two opposing military and civil factions in pre-war Germany: it was partly because of the internal opposition of the Civil Government that Germany's foreign policy did not yield to the lust for conquest, as Houston Chamberlain expected.

"Between 1900 and 1912, when England conquered South Africa, when France took Morocco, and Italy, Tripoli, Germany made no such acquisition by force of arms. It had withdrawn from Morocco before France, in Persia before England and Russia.

"Towards the end of the century Germany had refused a Franco-Russian offer to unite against England, who was then involved in the Boer War. Then when Russia and France concluded a pact directed against Germany, the latter, in 1904 and 1907, allowed the tempting opportunity of waging a lightning invasion of France to slip away, although Russia was at that time hard pressed by internal revolution and the defeat of Japan. Even the First World War did not begin as a German war of conquest." (*Der Führer*: Konrad Heiden.)

Austrian Throne, the Archduke Franz Ferdinand, and his wife the Duchess Sofia, were shot in Sarajevo by assassins belonging to an Occult Society called the "Black Hand", the international crisis arose which through fear and misunderstanding gave the Kaiser the holocaust for which he and Chamberlain had been praying.

At first few Germans believed that an assassination in Sarajevo could have any effect on their lives. Bosnia and the Balkans were far away and few people really cared about the murder of an Austrian Archduke. Although the German Government supported the Austrian view that the Serbians should be punished for such wickedness, it was assumed that the Russians could never mobilise in support of a small nation who had perpetrated a brutal assassination.

Throughout July the Kaiser remained aboard the Royal Yacht on a prolonged Norwegian cruise. General von Moltke, who was on holiday with his family in Karlsbad, had the uneasy feeling that Europe was on the brink of some terrible disaster.

On July 23rd when Austria delivered a belated but uncompromising ultimatum to Serbia, the whole world was surprised at the Tsar's abrupt reaction: "Russia cannot allow Austria to crush Serbia and become the dominant power in the Balkans."

The situation began to look ominous. And it was only then that the German Chief of Staff suddenly grasped the previously unseen weakness in the Schlieffen Plan. It did not allow any time at all for diplomatic negotiations which might avert a war.

"In truth, once the scarlet posters announcing general mobilisation were posted in Russia, nothing could save the peace, for Germany, faced with enemies on two sides, felt that she could not afford to wait until the Russian steam-roller began to move.

"In the last fateful days the dead hand of General Count von Schlieffen did more to guide German policy than the Kaiser or Bethmann-Hollweg (the Chancellor). Since the Schlieffen Plan called for the defeat of France while Russia was still assembling her armies, Russia could not be allowed to mobilise in peace.

Conversely, if war was declared on Russia, France would have to be invaded. Or so at least General von Moltke believed. The Plan called for it. No alternative existed. And even if France declared herself willing to abandon her ally and allow Russia to face Germany alone, could she be counted on to resist the temptation of attacking her old enemy once the German Armies were deeply committed in Russia."

Ludendorff: D. J. Goodspeed, (Rupert Hart-Davis.)

General von Moltke insisted that it was a military necessity to inform the Russians that the mobilisation of their armies would be regarded as an act of war. "Further continuation of Russian mobilisation measures will force us to mobilise and in that case a European War can scarcely be averted" read the official note which the German Ambassador handed to the Russian Government at St. Petersburg.

And there was yet another reason why Helmuth von Moltke began to feel personally responsible for the uncontrollable on-rush of events. His own personal amendments to the Schlieffen Plan demanded the immediate capture of Liège in Belgium at the very moment war was declared. The Liège forts had to be silenced before the French and British Armies could move by rail through Belgium into the heart of France. Any delay which allowed the enemy to prepare would lead to the failure of the whole plan. Von Moltke's Chief of Military Intelligence reported that both the Russian and the French mobilisation was fully under way. The situation was not only menacing, it had passed the point of no-return. Now there was no choice but war. If Germany did not mobilise according to the Plan and move immediately into the attack, the war would be lost before it was begun.

On July 31st the Kaiser with bristling moustache and triumphant countenance drove through Berlin amidst wildly cheering crowds. The evening newspapers announced Germany's ultimatum to Russia and 200,000 people gathered below the balcony of the Royal Palace. "The Sword has been pressed into my hand," he declared. "And now I commend you to

125

God. Go to the Churches, kneel before God and pray to him for help for our gallant German Army."

All night General von Moltke sat at his command desk at Supreme Headquarters as the lightning mobilisation plans he had prepared with minute care rolled on without a hitch.

> "All across Germany the reservists were reporting to their mobilisation depots. . . . At the railway stations the soldiers were quickly loading into troop trains, some of which were already chalk-marked with slogans 'Nach Paris', 'Nach Petersburg'. The reservists leaned out of the windows and waved at their families and relations, as, punctual to the second, the long trains pulled away. . . . Battalion after battalion, division after division, corps after corps were formed to strength, equipped with every last item needed, and entrained for predetermined localities. The marvellous German railway system, with four double lines running right across the country from East to West and with every subsidiary line designed with mobilisation in mind, handled the troop movements smoothly and efficiently. If there were any military errors in the first weeks of the war, they were not in the technical staff work."*

Standing before the master maps on the walls of the OHL in the Redhouse on the Königsplatz, General von Moltke issued a stream of directives ensuring that his army corps moved immediately into planned positions on the Eastern and Western Fronts. Every contingency which arose had been anticipated in his own personal amendments of the Schlieffen Master Plan. He knew that the future destiny of the Fatherland rested squarely in his hands and he felt competent to fulfil his tasks with the ruthless determination demanded of him.

It was at this moment when the well-drilled military machine was working with perfect Prussian precision that the Supreme Commander slumped across his desk in what outwardly appeared to be a stroke or a heart attack. A doctor was sent for whilst anxious aides carried their General to an armchair by the window overlooking the Königsplatz.

* ibid.

Helmuth von Moltke's sudden collapse was not the result of any immediately diagnosable illness. For some unknown reason he had swooned into a baffling condition of trance which, without any warning, overwhelmed his physical senses. His methodical and scrupulous German mind had not reckoned with the hand of fate which, at this critical moment in his career, now reached across a thousand years to bring him to a shattering realisation of the meaning of his personal destiny in the historical process.

THE POPE AT ARMY H.Q.: THE ARTISTRY OF DESTINY

Non corpore, tamen Spiritu
et Virtuti

"Among those raised to Papal dignity in the City of Rome since the time of Saint Gregory not one proved the equal of Pope Nicholas I (858–867).

"He issued his commands to Kings and tyrants and his relations with them was as authoritative as though he were the ruler of the whole earth.

"With Bishops and priests who observed their Lord's commandments in the right manner he was humble, kind, pious and gentle, but towards the Godless and as such as had strayed from the right way he was terrible and fierce in moral denunciation, so that it was justly held that by the will of God a second Elias had arisen in our time, *if not in body at any rate in spirit and in power* (Non corpore, tamen spiritu et virtuti).

Regino of Prune, Chronicler of the Ninth Century.

The anxious military aides who gathered round their Supreme Commander in the OHL thought at first that he was dying. His breathing was so light as to be barely audible and there was only the slightest trace of heartbeat. The open eyes had a vacant, lifeless look as though all consciousness had been extinguished.

Whatever his outward appearance Quartermaster General Helmuth Ludwig von Moltke was very far from the eclipse of life and consciousness which they attributed to him. On the contrary, he was experiencing a new-born awareness so concentrated, sharp and vivid that it took him to the edge of pain as his soul was transported on a journey back through Time across a thousand years.

With all the mobile and colourful imagery of dreams, and with that same magical quality with which dreams slip through the barriers of sequential time and three-dimensional space, he found himself reliving vital episodes in the life of a medieval Pope. And by means of some inexplicable process of higher memory which now awakened in his soul, he identified the life which he was experiencing as that of Pope Nicholas I upon whom fell most of the fateful decisions of the Roman Church in the Dark Ages.

Yet within the labyrinth of his expanded mind which arched across the centuries, he still retained his own twentieth-century identity as Chief of Staff. Indeed he was fascinated to behold how these two lives, separated by a thousand years of European history, seemed to dovetail into a living tapestry of cause and effect.

It appeared to him that the happenings in the life of this august Pontiff were woven by some law of magical metamorphosis into the sequence of events and personal relationships in his own life in contemporary times. And he was yet more astonished to discover that many of the faces of the Cardinals and Bishops surrounding this celebrated Vicar of Rome reappeared in the countenances of his immediate colleagues on the German General Staff!

One of the medieval figures which he recognised most clearly was his illustrious Uncle, the famous Field Marshal who had founded the General Staff and achieved the resounding victory over the French in the war of 1870. But his Uncle did not appear as he formerly remembered him, in the uniform of the German High Command, but in the garb of a medieval Pope.

Needless to say there were certain dissimilarities in the two faces separated by ten centuries, but the act of recognition stemmed from the emergence of yet higher faculties which laid bare the secrets of the Karmic transformation of human physiognomy. In this manner he was able to identify him as Pope Leo IV, the great "Soldier-Pontiff" who organised the defence of Rome and led his own soldiers into battle.

An even greater surprise came with the appearance of the tall, thin and waspish General von Schlieffen in the guise of Pope Benedict II, the Pope who spent a lifetime scheming how to balance the hostile powers in the East and the West, persuading the Carolingian Emperors to honour their pledge to defend the Roman See against its assailants.

After von Moltke retired from active service in 1914, he wrote a detailed description of this extraordinary transcendent experience which he believed to be a genuine perception of a previous life on earth and a revelation of the inner workings of Karma and Reincarnation.

When he had the leisure to enable him to consider the significance of all that had been revealed to him through the sudden lifting of the veil of Time, it seemed to him totally irrational that a renowned Pope dedicated to the service of the Roman Church should have reincarnated as the Supreme Commander of an Army equally dedicated to waging war against the enemies of his Fatherland. He could make no sense of it all. But after many months of trying to unravel this mystery he at last began to find a whole chain of rational links between the succession of medieval Popes in the ninth century and the chain of Command of the German General Staff and its elite corps of officers in the nineteenth and twentieth centuries.

He found the key to the Karmic relationship between these two streams of personalities living a thousand years apart when he discarded the idea that the "religion" of the Popes was a significant factor. He looked instead for a repetition of the way of life of the medieval Churchmen amidst the contemporary scenes and daily routines of the Staff Corps. For instance, such things as customs, habits, the quality of personal relationships, bearing and gestures.

He perceived how the Officers of the General Staff also lived almost totally sequestered lives cut off from the main stream of life around them. And he realised that in many ways they appeared to be as withdrawn as the Roman Curia, living isolated but dedicated lives like Popes and Cardinals and intent only on administering the equivalent of a supreme religious order.

Like august Churchmen, all ranks of the elite Staff Corps were haughtily aloof from the pollutions of the secular scene, and completely oblivious of what was going on around them —such things as the great industrial expansion of modern Germany and the new wave of bourgeois prosperity.

After the manner of an exclusive Papal circle they also managed to unite harmoniously the opposing principles of absolute autocracy and the most liberal form of democracy. As in the Roman Curia, they also regarded rank less highly than intelligence or genuine talent. All ranks from the highest General to the most lowly Captain joined together freely and often heatedly in discussion up to the very second a decision was made. And although junior officers were expected to carry out orders instantly and without question, they were also expected to advise their seniors honestly and without subservience in a manner similar to medieval prelates of the Roman See.

It was the similarity of the basic mission of the ninth-century Popes and the modern Chiefs of Staff which struck von Moltke most forcibly. He assessed the primary task of the Popes to have been the balancing of power between East and West in which the very existence of the Roman See was perpetually at stake. And not unlike the succession of Popes a thousand years earlier, the chain of Chiefs of Staff also had one common intent handed down generation by generation. They sought to protect the destiny of Central Europe, the continually threatened fulcrum between two contrasting and potentially hostile civilisations in the East and West. And the lives of the Supreme Commander and his Staff Corps pivoted round the execution of the Schlieffen

Master Plan which anticipated a war to be fought on two fronts, a titanic struggle in which the very survival of the Fatherland was at stake.

Pre-armed with von Moltke's own conclusions regarding the veracity of his transcendent visions, the reader may find the actual content of it a little more credible. Perhaps it is relevant at this juncture to point out that the German Supreme Commander was a man known for his scrupulous honesty who angrily denounced all forms of unfounded speculation, while his love of truth and meticulous attention to detail were widely respected. He himself insisted that his awareness throughout the whole period of mind expansion was clearer and sharper than everyday consciousness of the phenomenal world, claiming that the sense of truth and reality exceeded in intensity anything he had previously known.*

The central pivot, which gave a theme of meaning to the wide and rich content of Helmuth von Moltke's transcendent experience, was the Spear of Destiny. Several months earlier, while on a visit to Vienna he had visited the Schatzkammer to see it.

At that time he was attending a joint meeting of the Staffs of the German and Austrian Armies. The courtesy visit to the Hofburg had been arranged so that he could take a close look at this "Heilige Lance" through which Houston Stewart Chamberlain had been inciting Kaiser Wilhelm to visions of world conquest.

He entered the Schatzkammer in the company of the Austrian Chief of Staff, General Conrad von Hotzendorf, a friend of many years standing. While the two men walked around the gangways looking at the Hapsburg Regalia, they continued to discuss the critical International situation, the armaments race and the likelihood of war. Hotzendorf ex-

* In many ways we have here a comparable situation to that faced by Lord Dowding, the Air Marshal whose foresight as Chief of R.A.F. Fighter Command saved the English nation during the Battle of Britain. He also had many deep spiritual experiences for which he was ridiculed for many years until a new generation arose to acclaim loudly both his spiritual wisdom and his integrity.

pressed his opinion that the encirclement policy of Britain, France and Russia showed a clear intent to dominate the German-speaking peoples and that war was now inevitable.

It was at this juncture, when the two Generals were standing before the Spear of Longinus, that von Moltke said: "If war must be our fate, any adjournment will unfortunately have the effect of diminishing our chances of success."

The Spear made a profound impression on him. Yet it was not only Christian feelings of awe and compassion for the supreme sacrifice of Jesus Christ that were evoked in his heart. The Spear also seemed to raise strange recollections and un-answered questions to the threshold of his consciousness. He later told his wife, Eliza von Moltke, that he believed that the Nail secured within the blade of the Spear held the answer to the riddle of *fate and free will.*

And now, in the transcendent awareness in which he was re-living the life of Pope Nicholas I, he was astonished to discover that just this very question of the conflicting factors of fate and freewill had tormented the medieval Pontiff.

In the heated controversy regarding the manner in which man himself reflected the Holy Trinity of Father, Son and Holy Spirit, Pope Nicholas had come to the conclusion that human fate befell to man out of the necessity of the Father God, whilst the possibility of human freedom stemmed from the sacrificial love of the Son. According to Nicholas, a man was led into debt and illusion when he failed to understand how fate and freedom were intermingled in human destiny. He achieved blessedness only when he discovered how divinely regulated fate and human freedom together ruled his personal destiny.

At the zenith of his transcendent vision, General von Moltke grasped the true significance of the Spear of Destiny which now appeared to him in the form of a mighty apocalyptic symbol.

He understood how the blade represented fate, the working of the law of moral consequence which transformed the hap-penings of earlier centuries into new patterns of world events. And he realised that the Nail enclosed in it symbolised the des-tiny of each individual man inextricably bound into the fabric of the historical process. The only measure of freedom rested in the motives and manner in which the individual reacted to his allotted fate. And yet each pattern of personal destiny, when embraced with Christian love, contained within it exactly those possibilities which paved the way to Self Knowledge.

Looking forward into the future from the ninth century, Nicholas could even then see the advent of modern materialism as the result of an inescapable fate which must befall Western humanity. It appeared to him as inevitable in the evolution of human consciousness that the Europeans should sink yet more deeply into the three-dimensional world of the senses.

Cardinal Anastasius (Biblothecarius), his friend and councillor, believed that only through such a descent could Western man become a strong and independent Ego and develop the analytical intellect in order to gain a scientific mastery of the Earth. Yet, at the price of such a scientific outlook which would bring about the machine age, man would have to cut himself off entirely from all knowledge of the spirit-worlds and fall back entirely on the revelations of the Gospels.

Both Nicholas and Anastasius envisaged the time when the inner longing in the souls of individual men in a future materialistic age would inspire them once again to search in freedom for the Spirit. And it was these considerations, quite apart from the presentation to the Roman See of the "Pseudo-Isodoric Decretals," which finally persuaded Pope Nicholas I to eradicate the Individual Human Spirit from the original Trichotomy of Man.

Anastasius, gifted with the vision of celestial Spirits, could perceive how evil Spirits had been cast down out of the Macrocosm into the souls of men. And that these spirits of the second hierarchy of the Trinity of Evil would temporarily seduce man into the illusion that the physical world was the only reality.

After the death of von Moltke, Dr. Rudolf Steiner, a man of exceptional spiritual gifts who could read at will the 'Cosmic Chronicle', confirmed the essence of the General's vision. In a letter to Dr. Walter Johannes Stein, Eliza von Moltke gave permission for this confirmation to be published.

134

Friedenau.
3rd December 1927

Dear Dr. Stein,

I willingly put the following notes at your disposal for your book:

Letter from Dr Rudolf Steiner, 28th July, 1918 to Eliza v Moltke on Pope Nicholas and his Counsellor:

In the ninth century the Counsellor stood at the side of Nicholas surveying the map of Europe. It was encumbent upon Nicholas at that time to grasp the ideas which were to separate East from West. In this separation many people were involved. . . . The Counsellor with his survey gave judgement on this. But at the same time man still stood near the spiritual worlds. It occasioned no surprise that Spiritual Beings come and go. The dwellers in Mid and Western Europe were, however, striving away from the Spiritual Hierarchies. For they were to prepare themselves even then for materialism. For Nicholas and his Counsellor in the ninth century there was much of a directly perceptible spirit influence. The Counsellor often said: The Spirits will withdraw from Europe, but the Europeans will later on long for them. The Europeans will create the machine and their contrivances without the Spirit. Therein they will become great. Thereby they will, nevertheless, rear within their own womb, as it were, the Western Man who will bring the Ahrimanic culture to its highest point for them, and then take their place.

(signed) Eliza v Moltke
Geb. Gräfin Moltke Huitfeldt.

Friedenau.
10 December, 1927.

Dear Dr. Stein,

I willingly send you the following notes for use in your book:

A conversation between Pope Nicholas and his Counsellor, the Cardinal, reported to Eliza von Moltke by Rudolf Steiner, 17th June, 1924:

The Pope: Shall we lose that which brought the spiritual to us when the Gospel of the Crucified brought Heaven down to Earth?

The Counsellor: What has grown old must wither away; Death is

135

merely new life. Out of the downfall of Asia I see the life of Europe arise.

The Pope: The decision will be difficult.

The Counsellor: But it is the will of higher spirits, in order that Ahriman may be shown the right way into the soul life that shall light up from the Franks to the East. The Northern Light has also told it to me, when, on a fair summer night, among the rock of my home country, I heard the voice which comes from Gabriel, who will bring forth a new Europe.

The Pope: Are you certain?

The Counsellor: The utterance of higher Spirits is the only certainty. I am certain they speak clearly.

The Pope: May they speak clearly! But I know too that the centuries to follow will weigh heavily upon our souls.

(signed) Eliza von Moltke
Geb. Gräfin Moltke Huitfeldt.

A vast panorama encompassing a thousand years of European history arose before the transcendent vision of General von Moltke, illustrating how, as the result of the Papal denial of the Individual Spirit he had himself made in a former incarnation, mankind had been led step by step into virtual imprisonment in the phenomenal world of measure, number and weight, the very existence of the human soul itself becoming a matter of doubt and debate.

He witnessed how a great sleep had descended upon the earth in the materialism of the eighteenth and nineteenth centuries so that the spiritual origins of humanity were forgotten, and the flow of onward history was regarded as a blind accident of a Darwinian evolution. Unable to find the path back to the recognition of the Spirit, the masses had been tricked into believing that patriotism was the highest ideal. And it was out of such misplaced national pride that the armies of the nations were now mobilising to slaughter one another.

When the Quartermaster General recovered consciousness, he found himself peering up from a chair into the face of an Army physician who was in the process of examining him. Though he had been outwardly unconscious for nine minutes, nothing more serious was diagnosed than physical collapse due to excess strain and exhaustion.

Staff Officers of all ranks hurried back to their duties while expressing relief that their Supreme Commander needed no more than a sound sleep before returning to his post. General von Moltke alone knew the terrible dilemma with which he was now faced.

He was in command of the greatest fighting force the world had ever known. Two million "sleeping" men hurtling according to plan towards the frontiers of Germany to confront and annihilate millions of other "sleeping" men of the French, Russian and British armies. The great fear in the hearts of these men of all nationalities was the same—the dread of awakening to the Individual Spirit within them through which they would see that all their cherished patriotic ideals were no more than a deadly tissue of dreams.

And worst of all, it appeared that the working of fate itself would now demand a prolonged nightmare of death and mutilation in a veritable hades of trench warfare. For now the Pope at Army H.Q. inwardly feared that only a long drawn-out war of unprecedented magnitude and suffering could awaken mankind to the falsity of its beliefs and values.

CHAPTER TEN

A *BLITZKRIEG* FOR MERCY'S SAKE

The Inescapable Hand of Fate

"My Master Plan is foolproof. Our enemies will never withstand its brutal and robust simplicity. In the iron hands of a ruthless and determined Commander-in-Chief it cannot fail."

General von Schlieffen.

General Helmuth von Moltke now faced a terrible dilemma. In the light of his newborn understanding of the real meaning of personal destiny within the fate of the historical process, the death of a single soldier, whether German, French, Russian or British, weighed on his soul like a personal tragedy.

And yet at the same time it was unthinkable that he should desert his post as Commander-in-Chief at such a time of crisis. Over a period of two years, the strategy, tactics and mobilisation procedures of the entire German Army had been geared to striking a victorious blow with the Schlieffen Plan. And because he had amended personally the Plan so that it included a lightning strike through Belgium and had masterminded every detail of it, there seemed no doubt that he was duty bound to retain command.

According to the Schlieffen Plan, Paris would fall and the outflanked French Armies would capitulate on the thirty-sixth day after the first mobilisation order. If he could take the initiative with an iron hand and ruthless determination, it was still possible that he could avert a war of attrition which would cost untold millions of lives.

He decided upon a *Blitzkrieg* for mercy's sake.

Once the decision was made, General von Moltke was astonished to discover that his spiritual enlightenment had in no way changed his personal destiny. Everything continued as before, only his motive for action had changed. And so it came about that he acted in a somewhat similar manner to the Roman Centurion, Longinus, for he, too, had undertaken a martial act out of a motive of mercy.

The robust and brutal simplicity of the Schlieffen Plan worked with terrifying effect as the German Armies cut through the very heart of Belgium into France. While a minimum force held the Russian Armies on the Eastern Front, the bulk of the German Armies swept forward, pivoting on Metz like a giant-swinging scythe. On the extreme right, General von Kluck's Army cut across the Marne reaching positions within sight of Paris.

'Victory according to schedule' appeared beyond doubt. General von Moltke issued a bulletin: "The enemy, beaten all along the line, is in full retreat and is not capable of offering serious resistance to the German advance."

And then there happened in the course of a single day that mysterious series of misunderstandings and events which were to leave their bloodstained mark on history.

The repetition of Hannibal's "Battle of Cannae" had been the dream of General von Schlieffen. But now it failed to materialise as he had planned it because the right wing of the German Armies failed to envelop the French and British forces.

General von Kluck, a vain and swashbuckling character who liked to compare himself to Attila The Hun, failed to obey orders. In pursuit of personal glory he was tempted into attacking the exposed flank of the retreating French Army and he wheeled round in front of Paris instead of going behind it. His tactical error not only left a treacherous gap between the advancing German columns, it also exposed the naked belly of his troops to a fierce counter-attack from the more flexible French and British Corps.

The German troops were exhausted after their long advance, supplies were short and the tactical situation had become confused. General von Moltke suddenly saw a desperate need for a Reserve Army Corps to fill the ominous gaps between his wildly wheeling armies. But now he had no such reserves, for, in a flush of confidence, he had sent them to the Eastern Front to cope with the perilous-looking situation which was developing there against the Russians.

From OHL in Luxemburg, some 200 miles from the scene of battle, von Moltke despatched a Staff Colonel to assess von Kluck's tactical position, somewhat unwisely giving him full powers to order an advance or a retreat.

This trusted officer, Colonel Hentsche, was suddenly smitten with a serious bout of kidney illness which appears to have completely clouded his judgement. Instead of making the obvious decision at whatever the cost to order an immediate advance in accordance with the original plan, he advised a temporary withdrawal across the Marne for a short regrouping in preparation for a final assault.

It was the turning point of the war. Gone was any hope of lightning victory. The French resistance miraculously stiffened and they fought back with savage courage. After a race to the coast, the deadly stalemate of trench warfare stretched like a gangrenous wound across the breadth of France. Modern weapons proved themselves three times as effective in defence than in attack and a war of mutual attrition now began with a ferocity never before known.

Ahead stretched four years of mortal combat in the shell-pitted wastes and leafless stumps of Flanders. The only hope left to the soldiers of all nationalities who lived through this murderous deadlock was the forlorn hope that they were fighting a war to end wars.

The trap was sprung. What the world had refused to hearken

in freedom, it was now to learn from the bitter cup of fate. Millions, who had turned aside from the battle within, were now faced with those monstrous actions in which hundreds of thousands were killed in a single day to gain ten yards and exchange one rat-ridden trench for another.

General von Moltke, a broken man relieved of his Command, wept for a world in which only slaughter on such an unmitigated scale could serve to awaken mankind to the recognition of the Spirit.

CHAPTER ELEVEN

THE WISDOM OF HINDSIGHT:
A PANORAMA OF THE FUTURE

General von Moltke became the scapegoat not only for the failure of the Schlieffen Plan but also for the advent of the murderous insanity of the trench-warfare that followed.

His staff had noticed how reports of the early victories in the first long successful drive into Belgium and France only brought tears to his eyes. "He looked worn, with haunted eyes and deeply etched lines on his face," said Colonel Eric Ludendorff after a visit to von Moltke's headquarters. "There was nothing in the sad countenance to suggest the victorious commander."

His fellow Generals, unaware of a new dimension on Christian conscience which had come to birth within him, interpreted his conduct as a sure sign that all the doubts and irresolutions which had originally beset him when first offered the post as Commander-in-Chief had now returned. What use, they said, is a Commander without confidence in his own star, a man so sensitive that he is tortured by the prospect of the human suffering which must inevitably result from military decisions in times of war?

Replaced by General Eric von Falkenhayn, he made no attempt to defend himself against the accusations which sought to make him solely responsible for creating the murderous stalemate which he above all had foreseen and sought to avoid.

It was not until *after* his death in 1916 that he gave the real explanation of everything which had happened, describing it from a higher vantage point from which he could see without personal prejudice exactly why the Schlieffen Plan had been fated to fail.

The close bond between the General and his wife was not severed at his death. Eliza von Moltke, who had by this time also awakened within herself higher faculties, remained in a deep communion of spirit with him. And it was through the faculty of "Inspiration", that which St. Paul calls "speaking with tongues", that the dead General was able to speak through her from higher levels of time and consciousness.

Many of the closest friends of the Moltke family assembled regularly and in secret to hear descriptions of what he could behold in the "Cosmic Chronicle", the eternal tapestry of world destiny in which past, present and future are inseparably woven.

Eliza von Moltke insisted that there was nothing of a mediumistic nature about her communications with her husband. According to her summing up of modern spiritualism, mediums in a condition of trance were unaware of the communications revealed through them. In many cases she believed that this amounted to demonic possession, for such mediums could not identify the nature of the intelligences which had overwhelmed their consciousness and taken over their bodies. In contrast, she herself claimed to be in a condition of normal everyday consciousness when her husband communicated through her. Though his words were spoken in her voice, the circle who listened had no doubt at all that the manner and style of delivery was characteristic of the deceased Chief of Staff.

These communications, which were written down in 1916, contain General von Moltke's prophetic vision of the events destined to take place in the later decades of the twentieth century. Enveloping himself in the Akashic Record he described what he saw as the fate of Europe between 1916 and the year 2000 A.D.

He described how a further giant stride in the evolution of human consciousness was to take place in the twentieth century when millions of men and women would begin to experience within themselves the birth of an individual spiritual identity

(Higher Self) and with it a new sense of moral freedom and equity which would altogether transcend prejudiced forms of nationalism.

He described in great detail how Germany would lose the war and the type of conditions which would emerge in the aftermath of defeat under the shadow of the Versailles Treaty. He foretold how the working classes would awaken to the truth that the war had been fought against their interests and the interests of mankind as a whole. And how the great majority of the veterans of the German Army would realise that they had been no more than dispensable pawns in a senseless war forced upon them by the power politics of the West and by the Kaiser himself and the great Junker families.

He could see how the dreadful scenes of massacre in the trenches would illustrate the utter futility of misplaced patriotism in the "Fatherland Idea" and unquestioning loyalty to the leaders of the nation.

He prophesied, too, the fall of the Romanovs and the Hohenzollerns and the other great Dynasties which had held sway for a thousand years and which would be swept away by new ideologies with an international connotation—Fascism and Communism.

He foretold in exact detail how Lenin would establish a Communist regime in Russia and the manner in which Nazism would arise in Germany. Perhaps the most convincing aspect of these staggering prophecies spoken through the mouth of Eliza von Moltke, was the naming of Adolf Hitler as the future Führer of the Third Reich, for at that time he was an unknown and totally insignificant Meldeganger in the Lizt Regiment on the Western Front.

The naming of the then unknown Hitler as the coming Dictator of Nazi Germany, and the exact pre-vision of the whole sequence of events, cunning political manoeuvres and the racist doctrines through which he would come to power, was not the result of some inexplicable and ghostly guessing game from beyond the grave. That is to say, the communications received through Eliza von Moltke were not of the same nature as the sensational hit and miss predictions of a contemporary "Prophetess" from New York who, by mysteriously channelising unidentified powers, was able to foretell the tragic murder of President Kennedy.

The detailed prognostications describing in astonishing detail the coming Hitler regime were perceived by Helmuth von Moltke as an integral part of a gigantic vista, which included both the past history and the future fate of Europe, the manifestation of an immense "Time Organism" which arched across the centuries from medieval times to the present age.

Within this Time Organism he saw how the coming events of the twentieth century were the Karmic metamorphosis of the historical scene which had taken place a thousand years earlier. And he was able to distinguish how the same leading personalities who had confronted one another in the struggle to guide the destiny of Europe for good or evil in the ninth and tenth centuries were now reappearing on Earth again to work out the moral consequences of their former deeds.

The Moltke "Mitteilungen" are very extensive and amount to several hundred pages of typescript, photostats of which are still circulating secretly among hidden Grail Groups in Germany today. They include an identification and description of the former incarnations of many of the most important personalities on the scene of world politics in the twentieth century. We will confine ourselves to four of the people he mentions who are within our context of the story of the Spear of Longinus and the role it has played in changing the course of history in the twentieth century: Adolf Hitler, Kaiser Wilhelm, Houston Stewart Chamberlain and General Eric Ludendorff.

Von Moltke named Adolf Hitler as the reborn Landulf of Capua, the defrocked and excommunicated Archbishop who took refuge in Kalot Enbolot in Sicily from where he wielded the most fearsome black magic powers. The very same "Klingsor" figure whom Hitler also believed himself to have been in a previous life on earth And he describes how the monstrous black magic practices of the circle of Adepts, of whom this Count of Terra de Labur was the dominant figure, would reappear as the demonic occultism of the inner core of the Nazi Party.

His pre-vision of Hitler's meteoric career which would take him from obscurity to the heights of infamy and power included the staggering prediction that he would become the new claimant to the Spear of Longinus from a defunct Hapsburg Dynasty, embarking on a world war with this Spear as his talisman of power—a war which would reduce Germany to both moral degradation and into a heap of smoking ruins!

Kaiser Wilhelm appears in these communications as the reincarnation of Bishop Rothard, the Fox of Soissons, a most unsavoury character and the figurehead through whom the "Pseudo-Isodoric-Decretals" were presented as genuine documents to Pope Nicholas I in Rome. Moltke attributes the Kaiser's withered arm to the Karmic retribution for this deed of treachery in the ninth century.

The original motive for forging the whole series of Decretals which appeared in the ninth and tenth centuries was to establish a false claim to support the idea of the supreme power of the Roman Church above the secular powers of Emperors and Kings. These Decretals paved the way for centuries of bloody inquisition in which the Vicar of Rome exercised powers of life and death over those who dared to question the dogmas of his Church. According to von Moltke, the same devious personalities who perpetrated these crafty medieval falsifications reappeared on earth in the nineteenth and twentieth centuries to establish the equally fallacious conception of the "Inequality of Races" in opposition to the genuine Christian ideal of the equality of all mankind.

The wily exponent of this false racial philosophy was Houston Stewart Chamberlain, the man who cunningly united Wagner's racist doctrines with Nietzsche's concept of the coming "Superman" in order to create the dream of an Aryan Master Race. And von Moltke once again predicted correctly when he prophesied that it would be Houston Stewart Chamberlain who would declare Adolf Hitler to be the long-awaited "German Messiah"

146

William Shirer describes the first meeting between Adolf Hitler and Houston Stewart Chamberlain:*

It was on the Third Reich which did not arrive until six years after his death but whose coming he foresaw, that this Englishman's influence was the greatest. His racial theories and his burning sense of destiny of the Germans and Germany were taken over by the Nazis, who acclaimed him as one of their prophets. . . . It is likely that Hitler first learned of Chamberlain's writings before he left Vienna. In *Mein Kampf* he expresses the regret that Chamberlain's observations were not more heeded during the Second Reich.

Chamberlain was one of the first intellectuals in Germany to see a great future for Hitler—and new opportunities for the Germans if they followed him. Hitler had met him in Bayreuth in 1923, and though ill, half-paralysed and disillusioned by Germany's defeat and the fall of the Hohenzollern Empire— the collapse of all his hopes and prophecies!—Chamberlain was swept off his feet by the eloquent young Austrian.

"You have mighty things to do," he wrote Hitler on the following day. . . . "My faith in Germanism has not wavered for an instant, though my hope, I confess, was at a low ebb. With one stroke you have transformed the state of my soul. That in the hour of her deepest need Germany gives birth to a Hitler proves her vitality; as so the influences that emanate from him; for these two things—personality and influence— belong together. May God protect you!"

The hypnotic magnetism of Hitler's personality worked like a charm on the ageing, ill philosopher and renewed his faith in the people he had chosen to exalt. This remarkable Englishman's seventieth birthday, on September 5th, 1925, was celebrated with five enconiums in the Nazi *Völkischer Beobachter*, which hailed his "Foundations of the Twentieth Century" as "The Gospel of the Nazi Movement", and he went to his grave 16 months later with high hopes that all he had preached and prophesied would yet come true under the divine guidance of this new German Messiah."

* *The Rise and Fall of the Third Reich.*

The mystery of the nature of the blood of Jesus Christ and the legend of the Spear which shed it is believed to have been the main theme of the discussion between the ageing Chamberlain and Adolf Hitler when they met at Wahnfried, the home of the Wagner family. And it was Alfred Rosenberg, the prophet of the Anti-Christ of *The Protocols of the Wise Men of Zion*, who introduced the ex-Corporal with the hypnotic voice to the man who was chased by demons.

Chamberlain's teachings conceived Aryan blood to be the essential factor in the breeding of a future Master Race. From birth a man was destined according to the quality of the blood in his veins to become an exalted member of the Herrenvolk or to be condemned to a life of slavery as a 'sub-human'. Such a thesis anticipated the Gestapo, the Totenkopf SS and the Concentration Camps—even the gas ovens! And yet none of this could ever have come to pass without first establishing that Christ himself was of Aryan lineage. Once it was established that Jesus Christ was an Aryan God, the persecution of inferior races could become a religious crusade. A Himmler, a Heydrich and an Eichmann would then be able to organise the mass murder of sub-humans in fulfilment of religious duty—the Inquisition of Inferior Blood.

Though the whole content of this discussion between the two men who shared the secret of the Spear of Destiny has never been reported, it was the implication of Chamberlain's words which later inspired Rosenberg to write the racial bible of Nazism: *The Twentieth Century Myth*. One thing is certain. Chamberlain convinced Hitler that religion and politics could be fused together to support the new image of the Herrenvolk.

Chamberlain, whose clairvoyant faculties had mysteriously dispersed at the disastrous failure on the Western Front at the outbreak of World War I, was now seized anew with a strange excitement which mysteriously enkindled his former vision for the remaining years of his life.

Was it Hitler's moment of evil transfiguration before the man who was to proclaim him as the German Messiah? Perhaps he saw the Spirit of Lucifer hovering above the ex-Corporal with the hanging forelock and the banal moustache. "Hitler is an awakener of souls, the vehicle of Messianic powers," Chamberlain proclaimed. "Here is the new Leader sent by God to the German people in their hour of greatest need."

The final link in the chain had been wrought. The prophet of Aryan Christianity had joined hands with the vessel of the Anti-Christ in an unholy crusade to vanquish the free spirit of mankind.

Von Moltke considered that the greatest mistake of his whole life had been the handing of unlimited power to the one man who above all others would herald the Nazi Regime—General Eric Ludendorff.

Von Moltke had been one of the very first to note the tremendous executive abilities and military dedication of Ludendorff while he was still a comparatively junior officer on the Staff Corps. It was Ludendorff to whom he had entrusted the administration of the mobilisation schedules and the plan to advance through Belgium. Later Colonel Ludendorff had been overzealous and broken the golden rule of the Staff Corps when he secretly entered the political arena in an attempt to lobby for an increase in the numerical strength of the German Army. Von Moltke had been unable to protect his protégé when the Minister of War demanded his subordinate's instant return to regimental duties.

His first move at the moment of mobilisation was to bring back Ludendorff on to the Staff and give him unlimited power to oversee the assault through Belgium, a task which he performed with ruthless efficiency. It was at this juncture that Von Moltke made the fateful decision to promote Ludendorff to the rank of General and despatch him to the Eastern Front as Chief of Staff. Hindenburg, an aged Infantry General, was brought out of retirement to act as a mere figurehead through whom Ludendorff could issue his own orders.

Ludendorff's brilliant and decisive triumphs at the Battles of Tannenberg and the Masurian Lakes were the two resounding

German victories of World War I. Russian Armies outnumbering the Germans by four to one were enveloped and annihilated. It was the beginning of Ludendorff's meteoric rise to power. Within two years he had become the virtual military Dictator of Germany.

While he was still alive Moltke had not regretted promoting this man who had proved himself to have unquestionable strategic and tactical genius, an astonishing flair for making timely and decisive decisions and a determination to see that his orders were carried through to the letter.

It was only after von Moltke's death that he spoke forth about the evil which would inevitably come to pass through Ludendorff whom he now identified as the reincarnation of Pope John VIII, the Pontiff with the blackest record in the entire history of the Roman Church, who had been the fellow conspirator of Landulf II of Capua in the ninth century.

Were it not for his uncannily accurate pre-vision of the unfolding future events of the twentieth century, one might be tempted to believe that Eliza von Moltke, who claimed to speak her husband's after-death experiences, was dangerously deluded if not actually off her head. However, such an attitude is confounded by the fact that the words from her lips anticipated correctly all the later salient events in the life of Ludendorff, including how he would be instrumental in helping the then unknown Adolf Hitler to power.

Considered only from a purely conventional viewpoint, it is simple enough to assess the dire consequences for mankind which resulted from Ludendorff's evil genius, his decisions and his actions.

For instance, Eric Ludendorff not only planned every detail of the tactical breach of Belgian neutrality in 1914, but he it was who called from the field of battle for the first air raid of the century, the bombing of the civilian population of Liège.

From Ludendorff, too, came the plan to tempt the French into the breach-head at Verdun with the aim of tricking the enemy into the most fruitless slaughter the world has ever seen. And from Ludendorff, too, came the first execution of defence and attack in depth which anticipated the mobile tactics of infiltration which were to characterise World War II.

As Military Dictator of Germany he was also responsible for harnessing every aspect of life and activity of the German nation towards a total war effort. The form of military government which arose provided the blueprint for the totalitarian administration of Adolf Hitler's Third Reich. The first seed of the later persecution of the Jews came about at this time after Ludendorff had publicly announced that thousands of young Jews had evaded the call-up to the Colours and that the majority of Jews in Germany were concerned in businesses which made no positive contribution towards winning the War.

Ludendorff's decision to order German U-boats to sink on sight all vessels trading with Great Britain, regardless of nationality, brought America into the War. It made certain not only that Germany would be ultimately defeated, it also gave the moronic President Wilson the main say in the terms of the Versailles Treaty which was the cause of seething and justified discontent in the aftermath of the conflict.

The most drastic single decision of the century was made by Ludendorff when he sent Lenin and his 'cell' of thirty Marxists through Germany in a sealed railway carriage on their way from Switzerland to Russia. Lenin himself had refused to go. Only Ludendorff's large gifts of cash and assurances of his personal safety persuaded the reluctant Lenin to make the trip. Ludendorff's motive was to set up a Fifth Column in the heart of Russia. Yet through Ludendorff and Ludendorff alone, the pawn was queened. The Communist bloc and, later, the iron curtain appeared like the finger of fate through the decision of a German General. And yet Ludendorff became the foremost voice in post-war Germany in condemnation of the "Jewish-Marxist" menace.

Ludendorff's greatest crime was perpetrated against his own people, for he knew already in 1917 that the German Armies could never gain ultimate victory. Despite this knowledge, and perhaps to prolong his own personal power, he sent millions of Germans fruitlessly to their deaths in the stalemate of trench warfare. And finally when he saw that the war was irretrievably lost, he pushed the responsibility of ending it into the hands of the Social Democrats. In so doing, he managed to place the responsibility of surrender on to the shoulders of the civilian administration. Thus arose the myth that Germany had been stabbed in the back.

Ludendorff needed little persuasion to support the emerging National Socialist Party when he came to settle at Ludwig-shoehe in Bavaria in 1919. Captain Ernst Röhm, whose heroic wartime exploits were known to Ludendorff, introduced him to Adolf Hitler. The two men, the General and the Corporal with the Iron Cross, First Class, discovered an instant rapport in their similar racial ideologies, their intent to down the Weimar Republic, and their mutual hatred and contempt for the Jews.

Soon Ludendorff was appearing in uniform to inspect parades of Nazi *Sturmabteilung* and speaking in support of Adolf Hitler at demonstrations and rallies. Hitler was quick to grasp the prestige value of the name and renown of Germany's greatest living General. His presence at their meetings made the Nazi Party appear respectable in the eyes of the Officer Class and right-wing political supporters throughout Germany.

Hitler was wary not to let Ludendorff take over the Party to lead a counter-revolution, for he did not wish to play second fiddle to a political figurehead. He had come to an early conclusion that Ludendorff himself was completely lacking in political sense. The vital realisation which Hitler grasped through his discussions with Ludendorff was that the leaders of the elite German Staff Corps were not only approachable but could be handled like "babes in arms" in the political arena. There can be little doubt also that the real victor of Tannenberg, who considered the Slavs as an inferior race, opened Hitler's eyes to Eastern horizons and dreams of conquest and occupation of huge tracts of Russia.

When the Nazis attempted to take over the Bavarian Government in the so-called von Kahr *Putsch* in 1923, it was the very presence of General Ludendorff which gave authority to the dangerous undertaking. The whole affair, lacking the kind of planning which makes for successful revolutions, failed to succeed because Hitler omitted to concentrate his men in the obvious strategic strongpoints. Instead, the great column of Nazis led by Ludendorff and Hitler marched towards the centre of Munich where they were caught in a bottleneck as they approached the Marienplatz Square. When the police opened up with volleys of rifle shots Hitler turned and fled, leaving Ludendorff as the single, solitary figure to march on and brush the police carbines contemptuously aside.

Though the *Putsch* was a fiasco, the trial which followed gave Adolf Hitler the opportunity to make his name known beside that of the famous General. Using the dock as a political platform to discredit the compromised von Kahr Government, Hitler's words were, for the first time, heard beyond the borders of Bavaria and his name was emblazoned across the headlines of the newspapers of the world. Stealing the limelight from the greatest military figure of World War I, Hitler turned the trial into a triumph and forged the final link through which his own budding Nazi Party could shake hands in patriotic fervour with the most highly principled section of the German population.

While Hitler went off to serve one year of a five-year sentence in Landsberg Fortress, where he wrote the first volume of *Mein Kampf*, General Eric Ludendorff retired quietly to his Ludwigshoehe, complaining that the German Army had obstructed the *Putsch* and swearing he would never again put on the uniform of a German Officer because it had been so debased by their perfidy. He spent his years in retirement writing pamphlets against the Jews, the Freemasons and finally against the evils of Roman Catholicism, proclaiming the succession of Popes as the arch enemies of mankind! Out of the hidden depths of his subconscious mind he was condemning the ninth-century Pope, John VIII, the sinister personality of whom General von Moltke proclaimed he was the reincarnation.

THE MAN WHO WAS SMOOTH BETWEEN THE LEGS

Twentieth-Century Klingsor

"In the famous castle of Kalot Enbolot he became the mock of the world.

"The king found Klingsor with his wife, sleeping in her arms. If he found a warm bed there, he had to pay a heavy price that by the hand of the king he was made smooth between the legs.

"The king thought that was his right. He clipped him in such a way that he can never more give pleasure to any woman. But this has meant suffering for many people.

"It is not in the land of Persia, but in a city called Persida, that magic was first invented. To that place Klingsor travelled, and brought from there the magic art of how to do whatsoever he will.

"For the shame done to his body he never again bore good will toward anyone, man or woman, and when he can rob them of any joy, especially those who are honoured and respected, that does his heart good."

Parsival: Wolfram von Eschenbach.

Dietrich Eckart has been called the spiritual founder of Nazism. Whether this be true or not, for Houston Stewart Chamberlain has also been credited with this title, Adolf Hitler himself considered Eckhart as the most important single influence on his life and the fulfilment of his mandate. He describes Dietrich Eckart in *Mein Kampf* as "one of the best who devoted his life to the awakening of our people, in his writings, his thoughts and finally in his *deeds*".

Behind the apparently innocuous epitaph with which Hitler concludes *Mein Kampf* an unsuspected and dreadful secret lies hidden, for Eckart's final *deed* before he died was to initiate Hitler in a monstrous sadistic magic ritual similar to the rituals performed by Landulf II at Kalot Enbolot in the ninth century.

A description here and now of this ritual, when Hitler's occult centres were opened amidst participating members of the Thule Group, would be barely comprehensible, let alone credible, to the reader without some knowledge of the history and practices of ritual magic. For this reason our immediate endeavour will be to present a minimum background against which this all-important moment in the life of Adolf Hitler can be fully understood. We will begin by giving a few salient biographical details about Eckart before considering the occult anatomy of the Thule Gesellschaft and its various levels of activity, and the manner in which its secret inner core came to practice such a horrific form of "Astrological Magic".

Dietrich Eckart and Adolf Hitler quickly discovered that they were natural soul mates because they shared so much in common during the early background of their lives. For instance, Eckart, a brilliant student, failed to attain his Doctorate at Law because he had too many outside interests and a tendency to drink too much.

Konrad Heiden, the Munich journalist who knew Eckart, has described him as "the same sort of uprooted, agitated and far from immaculate soul. In Berlin, already in his thirties, he had led the life of a vagrant who believes himself to be a poet. He could tell Hitler that he (like Hitler himself) had lodged in countless flophouses and slept on park benches because of Jewish machinations which, in his case, had prevented him from becoming a successful playwright."*

* *Der Führer* by Konrad Heiden. Victor Gollancz.

Like Hitler, too, Dietrich Eckart had in the first instance achieved transcendent consciousness through the use of drugs. Although Eckart was basically a morphine addict, many times hospitalised to cure his addiction, he also experimented with numerous other drugs including substances evoking what we call today "psychedelic experience".

Twenty years earlier (1886) a German pharmacologist, Ludwig Lewin, had published the first scientific study of the Mexican Cactus and its startling effects on the mind and nervous system. Many people, including the English philosopher Havelock Ellis, were prompted by the publication of Lewin's research to experiment with peyote, the operative mind-bending factor in the Cactus. Dietrich Eckart belonged to one of the groups in Berlin who used peyote in their practice of Neo-pagan magic.

Eckart's reaction to drugs, and the violence of his behaviour during periods of withdrawal, finally led him to prolonged detention in a Berlin lunatic asylum, where his only companions were the mentally ill. It was there that he was at last able to stage a number of his rejected plays involving neo-pagan rituals, scenes from the Germanic sagas and the legends of the Holy Grail.

"His theatrical gifts," says Heiden, "had at last found a haven. In this place for the mentally deranged, he was able to use lunatics as actors." And, if our information is correct, one of these plays was written around the mysterious legend of the Spear of Destiny and how the Spear became a talisman of power in the Middle Ages.

It would be an error to believe that Eckart was without genuine talent, for he later made an excellent translation of Ibsen's *Peer Gynt* and his writings on Norse mythology found a wide and far from unintelligent public. In the years immediately following World War I he settled in Swabling, the artists' quarter of Munich, and from there he published a scurrilous propaganda "hand-out" called *Auf gut deutsch*, a witty, competent though sadly prejudiced weekly news-sheet.

Like Hitler, he had a historical cast of mind and his favourite subject, racist ideology apart, was the rise of Islam, his knowledge of the Mohammedan invasions of Europe and the art, architecture and religious symbolism of Arab culture being very extensive indeed.

Dietrich Eckart believed himself to be the reincarnation of Bernard of Barcelona, a ninth-century personality and a leading figure in the medieval collusion with the Arab world. He was reputed to have held at bay the Carolingian armies on the Spanish Mark by means of 'black magic' powers.

Eckart had journeyed widely among the Arab peoples in North Africa and had also visited the sites of the old Islamic strongholds in medieval Spain, including Granada and Barcelona. And, as we shall describe in some detail, he had made a special journey to Sicily, the melting-pot of the intrigues in the ninth century, to bring about the Arab occupation of Southern Italy, and the seat of Klingsor of the Grail legends.

With such interests Eckart was following in the footsteps of Friedrich Nietzsche, another keen student of Islamic culture. And in the Nietzsche tradition too he was a fervent admirer of Schopenhauer and had consumed many long hours of his life in the study of Oriental philosophy and the practise of Yoga.

It is not difficult to imagine how each and all of these diversified interests captivated the eager attention of Adolf Hitler and complemented and fulfilled his own self-tutored mind.

The forty members of the Thule Gesellschaft, who attended the historic meeting of German Workers' Party to take their first look at Hitler, were a very mixed assortment. Some, like Anton Drexler, were only politically orientated and had little knowledge of occultism, only a bare outline knowledge to back up their racist ideas; others, like Dr. William Guthbertlet who cast Adolf Hitler's horoscope for the occasion, were harmless cranks. Only a small nucleus, ordered to attend by Eckart himself, had graduated to a deeper knowledge of occultism through participation in many different orders, lodges, movements and societies more or less closely associated with the nineteenth-century renaissance of Oriental philosophy and ritual magic. It was this compact inner circle within the Thule Gesellschaft, the existence of which was unknown to the general membership, which was awaiting the imminent appearance of a German Messiah.

Perhaps it is more than coincidence that about this time the French philosopher Réné Guenon was warning the world that such Neo-pagan groups practising ritual magic were likely to become the unconscious tools of higher powers which would unleash untold horrors on mankind:

"The false Messiahs we have seen so far have only performed very inferior miracles, and their disciples were not very difficult to convert. But who knows what the future has in store?

"When you reflect that these false Messiahs have never been anything but the more or less unconscious tools of those who conjured them up, and when one thinks more particularly of the series of attempts made in succession in contemporary times, one is forced to the conclusion that these were only trials, experiments as it were, which will be renewed in various forms until success is achieved. . . . Not that we occultists or spiritualists are strong enough by themselves to carry out an enterprise of this nature. But might there not be, behind such movements, something far more dangerous which their leaders perhaps know nothing about, being in themselves in turn the unconscious tools of a higher demonic power?"

Dietrich Eckart was not among the earliest members of the Thule Group and he only joined it to use the movement for his own purposes. He had already made the acquaintance of the so-called Count Heinrich von Sebottendorf, who founded the Thule Gesellschaft as an offshoot of an anti-Semitic Lodge of the ancient Germanenorden. It did not take Eckart long to discover that this 'nobleman's' real name was Rudolf Glauer, or that he had been born the son of an engine-driver from Dresden. Rudolf Glauer claimed he had been officially adopted under Turkish Law by Heinrich von Sebottendorf and had a right to the title of Count. Eckart made no attempt to expose him for he did not wish to undermine the reputation and power the Group was beginning to establish in Bavaria.

Rudolf Glauer settled in Turkey (1901) at the age of twenty-six after an adventurous life as a merchant seaman. Throughout the thirteen years in which he was employed in Turkey as the engineer-cum-supervisor of a large estate, he divided his spare spare time between the practice of Sufi meditation and reading Oriental philosophy. He was also deeply influenced by contemporary Theosophical literature, especially the writings of Madame Blavatsky, and he drew his inspiration for recreating the Thule myth almost exclusively from her three-volume work, *The Secret Doctrine*.

Glauer himself was entirely lacking in spiritual faculty. He simply transposed Blavatsky's grotesque descriptions of the magical conditions prevailing in the vanished civilisation of 'Atlantis' to give a pre-historical background to the mythological world of the Edda in which Gods, giants, men and beasts were engaged in a bloodcurdling struggle for survival. In re-spinning the age-old legends of Niflheim, Muspellsheim and Midgard, he introduced Theosophical ideas about the magical relationship between cosmos, earth and man. He predicted that the latent powers and faculties slumbering in the blood of the Aryan race would unfold in the twentieth century when "Supermen" would reappear on earth to awaken the German people to the glories of their ancient heritage and lead them in the conquest of the world.

The original conception of the modern Thulists was extremely crude and naïve. The more sophisticated versions of the legend of Thule only gradually developed in the hands of Dietrich Eckart and General Karl Haushofer, and were later further refined and extended under the direction of Reichsführer SS Heinrich Himmler, who terrorised a large section of the German academic world into lending a professional hand at perpetuating the myth of German racial superiority.

"In the depths of his subconscious every German has one foot in 'Atlantis' where he seeks a better Fatherland and a better patrimony," said Hermann Rauschning, the defected Gauleiter, when he sought to explain the way in which the Germans were so easily excited by racist ideologies.

The "Fatherland Idea" had been heightened for Adolf Hitler in his childhood by his love for Teutonic mythology. In Vienna he had even written bloodthirsty dramas about the epic heroes of the Edda whose deeds he believed were living on in the German blood in his veins. Now through his new associates in the Thule Group he was plunged into the world of cosmology and magic which had inspired the twentieth-century rebirth of Thule.

The Thule legend, as old as the German race itself, was interpreted in endless different ways within the Thule Gesellschaft itself. And Hitler soon learned from Eckart to distinguish between the crude propaganda put out by the Society for mass consumption, and the various intermediate levels of involvement in its activities, as opposed to the hidden inner circle who gained higher levels of initiation through the practice of ritual magic.

Pauwels and Bergier, who failed to make the discrimination between the crude propaganda put out for mass consumption and the deeper hidden knowledge of the innermost strata of the Thule Gesellschaft, mistaking the former for the latter, have written a colourful piece on Thule in their best-selling book, *The Dawn of Magic*:

"Thule was supposed to be an island that disappeared somewhere in the extreme North. Off Greenland? or Labrador? Like Atlantis, Thule was thought to have been the magic centre of a vanished civilisation. Eckart and his friends believed that not all the secrets of Thule had perished. Beings intermediate between Man and other intelligent Beings from Beyond, would place at the disposal of the Initiates a reservoir of forces which could be drawn on to enable Germany to dominate the world again and be the cradle of the coming race of Supermen which would result from mutations of the human species. One day her legions would set out to annihilate everything that had stood in the way of the spiritual destiny of the Earth, and their leaders would be men who knew everything, deriving their strength from the very fountainhead of energy and guided by the great ones of the ancient world. Such were the myths on which the Aryan doctrine of Eckart and Rosenberg was founded and which these 'prophets' of a magic form of Socialism had instilled in the mediumistic mind of Hitler.

The inner core within the Thule Group were all Satanists who practised Black Magic. That is to say, they were solely concerned with raising their consciousness by means of rituals to an awareness of evil and non-human Intelligences in the Universe and with achieving a means of communication with these Intelligences. And the Master-Adept of this circle was Dietrich Eckart.

Despite the fact that the most significant early growth in the reappearance of ancient magic in the modern age took place here in England, it is the Western mind that finds it almost insuperably difficult to accept the existence of any kind of magic as a reality. Perhaps this is so because the basic concept behind all magical practice is a belief in a correspondence between the Universe and Man, that is, between Macrocosm and Microcosm. The Western mind grounded in materialism finds such thinking totally unscientific and, in the case of the older generation anyway, the average Englishman, like Shakespeare's Hamlet, can get no further than a belief in the existence of 'ghosts'.

The contrasting Germanic attitude in this regard is reflected in the opening lines of the dedication in Goethe's *Faust*:

> Again ye come, ye hovering Forms! I find you
> as early to my clouded sight ye shone!
> Shall I attempt, this once, to seize and bind you?
> Still o'er my heart is that illusion thrown?
> Ye crowd more near! Well then, be power assigned you
> to sway me from your misty, shadowy zone!
> My bosom thrills, by youthful passion shaken
> that magic breezes round your march awaken.

The Germanic soul is also steeped in the understanding of the relationships between heaven and earth, which appears at the very heart of Teutonic mythology and in the history of German literature and philosophy. Such a belief in the magical correspondences between Macrocosm and Microcosm also reaches its climax in the works of Goethe, and especially in his *Faust*:

> (Faust opens the book and sees the Sign of the Macrocosm)
> Ha! What a sudden rapture leaps from this
> I view, through all my senses swiftly flowing!
> I feel a youthful, holy, vital bliss
> in every vein and fibre newly glowing.
> Did once a God these signs and figures write
> that calm my inner violent feeling
> my troubled heart to joy unsealing;
> that work their will with secret might,
> the forces of great Nature, round about revealing?
> Am I a god?—so clear mine eyes!
> In these colour symbols I behold
> creative nature to my soul enfold . . .

> (He contemplates the Sign)
> How each the whole its substance gives,
> each in the other works and lives!
> See heavenly forces rising and descending
> their golden urns reciprocally lending:
> on wings that winnow sweet blessing
> from heaven through the earth they're pressing
> to fill the All with harmonies caressing. . . .

In Goethe's world conception, which is of a magical nature, both man's spiritual and physical existence is related to the whole Universe of Stars, Sun and Planets. Just as man is not limited to his physical body, which Goethe conceived as the garment of both soul and spirit, the stars are not considered as simply meaningless masses framed in a three-dimensional space-time continuum. Rather, Goethe regarded the heavenly orbs as the outer physical expression of Spiritual Beings, higher non-human Intelligences, which radiate spiritual and qualitative forces within their operative orbits.

Neither the Initiates of the ancient mystery knowledge nor modern occultists considered the Macrocosm in terms of space and time but rather in spheres of transcendent consciousness. The Adepts of Ritual Magic, both white and black, seek an expansion of consciousness in what they call 'the Astral Light' of the planetary spheres. The purpose of their magical rites is to channelise the cosmic forces or to awaken 'the reflection' of these powers from the depths of their own being. And as an aid to the fulfilment of this purpose a whole range of signs, symbols, colours and shapes are used as part of the rituals in order to guide the magician to communication with those particular powers he seeks to serve.

The next great principle of Western Magic is the belief that the properly trained human will is, quite literally, capable of anything. A quotation from the great seventeenth-century theologian Joseph Glanvill admirably summarises this doctrine: "And the will lieth therein, which dieth not. Who knoweth the mysteries of the will with its vigour? For God is but a great will pervading all things by nature of its intentness. Man doth not yield himself to the Angels nor to death utterly, save only through the weakness of his feeble will.

"The motivating power, then, in all magical operations, is the trained will of the magician. All the adjuncts of Ceremonial Magic—lights, colours, circles, triangles, perfumes—are merely aids to concentrating the will of the magician into a blazing stream of pure energy."*

In the light of this brief summary of the meaning and purpose of Ritual Magic, it will be seen how Adolf Hitler had already crossed the threshold into the experience of magic in his forma-tive years in Vienna, when he achieved not only levels of higher consciousness, but also slipped through the veil of the senses to commune with the Anti-Spirit associated with the Spear of

* *Ritual Magic in England*: Francis King, published by Neville Spearman.

163

Longinus. And more than this, while lying blinded by mustard gas in an enforced state of trance in Pasewalk Hospital in November 1918, he had become immediately aware of the correspondences between the Universe and the workings of the psychical and physiological processes in his own body. On a path of self-initiation he had already turned the postulates of would-be magicians into crucial and immediate experience.

The form of ritual magic through which Dietrich Eckart further initiated Adolf Hitler was similar to, and in part derived from, the horrible sexual magic of Aleister Crowley.

Aleister Crowley's Lodge, the Astrum Argentinum, was the end product of a short and highly dubious renaissance of astrological and ceremonial magic which took place in England in the latter half of the nineteenth century.

The origin of this astonishing re-emergence of medieval magic amidst the upper crust of Victorian society can be traced to a Freemason called Robert Wentworth Little, who founded the "Societas Rosicruciana" in 1865. His motive for incorporating the ancient Rosicrucian tradition and new rituals into Freemasonry had been to bring a fresh and living impulse into rites which had long lost their original meaning and vigour in a maze of dead symbolism. But what Little had not foreseen was that later members of this Lodge would create breakaway movements which were out of keeping with the highest moral traditions of Freemasonry. Such a breakaway movement was the Golden Dawn from which the Nazis were indirectly to derive demonic inspiration for their own special brand of occultism.

The Golden Dawn was founded under a shroud of mystery, and to this day numerous versions regarding its origin are still circulating. One thing alone is sure, it arose through the apparently chance finding of documents from a Nuremberg source which contained hitherto unknown and highly potent Initiation rituals.

Within the ranks of its Five Temples situated in England and Paris were many notable people including Nobel Prize winner

W. B. Yeats, Florence Farr, Director of the Abbey Theatre and close friend of Bernard Shaw, and Sir Gerald Kelly, President of the Royal Academy.*

The Golden Dawn faced a great crisis in its further development in 1892. The Order had obtained its original Charter and the rituals for the first five grades from a parent Lodge in Germany with which it carried on a voluminous correspondence. Yet not a single member of the Golden Dawn had ever visited the German Lodge or met any of its members. The enthusiastic would-be magicians were already treading dangerous ground. There was consternation when the Nuremberg Lodge refused to hand over the four ascending Adeptus Grades which lead directly to communication with hierarchies of higher Intelligences.

Perhaps the Golden Dawn would have come to a quiet and undramatic end if a certain Samuel Liddell Mathers had not offered to come to the rescue of his fellow magicians. At a general meeting of the Lodge, he announced to his astonished audience that he himself had established communication with the Powers, who had themselves presented him with the requisite Grades and Rituals of the Second Order. However, it was not with the celestial hierarchies that he had been in communication but with a hierarchy of "Supermen"—"The Secret Chiefs of the Third Order."

Mathers, son of a London clerk, with a grammar school education had gradually built up for himself a sound reputation for scholarship in occult matters. Yet, despite a fine intellect and a rich occult knowledge, he had never been liked by his fellow members. Though he had undeniable spiritual gifts, his colleagues now wondered whether he could be trusted in a matter of such vital importance. But when his startling disclosure was put to the vote, his new rituals and their authenticity were overwhelmingly accepted.

---

* Other members included Algernon Blackwood, Annie Horniman, an intimate friend of Yeats, Sax Rohmer, Bram Stoker, the author of *Dracula*, Arthur Machen, and Peck, the Astronomer Royal. See also *The Golden Dawn* by R. G. Torrens. (Neville Spearman.)

Like the majority of those present, Mathers had been influenced by Madame Blavatsky's *Secret Doctrine*. And in particular by her lofty descriptions of "the mighty Custodians of the Eternal Mysteries, the Great White Lodge of Supreme Adepts". And these Supreme Adepts, believed to be working invisibly behind the changing scenes of history, were supposed to have been the "Supermen" with whom Mathers had been in touch. Yet when we consider his personal descriptions of them we find a remarkable similarity to the intrepid and cruel Spirit which Adolf Hitler first beheld when standing before the Spear of Destiny.

" 'As to the Secret Chiefs of the Order, to whom I make reference and from whom I have received the wisdom of the Second Order, which I have communicated to you, I can tell you *nothing*,' said Mathers.

" 'I know not even their earthly names, and I have rarely seen them in their physical bodies. . . . My encounters with them have shown me how difficult it is for a mortal, however advanced, to support their presence. . . . I do not mean that during my rare meetings with them I experienced the same feelings of intense physical depression that accompanies loss of magnetism, on the contrary, the sensation was that of being in contact with so terrible a force that I can only compare it to the continued effect of that which is usually experienced by any person close to whom a flash of lightning passes during a violent storm; coupled with a difficulty of respiration similar to the half strangling effect produced by ether. As tested as I have been in occult work, I cannot conceive a much less advanced Initiate being able to support such a strain, even for five minutes without death ensuing . . . the nervous prostration after each meeting being terrible and accompanied by cold sweats and bleeding from the nose, mouth and ears."

Mathers later became the patron of one of the most infamous 'black magicians' of the twentieth century—Aleister Crowley. Crowley first heard of the Golden Dawn when he was still an undergraduate at Cambridge. He joined the Order in 1898. His progress through the preliminary grades was sure and swift but he was bluntly refused entry for the grade of Adept because of his unsavoury reputation. And when Mathers, who was quick to stop Crowley's potential as a Master-Adept, initiated him in the Paris Temple of the Order, it sparked off the fierce eruptions which brought about the speedy dissolution of the Golden Dawn.

When Aleister Crowley established his own Lodge, the Astrum Argentinum, he quickly shed the amateur techniques of the cult and began in earnest the effective practice of black magic in a new and effective form. Compared with Crowley, the entire membership of the Golden Dawn can be likened to sleeping puppets playing ceremonial charades.

Crowley gradually found the path to the type of black magic practised by Klingsor a thousand years ago. His studies concentrated on all forms of sexual illuminism and, by 1912, he had reached the Ninth Grade of a spurious and clandestine Lodge in Berlin, "Ordo Templi Orientis", concerned exclusively with sexual magic.

Working up through auto-sexual magic—a form of magical masturbation—he graduated to the highest degrees in which the sexual act took the central place in the ceremony, the participants partaking in an 'Elixir of Life' concocted from the mingling of male and female secretions.*

By the time Crowley had settled in the "Abbey of Thelema" (Thule Abbey), in Sicily, he had become involved in yet more perverse and highly sadistic sexual practices. His rites now included animal sacrifice, heterosexual orgies, bloody scourgings and sodomy, for he had discovered that indulgence in the most sadistic rituals awakened penetrating vision into the workings of evil Intelligences and bestowed phenomenal magical powers. He was now treading in the medieval footsteps of Landulf II of Capua, the Klingsor of the anti-Grail "who dominated all spirits, whether good or evil," from his eyrie in Castle Merveille. And it was on a nocturnal visit to the site of Klingsor's castle at Kalot Enbolot that Crowley first invoked the Anti-Christ into manifestation, the Beast of the Revelation

---

* See *Ritual Magic in England* by Francis King.

called forth by Ernst Pretzsche and Guido von List in Vienna, the same Apocalyptic Spirit which had appeared to Dietrich Eckart and Alfred Rosenberg at the mediumistic seances of the Thule Group in Munich.

Richard Wagner has described the scene in which Klingsor, surrounded by seductive flower maidens in his magic garden, carried out the rites of Astrological Magic which were the source of all his power.

On a visit to Sicily Dietrich Eckart had searched for the seat of Klingsor's castle which Wolfram von Eschenbach calls Kalot Enbolot and which other medieval Grail Sagas call Chateau Merveille (Castle of Wonders).

In the heights of Monte Castello in south-west Sicily he discovered the derelict Temple of Erix at which Priestesses of Antiquity had once guarded the Oracle of Venus, the Goddess of Love. And Eckart identified this eyrie in the fastness of the mountains as Qal'at al-Bellut, the Fortress of the Oaks, which had been seized and captured in A.D. 840 by the troops of Abu-I'Kal-Aghlab-ihn-Ibrahim, the Arab Sultan who conquered Palermo and established African Mohammedism throughout the island.

According to the medieval Chronicler Echempertus this was the eyrie to which Landulf II had fled when his collusion with invading Islam was unveiled. There, consumed with bitterness, after castration by the husband and brothers of a noblewoman he had raped, the Landulf carried out the satanic rituals of Arabian star magic which terrorised Southern Europe and changed the course of history in the ninth century.

There can be little doubt that Dietrich Eckart had made a close study of the similarity between Crowley's sexual magic and the 'Astrological Magic' of Landulf II. Although Crowley's potent and effective form of magic brought into manifestation a whole range of evil spirits and released powerful forces to his command, all the humans who participated in these rituals came out unscathed. That is, there were no innocent and unwilling victims in these rites. The Magic of Landulf II, on the other hand, involved human sacrifices.

If the legends that have come down from these dark centuries of European history are true, these rituals carried out at Kalot Enbolot included terrible tortures such as the slitting open of the stomachs of sacrificial victims and the slow drawing of their entrails, the driving of stakes through the orifices of their bodies before disembowelling them, and the invoking of Spirits of Darkness (Incubi) to rape young virgins kidnapped from their families.

The nature of each horrific rite was conditioned by the type and hierarchical grade of the Satanic Spirits called forth, and the corresponding astrological signs and symbols were set out accordingly. Through such vile means, the ninth century Klingsor opened the centres in the astral bodies of his own neophytes to a vision of the Macrocosm and gave them power over all realms of elemental spirits between heaven and earth.

It is a well-known fact that the Thule Gesellschaft was among other things a "Society of Assassins". That the Thule Group held its own secret courts at which many innocent people were tried and condemned has also been fully documented. Their activities were well known also to the Police authorities, for many senior Police Officers at this time were themselves either Thulists or fellow travellers. For instance, Pohner, the Police President of Munich was himself a member of Eckart's innermost circle. Professor Alan Bullock has quoted Pohner's famous reply when officially asked if he knew about the existence of political murder gangs in Bavaria: "Yes, but not enough of them!" Also only too aware of these murders and suppressing any attempt to solve them and arrest the culprits were Assistant Police Chief William Frick, later Hitler's Minister of the Interior and for a while Heinrich Himmler's immediate boss, and the Bavarian Minister of Justice, Franz Gürtner, rewarded for his early co-operation with the Nazis with the position of Minister of Justice to the Third Reich.

Quite apart from the 300 or more political murders which were perpetrated between 1919 and 1923, there were also a very large number of people in the area of Munich who were reported as missing under mysterious circumstances. And it was from among these missing persons, most of whom were either Jews or Communists, that we must look to find the 'sacrificial victims' who were murdered in the rites of 'Astrological Magic' carried out by Dietrich Eckart and the innermost circle of the Thule Gesellschaft.

Though a number of books have appeared suggesting such rites took place, there is no conclusive circumstantial evidence that hapless victims were tortured and put to death as a part of these magical initiation rites. There is, however, evidence of another kind from a secret circle of Grail Initiates who were able to behold these rituals in that higher form of consciousness which is known to occultists as Astral Projection.

The leader of these Adepts, as we shall fully describe later, was a certain Dr. Rudolf Steiner, the most highly initiated Christian Adept in Europe.* And it was from one of his closest associates, Dr. Walter Johannes Stein, that I first heard a description of the atrocities which were carried out as part of the ritual magic in which Dietrich Eckart opened the centres of Adolf Hitler to give him a vision of and a means of communication with the Powers. No attempt will be made to repeat them here, suffice it to say that they were indescribably sadistic and ghastly. Indeed, many times more horrible than the treatment later handed out to the circle which attempted to murder Hitler, who ended their lives slowly strangling to death from piano wires suspended from butchers' hooks in a Berlin abattoir.

Hermann Rauschning, the Nazi Gauleiter who defected to the West, came closest to seeing Adolf Hitler as the twentieth-century Klingsor:

* It was because Adolf Hitler was unable to hide any of his activities from Rudolf Steiner's spiritual vision that he declared him to be the greatest enemy of the Nazi Party, and the first unsuccessful attempts were made to murder Steiner on Munich Railway Station in 1922.

Kunsthistorisches Museum, Vienna

1. The Imperial Crown, Apple, Sceptre, Crosses, the Imperial Sword and the Sword of St. Maurice. These items of the Imperial Regalia known collectively as the "Reichkleinodien" are on view in the Treasure House in the Hofburg in Vienna. The Sword of St. Maurice was later mistaken by the Nazis for the Spear of Longinus (seen below).

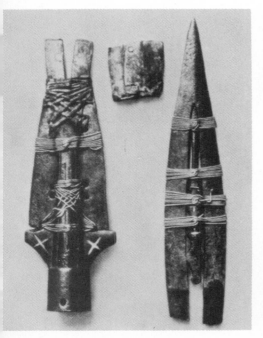

2. The Spear of Longinus, often named the Maurice Spear, now consists of two parts held together by a silver sheath. A nail from the Cross of Christ has been inserted into the blade and is held in place by gold, silver and copper threads. The base of the spearhead is embossed with gold crosses.

WELTGESCHICHTE
IM LICHTE DES HEILIGEN GRAL ·

BAND I
DAS NEUNTE JAHRHUNDERT

WALTER JOHANNES STEIN

1928

ORIENT-OCCIDENT-VERLAG
STUTTGART — DEN HAAG — LONDON

3. *World History in the Light of the Holy Grail by Dr. Walter Johannes Stein.* Heinrich Himmler, Reichsführer SS, ordered Dr. Stein's arrest in an attempt to force him to work for the Ahnenerbe, the Nazi Occult Bureau. After his escape to England, they printed a pirate edition in Berlin in 1938.

Bildnis des Papstes Nicolaus I.
s „Ciaconlus, A., Vitae et res gestae Pontificum Romanorum . . .ʺ
Romae 1677, Tom. I).

4. A coin stamped with the head of Pope Nicholas I and a picture of the same Pope painted some 500 years after his death. See chapter entitled "The Pope at Army H.Q.—The Artistry of Destiny."

5. Walter Johannes Stein, a Vienna-born scientist who died in Britain in 1957, knew more about the personal life of Adolf Hitler than any man alive. He followed the career of Hitler from student days in Vienna to the moment when he became the personal claimant to the Spear at the Anschluss in 1938. Throughout World War II Stein acted as personal adviser to Sir Winston Churchill regarding the mind and motives of the Nazi Führer.

6. The Skull of Lazarus in the Grail Chapel at Ansbach, Germany. (See chapter entitled "The Spear as Symbol of the Cosmic Christ.")

7. The Camel carrying the Cross containing a relic of the Blood of the Circumcision of Jesus from Tours to Niedermünster. (See chapter entitled "The Camel's Hump": a new technique in historical research.)

8. The unguided Camel finally came to a stop at the Church of St. Odille at Niedermünster which became the centre of the Holy Grail in the Ninth Century.

Berlin Friedenau 26 November 1927.

Sehr geehrter Dr. Stein!

[handwritten letter in German cursive]

Eliza von Moltke
geb. Gräfin Moltke-Huitfeldt

9, 10, 11, and 12. Four letters written to Dr. Stein by Eliza von Moltke, the wife of General von Moltke, Chief of the Imperial General Staff of the German Army in World War I.

Friedenau 3. Dezember 1927.

Sehr geehrter Dr. Stein!

Auch die folgende Notiz stelle ich Ihnen gerne für Ihr Buch zur Verfügung. — Brief von Dr Rudolf Steiner am 28 Juli 1918 an Eliza von Moltke — über Papst Nikolaus und dessen Ratgeber

"Im 9. Jahrhundert stand "der Rater" an Nikolaus Seite mit dem Überblick über die Karte von Europa. Es oblag Nikolaus damals die Ideen zu fassen, welche den Osten von dem Westen trennen sollten. In diese Trennung waren viele Menschen verwickelt. —
Über diese urteilte "der Rater" mit seinem Überblick. Aber damals stand man der geistigen Welt noch nahe. Man hatte das Bewusstsein geistige Wesen kommen und gehen. Doch die Bewohner Mittel = und Westeuropas strebten von den geistigen Wesen weg. Sie mussten sich für den Materialismus schon damals vorbereiten. Bei Nikolaus und seinem Rater war im 9. Jahrhundert viel unmittelbar wahrnehmbarer geistiger Einfluss. Da sagte der Ratgeber oft: "die Geister werden sich von Europa zurückziehen, aber die Europäer werden sich später nach ihnen sehnen. Ohne die Geister werden die Europäer ihre Maschinen und ihre Einrichtung machen. Darin werden sie gross sein. Doch sie erziehen sich dadurch in ihrem eigenen Schoße die Westmenschen, die ihnen die ahrimanische Kultur bis zum höchsten Gipfel treiben und die sich an ihre Stelle setzen "

Ihre sehr ergebene

Eliza von Moltke
geb: Gräfin Moltke Huitfeldt.

Friedenau 10 Dezember 1927.

Sehr geehrter Dr. Stein!

Auch die folgende Notiz stelle ich Ihnen gerne für Ihr
Buch zur Verfügung:

Ein Gespräch zwischen dem Papst Nikolaus und einem Rater, dem
Kardinal, von Dr. Rudolf Steiner am 17 Juni 1924 an Eliza
von Moltke mitgeteilt:

Der Papst: Sollen wir verlieren, was uns Spirituelles brachte, nachdem
die Hunde von dem Gekreuzigten den Himmel auf die Erde senkte.

Der Rater: Was alt geworden, soll vergehen, ist ja der Tod nur neues Leben.
Ich sehe Europas Leben ersteigen aus Asiens Niedergang. —

Der Papst: Es wird der Entschluss schwer.

Der Rater: Doch höhere Geister wollen ihn, um Ahriman die rechte
Richtung zu weisen, im Seelenleben — das von Franken nach dem
Osten leuchten soll. Das Nordlicht, das auch eine Seele hat,
das hat es mir gesagt, als ich in heller Sommernacht auf
heimatlichen Steinen der Stimme lauschte, die von Gabriel
kommt, die ein neues Europa gebären will ——.

Der Papst: Bist du sicher?

Der Rater: — Aber es gibt nur Sicherheit, wo die höheren Geister sprechen,
und ich bin sicher, dass sie deutlich sprechen.

Der Papst: Deutlich mögen sie sprechen, aber ich weiss auch,
dass die Jahrhunderte, die da folgen auf unseren
Seelen lasten —. —

Eliza von Moltke
geb: Gräfin Moltke Huitfeldt.

Arlesheim 27. 12. 27.

Sehr geehrter Dr. Stein!

Ich freue mich sehr in der Lage zu sein, Ihnen konkrete
Antwort auf Ihre Frage geben zu können —. Sie fragen, ob
ich weiss welchen Berg Herr Dr. Steiner in seiner Mitteilung
vom 31. August 1917 mit den Worten bezeichnet: „der Berg,
der vis à vis unserem Dornacher Bau steht." — Ich kann auf
diese Frage sehr genaue Antwort geben, da Dr. Steiner gelegentlich
meiner ersten Anwesenheit in Dornach im Spätherbst 1917
mich zu einem Gang mit ihm nach der Ermitage aufforderte
und dort an Ort und Stelle wo man vom Kloster aus den
Dornacher Bau liegen sieht mir sagte: „Hier dieser Berg
ist die Stelle zu der Odilie geflohen ist!"

Mit freundlichem Gruss Ihre sehr ergebene —

Eliza von Moltke
geb: Gräfin Moltke Huitfeldt.

13. An illustration from the works of Basilius Valentinus, Alchemist and Occultist. The picture shows Parsival, Gawain and Feirifis, three heroes in search of the Grail, standing before the Hermitage of Treverezent. The symbols on the path up the mountain depict the disciplines and trials confronting a Knight searching for Grail Initiation. The Alchemy of the Quest for the Grail is fully explained in the chapter entitled "The ABC of the Grail with Black Magic."

14. Dr. Rudolf Steiner. The picture was taken shortly after he graduated at Vienna University.

15. The first Goetheanum built by Dr. Rudolf Steiner was burned down by the Nazis on New Year's Eve, 1922–1923.

Anthroposophical Society

Anthroposophical Society

16. A drawing made by Rudolf Steiner illustrating the "Doppel-gänger". A motif for the stained glass windows of the Goetheanum in Dornach, Switzerland.

Anthroposophical Society

17. Dr. Rudolf Steiner working on the figure of Jesus Christ as the Representative of Humanity. On the left of the picture is a clay model of the projected woodcarving which stands 32 feet high. The carving shows Christ at the moment of conquest of the hierarchies of Evil—Lucifer, Ahriman and the Azuras.

18. The head of Ahriman carved by Dr. Rudolf Steiner who prophesied the birth of the Anti-Christ in America in the second half of the 20th century.

Anthroposophical Society

19. Lucifer, the Spirit of False Pride and (above) the Anti-Spirit of the Time.

Anthroposophical Society

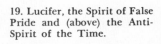

20. Houston Stewart Chamberlain. The Englishman who won the Iron Cross and later
proclaimed Hitler as the German Messiah.
Wiener Library

21. Dietrich Eckart who claimed to have
"opened" Hitler's Occult sight.
Wiener Library

22. Professor Karl Haushofer who inspired
Hitler to achieve world conquest.
Wiener Library

23. Albrecht Haushofer with his father whom
he claimed had unleashed the Beast of the
Apocalypse upon humanity.
Wiener Library

24. General Helmuth von Moltke, the Army Chief who sought the Holy Grail and believed himself to be the reincarnation of Pope Nicholas I in the Ninth Century.

Wiener Library

25. General Eric Ludendorff, Military Dictator of Germany in World War I who supported Adolf Hitler in the Munich Putsch in 1923.

Stadtarchiv Nürnberg

26. The posse of Nazis responsible for burying the Spear of Destiny beneath the Nuremberg Fortress where it was discovered on the day Adolf Hitler shot himself in the Berlin Bunker on April 30, 1945. From left to right: Karl Holz (man in background not known), Julius Streicher, Willi Liebel, Hans von Obernitz, Dr. Benno Martin.

"Most of all Hitler is the reeking miasma of furtive, unnatural sexuality which fills and fouls the atmosphere around him, like an evil emanation. Nothing in his environment is straightforward. Surreptitious relationships, substitutes and symbols, false sentiments and hidden lusts—nothing in this man's surroundings is natural and genuine, nothing has the openness of a natural instinct. 'Oh, if only Hitler knew how it does one good to have a fresh natural girl!' said Forster, another of Hitler's Gauleiters."
(*Hitler Speaks:* Hermann Rauschning.)

Rauschning has described his first visit to see Adolf Hitler in his mountain eyrie, Barbarossa, and what he found there. After walking through a rocky ravine and ascending several hundred feet in a lift, he entered the glass-walled building which nestled in the snowbound wilderness of the Bavarian mountains. But when he entered Hitler's holy of holies he was immediately faced with a monstrous incongruity which left him baffled and horrified.

High above the world, far beyond the reach of ordinary mortals, Hitler sat enthroned "looking out to eternity and challenging his Aeon". But on the walls of this eyrie where Hitler dreamed of world domination, convulsed by paroxysms of hate and on the verge of insanity, there were pictures of obscene nudes, concealing nothing, pictures without artistic intention or appeal illustrating the crudest sexual deviations.

Apart from Rauschning, the other leading biographers of Hitler have been unable to perceive that sexual perversion took the central place in his life. They deal with the question in a fragmented way under such headings as "Was Hitler Impotent?" or "Hitler's attitude to Women". They fail altogether to understand that a monstrous sexual perversion was the very core of his whole existence, the source of his mediumistic and clairvoyant powers, and the motivation behind every act through which he reaped a sadistic vengeance on humanity.

Wolfram von Eschenbach describes in *Parsival* (Book VIII) how the castration of Klingsor, while still a young man, led to a similar sexual perversion and bitter hatred for humanity and a reaping of vengeance through the attainment of magical powers:

> "Never did youth reach old age with such womanly honour. Sir his marvels here are but small by the side of the mighty marvels he still has in many lands. . . . I will tell you what he is like: he has become bitter toward many people. His land is called Terre de Labur, and he is descended from one who had also learned how to work great marvels, from Virgil of Naples.
>
> " 'I shall tell you about Klingsor. His capital was Capua. He took the high path to fame and did not go unrewarded. Klingsor, the Duke was in the mouths of all, both men and women, until he fell into disgrace. Sicily had a noble King called Ibert, and Iblis was his wife, the loveliest woman ever weaned from a mother's breast. Klingsor served her until she rewarded him with love. For this the king robbed him of his honour. If I am to tell you his secret, I must ask your forgiveness, for it is unseemly for me to say such things. One cut of the knife, and Klingsor became a eunuch.'
>
> "Then she told him still more. 'In the famous castle of Kalot Enbolot he became the mock of the world. The King found Klingsor with his wife, sleeping in her arms. If he found a warm bed there, he had to pay a heavy price that by the hand of the king he was made smooth between the legs. He clipped him in such a way that he can never give more pleasure to any woman. But that has meant suffering for many people.
>
> " 'It is not in the land of Persia, but in a city called Persida that magic was first invented. To that place Klingsor travelled, and brought from there the magic art of how to do whatever he will. For the shame done to his body he never again bore good will toward anyone, man or woman, and when he can rob them of any joy, especially those who are honoured and respected, that does his heart good.' "

There can be no doubt that Adolf Hitler was equally as impotent as Klingsor, who was "smooth between the legs" for he, too, was incapable of achieving orgasm through normal sexual relations. Although Adolf Hitler only had one testicle, a condition noticed by Dr. Stein when bathing with Hitler in the Danube and later confirmed by the Russian medical authorities on examination of Hitler's burned corpse outside the Berlin Bunker in 1945, there is no reason to believe that he suffered any organic incapacity to perform normal sexual intercourse.

Rather his impotency had a deep psychological foundation. He only knew sexual fulfilment through the extremes of sadism and masochism, sexual delight either through inflicting pain on others or from suffering such pain himself. In his formative years in Vienna, we see him dreaming romantic dreams about his sweetheart in Linz with whom he never sought to establish a normal relationship. And in contrast to these unrealistic masturbations, he would furtively retire to the red-light district of the City to have himself tied up and whipped by any prostitute who was willing to earn a few miserable *hellers*.

It is claimed that Adolf Hitler was for a time genuinely in love with his niece, Geli Raubal, whom he brought from Vienna to live with him at the Villa Wachenfeld on the Obersalzberg above Berchtesgaden. But can one call it love in the true sense of the word when his attentions finally led to her tragic death?

After six months in which their relationship appeared to be harmonious, Hitler installed her in a luxurious apartment in the Prinzregentenstrasse in Munich where a more intimate relationship began and immediate disruption followed.

Hitler became insanely jealous and accused her of having affairs with other men, including his ex-convict bodyguard and chauffeur Emil Maurice. On the one side he established a reign of tyranny over every aspect of her life, even refusing to permit her to talk to anybody. On the other side, he longed to be enslaved by her in their sexual relationship and begged her to physically maltreat him and use him at her will. On one occasion he was indiscreet enough to compose a letter in this vein, which later came into general circulation and brought a gruesome end to all those who were unfortunate enough to have read it.

Finally, when Geli Raubal was on the verge of a complete breakdown and entreated Hitler to permit her to return home to Vienna, he locked her in her room where she is supposed to have shot herself. Though the Coroner's verdict was 'Suicide', even high-placed Nazis believed that Hitler had murdered her himself in a paroxysm of fury, or that Heinrich Himmler had himself shot her because her very existence had become a threat to the future of the Party.

It is common knowledge that Hitler's whole relationship with Eva Braun, a vain and stupid woman, followed more or less the same pattern. She suffered his tyranny at all other times except in the bedroom where she became the all-powerful mistress and he the grovelling slave.

Rauschning describes how he was present one day when a far-sighted woman in Adolf Hitler's circle said to him warningly: "My Leader, don't touch Black Magic! As yet both white and black magic are open to you. But once you've embarked on black magic it will dominate your destiny. It will hold you captive. Don't choose the quick and easy successes. There lies before you the power over a realm of pure spirits. Do not allow yourself to be led away from your true path by earthbound spirits, which will rob you of your creative power."

Rauschning himself knew only too well that Hitler had abandoned himself to forces which were carrying him away—"forces of dark and destructive violence!" And in this respect Rauschning's insight into the soul of Adolf Hitler was both penetrating and significant.

"He imagined that he still had freedom of choice but he had long been in bondage to a magic which might well have been described, not only in metaphor but in literal fact, as that of Evil Hierarchies of Spirits. Instead of a man emerging step by step from the obscurity of youth, and freeing himself from its dross on an upward course, we witnessed the development of a man possessed, the helpless prey to the Powers of Darkness. . . . The reason he pursued the path to the Abyss lay in the infirmity of his Will,"

Though Rauschning recognised that Hitler was developing the powers of a supreme magician, he himself knew next to nothing of the black arts and he had never belonged to that hidden inner circle in which such arts were practised. In one of his later interviews with Adolf Hitler, the Führer told him that the Nazi Party would bring the medieval ages to a close. "The intellect has grown autocratic and has become a disease of life," Hitler told him. "We are at the outset of a tremendous revolution in moral ideas and man's spiritual orientation. A new age of the magic interpretation of the world is coming, an interpretation in terms of will and not the intelligence."

On another occasion Hitler openly discussed the question of Freemasonry and the rituals of Ceremonial Magic. And although Rauschning could not fathom the deeper significance of what his Führer was saying, he nevertheless recorded it faithfully in his diary.

Apparently Hitler believed that traditional Freemasonry had largely descended into "just a harmless union for the mutual protection of interests." "But there is one dangerous element," he said, "which I have copied from them. They have developed an esoteric doctrine, not merely formulated it, but imparted it through the medium of symbols and mysterious rites. . . . That is to say without bothering their brains but by working directly on the imagination through the symbols of a magic cult. All this is the dangerous element I have taken over. Don't you see that our Party must be of this character. An Order that is what it has to be. An Order, the hierarchical Order of a Secular Priesthood."

Rauschning is surely the only authentic biographer of Adolf Hitler. To read his works *Hitler Speaks* and *The Beast from the Abyss*, one is struck with the similarity between his descriptions of Hitler and passages about the Landulf of Capua from the manuscripts of the medieval Chronicler Echempertus. By comparing the two sets of documents separated by a thousand years, one is struck by the resemblance in the characters, lives and attitudes of the German Führer and the medieval Klingsor, whom Hitler believed himself to be the Reincarnation.

"Hitler used to like to be seen with a riding whip in his hand; he has given up the habit. But the qualities it revealed remained— contemptuousness, arrogance, brutality and vanity.

"Hitler is full of resentments. A chance word, an association of ideas, may arouse him at any time. He is not only sensitive but brutal and vindictive. He lives in a world of insincerity, deceiving and self-deceiving. He is entirely without generosity. Hatred is like wine to him, it intoxicates him. Brutal and vindictive, he is also sentimental, a familiar mixture. He loved his canaries and cried when one died. But he would have men against whom he had a grudge tortured to death in the most horrible way. He has the instincts of a sadist finding sexual excitement in torturing others.

"Even in the praise of others, he is so self-centred that it is only his own self that he thus honours. . . . So convinced is he of his Godlike stature he is grateful for every bit of praise and for the crudest flattery. . . . He depends at all times on the agreement of those around him and it is to women's encouragement that he owes his self-assurance. Women with more than a touch of hysteria are selected before all others.

"A thorough knowledge of the weaknesses and vices of each one of his opponents is regarded as the first condition for success. . . . He believes he will only achieve his aims by the systematic corruption of the influential and governing classes. He does not care if people brand him as a bloodthirsty tyrant for he claims that all rule is at the bottom tyranny. He carries on power politics with a naked ruthless force and does not see what earthly difference it can make to use every form of trickery and misrepresentation. He commends the deliberate use of power at a time when there are still illusions abroad as to the forces which mould history. . . .

" 'We are awake,' he says, 'let others sleep.' "

(A cameo of extracts from *Hitler Speaks* and *The Beast from the Abyss:* Hermann Rauschning.)

CHAPTER THIRTEEN

THE DEMONIC MEISTERSINGER

A Pied Piper from the Flophouse

"Hitler's gestures and the emotional character of his speaking, lashing himself up to a pitch of near hysteria in which he would scream and spit his resentment, had the same effect on his audience. . . . He succeeded in communicating a passion to his listeners, so that men groaned and hissed and women sobbed involuntarily, if only to relieve the tension, caught up in the spell of powerful emotions of hatred and exultation, from which all restraint had been removed. . . . His power to bewitch an audience has been likened to the occult arts of the African Medicine-man or the Asiatic Shaman; others have compared it to the sensitivity of a medium, and the magnetism of a hypnotist."

Hitler—A Study in Tyranny: **Alan Bullock.**

Hanisch, a fellow tramp from the Vienna flophouse, has recalled the extent to which Hitler was fascinated by the power of rhetoric even in the days of his impoverished obscurity.

"One evening," recounts Hanisch, "Adolf Hitler went to the cinema where Kellermann's *Tunnel* was being shown. In this film an agitator appears who rouses the working masses with his speeches. Hitler almost went crazy. The impression it made on him was so strong that for days afterwards he spoke of nothing else but the power of the spoken word."

Even in his early teens Hitler had delighted in stories about the great orators of history. Gustl Kubizek mentions how the power of oratory illustrated so dramatically in Wagner's opera *Rienzi* had elated Hitler into the excited confession about how he believed he too would one day hold the masses spellbound with the magic power of the word.

Hitler speaks in *Mein Kampf* about the importance of oratory. "The power which has always started the greatest religions and political avalanches in history rolling has from time immemorial been the magic power of the spoken word. The broad masses of the people can be moved only by the power of speech. All great movements and popular movements, volcanic eruptions of human passions and emotions, were stirred by the firebrand of the word hurled among the masses. . . ."

And Hitler even comes near to revealing something of his magical technique when he talks about overcoming emotional resistance in a crowd. He says that this cannot be achieved through argument but only by appealing to 'hidden forces'. "He will always follow the lead of the great mass in such a way that from the living emotion of his hearers the apt word which he needs will be suggested to him and in turn this will go straight to the hearts of his hearers."

Otto Strasser, himself a brilliant speaker but never a member of the inner Nazi hierarchy, understood something of the magical power behind Hitler's ability to communicate the wildest passions to his audiences:

"Hitler responds to the vibration of the human heart with the delicacy of a seismograph, or perhaps a radio receiving set, enabling him, with a certainty with which no conscious gift could endow him, to act as a loudspeaker proclaiming the most secret desires, the least admissable instincts, the sufferings, and personal revolts of a whole nation."*

Strasser thinks little of Hitler's intellectual arguments based on books he has imperfectly understood. "But let him throw away his crutches and step out boldly, speaking as the spirit

* *Hitler and I:* Otto Strasser.

moves him, and he is promptly transformed into one of the greatest speakers of the century. . . . Adolf Hitler enters a hall. He sniffs the air. For a minute he gropes, feels his way, senses the atmosphere. Suddenly he bursts forth. His words go like an arrow to their target, he touches each private wound on the raw, liberating the mass unconscious, expressing its innermost aspirations, telling it what it wants to hear."*

Professor Alan Bullock perhaps comes far nearer to the truth than he himself realises when he writes: "Hitler's power to bewitch an audience has been likened to the occult arts of the African medicine-man or the Asiatic Shaman; others have compared it to the sensitivity of the medium, and the magnetism of the hypnotist." Yet external observation alone could never reveal the real source of the magical faculties with which Adolf Hitler hurled the firebrand of the word into the hearts of the German people to incite them to follow the Nazi racial cause.

Adolf Hitler's clairvoyant gifts, arising from the ritual 'opening' of his centres of vision, were of an atavistic nature. That is, he was unable to control or direct his vision. Nor were his perceptions immediately associated with the spiritual realities which stand within the phenomenal world. The activation of the centres in Hitler's astral organism came about involuntarily when he had whipped himself up into a frenzy of emotional excitement. Perhaps one can with a measure of justification compare his vision to the deepest kind of mescalin or 'LSD' trip in which the subject becomes involved in a mobile continuum of ever-changing colours and forms, as each vibrating 'Chakra' makes its specific contribution to the total transcendent experience.

On the genuine path to the Grail these centres are developed through disciplines of meditation in which purified thoughts and feelings nurture the budding organs of vision in the same manner as sunlight and water nourish the growth of a plant from a seed. The obvious comparison of the fruition of these Chakras

* Ibid.

to the laws of growth in nature and the unfolding of the blossoms inspired the ancients to call these organs of clairvoyant vision by the name of 'Lotus Flowers'.

These slumbering capacities are awakened by the development of specific capacities, the acquisition of moral qualities, and the mastery of hidden functions within the soul. Each centre comes to fruition as the result of the acquisition of a specific number of attributes. For instance, the Buddhist 'Eightfold Path' leads to the acquisition of eight attributes through which the eight-petalled Lotus Flower associated with the thyroid glands is brought to fruition and activated to vision.

Each of these organs based upon the seven endocrine glands yields a different type of vision. For example, the Chakra which interpenetrates the Thymus Gland permits vision of the changing sentiments and disposition of others, while the ten-petalled organ situated in the Solar Plexus opens up a vision of the talents and capacities and gives intercourse with Spiritual Beings. Yet other centres reveal the hidden thoughts and secret motives of others, revealing the inner life of total strangers like an open book.

We have briefly described the objectionable and totally illicit manner through which Adolf Hitler's centres were opened in obscene and sadistic initiation rituals under the direction of the Dietrich Eckart and the innermost circle of the Thulists. And there can be no doubt that during Hitler's mesmerising flights of oratory these slumbering faculties became awakened so that like an inspired Pied Piper he was able to gain an instinctive mastery of his audiences; an Oriental Shaman screaming forth his deadly mantrams to ignite his listeners into explosions of uncontrollable emotion like Subudists at a Latihan.

Unlike contemporary materialists, Adolf Hitler had never dryly and unimaginatively accepted the faculty of speech itself as just another mode of human behaviour. The revelation of Hitler's powers of oratory can also be found in von Eschenbach's *Parsival* about which he had a surprisingly penetrating knowledge.

At the very heart of this fascinating medieval romance, itself a profound initiation document, there is a wonderful description of how the human word is also a sword which proceeds out of the mouth of man. It is mentioned as a "Word-Sword" which has grown old, atrophied, shattered and lost its power. Only by discovering the original source of its power can this "Word-Sword" be renewed.

Hidden in one significant passage of *Parsival* this secret source stands revealed:

> "The sword will withstand the first blow; at the second it will shatter. If you then take it back to the Spring, it will become whole again from the flow of water.
>
> "You must have the water at its source beneath the rock, before the light of day has shone upon it. If the pieces are not lost and you fit them together properly, as soon as the spring water wets them, the sword will become whole again, the joinings and edges stronger than ever before, and the signs (of the constellations) engraved upon the blade will not lose their shine. The sword requires a magic spell. I fear that you forgot to learn it. But if your mouth did learn the words, the power of fortune will sprout and grow forever."

The minnesinger later described the Well of Kunneware, which is guarded by a Dragon, as the source of the magic spring: above the well was a globe, and upon it sat a dragon.

In this wonderful grail symbolism the Well represents the sex glands—the gonads. It is here that the globe (or Chakra) is seated, the highest spiritual organ which the ancients designated by the four-armed Swastika.

The Dragon, which guards the Well, symbolises the undiluted savagery of the blood of the race, the most primitive sexual instincts which must be overcome and transformed before the spring will yield its virtue—the creative healing power of the Word.

Here, at the Well of Kuneware, a man must not only overcome deep-seated egoism and racial pride, he must also fit together the broken pieces of the Sword. And these pieces must fit in such a way that each piece goes into its rightful place to make up the Signs of the Zodiac; a sort of spiritual jig saw puzzle in which the fixed constellations must reappear in their right order and position. "Not one piece must be lost."

The Grail Knight must accomplish this beneath the rock before the light of day. That is, he must achieve it in transcendent awareness unilluminated by the light of waking consciousness in the three-dimensional world of the senses.

It is pertinent that this passage follows almost immediately after Parsival's first unsuccessful visit to the Castle of the Grail when he fails to ask the compassionate question of the wounded Anfortas: "Brother, what ails thee?" For the magic spell which welds together the shattered word-sword is *LOVE*, the Love of Christ, the Word made flesh. And only through such love, which transcends all prejudice of race, colour, nation, creed and sex, can the Individual Human Spirit come to birth in man.

Well versed in the whole story and historical background of *Parsival*, Adolf Hitler was aware of the medieval doctrine of correspondences between Macrocosm and Microcosm in which man is spoken of as the concentrated image of the whole Cosmos. And how the creative principle (Word) of the Universe has been implanted in man and comes to expression in the tremendous faculty of human speech.

In this sense it is beyond doubt that Adolf Hitler realised that the shattered word-sword with the constellations engraved upon it was man himself. But he did not wish to follow the path of Christian renewal through which the Word will more and more express itself in moral inspiration and healing powers of love. He sought to use the magical powers inherent in the word for destructive motives to incite hatred, division and enmity among men.

It was with the powers of Nazism that Hitler sought to lead mankind away from the realisation of the individual human spirit. In his frenzied orations, public performances of astrological magic for those with eyes to identify it, he evoked the brutal instincts and primitive savagery in the blood of the race. The sole motive of the Luciferic Spirit, which possessed Hitler's deluded soul like a puppet, was to seduce the German people to give up their spiritual birthright for the tempting idea of racial superiority.

> "People set us down as the enemies of the Spirit. We are. But in a much deeper sense than the conceited bourgeois dolts ever dreamed of. What should I care for the Christian doctrine of the infinite significance of the individual spirit and of personal moral responsibility? I oppose it in icy clarity with the saving doctrine of the nothingness and total insignificance of the individual and of his continued existence only in the visible mortality of the blood of the race. . . . I am liberating man from the demands of spiritual freedom and personal independence which only a few people can bear. . . . A German Christianity is a distortion. One is either German or Christian."
>
> (Extracts from Hitler's talks with his Gauleiters).

Richard Wagner, with the insight of genius, dramatised the figure of Klingsor as a wizard of the black arts wielding the Spear of Destiny like a mighty phallic wand. And in the light of Wagner's Grail opera, we can see Adolf Hitler as the twentieth-century Klingsor stepping on to the stage of history to pour out his torrents of magically inspired sexual venom to blind mankind to the meaning of individual destiny in the historical process.*

When comparing Hitler with Landulf II of Capua, it is fascinating to discover that this Duke of Terra di Labur not only coveted the Spear for his own demonic ends but also made the Hagenkreutz or disguised Swastika into his heraldic emblem.

The traditions and legends about the figure of Klingsor do not end in the ninth century. For the name of Klingsor makes another appearance at the Wartburg Krieg in 1207. A certain Bishop Klingsor is said to have surpassed all the Minnesingers of Europe in this contest, even Wolfram von Eschenbach himself.

---

* In a scene from Wagner's *Parsival*, Klingsor throws the Spear at Parsival who catches it. Parsival, the representative of the Individual Human Spirit can not be harmed by Klingsor's magical powers. In the hands of Parsival, the Spear serves the powers of the Holy Spirit.

In the account of the Wartburg, which inspired Wagner's opera, *Tannhäuser*, indications are given that Bishop Klingsor had united himself with demonic powers which he had learned to control. The Luciferic Spirit which was the source of his astonishing talents was once again known as Nazim or Nasion. Von Eschenbach, who sang out of the purified feelings of the heart, proved to be no match for the wizard's cold occult wisdom and arts of astrological magic.

No historian has yet positively identified this figure of the Bishop Klingsor, but he is believed to have been the Count of Acerra, the Lord of Terra di Labur and Capua.

The Count of Acerra is known to have been an evil man and an adept of magic. It was rumoured that his sister, Sybilla, Queen of Sicily, had given birth to a son conceived in demonic rites. When she fled from Emperor Henry VI and took refuge at the eyrie of Kalath-el-Bellut, her terrible secret was discovered. Her son was castrated and the Count of Acerra, who had called forth the unclean spirit who had sired him, was condemned to a horrible death. Though he was supposed to have died on the rack in 1197, there were rumours at that time he had escaped and found refuge in Hungary.

Klingsor of Hungary, like Landulf II some four centuries earlier, was the central figure of a circle of adepts, among whom were some of the leading ecclesiastical personalities of the time. And it was through this circle that the whole process of the Inquisition came into being.

Bishop Klingsor was gifted with pre-vision and forecast the birth of Saint Elizabeth of Thuringen, who has been described as a sort of sister soul to Saint Francis of Assisi. It was through her Confessor, Conrad of Marburg, that the first fury of the Inquisition broke loose. The extermination of the Albigenses and Cathars took place the year after the Wartburg contest. Seven years later (1215) the heretic laws were established at the Lateran Council.

During the lifetime of Bishop Klingsor the fable of the Pied Piper arose in central Europe and some historians have associated its origin with him. It tells of a rat-catcher who became incensed against the whole population of the town of Hamelin. To avenge himself against them, he began to play his flute and all the children in the district gathered around him. Hypnotised by the magic of his music, they followed him beyond the walls of the town and into a deep cavern in the hills, where they vanished and were lost for ever. This legend describing the slaughter of innocent children signifies the working of hidden forces in history which sought to lead mankind from its true spiritual aims. The legend was also prophetic of the magic powers of oratory with which Adolf Hitler would rob the German people of the fulfilment of their true destiny, stripping them of their independence, and leading them into moral degradation through distorted racial ideologies.

Through a fascinating source we have come to know that Adolf Hitler also considered himself to be the reincarnation of Count of Acerra. After he had come to power and established the Third Reich, Adolf Hitler sent Hermann Göring on a special mission to see the famous Swedish doctor and author, Axel Munthe, who had rebuilt the Temple of Tiberius on the heights of Capri, overlooking the Bay of Naples.

Axel Munthe, author of the pre-war best-seller *The Story of San Michele*, began restoring the ancient Temple of Tiberius whilst he was going blind and his sight failed before he could complete it. He never saw the beauty of the restored San Michele which he had worked so hard to achieve.

In August, 1937, whilst on a visit to Rome for talks with Count Ciano, the Italian Foreign Minister, Göring slipped away in civilian clothes to Naples and took the steamer to Capri.

Munthe, perturbed at a visit from the Vice-Chancellor who had founded the Gestapo, was reluctant to open his doors. But after an assurance from Göring that he had come as Hitler's emissary to make an offer to buy San Michele, Axel Munthe agreed to speak with him. The Swede was amazed to discover Göring's remarkable knowledge of history and art and the two men remained in deep discussion for several hours.

Later that year on a short stay in London where he finally

settled when war was declared, Axel Munthe paid a visit to the Kensington home of Dr. Walter Johannes Stein, a friend of long standing, to whom he recounted the full details of his strange conversation with Hermann Göring.

Apparently, when Göring discovered that Axel Munthe was himself an occultist with awakened faculties and penetrating perception, he spoke openly about Hitler's reasons for wanting to buy San Michele, where he intended to retire in his old age.

Hitler, said Göring, not only considers himself to be the reincarnation of Landulf II and Count Acerra, both Lords of Naples and Capri (Terra di Labur), he also thinks himself to be the reborn Tiberius, the Roman Emperor who retired to the island to spend the last year of his life in seclusion.*

During the course of their day-long discussions, Göring proudly stated that he had always incarnated beside his Führer. He claimed to have been Count Boese (bad),† the personal friend and confidant of Landulf II in the ninth century. In the thirteenth century he claimed to have been reborn as Conrad of Marburg, the close associate of Bishop Klingsor, the wizard of the Wartburg. Goebbels was mentioned in the same context as the reincarnation of Eckbert of Meran, the thirteenth-century Bishop of Bamberg, who introduced the Count Acerra to the Court of King Andrew of Hungary under whose jurisdiction the "Battle of Song" took place.

Göring became an active member of the Edelweiss Society while he was living in Sweden in 1921. The Edelweiss Society, an offshoot of the Golden Dawn, awaited the appearance of a Nordic Messiah. When he first heard Hitler speak, he had no doubts that he was listening to the "Saviour of Germany".

---

* Adolf Hitler offered Munthe a very high price for San Michele. Dr. Stein told me that Axel Munthe refused to sell because he believed himself to be the reincarnation of Tiberius Caesar about whose life he claimed to have had transcendent memories.

† Hermann Göring constructed an entirely fictitious Genealogical Tree which traced his ancestry back to Count Boese, a noble of Royal Carolingian blood, and to Conrad of Marburg, the confessor of Elizabeth of Thuringen. This spurious family tree has been reported by most of Göring's biographers yet none of them ever gleaned his real motives for making it.

"Hitler's convictions were spoken word for word as though from my own soul," he said. "When I introduced myself, Hitler said it was an extraordinary turn of fate that we should meet. We spoke at once about the things which were close to our hearts."

But it was Goebbels, who first heard Hitler speak at a Party Rally in Bamberg, who had been the prophet of the new leader as a magic Meistersinger. Goebbels, the lame child of a humble printer in Rheydt, had secured the patronage of the Albertus Magnus Society, to pay his way through University. In a degree course in history and literature, he attended five different Universities. While in Freiburg in the summer of 1918, he had made a study of the medieval history associated with the mystery of the Holy Grail. During his life as a student he began a novel called *Michael* which resembles the diary of a hero who combines the occupations of soldier, poet, lover, patriot and revolutionary, a youth who is "anxious to grasp life with every fibre of his being". The hero places the whole responsibility for the pitiable plight of Germany in defeat on the Jews—"They have raped our people, soiled our ideals, weakened the strength of the nation, corrupted morals. . . . They are the poisonous eczema on the body of our sick nation. . . . Their intellect has poisoned our people." When the hero reaches the depths of despair regarding the destiny of the German people, he is suddenly awakened to new hope by the appearance of a messianic orator:

"I sit in a hall I have never been in before. Among utter strangers. Poor and threadbare people most of them. Workers, soldiers, officers, students. I hardly notice how the man up there begins to speak, slowly, hesitatingly at first.

"But then all of a sudden, the flow of his speech is unleashed. Its light a light shining above him. I listen. I am captivated. Honour! Work! The Flag! Are there still such things in this people from whom God has taken His blessing hand.

"The audience is aglow. Hopes shine on grey faces. Someone clenches his fist. Another wipes the sweat off his brow. An old officer weeps like a child.

"I am getting hot and cold. I don't know what has happened to

187

me. I seem to hear guns booming. A few soldiers get up and shout 'hurrah', and nobody seems to notice it.

"And the man up there speaks on, and whatever was budding in me falls into shape. A miracle!

"Among the ruins is someone who shows us the flag.

"Those around me are no longer strangers. They are brothers. I go up to the rostrum and look into the man's face.

"No orator he! A prophet!

"Sweat is pouring down his face. A pair of eyes glow in the pale face. His fists are clenched. And like the last judgement word after word is thundering on, phrase after phrase.

"I do not know what to do. I seem demented.

"I begin to cheer. And no one seems astonished.

"He on the rostrum glances on me for a moment. Those blue eyes scar me like a flame, that is an order.

"I feel as if I was newly born. I know now whither my path leads me. The path of maturity. I seem to be intoxicated. All I remember is the man's hand clasping mine. A vow for life. And my eyes meet two great blue stars."

In such a manner did the unfolding destiny pattern of Joseph Goebbels anticipate his fated meeting with Adolf Hitler, the reappearance of the demonic Meistersinger of the Wartburg.

The impact which Adolf Hitler made on Goebbels on the day they met in Bamberg was found in the diary of the Nazi Minister of Propaganda which was impounded by the Allied Intelligence after the fall of Berlin in 1945:

"I thank fate that there is such a man! . . . He is the creative instrument of fate and deity. I stand by him deeply shaken. . . . That is how it is. . . . I recognise him as my leader quite unconditionally. . . . He is so deep and mystical. He knows how to express infinite truth. . . . He seems like a prophet of old. And in the sky a big white cloud seems to take the shape of a Swastika. Is this a sign of fate? How much elementary strength in this man compared to the intellectuals. On top of it all, his overwhelming personality. . . . With such a man one can conquer the world. To him I feel deeply linked. My doubts vanish. . . . I could not bear to have to doubt this man. Germany will live. *Heil Hitler!*"

PART THREE

THE BLOOD AND THE ASHES

Wagner has proclaimed the eternal tragedy of human destiny. He was not merely a musician and a poet; he was the supreme prophetic figure among Germans. I came early to Wagner by the disposition of Providence. All I found in Wagner was in agreement with my innermost, dormant convictions.

We must interpret Wagner's *Parsival* in a totally different way to the general conception. Behind the absurd externals of the story, with its Christian embroidery and its Good Friday mystifications, something altogether different is revealed as the true content of this profound drama.

It is not the Christian religion of compassion that is acclaimed but pure noble blood, in the protection and glorification of whose purity the brotherhood of the Initiated have come together.

The King Anfortas is suffering from the incurable ailment of corrupted blood. The uninitiated but pure man is tempted to abandon himself in Klingsor's magic garden to lusts and excesses of corrupt civilisation instead of joining the élite of Knights who guard the secret of life, pure blood.

All of us are suffering from the ailment of mixed corrupted blood. How can we purify ourselves and make atonement? Shall we form a select company of the really initiated? An Order—The Brotherhood of the Templars round the Holy Grail of pure blood!

Note that the compassion through which man gains comprehension is only for the corrupted man at issue with himself, And that this compassion only knows one treatment—the leaving of the sick person to die. The eternal life granted by the Grail is only for the truly pure and noble.

A cameo of extracts from *Hitler Speaks*:

Hermann Rauschning.

CHAPTER FOURTEEN

THE NAME INSCRIBED
ON THE STONE

The Spiritual Lineage of Reincarnation

"You say you yearn for the Grail. You foolish man, I am grieved to hear that. For no man can ever win the Grail unless he is known in heaven and called by name to the Grail. This I must tell you about the Grail, for I know it to be so and have seen it for myself.

"A valiant host lives there (at Montsaelvaesche), and I will tell how they are sustained. They live upon a *Stone* of the purest kind. If you do not know it, it shall be named unto you. It is called Lapsit Exillis. . . .

"By the power of that *Stone* the phoenix burns to ashes, but the ashes give him life again. Thus does the phoenix moult and change its plumage, which afterward is bright and shining and as lovely as before. . . . Such power does the *Stone* give a man that flesh and bones are at once made young again. The *Stone* is also called the Grail.

"This very day there comes to it a message wherein lies its greatest power. Today is Good Friday, and they await there a Dove, winging down from heaven. It brings a small white wafer, and leaves it on the *Stone*. . . .

"Hear now how those who are called to the Grail are made known. On the *Stone*, round the edge, appear letters inscribed, giving the name and the lineage of each one, maid or boy, who

191

is to make the blessed journey. No one needs to rub out the inscription, for once he has read the name, it fades before his eyes."

(Thus spake the hermit Treverezent to Parsival.)

Parsival: Wolfram von Eschenbach.

Walter Johannes Stein went to war with a haversack stuffed with books. He joined the Imperial Austrian Army as a humble gunner and completed his service as a Staff Captain. He left home as a gangling novice in search of the Grail. He returned from the war as an Adept who had read his name inscribed round the edge of the Stone.

Though he saw continuous action in the bitter fighting against the invading Russian armies, gaining a decoration for gallantry and mentions in despatches, he somehow contrived to find time to write the dissertation for his Doctorate. It was a thesis on time and consciousness describing the physiological processes of the human body as the potential seat of nine higher dimensions of transcendent awareness

When he went off to the battle front in 1914, he had not yet found a path to the attainment of higher consciousness. He was faced with the same problem which has baffled most students of the occult: how to awaken dormant powers in the soul which will lead to genuine spirit-vision. It was obvious enough to him that such vision could only be achieved by meditation. But what kind of meditation and how to find time to carry it through under conditions of modern warfare?

He came to the conclusion that, because he was intent on reaching a kind of thinking no longer dependent on the brain, the content of his meditation should be of a sense free nature too. He chose the ancient Rosicrucian meditation of the Black Cross and the Seven Red Roses. The separate symbols never appearing together in the sense world, such a form of meditation was already a step towards sense-free experience. Besides this, the whole thought process of this particular meditation embraced the inner significance of the blood, the central theme of the search for the Grail.

Whatever the immediate tactical situation of his Battery, advance or retreat, or simply the crucifying deadlock of artillery barrage between Austrian and Russian guns, he forced himself to find time on three occasions each day for a spell of concentrated meditation. This in itself was quite an achievement.

By perseverance with the meditation, he summoned up from the depths of his soul far stronger forces than he was accustomed to employ in the everyday process of thinking. Gradually, little by little, he became aware during these periods of sustained meditation that his soul was liberating itself from the body in a similar way to entry into a condition of sleep. Yet, instead of passing over into unconsciousness, he found himself awakening to a heightened awareness of another level of existence.

After little more than a year at the front, the buds of a genuine clairvoyance of the spirit worlds began to blossom forth in a faculty which occultists call Imaginative Cognition.

It was at this stage in his inner development that he was sent home from the fighting on a brief compassionate leave to comfort his mother in her grief over the loss of her eldest son. Fritz, Walter's brother, had been posthumously awarded the highest decoration for bravery and devotion to duty. He died defending a fortress from Russian attack, blowing himself up along with the fort when the enemy penetrated its defences. The two brothers had been very close. He, too, felt the loss acutely. Both had considered the multi-racial basis of the Austro-Hungarian dynasty worth fighting for, but death was a high price to pay.

During his short leave Walter Johannes decided to pay a brief visit to the Hofburg in order to stand once again before the Spear of Longinus, the ancient weapon associated with the strange legend of world destiny. It was a beautiful late summer day as he walked across the almost deserted Ring and climbed the steps up to the Weltliche Schatzkammer.

The attendants, mostly retired soldiers too old for further service with the colours, saluted the young Lieutenant as he marched down the gangways of the rococo hall. He took in the

193

now-familiar scene of the Hapsburg regalia and the Reich-kleinodien and made his way directly to where the solitary looking Spearhead still rested on its red dais within a glass case.

It was more than two years since he had stood in the same spot beside Adolf Hitler, who did not at this moment even enter his mind. Instead he found himself thinking how his fellow science students at the University would have mocked him for his belief in the legend of the Spear of Destiny. Any suggestion of a meaning to personal destiny would have been scorned as a pathetic joke. And for this reason he had never discussed his researches into the history of the Spear with anybody other than his mother and his brother Fritz, now dead.

The very sight of the Spear made him aware of the extent to which he had become a divided personality, holding tenaciously to two apparently contrasting viewpoints and unwilling to let go of either.

On the one side, his mind was dominated by the atomistic hypothesis of modern physics and the new scientific method which sought to explain man only in terms of the physical world in which he lives. His whole science course at the University had taught him about a world devoid of spirit, a Godless world of measurement in which man shrank to utter insignificance; the earth itself appearing as no more than a speck of cosmic dust in a dying galaxy.

On the other side his emerging clairvoyance awakened him to a spirit existence where perceiving was in itself knowing, and intellectually derived thought had no place. He described himself at this time as "half sceptic, half visionary". And yet he could find no bridge between these conflicting standpoints which might explain how matter was fashioned by spirit and sustained by it.

Despite this dilemma, he had an unshakeable inward conviction that a moral order reigned throughout the Universe and that judgement and consequence were at the heart of both the historical process and the unfolding of personal destiny. Day by day as the casualties mounted and many of his former student friends lost their lives, a sense of inner certainty grew within him that he would survive the war to fulfil some form of spiritual mission.

While these thoughts were running through his mind he had been examining the ancient Spearhead which had inspired so many different personalities in the history of Christendom. He ran his eyes over the odd-shaped phalanges which had been added to symbolise the wings of a dove, the golden crosses engraved on the dull metal, the hammerheaded Nail secured in the central aperture of the blade, the long tapering point.

Was this indeed the Spear which the Roman Centurion had thrust into the side of Christ as an act of mercy?—he asked himself. Or had some of the greatest personalities of world history been victims of a delusion?

He had not reckoned with the powerful effect this talisman of the Blood of Christ would now have on his emerging clairvoyant faculties. Quite suddenly he became aware of its psychometric qualities. It seemed to emanate mystical vibrations which had the power to evoke powerful imaginations. Before he could summon the strength to cast it off, he was deep in the grip of an experience which overwhelmed his senses. He found himself pulled out of the earthly space-time continuum with an almost savage abruptness and precipitated into a higher level of awareness.

The immediate surroundings of the Treasure House melted away as he was whisked through Time like some unwilling captive on a magic carpet bound for the unknown. He found himself transported into the very midst of an astounding scene which forcibly clothed itself in his spiritual imagination. And with this newly-born cognition he found himself a witness to a Manichaean War of Worlds between Spirits of Light and Darkness.

Above him in the distance he could discern a mighty figure leading an array of angelic hosts, a translucent Spirit girded around the breast in white raiment which fell in folds of living beauty, an outward expression of absolute purity of heart. In joy and wonder he beheld the majesty and spirit power of this heroic Being whose countenance was 'the Countenance of the Lord'.

He knew with immediacy that he was standing before the Archangel of the Grail, the *Zeitgeist*. His helmet sparkled and shone with the consecrated fire of molten iron in a cosmic forge. In his right hand he grasped a blade of light which he smote across the heavens with immeasurable purpose and Divine will; lightning flashing forth from the blade forked down to strike clusters of demonic spirits who sought to penetrate the celestial worlds from which they had been cast out.

As the battle came nearer, like the approach of a terrifying cosmic thunderstorm, he too felt himself within the range of the purging sweep of this spiritual Excalibur. Though accustomed to the temper and stress of physical battle in earthly war between men, with all its accompanying sights of horror, he had experienced nothing remotely resembling this incredible scene in which the evil spirits were thrown back in flames of desolation before the uncompromising might of this Guardian of the Threshold of the Macrocosm.

And now he was tempted to flee in panic along with the grotesque creatures surrounding him on all sides, who seemed to have come alive from the nightmare paintings of Hieronymus Bosch or the canvas of Orcagna's hell. Somehow he found the moral courage to remain. And more than this, he knew he must reach out and open himself to the purging fire. Searing pain and anguish arose in his soul as the lightning struck him. He felt as though he was being hollowed out as the evils of false pride and materialism were burned out of his soul. When he could withstand the agony no longer, he swooned into unconsciousness.

As suddenly as the transcendent experience had overcome his physical senses, he now found himself back with an equally breathtaking abruptness within the four walls of the Treasure House. His right hand was fully extended as though he was grasping at something, the fist clenched so tightly that his fingernails had drawn blood in the palm. How long he had been standing there in a trance he did not know. It could have been minutes or but brief seconds. Nobody seemed to be paying him any special attention. The Spear lay there before him on its velvet dais within the glass case. The sun was shining through the high windows of the rococo hall, illuminating the gaudy colours of the Hapsburg Regalia. The contrast between the peaceful scene of the Schatzkammer and the wrathful energy of the War of Worlds from which he had just emerged, stretched his mind to its utmost limits.

As he walked back across the Ring he remembered that it was Michaelmas Day. And he recalled the Michael verse in Goethe's *Prologue in Heaven* which almost perfectly described his own shattering experience.

> MICHAEL: And rival storms abroad are surging
> from sea to land, from land to sea,
> a chain of deepest action forging
> round all, in wrathful energy.
> There flames a desolation blazing
> before the thunder's crashing way.
> Yet, Lord, Thy messengers keep praising
> the gentle movement of Thy Day.

And was it a similar vision which had inspired that martial and mysterious verse in the Revelation of St. John?: "And there was war in heaven: Michael and his angels fought against the dragon; and the dragon fought and his angels, and prevailed not; neither was their place found any more in heaven" (*Revelation* 12, 7 and 8).

It was baffling that such magical imagery should clothe itself as a cognition in human imagination and yet be of the nature of a temporal experience. But he knew that the Beings involved, both good and evil, were real in the truest sense of the word—more real indeed than the very pavement upon which he was walking.

The vision of the Archangel of the Grail had been in itself a kind of spiritual recollection. He felt in Spirit that he had served this sublime Being in his pre-earthly existence before birth and also throughout countless former lives on earth. He knew at last what it really meant to be a Knight of the Grail.

Above all he was now aware that his whole life must be dedicated to the fulfilment of its aims on earth, and that he should strive to prepare himself for the tasks that lay ahead. Like a Knight of the Holy Grail in the Middle Ages he made a solemn vow to serve this Spirit of the Most High, even at the cost of life itself.

During the months which followed his first vision of the Time-Spirit, the Spirit of the Spear of Destiny, he put new heart and resolution into his daily meditation, strengthening further the capacity to create vivid images and to wield thoughts as though they were things. The reward of his labours came about in a most surprising manner on a bitter December day in 1916 while he was up in the line as forward observation officer for the guns of his battery.

He found himself in the middle of a deadly box barrage in which shells were exploding uncomfortably close all around him. The long-awaited moment of occult illumination came when a shell plunged into the trench right beside him and failed to explode.

In a single instant he saw his whole life pass in review before him in a great tableau. And he witnessed this life panorama with the uninvolved spectator consciousness of the Higher Ego. Yet the events of his life were not beheld in a kind of speeded-up version of successive time consciousness. On the contrary, the tableau appeared as a huge interweaving pattern of cause and effect which he comprehended as a Unity from a higher level of consciousness. Somehow he had been precipitated out of earthly time in which events happen one after the other in succession. Instead, he experienced himself as a Time Being rather than a soul trapped in time.

The next step on the path to the Grail demanded that he learn to wipe out all thought images from his consciousness. He had reached the stage where he was faced with the great enigma of the anatomy of emptiness in which the soul must seek immeasurable fullness in an apparent void. The time had arrived for him to hold his mind in expectant emptiness whilst maintaining the heightened feelings of reverence and humility of a soul who awaits upon the grace of God.

In these moments of silent and imageless absorption, a vision of the spirit-world was born, the world of the hierarchies of supersensible Beings. And gradually, step by step, Walter Johannes acquired the gift of being able to empty his consciousness at will so that he could enter that invisible world from which creative Beings fashion and sustain the world of the senses.

In his first tenuous excursions into the Macrocosm the would-be Grail Initiate confronts the task of orientating himself in a new world in which he must learn to recognise and identify the ascending hierarchical grades of celestial spirits. He must not only gain an understanding of the nature and faculties of each separate grade but also differentiate between the endless ways in which they send forth their activities into the three-dimensional world.

Above all Walter Johannes was astonished by the manner in which these lofty celestial spirits stood in ever-changing relationships to one another. Like letters of the alphabet, their groupings and swiftly varying order seemed to express a symphony of the creative word, a new language of the spirit with an infinite depth and variety of meaning. It was with some satisfaction that he realised how Wolfram von Eschenbach had described the faculty of interpreting these changing inter-relationships and groupings as the "Learning the ABC's but without the aid of Black Magic".*

The vision of the celestial hierarchies, which has inspired a hidden thread of Grail Initiates since the days of Joseph of Arimathea, stimulates an ineffable longing in the human soul to rise beyond the activity of a mere preception of the spirit world. And Walter Johannes now sought to enter into direct communication with these sublime spirits who serve the purposes of the Divine Trinity.

Whereas the development of Imaginative Cognition had been

---

* The modern astrologer who attempts to predict the future through the positions and inter-relationships of the visible planets against the fixed stars, and uses them as a kind of alphabet of inner meaning, is materialising the last echoes of a sublime and ancient wisdom.

achieved through the acquisition of sense-free thought independent of the brain, and the faculty of Inspiration through the purification of the life of feeling, the final step to intuitive identification with supersensible spirits now demanded a strengthening of the moral powers of the will.

In this ascent to the ultimate realisation of the Grail, a man becomes aware of the real nature of his Individual Spirit. He discovers that his earthly ego, which he had previously regarded as the centre and core of his being, is but a reflection of the Eternal Self which overshadows it.

Walter Johannes was on the brink of reading his name inscribed around the edge of the Stone which is also called the Grail. For the Individual Spirit is also the guardian of the higher memory of a whole series of lives which the soul has lived previously on earth.

> "Hear now how those who are called to the Grail are made known. On the *Stone*, around the edge, appear letters inscribed giving the name and the lineage of each one, maid or boy, who is to make the journey."—*Parsival*.

Of course this lineage mentioned by Wolfram von Eschenbach is not a genealogical tree of an earthly blood line, but a lineage of successive incarnations on the earth, the memory of which is retained by the Spirit-Ego until the maturing soul has made itself ready to receive it.

The Sign of the Holy Grail, as we have mentioned briefly in an earlier chapter describing the alchemical symbolism of the quest, is a Dove winging across from the Sun into the invisible disc held within the arms of the Crescent Moon. And Walter Johannes, now himself aware of the relationships between Macrocosm and Microcosm, discovered the same configuration in man. The Dove represents the purified feelings of the heart (Sun), which arise to permeate the cold intellectual thinking of the brain (Moon), thus to free it from a soulless three-dimensional conception of the Universe.

This process, known in Occultism as the "Aetherisation of

the Blood" can be clairvoyantly perceived as an ethereal rose light which arises from the blood in the human heart and initiates an alchemical process in the brain, and especially within the Pineal gland, which then becomes the organ of higher memory—the Third Eye. It is with the Third Eye that the soul perceives its name inscribed on the Stone.

Each single letter appearing round the edge of the Stone is perceived by the activated Pineal gland to represent a former life on earth. Together these letters spell out, as it were, the whole spiritual biography of the soul in its striving from life to life in the evolution of consciousness within the historical process. The inner realisation of the spiritual biography of the Eternal Self is the fruit of the reading of the name around the edge of the Stone.

Walter Johannes now understood why the legitimate quest for the Grail could never be undertaken by a character like Adolf Hitler who had no compassion for the sufferings and tribulations of others. Only a soul which had become the sacrificial vehicle of the Love of God could awaken to the comprehension, without black magic, of his own Individual Spirit. And this was indeed the true interpretation of the sublime motto of the Grail Knights: *Durch Mitleid wissen.*

The lineage which Walter Johannes perceived around the edge of the Stone embraced a spiritual biography reaching back for 5,000 years and beyond. Faces, some men, others women, appeared to him one by one out of the history of the ancient world—Persia, Egypt, Chaldea, Palestine, Crete, Greece and Rome. Figures also appeared before his spiritual gaze from the centuries of the Early Church Fathers, the Fall of the Roman Empire, the Carolingian Dynasty, medieval England, the era of Scholasticism, the age of discovery and so on, right through to the French Revolution and the Napoleonic Wars.

An array of human beings inter-connected by a tapestry of moral cause and effect, as though each one had laid the foundation of both inward character and outer event for its future appearances on earth.

He beheld the journey of his soul through the centuries with the eyes of the Spirit. It was an act of Grace which would not recur in this form again. As soon as each figure had manifested to his vision, it melted away. On another level of consciousness he remembered the words of Wolfram von Eschenbach: "No one needs to rub out the inscription, for once he has read the name, it fades before his eyes."

The face of each personality had left an indelible impression on his mind. If he had seen the faces as coloured illustrations in a book, he would have regarded them as merely faces out of past history. Something dead and gone. But now he realised that all these faces had been his faces, expressions of his own identity; their joys and sufferings, loves and hates, ambitions and striving, successes and failures, had been his very own.

THE CAMEL'S HUMP AND THE SPHINX'S INSCRUTABLE SMILE

A new technique in Historical Research

History had become a very personal affair for Walter Johannes Stein. He realised to what extent the entire contemporary world was fast asleep to the real meaning of the historical process. History was something the living themselves had helped to create in their former lives on earth. They bore the whole responsibility for what the world was, what it is, and what it will become.

Apart from the brief glimpse of his own spiritual lineage, he wondered how it was possible to recapture the whole experience of a former life with the same clarity and fullness of detail with which he remembered his present life. He had not long to wait.

In the succeeding weeks another form of memory began to arise. It also emerged in the form of a vivid picture consciousness. Memory after memory flooded into his soul of the life of a nobleman at the Frankish Court in the eighth and ninth centuries. He never knew when the next piece of the jigsaw would fit into place. And at first he did not understand what sparked the process into life. It appeared that events in his own life, as they happened, were in themselves a stimulus, which evoked memories from the life of this personality who had lived a thousand years earlier.

Although he began to perceive the life of this medieval knight in vivid pictures, the whole process was not unlike the working of ordinary memory in which the eye of the mind calls forth remembrances. Only he could not himself call forth these higher memories but had to wait until they appeared spontaneously. Nor did these memories appear in chronological order. That is, they did not appear to follow a time sequence from birth to old age, and they seemed to deny what we know as the law of cause and effect in successive time. For instance, the moral consequence of any act was known before the act itself was perceived. Above all he learned not to try and speculate or intellectualise the experience but let it come to birth without any egoistic interference.

By the time hostilities were over, he knew almost as much about a former incarnation in the age of Charlemagne as he did about his own contemporary life in the twentieth century. And yet much that he remembered conflicted with the generally accepted history of the ninth century. When he returned home to Vienna to find the ancient city in the storm of revolution following the death of Franz Joseph, he set himself one all-important task—to search the archives of Europe for extant records of medieval history in order to find proof of everything his newly-won faculties had revealed to him.

He knew that historical evidence of his ninth-century incarnation would prove immensely difficult to unearth. He had a shrewd suspicion that there had been a conspiracy at that time and in later centuries to expunge his former name and his deeds from all historical records.

The life that he could now recall in such detail concerned a certain Count Hugo of Tours (Hugo von Touron) whom he had discovered to be one of the leading Initiates of the Holy Grail in the Dark Ages, and a man both feared and hated by the Roman See.

Walter Johannes had been shattered to learn that this same Hugo had been Charlemagne's closest friend and confidant, and a man whose advice the Emperor of the Franks valued beyond all others. And yet Einhard, the best known biographer of Charles The Great, did not even consider Hugo of Tours worth a mention. Nor indeed did later biographers, possessed with similar intense loyalties to Rome, record a single word about this Knight and scholar in their descriptions of the Carolingian era.

Hugo of Tours had been present at the High Mass in St. Peter's in Rome on Christmas morning in A.D. 800 when Pope Leo III tricked Charlemagne into identifying himself totally with the Roman See. It had been a carefully planned and cunning attempt to make Charles subservient to Rome in exchange for the title of "Caesar Augustus".

Walter Johannes had seen vivid pictures of this scene when the Pope without warning placed the crown on the head of Charles while a well-primed crowd shouted: "To the divinely crowned Emperor Carolus Augustus long life and victory."

He could remember how Charlemagne was taken by surprise and stood there hesitant and shocked with a look of distaste on his face. Up to this moment Charlemagne's only consideration regarding the Roman Church was that he himself should have the decisive voice in the choice of Pope and in the governing of Rome. He had just concluded a war with the Lombards in order to silence rebellion and bring back the Pope who had been driven away from his own capital city.

Charlemagne had become the recipient of the full Grail wisdom through his grandfather (on his mother's side) Charibert, Count of Laon, who had implanted in the bloodstream of his descendants a capacity for clairvoyant vision. And it was because of his fascination with the search for the Grail that Charlemagne had surrounded himself with adepts of the Grail knowledge. From Hugo of Tours Charlemagne had learned of the hierarchies of celestial Spirits and the part they played in the destiny of mankind. And it was through clairvoyant faculties that Charlemagne had himself seen the Spirit of the Spear of Longinus, the Spear which became the very talisman of his personal destiny and the symbol of his power to rule an Empire as powerful and extensive as that of Caesar Augustus a thousand years earlier.

Yet Charlemagne was not a learned man. Although he had a kind of native shrewdness and a deep sense of justice, he himself had never learned to read and write—indeed, all attempts to do so had proved unsuccessful. And yet he somehow contrived to learn to speak Latin and some Greek. In consequence of his own academic shortcomings, he was deeply impressed by men of letters and surrounded himself with some of the greatest scholars of the age.

At his capital in Aachen, on his almost ceaseless campaigns against the marauding Saxons, and in the schools of learning which constantly moved around with his retinue, there were always leading advocates of both the orthodox Roman and the Grail Christianity. Charlemagne had an almost equal sympathy with both.

The King had been especially moved by St. Augustine's *City of God*, passages of which he would have read to him every day. And it was this very same Augustine of Hippo, the greatest of the early Fathers of the Church, who had refuted Manichaean Christianity which had within its system many similarities to the quest for the Grail.

The situation at the Carolingian Court developed into a sort of running battle between the advocates of faith in dogmas which the intellect was unqualified to refute, and a path to the vision of spirit-worlds in which perceiving and knowing were a unity.

However, Charlemagne was a man with a sense for history who believed beyond all else in his own indispensability and fated greatness. And in this matter of personal pride lay his one great weakness. Pope Leo III had learned from his spies the nature of this Achilles Heel of the King of the Franks. By crowning him without warning at the High Mass at St. Peter's as a 'divine act' of ritual—itself a form of powerful magic—Charlemagne was won over to the Roman cause from which he never escaped. This moment marked the eclipse of the Christianity of the Holy Grail which within decades was to be

banished from the face of European history. Charlemagne, at
first angered by the Pope's gesture, finally became in all
religious matters a vassal of Rome. The Pope regarded himself
as the leader of the renewal of the Roman Empire in the West,
a view which he emphasised on coins, inscriptions and seals. A
saddened and disillusioned Hugo of Tours was despatched to
Byzantium to conciliate the Emperor of the East and persuade
him to acknowledge Charlemagne's coronation as Holy
Roman Emperor of the West. Thus the power of Christendom
flowed from Greece to Rome.

Hugo of Tours fell into royal disfavour as a result of the
intrigues of the rival faction at Court who persuaded the Emperor that his former favourite sought to kill him.

Walter Johannes could remember the imprisonment of Hugo,
his trial and how he had been sentenced to death. He could
even recall vividly how the executioner for some inexplicable
reason had been unable to lift the axe to sever his head. And
how the infuriated Emperor had run forward to execute him
with his own sword but proved equally incapable of striking the
blow. As a result of this miraculous interference which Charlemagne had attributed to the Archangel of the Grail, he had
recognised that the very hand of God was protecting an innocent man. The Emperor had implored forgiveness of his former
friend and adviser, offering him any gift he should desire as a
sign of royal grace. Hugo had asked Charles for the most
precious reliquary in Christendom, the Praeputium Domini,
the relic of the first shedding of the blood at the circumcision of
Jesus.

No such events as these were to be found in known historical
records. Walter Johannes began to study the legends of the
whole Carolingian age in the hope that some vestige of these
strange happenings in one of his previous incarnations might
not have been expunged from them. After a long search in both
France and Germany, he found what he was looking for in a
little-known document in the archives of the library at Strasburg.

The legend written by a certain Peter Lyra was extant in

both Latin and German. It had been written down as late as 1672 but had been copied from a much earlier manuscript dating back to 1434 which had been destroyed by fire in Strasburg in 1870. And this document also had been copied from an even earlier work dating back to the early thirteenth century at the time that Wolfram von Eschenbach had sung his *Parsival* across Europe.

The enchanting manuscript of Peter Lyra, although in some instances historically inaccurate and exaggerated, contained a great deal of the life of Hugo of Tours as Walter Johannes himself had remembered it. For instance, the exalted position of Hugo at the Court of Charlemagne was both clearly and correctly stated.

"It was the custom of Charles to tackle nothing that was of importance without the counsel and help of the most excellent, the wisest and the most experienced men.

"For military purposes he availed himself of the services of the brave, dauntless and well-proved heroes Gerald, Roland, Theodorious, Rudolf. His royal court was ruled by Echardus and Volradus. The city and municipal affairs were entrusted to Eschinobaldus and Eginadus. Alcuinius, Albinus and Clement helped the King in science and learning when matters of great import called for solution.

"Likewise in this time there lived in the Kingdom a mighty and wealthy knight, Hugo by name. He was wedded to a matron, pious and retiring, generous and impeccable both in word and deed, whose name was Aba. Her liege and spouse was the gentlest of all men; of noble birth, mighty in all matters of the world, peace loving at home, brave and daring in warfare, wealthy of estate, a patron of the poor, generous towards strangers, kindly and gracious towards his own kindred. He ranked first and foremost in the King's grace. None other's converse did the King like better, and none other's counsel sought he than Hugo's. He was the King's most confidential, chief and noblest, dearest servitor. Above all His Majesty felt assured that he was not only a constant lover of truth and justice, but also intelligent, prudent, of good intent and wholly imbued with honesty."

Here too he found the story of the men who plotted the downfall of Hugo.

"The shadow is the disfavour of the body, but it is also the inalienable companion of virtue. With envious eyes it always watches the favour gained by chivalrous deeds and virtues. Socrates has well said, that for the ungodly nothing is harder to endure than the happiness of the pious. They are in truth the spider's brood, sucking poison from the loveliest flowers. At the price of great harm Prince Hugo learnt the nature of these malevolent men, and a heavy toll he paid for the lesson. His princely virtues which had gained for him the love of so many filled his enemies with the gall of bitter hatred, and the poison of envy. Wherefore as men of piety cannot dwell side by side with those of evil mind, some of the envious courtiers began to plot how they could best upset Hugo's chariot of honour. In order to achieve this they deemed it right above all to make Hugo hateful in the eyes of the King and to deprive him of the King's favour—thus they talked among themselves. Unless Hugo be lifted out of the saddle of grace, he will never be caught in the meshes of misfortune. For he who is protected by the favour of sceptre and crown is far too safe. . . ."

The manuscript told the whole story of the false accusations laid against Hugo, about his miserable existence in prison and how the King found him guilty of treason and condemned him to death. And then there followed a chapter entitled "How and in what manner Duke Hugo was released from death by the special help of God."

". . . Meanwhile Duke Hugo, humbly submitting himself to his death, had put off his apparel and bared his neck, and with eyes bound and knees bent, giving himself up to God, he offered his head to the stroke of the axe—in complete and willing expectation of the blow about to descend.

"But as the executioner approached from behind, raising the sword and intending to strike, a sudden unexpected fear, never before experienced, seized him in such a manner than he turned round and round and asked in astonishment: 'What is this? What does this mean? Whose voice is it? Whence this command? Am I to put my sword back in the sheath? Shall I, covered with shame, at the risk of losing my life, withdraw from this spot without having accomplished the deed? But I know not what this is; I feel within me no strength, no force, no power. I shall protest to all those present that I can go no further, you can do with me as you please, I can no more.' "

After describing the executioner's further reluctance to fulfil his task and the consequent wrath of the crowds, the manuscript goes on to tell of the King's personal reaction to this potentially seditious situation.

"Finally, when it was realised that all the cries of encouragement to the executioner were in vain, and as moreover, none could be found who would strike the blow in view of the miracle consummated before all eyes, the King was seized with a sudden pallor. Fearing he might become a laughing stock of his people and dreading that this might give rise to sedition and rebellion, the King was seized with great wrath which he vented thus: 'Have I lived to see the day when even the last of my subjects refuses to submit obediently to my orders? What? Am I to suffer in my realm, at my Court, in the midst of my most privy councillors,— the presence of a convicted traitor plotting the downfall of me and my crown? I will not tolerate it. I will not endure it. Hugo must die even if I should have to stain my royal hands with his blood.' "

But when the King drew his sword to despatch Hugo, his arm became rigid and immovable, and the sinews hardened, in such a manner that he was neither able to drop his arm nor his sword.

"Perceiving this the King took council with himself, recovered his spirit and decided to try other means. And thus he spake: 'Now I see how much I have erred, I acknowledge the just and mighty hand of the Most High, the Protector and Refuge of the innocent. Come hither, my beloved Hugo, let me embrace thee, thou whom God has protected against my injustice. Come hither thou faithful honest hero; through thy prayer reconcile me with God,

Who is rightfully angry, and beseech Him that it may please His Omnipotence to restore my arm to its former strength.' ''

When Hugo of Tours was released and the blindfold removed from his eyes, the King was miraculously healed. Charlemagne offered his friend anything he so desired in recompense of the wrong he had done to him.

"Whereupon great joy and jubilation broke out throughout the whole Court and spread throughout the whole city. This induced the King to make a new covenant with Hugo, offering him thereby not merely honour and rank but desiring to confer on him all royal grace."

Under the title "Of Duke Hugo's chosen relic and other precious gifts", Lyra's manuscript described a precious thing kept in a silver casket which Charlemagne had received from Patriarch Fortunatus.

"In as much as Hugo remembered well that such a treasure existed and although he knew it was held in high esteem by the King, he took no delight in anything else but in this precious and proven treasure.
" 'This alone I request and demand that your Royal Majesty may gracefully grant and bestow on me the gifts sent over from Jerusalem among which are contained a portion of the Holy Body of our Saviour and Redeemer, a piece of the Holy Cross and Blood shed for us, above all because this alone will blot out and make good all the insults poured on me.'
"This request stirred the King's heart. 'My dearest Hugo, thou demandest more than if thou hadst claimed my whole kingdom. Nevertheless, in order to fulfil my word I will command that thy request be granted even if it be though my loss. And what has been my comfort and joy shall henceforth be thine.' ''

The Austrian science graduate researching his former life in the Carolingian age could remember with exactness how Hugo and his wife, Aba, had kept the relics in a chapel in their own home while they decided where the precious items should rightfully be sent. And he could remember how Hugo had personally designed the Cross which was built to contain these relics.

> "After the work had been completed Hugo put inside it the Praeputium Domini of bloody circumcision of Our Lord; likewise a fragment of the true Cross, and some of the Holy Blood and several other precious relics, in order the better to preserve them."

It was just in his perception of how Hugo of Tours had found a resting place for this Cross that the young Austrian researcher had doubted his own supersensible faculties. For memories had flooded into his soul of Hugo setting the Cross containing the reliquaries on the hump of a Camel so that the *workings of fate* would lead the dumb animal to the place where the Praeputium Domini would be truly venerated as a sign of the chastity demanded of the Knights of the Grail.

He found confirmation of these strange happenings under the title: "How the Sacred Cross was laid on a camel and how Divine Providence was called upon to accompany it on its way."

> "Hugo remembered with approval what the Philistines had used of old when they placed the Ark of God, acquired by the sword, on a vehicle drawn by milch kine, with the behest that it would be brought to its destination without the help of man.
>
> "Whereupon he too placed his trust in Divine Providence and commanded that this treasure, given over and devoted to God, should be laid on a Camel, but with no driver or runner to accompany it, so that it might be led by God's grace and care.
>
> "In order to protect the sacred Cross from storm, rain and any other emergency on the journey, the sacred cross was enclosed in a chest, and books and writings were placed in another convenient box. Both were then fastened to either side of the camel, in undoubted hope and trust that it would convey the burden to that spot which should be pleasing to God.
>
> "But to secure news and to have some witness of the hoped for achievement Hugo thought it fit to send five trusted knights,

renowned for their rank and virtue, who were charged to follow the footsteps of the camel until they should reach the spot where the riderless animal chose to lay down his burden. . . ."

Hugo of Tours then addressed the Camel before it began its journey:

" 'Thou who bearest these sacred things and to whose care we have entrusted them, take heed of every step of the way in order that these treasures may not be dishonoured by a chance fall, nor suffer harm or damage of any sort. Go whither God lead and guide thee, without anything unforeseen befalling thee: Go over hill and dale, through forest and heath, through towns, boroughs and villages and, by means of the bells attached to the neck, ask where the resting place may be, and where that heir is to be found to whom the sacred treasure laid on thee is to be given over.' "

Finally Hugo gave his orders to the accompanying knights:

" 'And you witnesses, take care of this messenger, hasten not nor goad him on, let him not suffer hunger or thirst, at our expense provide for all his needs. Go in the name of the Lord and diligently take note of all your paths, the towns and boroughs, so that you might give account of all your journey.' "

The manuscript then described the unhindered journey of the camel:

"Having received this farewell greeting the camel bravely set out on its journey as if it had been given a special sign, and as if its path had been made smooth and even.

"It journeyed over meadows and fields, climbed over hill and dale, penetrated through forest and heath, took the road through Burgundy to France, and straight to its capital, Paris, rousing all men everywhere by its bells, so that all people ran to their windows in order to watch the strange procession and glorify God for what he had so wondrously ordained. . . . Each and every man prayed that the Camel might end its journey and that such

happiness might befall his own house so that the precious burden
might be laid down with him.

"The citizens and inhabitants of Paris would have welcomed it
if the camel had stayed with them for their protection, more
especially because handsome buildings and churches were already
there to receive the sacred treasure. But it was not the pleasure
of God that this should come to pass, rather did the camel still
continue the journey, nor could it be led astray or stopped."

The camel continued its journey through Alsace where it
ended its journey and laid down its burden in Niedermunster.

"The ever-spreading cry had gone so far that it seemed likely
that the conjecture would become truth, more especially because
the Camel departed neither to the left nor to the right, impressing
its footsteps in the hard rock as if it were wax, which might easily
have led the closely following worshippers to surmise that here
was the spot where the strange guest would halt.

"Whereupon they followed it all the more fervently until,
guided and directed by the tracks left in the Niedermunster
region, they clearly perceived the convent on the hill.

"The stranger led until now by Divine Providence, stopped in
view of the Convent it was nearing, just as if it wished to gaze at
the building in wonderment—but presently it again pursued its
way and when it came to the gate of the convent for noblewomen
it stamped on the ground with its feet and knocked at the gateway
by means of a ring which hung there, in order to enter into the
doors of justice and rest therein. . . . whereupon the stranger now
entered (for the gates had been opened to it), giving over the
heritage entrusted to its care, and demanding as it were, a token
or a testimony of its accomplished task.

When Walter Stein visited Niedermunster to continue his
researches, he found that according to an ancient tradition the
spot where the camel had halted was marked by an imprint of its
foot. A local historian, who did not himself know anything of
the historical background of the beast's journey, pointed out to
him the engraving of a camel's foot on a softly sloping rock in
the walled square of the ruins of the Chapel of the Knights of

St. James. (It is still to be seen there to this day near the curve of the road where the Hotel of St. James originally stood before being burned down.)

In following up this extraordinary chain of events recollected from a previous life on earth, he had not been motivated solely by curiosity, although this had played an important part. Nor because he now saw limitless possibilities for a new technique of historical research in which factual evidence was unearthed in the wake of transcendent memories of former incarnations. Beyond these considerations he was interested in the whole matter of the possession of the Praeputium Domini. By tradition the holder of this most unusual and precious relic of the first shedding of the blood was the leader of the whole impulse of the Grail in the ninth century.

It appeared to him to be of vital importance that the relic had been brought to the Niedermunster Convent which was under the patronage of St. Odile. St. Odile was the patron saint of the Knights who sought the Holy Grail and the Odilienberg was the very heart of the Grail territory in the Middle Ages.

Odilia was the daughter of Eticho (sometimes called Adalrich) who inherited the dukedom of Alsace in A.D. 666. When he discovered that his daughter had been born blind, he asked himself: "Who has sinned, the parents or the child?" When he heard whisperings at his Court that he himself was responsible for the child's blindness, he decided to put her to death. The mother escaped with the baby to Regensburg. Erhard, the Bishop of Regensburg, was inspired in a dream to seek out and baptise the child. At her baptism, her sight was restored. Bishop Erhard compared the miracle to that of Christ's healing the man born blind. "The Light of the World" has bestowed the grace of sight upon her, he said, and thus he named her Odilia, Sol Dei, Sun of God.

After her sight was restored Odilia was brought back to her father's Court at Adelrichsheim (Arlesheim) where all went well for her until she reached marriageable age but flatly refused her father's order to marry. On this occasion she went into hiding in the ancient hermitage which was later the retreat of Treverezent, the teacher of the Grail wisdom.

When reconciliation had been made between father and daughter, Odilia, now a mature and saintly character, founded Christian Cloisters in the Hochburg and in the valley below at Niedermünster. In the heights she meditated and was inspired by visions of the Revelation of St. John; in the valley she healed the sick who came to her from all parts of Europe. In both centres, and in the surrounding monasteries, the mysteries of the Holy Grail were cherished and guarded. Novices were prepared step by step (*graduale*) for Christian Initiation.

Walter Stein discovered a history of the Hohenberg (or Odilienberg) and a short biography of St. Odilia in the works of Dionysius Albrecht, who had himself unearthed the real significance and the mission of the line of St. Odilia which became the 'Grail Family':

> "This ducal line became widespread, as once the line of Jacob, viz.: from the centre of Alsace towards evening in France, towards the morning in Roman and Austrian realms, towards mid-day in Spain, and towards mid-night in Saxony and Brandenburg. Just as Jacob's seed, according to the stars in their order, spread to all points of the compass, so also did the race of Odilia."

It was in this point in his researches that Walter Stein began to understand the significant passages in Wolfram von Eschenbach's *Parsival* in which the origins of the Grail lineage are also described:

> "Kyot, the wise Master, set about to trace this tale in Latin books, to see where there had been a people, dedicated to purity and worthy of caring for the Grail. He read the Chronicles of the lands, in Britain and elsewhere, in France and in Ireland, and in Anschau* he found the tale. There he read the true story of Mazadan, and the exact record of all his family was written there."

---

* Anschau, nearly always wrongly associated with Anjou, is not a geographical place or territory. The realm of Anschau is the world of the revelation of the Archangel of the Grail, the Time Spirit.

216

In Albrecht's history of the Odilienberg, he found a full genealogy of the bloodline of the Grail family in whose blood was seated powerful clairvoyant faculties. He was delighted to find the name of Hugo of Tours inscribed in this magical genealogical tree. He also recognised the names of those personalities at the Court of Charlemagne and his successors who had been the close friends of Hugo; all men and women who had cultivated the devout spiritual life in search of the Grail in deep contrast to the dogmatic Christianity of Rome.

He wondered whether these members of the Grail family in the Middle Ages had also been born again in the nineteenth and twentieth centuries and if his destiny would bring him into close contact with them again. Though he did not know it at this time, he was shortly to meet and be reunited in mutual recognition with many of them. They were to become the circle of Initiates whom Adolf Hitler was to call his greatest enemies and the real spiritual antagonists of Nazi Germany.

In following up the bloodline of Odilia into later centuries, he discovered that nearly all the great dynasties of Europe could trace their origins back to the ducal line of Eticho in the seventh century. And he was staggered to find that all the holders of the Spear of Destiny from Charlemagne onwards until the death of Emperor Franz Joseph, the last of the Hapsburgs, had the blood of the Grail family in their veins. Adolf Hitler was to become the only holder of the Spear who could not claim this descent.

And now he understood with great clarity why Landulf II of Capua and the ring of black adepts reaching from Byzantium across Europe to Spain had sought to bring the members of this gifted family to spiritual blindness and moral degradation. And why their efforts to obliterate the spiritual guidance of Europe's Royal Houses was carried out with the complicity of Rome.

The most instructive recollections, which he experienced of his former life as Hugo of Tours, concerned this Frankish nobleman's journey to the East on which he visited Jerusalem and then proceeded to the Court of Haroun-el-Raschid in Baghdad. Hugo was accompanied on this embassy by Bishop

Haito of Basel. An earlier embassy had been instigated by Charibert of Laon, the grandfather of Charlemagne. At that time Europe was hard pressed by Islam, especially so through Spain and Southern France. And it was for this reason that Ambassadors were sent to the Persian Caliphs who still had the greatest influence over the Arab world. The Persians, who had earlier been defeated by Islam but had risen again on account of their wisdom and statecraft, were the natural allies of the Christian world.

By the time Hugo arrived in Baghdad, the whole situation was sadly reversed. Haroun-el-Raschid, on his return from a visit to Mecca, had murdered all the leading members of the noble Persian Barnicide family who had up to that time ruled the regime. Though El-Raschid had sent gifts and words of flattery to the famous Charlemagne, his sympathies were solely with the Muslim world and its encroachment on Europe from all sides.

During his long stay in Asia Minor, Hugo took every opportunity to learn the teachings of the Persian religion. He recognised in Zoroastrianism a star wisdom which had anticipated the Incarnation of Christ. In Baghdad too he learned about Manichaeism and about its great prophet Mani who had been cruelly martyred for his Christian teachings—teachings which bore a remarkable similarity to the path to the Holy Grail. And there also he studied the alchemical works of Aristotle, translated into Arabic, which had not at that time been seen in the West.

When Hugo returned to Europe, Charlemagne was dead. In the division of the Carolingian Empire, he supported Lothair who had married his daughter. For some years he resided in the middle kingdom of Lombardy. Finally, in his old age—he lived to be over a hundred years old—he retired to the lonely hermitage at Arlesheim where he became the teacher of the wisdom of the Holy Grail.

It was only after Walter Stein had discovered this hermitage in Arlesheim, where the aged Hugo had taught his Grail pupils the spiritual significance of the Blood of Christ and the real

218

mystery of the Sacraments, that he reached a yet higher level of transcendent consciousness and a further insight into even earlier incarnations. In this manner he was able to identify those other faces which had originally appeared to him inscribed around the edge of the Stone (or precious jewel) which is also called the Grail.

The central figure in this chain of earth lives interested him most deeply. It was the face of a bearded Rabbi. And now he knew that this was the face of Joseph of Arimathea. And by the grace of God he relived a few brief moments in the life of this almost legendary figure who became the first earthly guardian of the Holy Grail.

He was hurrying from the City of Jerusalem towards the Mount of Golgotha where Jesus Christ had been crucified that day. He carried with him a signed document from Pontius Pilate which gave him the right to bury the body of the Lord. In his hand he held the Jasper Bowl in which he would collect the Holy Blood—the same dish in which Jesus Christ had placed the consecrated bread and wine at the Last Supper which took place in the upper room of his (Joseph's) house.

And when he came near to the scene of the Crucifixion, he witnessed how the soldiers of the Pharisees were mutilating the bodies of the two thieves crucified on either side of Jesus Christ. A Roman centurion reined his horse and charged towards the central Cross, plunging a Spear into the side of the Saviour. And there flowed forth from the wound both blood and water. And immediately it was as though the very sun itself was eclipsed, for the world fell into total darkness and a mighty thunderstorm arose. And he fell to his knees and worshipped before the body of the Lord which shone with holy light in the darkness. . . .

CHAPTER SIXTEEN

ONCE IN A THOUSAND YEARS

"And when the thousand years are expired, Satan will be loosed from his prison."

Book of Revelation 20, 7

Famished, manacled and awaiting the death sentence, a young German Staff Major named Albrecht Haushofer sat in a cell in the Lehrterstrasse Prison in Berlin and meditated on the fate of the German nation.

Albrecht Haushofer had been arrested as a conspirator of the circle who had plotted the final abortive attempt to assassinate Adolf Hitler at the Wolf-Schanze Headquarters in East Prussia on July 20th, 1944.

Day by day throughout the latter half of 1944 and the spring of 1945, while he awaited his inevitable execution, news reached the prison of the terrible fate of all those concerned even indirectly with the bomb plot.

"The criminals will get short shrift from me," Adolf Hitler had raged with an unquenchable desire for blood-letting revenge. "No long speeches. No military tribunals. We'll drag these traitors before the People's Court with lightning speed. Two hours after sentence, they'll hang without mercy."

The first grisly session of the People's Court sent a Field Marshal, three Generals, and four junior staff officers to the gallows, personal friends of Albrecht Haushofer. That same night Hitler watched a film of their execution, gleefully applauding the spectacle of eight naked men slowly strangling in nooses made of piano wire and suspended from meat hooks.

Two months before the war ended the death roll included some 4,000 people who were believed to have had some connection with the conspiracy to overthrow the Nazi régime. Even Field Marshal Rommel was not spared, committing suicide by agreement with Hitler in order to save his wife and family from the People's Court.

General Henning von Tresckow on the Eastern Front, who led the conspiracy, summed up the feelings of his fellow conspirators: "Everybody will now turn on us and cover us with abuse. But my conviction remains unshaken—we have done the right thing. Hitler is not only the arch-enemy of Germany: he is the arch-enemy of the world. In a few hours I shall stand before God, answering for my actions and for my omissions. I thank God I shall be able to uphold with a clear conscience all that I have done in the fight against Hitler."

Worst of all, the pogrom had broken the backbone of the moral resistance to Nazi tyranny formerly provided by the élite of the Officer Corps. Leading generals, shamefacedly seeking to save their own skins, handed over hundreds of their fellow officers to be tortured by the Gestapo and butchered by the Totenkopf SS.

Because the General Staff had failed to close its ranks against the threats of the brutal ex-Corporal and his henchmen, the great traditions of the German army were dishonoured and disgraced. All officers were now forced to give the Nazi salute and to swear undying loyalty to Adolf Hitler and the Nazi cause. The last moral stronghold within the Third Reich had permitted itself to be trampled down.

What baffled Albrecht Haushofer, a student of Oriental philosophy who had spent a year with the lamas in Tibet, was why such a crude and demented personality as Hitler, a conscious tool of evil powers, was allowed to escape unharmed as if by a miracle, though his continued survival meant the prolonging of the war and an unimaginable mountain of destruction throughout Germany.

In a sudden flash of intuition he perceived why it was that Adolf Hitler *had* to survive until Germany had been totally over-run by her enemies. How else could each and every German be taught the price of the failure to evaluate correctly the meaning of individual spiritual freedom and the duty to shoulder squarely a sense of personal responsibility towards his neigh-bour, unless every town, village and hamlet over the length and the breadth of the Fatherland was reduced to ruins and occu-pied by enemy troops. Only in such a manner could the entire population be given a savage visual image of the ultimate consequence of permitting the demonic Nazi regime to arise in their midst.

He now understood clearly that if Germany had been pre-maturely freed as the result of the assassination of Hitler, the insidious idea of "the stab in the back" would have arisen once again to mould future scenes of tyrannical dictatorship and further attempts at world conquest. And beyond this, he realized now why it was that his beloved officer Corps and the General Staff Corps had to be brought so low in the eyes of the nation. For it was in the officer Corps and the General Staff that this dangerous myth had been nurtured after it had originated from the lips of General Erich Ludendorff.

It was common knowledge throughout Germany that Hitler's life had been saved by a miraculous coincidence when he should have been blown to pieces by the bomb explosion at the OKW.

The courageous leader of the assassins, Colonel Stauffen-berg, had placed the bomb in a bulging brief case right under the table where Hitler was standing. In the final seconds before the time mechanism set off the bomb, an officer on Hitler's staff found that the brief case obstructed his leg-room under the table. Hardly aware of what he was doing, he shifted the case out of the way, shoving it over to the other side of a stout table support. This last-second act, performed subconsciously, saved Hitler from instant obliteration.

Adolf Hitler publicly proclaimed that his life had been saved by providence so that he should continue his world-historic mission as leader of the German people. But Albrecht Haus-hofer knew only too well the real nature of the evil powers working through and around Hitler, for his own father, Pro-fessor Karl Haushofer, the Master Magician of the Nazi Party, had been instrumental in initiating the Führer into a percep-tion of *how* the evil powers worked within the historical process. It was his father, too, who had unwisely advised Hitler to remove the Spear of Destiny from the Hofburg in Vienna and to place it in Nuremberg, from whence its evil powers could emanate from the very heart of the Nazi Movement.

According to the ancient legend, the life of an evil adept hold-ing the Spear of Destiny was protected until the very moment it passed from his possession. It was not difficult to under-stand how the black magic powers associated with this talisman were working to protect the person of the Führer against his adversaries. But what amazed Albrecht Haushofer was the dis-covery that yet higher and beneficent powers used the working of the evil to bring to fruition their own moral aims and pur-poses for humanity. In this case, the prolonging of Hitler's life by the powers of evil would cause just that measure of destruc-tion and degradation which would ultimately be the moral sal-vation of the whole nation. Along such lines of thought, Albrecht Haushofer gained a deep insight into the workings of the Law of Karma in moulding the fate of an entire people.

Once a convinced Nazi, Albrecht had first become dis-illusioned when he grasped the real nature and extent of Adolf Hitler's personal ambitions. It was not long before he became convinced that Germany had fallen into the hands of demonic powers. The extent of his disillusionment reached tragic pro-portions when he came to realise that his own father had been responsible for unleashing the Beast of the Apocalypse upon humanity.

During the last four years of his life, he set down his thoughts in the form of sonnets, which may one day find a worthy place in the history of German literature. He wrote his last sonnet in the condemned cell. It was discovered in his jacket after a detachment of SS had machine-gunned him down beside Klaus

Bonhöffer, the brother of Pastor Dietrich Bonhöffer, one of the very few churchmen in Germany prepared to pay the ultimate price for his Christian convictions.

The sonnet entitled *The Father* recalls an ancient legend of the Orient which bears a striking resemblance to a verse in the *Book of Revelation*: "And when the thousand years are expired, Satan will be loosed from his prison" (Chapter 20, verse 7).

According to this Eastern legend which Albrecht Haushofer had learned in Tibet, the Spirits of unholy Powers were incarcerated, sealed countless fathoms below in the darkness of the ocean. There they remained imprisoned by the beneficent hand of God, until, *once in a thousand years*, it was fated that a fisherman had it within his free choice to release the dreaded fiend, unless he cast his terrible catch straight back into the depths.

> For my Father the lot was cast . . .
> Once again the demon had to be repulsed
> and thrust back into his prison . . .
> My father broke the seal—
> He sensed not the breath of the Evil One
> But set him free to roam the world.

THE MASTER MAGICIAN

The Two Faces of Karl Haushofer

It is understandable that Albrecht Haushofer did not wish to believe that his own father had sensed the real nature of the Luciferic Principality inhabiting the soul of Adolf Hitler. Yet there can be no doubt that Karl Haushofer not only felt the breath of the Apocalyptic Beast possessing the demented ex-Corporal, he also sought quite consciously and with malicious intent to teach Hitler how to unleash its powers against humanity in an attempt to conquer the world.

A heated controversy has arisen in recent years as to whether, in fact, Karl Haushofer had any influence at all upon Adolf Hitler. Such a controversy has only come about because uninformed circles are totally unaware that this remarkable and enigmatic man had two entirely separate facets to his character.

The figure of the energetic and incontestably brilliant Professor of Geo-Politics is well known to everybody, and this side of his life is fully documented. But Karl Haushofer took every possible precaution to conceal the other side of his nature and his activities as the leader of a secret community of Initiates and an authority on every aspect of the "Secret Doctrine". And yet for anybody with a modicum of genuine occult insight, the hidden initiate is implicit in every word the Professor wrote and in his every act carried out on the political scene in Munich in the years immediately following the end of World War I.

We will begin by describing briefly his work and background from a purely external point of view, so that we can follow up by tracing within it that esoteric stream of satanism through which he sought to raise Germany to a pinnacle of world power.

Karl Haushofer was born in Bavaria in 1869. He chose a career as a professional soldier, his intellectual gifts and meticulous attention to detail quickly gaining him an appointment to the Staff Corps. An outstanding grasp of Oriental affairs led to a series of appointments with the German Intelligence Service in India and Japan. He studied several Eastern languages including Japanese which he learned to speak fluently whilst serving as a senior military observer at the German Embassy in Tokyo. He also mastered Sanskrit and made his own translations of some of the Hindu and Buddhist texts, became an authority on Oriental mysticism, and confessed himself to be an uncompromising disciple of Schopenhauer.

It was not until the age of forty-five, and only then because certain dispensations excused full attendance at University, that he obtained his doctorate with a brilliant thesis on Political Geography. He served on the Western Front throughout World War I and earned a reputation as one of Germany's most outstanding young Generals.

The theme of his thesis in Geo-Politics was a development of Ratzel's idea that the decay of every nation was the result of its declining space concepts. "Space is not only the vehicle of power; it is power," he told his first group of students, which included Rudolf Hess as well as some others who also became leading Nazis. "I intend to teach Political-Geography as a weapon to reawaken Germany to fulfil its destined greatness. I shall re-educate the whole nation to an awareness of the role of geography in history so that every young German shall cease to think parochially but think instead in terms of whole continents."

This was powerful medicine to the students of a defeated nation which had just been forced to hand over part of its own home territory and all its colonies to the victors.

226

One single magic word originated in Haushofer's first lecture to a crowded auditorium at Munich University—a word which was to justify a new wave of aggression from a people who considered themselves stabbed in the back—*Lebensraum*!

His ideas went far beyond the limited scope of all his predecessors in the field of Political Geography. He was not in the least interested in an objective analysis of geographical facts but associated geographical ideas only with a provocative theory of aggressive territorial expansion on a global scale. His appeal for *Lebensraum* for the German people and his plans to achieve it were no more than a justification for international brigandage on a grand scale, virtually a blueprint to world conquest.

At the same time he clothed geography in a veil of racial mysticism, providing a reason for the Germans to return to those areas in the hinterland of Asia from which it was generally believed the Aryan Race originated. In this subtle way he incited the German nation towards the conquest of the whole of Eastern Europe and beyond to that vast inner area of Asia which extends 2,500 miles from west to east between the Volga and the Yangtze rivers and includes in its most southerly aspect the mountains of Tibet. It was Haushofer's opinion that whoever gained complete control of this heartland, developed its economic resources and organised its military defence, would achieve unassailable world supremacy.

His theories spread like wildfire throughout Germany and became the evil nourishment of that false sublimation of the German Folk-Soul which followed the degradation of defeat in war. By 1935, Geo-Politics were taught to every schoolchild in the Third Reich and this stimulation to geo-political consciousness throughout the whole German people was a propaganda feat that even Goebbels was never able to match.

"Every single one of us is in some way an actor on the stage of world politics," Haushofer proclaimed over the radio to millions of eager listeners. "Even in the most humble place, as the willing follower of a God-given leader, we help shape the future of our people, be it only the right echo at the right time and in the right place. . . . "Do not be narrow-minded but think in terms of great spaces, in whole continents and oceans, and thereby direct your course with that of your Führer."

The ex-General with an academic flair for turning dull facts into patriotic inspiration wrote altogether forty volumes and 400 essays and founded the *Geo-Political Review*. In the wake of his personal inspiration some 3,420 books on Geo-Politics were catalogued between the two World Wars!

It is widely known that Rudolf Hess introduced Karl Haushofer to Adolf Hitler, and that the professor, armed with tomes on Geo-Politics, frequently visited Hitler while he was writing *Mein Kampf* in Landsberg Fortress after the failure of the Munich *Putsch* in 1923.

"What Haushofer contributed at a given point in Hitler's psychological evolution was a line of argument, a thesis, and a series of geographical facts heavily weighted with political significance. In *Mein Kampf* a new strain appears. In addition to the old clichés we find frequent invocation to *Lebensraum*, discussions between living area and outward security, evaluation of space as furnishing depth in defence, appeals for natural frontiers, a balance of landpower versus sea power, and the place of geography in military strategy. This graduation from rabble rousing in earlier chapters of *Mein Kampf* to the elementary stages of Geo-politics is too striking and too circumstantial to be a mere coincidence, in view of the type of reading matter that Haushofer admitted he had brought to Hitler and Hess in Landsberg prison. In chapter 14 of *Mein Kampf* one can almost feel the presence of Haushofer, although the lines were written by Hess at the dictation of Hitler. . . .

"What Haushofer did was to hand a sheathed sword of conquest from his arsenal of scholarly research. Hitler unsheathed the blade, sharpened the edge, and threw away the scabbard. . . ."

"Geo-Politics would now function in the formation of an élite in Hitlerian Germany in much the same manner as the twin hypothesis of class war and dialectic materialism had served in rationalising Communism in Soviet Russia. The spurious science gave a respectability to a conspiracy which began in a Munich Beer

Hall until its final evolution in an Empire bigger than that of Genghis Khan."

(*Total Power:* Edmund A. Walsh. Faber & Faber.)

After Adolf Hitler came to power in 1933, Professor Haushofer was instrumental in preparing the spadework for the Tripartite Alliance. Though he did not himself actually make the agreements which enlisted Japan's co-operation in a plan for world conquest, all the conferences between Japanese officials and Nazi statesmen took place at his home near Munich. He called these cosy get-togethers "Cultural Co-operation". He saw Japan as the brother nation to Germany, the *Herrenvolk* of the Orient. It was no mere coincidence that Matsuoko, Japanese Foreign Minister, returned to Tokyo after discussion with Haushofer to voice the opinion: "A nation is only offered the opportunity to greatness once in every thousand years." The opportunity was "Pearl Harbour" and there can be no doubt that this carefully planned and unscrupulous attack without declaration of war was the inspiration of Karl Haushofer.

All the Nazi invasions, one after the other, followed the broad pattern of his teachings, and Adolf Hitler used his methods of geo-political strategy, his vocabulary, his maps and his arguments.

Some people have sought to excuse Haushofer on the grounds that he merely produced certain new theories in political geography which the Nazis put into operation in a manner he never anticipated. But there can be no doubt whatsoever that he was only too conscious of the terrible implications of every word he wrote, aware that the fruition of his master-plans would involve rivers of human blood and suffering among the enslaved minorities of the so-called inferior races (his terminology) after the German war machine had pounded them into surrender. For Haushofer was a member of the Academy of German Law, and, as such, became a leading participant in the work group which prepared the tyrannous legislation imposed on conquered peoples. In this way he made the preparation for the Concentration Camps in which mass killing was to become a state industry with by-products. And yet, as if this unenviable record of his public deeds were not in itself gruesome enough, there stood behind the fine upright figure of the German General and the studious countenance of the Bavarian professor, another far more sinister figure—the scheming Master-Magician who contrived to unleash the full fury of the Beast of the Apocalypse upon humanity.

We have described how Dietrich Eckart contrived to develop and open the centres in the astral body of Adolf Hitler, giving him the possibility of vision into the macrocosm and means of communication with the powers of darkness. And the manner in which he aided his pupil in defining and utilising his memories of a past incarnation as the Landulf of Capua in the ninth century. It was now the turn of Karl Haushofer to contribute degrees of initiation of a far higher order, which served to expand and metamorphose the 'time organism' (etheric body) in Hitler teaching him to consider the evolution of man in tremendous vistas of time.

What in fact he was unveiling for Hitler in this respect were the teachings of the 'Secret Doctrine', of which his system of Geo-Politics was but a cunningly pointed exteriorisation, a means to channel the race consciousness of the German people in order to prepare the nation for an attempt to conquer the world.

By divulging *The Secret Doctrine*, Haushofer expanded Hitler's time consciousness and presented to him a global panorama of earth evolution, tracing the working of the hierarchies of evil and illustrating the manner in which such powers have opposed the true development of mankind at every stage in the evolution of human consciousness. Through such instruction, Haushofer awakened Hitler to the real motives of the Luciferic Principality which possessed him so that he could become the conscious vehicle of its evil intent in the twentieth century.

And finally, Haushofer himself took on the role of Mephistopheles when he initiated Adolf Hitler into the occult significance of the blood and the part which occult blood rites would play in creating a magical mutation in the Aryan Race, a mutation which would bring about a new stage in human evolution, the birth of the "Superman".

During the first two decades of the present century there arose the feeling within the nucleus of German intellectual life that the God-given direction of human evolution had come to an end, and that man would be forever trapped in the intellectual sterility of three-dimensional consciousness, unless he took the responsibility for his future development into his own hands.

Out of the despair which followed disillusionment in the dialectic materialism of the nineteenth century, there emerged the recognition that a new age of freedom had been born in which man himself held it within his own hands to bring about the redemption and re-animation of every aspect of life. At the same time it was believed that this new leap in human development could not take place without the appearance on earth of quite exceptional individuals who would carry a spiritual renaissance into every sphere of science, art and religion. It was within this atmosphere of prophetic awareness that the idea of the coming German Messiah was born.

Many different prophecies were made regarding the nature of the new Messiah, or indeed a whole number of Messiahs, who would bring about a renewal of philosophy, religion, medicine, poetry, music, painting, sculpture, indeed, every facet of human activity.

Among the various groups of intellectuals who believed that no aspect of human life could be awakened and redeemed without the appearance of a personal saviour were the Pan-Germanic and racially orientated fraternity. Here the concept of Friedrich Nietzsche's "Superman" came to the forefront, the manifestation of the Man-God who would lead the Aryan race in the conquest of the world and set up a new order which would last for a thousand years.

It is only within this context of messianic expectation that we can understand the real significance of the strange 'Essay Competition' which took place at Munich University in 1920. A German millionaire living in Brazil offered a large cash prize to the student who rendered the best thesis on the theme: "How must the Man be constituted who will lead Germany back to her former heights of glory?"

The winner of this competition was a certain Rudolf Hess. His much-praised essay painted the picture of a coming Messiah bearing a quite remarkable similarity to the 'Anti-Christ' of the *Protocols of Zion*. It also bore the stamp in every line of the thinking of Professor Karl Haushofer, personal tutor to Rudolf Hess at the Geo-Political department of the University.

Rudolf Hess had spoken in great detail about Adolf Hitler to Karl Haushofer who appears in the first instance to have been singularly unimpressed by the rabble-rousing leader of the Nazi movement. The ex-General refused to believe that the Corporal with the Chaplin moustache and outlandish manners could ever become the saviour of the German peoples. It was only when Haushofer attended the trial after the unsuccessful Nazi *Putsch* in Munich in 1923 that he began to grasp the real measure and potentiality of leadership in Adolf Hitler.

Sitting in a seat reserved for him at the Court held in the old Infantry School in the Blutenbergstrasse, Haushofer was mesmerised by the oratory and audacity of this then unknown revolutionary whose very presence seemed to belittle the famous figure of General Ludendorff in the dock beside him.

> "The man who is born to be a dictator is not compelled" cried Adolf Hitler before the assembled correspondents from the world press. "He wills it. He is not driven forward, but drives himself . . . . The man who feels called upon to govern a people has no right to say, 'If you want me or summon me, I will co-operate.' No! It is his duty to step forward."

Day by day as he fenced and lunged back at the judges and prosecutors, Adolf Hitler rose higher in the estimation of the Professor who watched him with his customary cold detachment. On the final day of the trial Haushofer had already come to the conclusion that he was listening to the words of the man who would one day lead Germany in the conquest of the world.

"The army we have formed is growing from day to day," shouted Hitler. "I nourish the proud hope that one day the hour will come when these rough companies will grow into battalions, the battalions to regiments, the regiments to divisions, that the old cockade will be taken from the mud, that the old flags will wave again, that there will be a reconciliation at the last great divine judgement which we are prepared to face."

Adolf Hitler's final words which he flung at his judges before they pronounced judgement were particularly impressive and significant:

"It is not you, gentlemen, who pass judgement on us. That judgement is spoken by the eternal court of history. What judgement you will hand down I know. But that Court will not ask us 'Did you commit high treason or did you not?' That court will judge us, the Quartermaster General of the old Army, his officers and soldiers, as Germans who wanted only the good of their own people and Fatherland, who wanted to fight and die. You may pronounce us as guilty a thousand times over, but the Goddess of the eternal court of history will smile and tear to tatters the brief of the state prosecutor and the sentence of this court. For she acquits us."

Adolf Hitler was despatched to Landsberg Fortress to serve a five-year sentence, where he was joined by Rudolf Hess who had belatedly given himself up and confessed his part in the attempt to overthrow the Bavarian Government. Hitler was treated more like an honoured guest than a prisoner. He was given a large room with a splendid view over the River Lech where a thousand years before Otto The Great had mustered his armies to move under the talisman of the Spear of Longinus against the fury of the marauding Magyars.

Although there was a careful watch over all of Adolf Hitler's activities within the fortress and a special scrutiny was kept on the identity and background of his guests, nobody objected to the apparently innocent visits of a professor of Political Geography from Munich University. Yet here in the summer of

1924 in the presence of Rudolf Hess, Karl Haushofer initiated Adolf Hitler into the "Secret Doctrine", a deed which was to have the most profound and shattering consequences for the whole world.

It is not within the scope of this book to give more than the very briefest details regarding the teachings of *The Secret Doctrine*, and in so doing, we must confine ourselves to the broadest outline of those aspects which shed especial light on the satanic nature of the occultism of the Nazi Party.

CHAPTER EIGHTEEN

THE SECRET DOCTRINE

The Origin of the Aryan Race in Atlantis

"There were *Giants* on the Earth in those days; and also after that when the *Sons of God* came in unto the daughters of men, and they bare children unto them, the same became mighty men which were of old, men of renown."

Genesis 6, 4.

When *The Secret Doctrine* first appeared among the initiates of ancient Tibet some 10,000 years ago, it was not taught in an intellectual manner nor passed down as a teaching from generation to generation. Only when the centres in the astral body of a novice had been brought to fruition and his etheric organism fully expanded could *The Secret Doctrine* be revealed to him.

In final preparation for such a moment of revelation the would-be initiate learned step by step to read the cosmic script, precisely the same process which the later traditions of the Grail called "learning the ABC's but without the art of Black Magic."

When the Third Eye had been opened to a full vision of the Akashic Record, the initiate became a living witness of the whole evolution of the world and of humanity. Travelling back through tremendous vistas of time, the very spirit origin of the earth and of man was unveiled to him, and he was able to follow the unfolding destiny of mankind through ever-changing conditions of life and cycles of development.*

The aspects of *The Secret Doctrine* which Haushofer passed on to Adolf Hitler concerned mainly the origins of the different races of mankind in that period of pre-history known to occult science as Atlantis, a civilisation which ran its course through many millennia in a lost continent on what is now the floor of the present Atlantic ocean.

Many of the valid descriptions which Karl Haushofer repeated to Adolf Hitler regarding the conditions of life in ancient Atlantis must appear fantastic and startling to minds which have been conditioned uncompromisingly to the sterile and petrified concepts of modern materialism.

Something of the astonishing nature of the environment, the extraordinary conditions of form, faculty and consciousness, and the magical powers and capacities which prevailed in Atlantis have lived on in the fabulous mythology of the peoples of northern Europe.

Atlantean man was not the crude and primitive creature of the kind of pre-history erroneously envisaged by modern science and contemporary anthropologists. Some of the many and varied civilisations in Atlantis reached heights of social and technological perfection in which science, education and the arts were fostered with great care and integrity. Atlantean scientists discovered means of extracting life-power from seeds

---

* The Tibetan Initiate 'reading' the Cosmic Chronicle saw that man had *not* in fact evolved out of lower forms of animal existence, which have themselves arisen out of elementary forms of organic physical processes. He recognised within the total development of mankind a sort of dual evolutionary process. On the one hand, he beheld the evolution of a physical-material world towards a condition in which man could descend to live as a physical being; and, on the other hand, he witnessed how man's psycho-spiritual organism had been created by spirit hierarchies in preparation for the descent from the Macrocosm into microcosmic earthly existence. An ancient Tibetan, if he were alive today to describe such a concept of evolution, would be forced to speak both in the physical terminology of Darwinism and the Biblical mythology of *Genesis*. Only by wedding these apparently opposed conceptions could he reveal an inkling of the realities revealed in the Secret Doctrine.

and made these forces available to large-scale commercial enterprises which arose throughout the continent. Means of transport not only included huge power-impelled ships but also flying craft with various types of sophisticated steering mechanisms.

One of the most difficult things for the modern mind to comprehend about the conditions of the environment in Atlantis is that the very nature of the elements and their manner of combination was totally different at that time. One can say with real justification that water at that stage in the evolution of the earth was much 'thinner' than water today, and air correspondingly far more 'dense'.

To contemporary sense perception Atlantis would have appeared as veiled in heavy mists. Yet the Atlanteans were by no means handicapped by this situation because they did not gain their experience of the phenomenal world through direct sense perception. They lived in a kind of vivid picture consciousness in which colourful images exactly mirrored the actualities of the sense world.

The sharpest distinction between contemporary man and the ancient Atlantean exists as a result of the tremendous changes in the evolution of human consciousness which have taken place since that time.

Whilst modern man is most conscious when 'awake' in the phenomenal world, he experiences a total obliteration of self-consciousness in sleep. But the Atlantean experienced a lowering of consciousness during the day while he worked in the phenomenal world. At night he experienced a great heightening of consciousness in which he lived in direct self-conscious vision of the celestial hierarchies in the Macrocosm with whom he had a magical means of communication.

The Atlantean Age passed through seven epochs in which seven sub-races developed in succession, each one maintaining itself while the others developed beside it. According to the Secret Doctrine these seven sub-races of Atlantis were named Rmoahals, Tlavatli, Toltecs, Turanians, *Aryans*, Akkadians and Mongols.

Adolf Hitler had gleaned something about Atlantis through members of the Thule Gesellschaft but he had only heard the most garbled ideas which had been developed out of an intellectual analysis of Nordic and Teutonic folklore. There can be no doubt that he was fascinated by everything that he now learned from Haushofer regarding the faculties and powers of the early Atlanteans which were wholly magical.

The source of the magical powers of the Rmoahals, Tlavatli and Toltecs was a fully expanded etheric organism which reached far beyond the confines of the physical body. Their speech, for instance, was intimately connected to the forces of nature. Their words could not only advance the growth of plants and tame wild beasts, but also bring about immediate and miraculous healing to the sick and terrible forces of destruction in times of enmity.

What Karl Haushofer had to say about the leaders of the Atlanteans was to have the most marked and significant effect upon how Hitler came to regard his later role as the leader of the German people. For the leaders of the sub-races of Atlantis were not in the ranks of ordinary evolving human beings. Of course, they belonged among their fellows in a certain respect. But because physical bodies were softer and had greater plasticity in that age, more pliable and malleable, as it were, it was possible for lofty Spirit-Beings to assume human form. They had mental and spiritual qualities of a superhuman kind and appeared to their contemporaries as Supermen. One could call them divine-human hybrid beings, sort of God-Men. They were greatly venerated by all lesser mortals who accepted their guidance gratefully and obeyed their commandments without question.

Such Supermen instructed the people in the sciences, the arts, law and religion, and taught them the techniques of tool-making and the practice of crafts.

These Supermen were also familiar with the laws appertaining to the formation of new races. At their Oracles, they selected special pupils who were sent off to isolation at training centres. There the pupils were schooled to develop those qualities which were needed in the breeding of a new race. Such carefully devised mutations, which controlled the birth and succession of the sub-races throughout the Atlantean epoch, were in great contrast to the appearance of other types of mutants of an entirely different nature.

The size, form and plasticity of the body in this pre-historic period were more intensely influenced by actual qualities of soul than by the forces of heredity. Where magical forces had been misused to serve the egotistical satisfaction of instincts, passions and desires, human figures arose that were altogether monstrous and grotesque in their shape and size. The existence of these 'self-mutants' has come down to us in the descriptions of the giants in many northern mythologies, especially in the Edda which was studied with such enthusiasm by Dietrich Eckart and the Thule Gesellschaft.

The whole trend in the evolution of consciousness throughout the first half of the Atlantean epoch worked towards the refinement of the powers of memory. Because the ability to think in concepts did not yet exist, personal experience could be gained through memory alone. When an image appeared before the soul of an early Atlantean, he remembered a whole number of similar images which he had already experienced. In this way, wisdom was stored up and personal judgement was directed accordingly.

It was the faculty of memory also which began to shape communal life on this lost continent. Groups of people elected as their leader a man who had gained a rich storehouse of memories. Racial identity was basically a facet of communal memory.

A further stage was reached when memory could be passed down through the generations in the form of a kind of 'blood memory'. Men recalled the deeds of their forebears with the same clarity with which they remembered their own lives. Rulers passed down their wisdom to sons and grandsons. Ancestor cults developed on somewhat similar lines to that which appeared many millennia later in ancient China. Dynasties of Kings built up vast kingdoms and empires, the continuous thread of rulership increasing the store of regal memory from which judgements could be made.

Yet it was just this power of memory which brought with it a pre-eminent and disastrous personality cult in which personal ambition was inflamed to extremes. The greater the personal power of a ruler the more he wished to exploit it. And because the Atlanteans had a magical mastery over the life forces in nature, its misuse led to disastrous consequences. The forces of growth and reproduction, when torn from the context of their natural functions and employed independently, stand in a magical relationship to the elemental powers at work in air and water. Many of the most powerful Turanian Kings had been initiated at the Oracles into the working of elemental spirits. Now they betrayed this knowledge. It was the egotistical abuse of the teaching of the Oracles, in which holy fertility cults originated, that brought about the most terrible disruptions. Black magic rituals, involving the perversion of the powers of human reproductions, let loose mighty and ominous forces and led to the eventual destruction of the whole continent in catastrophic storms of wind and water.

At this critical juncture in the history of Atlantis a new race was founded which was to protect the spiritual essence of man from extinction and guarantee the rightful progress of mankind for thousands of years to come, right into the first half of our own Post-Atlantean Age.

The destructive powers inherent in the magical faculties of the degenerating peoples of Atlantis could only be halted by the emergence of a superior faculty—*the faculty of thought*.

The power of thinking transcends even a magical remembrance of the past. Through thinking man can compare his experiences and he can improvise. As a result of thinking the faculty of moral judgement arises which can check and regulate the otherwise insatiable powers of instinct, impulse and desire. Only the emergence of such thinking powers and a capacity to listen to the inner voice of conscience could put an end to the Atlantean urge towards egotistical satisfaction of perverse appetites which was gradually destroying the continent.

Under such circumstances of dire urgency the "Master-Race" of Atlantis was founded. But this new race, *the Aryan Race*, was not formed by mere refinements of the previous sub-races of Atlantis. A sort of leap in the whole process of human evolution was achieved in order to fashion the Root Race which would live on in the new conditions of environment following the total destruction of the Atlantean continent.

The old type of picture consciousness which had mirrored in coloured imagery the unseen realities of the physical world was replaced with the capacity to see the phenomenal world in direct sense perception.

The etheric organism in the new type of Aryan man was contracted to bring about the metamorphosis to personal intelligence and a direct vision of the sense world. But these faculties of thought and sense perception were gained at the price of a total loss of all magical powers over nature and over the life-forces in the human organism. Even the basic form of man was radically changed. The former plastic, pliable, malleable, soft cartilaginous bodies of the Tlavatli, Toltecs and Turanians were replaced by what we know today as the form of modern man, the basis of which is the bony skeleton.

The breeding of the new race took place amidst the bitter weather conditions of the mountainous regions in the far north of the continent. Only gradually with the passing of many generations was a body bred out which was firm enough to withstand the effects of the adverse soul powers which had disfigured the earlier races of Atlantis. The correspondingly gradual contraction of the etheric organism denuded the new progeny of all magical powers over nature. But that portion of the life-body which now united with the physical body began to transform the physical brain into the essential instrument of thought. As this process continued the new generations began to feel the 'I' or ego in the physical body and the first human experience of 'self-consciousness' was awakened.

Those selected to be warrior leaders were isolated in mountain training centres where they received the most rigorous schooling under the rule of uncompromising discipline. Here they were taught that everything which confronted them visibly on earth was directed by invisible powers in the macrocosm and that they should dedicate themselves and put themselves without reservation at the service of these powers. Their education at the hands of the hybrid God-Men, or Supermen, brought them to the point where they could grasp in thought the principles upon which the Aryan Race was to be further developed. Above all, they were taught to respect and protect the purity of their blood. Their powers of moral will were strengthened and tested so that they should put aside all cravings and desires of a selfish nature. In this way the best qualities in the best specimens of the race were developed, and thus the refinement of the Aryan peoples progressed.

The great rulers of the degenerating races in the south of the continent saw the dangers of allowing the new race of Aryans to develop and made war upon them. Out of the mists surrounding the foot of the mountains the Aryan warriors were confronted by terrifying hordes of marauding peoples, many of whom were huge in size and grotesque in shape, manifesting the most fearful magical powers and capable of feats of superhuman strength. Against them the Aryans pitted their newborn intelligence and the ability to improvise proved superior to all the magic thrown against them. An echo of the ferocity of these prehistoric battles which were waged between the first self-conscious human beings and these monstrous and magical creatures has come down to us through the myths, especially those which tell of the outwitting of the giants.

The most radical difference between the Aryans and the earlier sub-races of the continent was in the nature of consciousness itself. The masses of the new race were entirely cut off from any form of direct perception of the spirit. At night they entered the void of sleep and during the day they were blind to the workings of the spirit in nature. The earlier magical power of memory dwindled and each new generation became further isolated from all knowledge of man's spiritual origins. In many ways these Aryans bore a certain resemblance to modern man, though they were not trapped like we are today in three-dimensional consciousness, for they experienced their thoughts as something given by divine powers. The personal ability to direct and combine thoughts in an intellectual manner did not then exist. Rather thoughts appeared to flow into them from higher entities in order to guide them and influence their will.

In order to remedy the spiritual blindness of the Aryan people which had arisen through total confinement to the sense world, the élite of the race were prepared for Initiation at the "Sun Oracle". After a further and yet more rigorous training in self-discipline and obedience, the centres in the astral bodies of the chosen few were matured and opened to the vision of the spiritual hierarchies. Under the symbol of the "Sun Wheel" or "Four-Armed Swastika", the new Initiates took over the leadership of the race and became the mediators between the masses of the people and the unseen higher powers. They taught a new religion which sought to bring every facet of life into relationship with the divine universal order in the world.

The Aryan Peoples were led out of Atlantis by the great Manu, the last of the Sons of God or Supermen. The migration took them across Europe and Asia into the area of the Gobi Desert and from thence to the heights of the Himalaya in Tibet. There, on top of the world, a Sun Oracle was founded which was to mastermind and direct the Seven Civilisations of the Post-Atlantean Age. Initiates trained at this Oracle, reincarnating as the leaders of the many and various peoples who also survived the Flood and settled in all parts of Europe, Asia and America. The large majority of the best-bred Aryan peoples settled in India.

It is not difficult to imagine the effect that these revelations from *The Secret Doctrine* had in further shaping the fertile and satanic mind of Adolf Hitler. And, as we shall later describe, the racist teachings he received from Haushofer in Landsberg Fortress were to be implemented in the training of the SS formations and in the Burgs from which it was intended that a new brand of Nazi superman should emerge.

THE CRITICAL TURNING POINT IN TIME

Vessels for the Hosts of Lucifer

"I am founding an Order," Adolf Hitler confided to Rausch-ning. He was speaking about his plans to establish the Burgs where the second phase in the breeding of a new race was to take place. "It is from there that the final stage in human mutation will emerge—The Man-God!"

Karl Haushofer had not only made a special study of the origins of the Aryan race in Atlantis and the manner in which it was moulded to fulfil a world historic destiny. He was also the source of the whole biological mystique of the racism of the Nazi Party and was immediately responsible for inspiring the whole idea of breeding experiments and the special schooling in the Burgs from which a new race of Supermen was to appear.

After initiating Adolf Hitler into *The Secret Doctrine* in Lands-berg Fortress, Haushofer became the leading figure in a secret society called the "Vril" or "Luminous Lodge" which was founded in Berlin. Attainment of a certain high degree of initiation into *The Secret Doctrine* was the only acceptable qualification for entry into this exclusive satanic circle.

The Luminous Lodge not only assembled its members from all the leading occult movements in Europe, it also attracted Initiates from all quarters of the globe including Tibet, Japan,

India, Kashmir, Turkistan and Ceylon. At the headquarters of the Society in Berlin, Tibetan lamas, Japanese Buddhists and members of other Oriental sects rubbed shoulders with former students of Gurdjieff, members of various spurious Rosicrucian Orders, former associates of the Paris Lodge of the Golden Dawn, and dubious personalities from Aleister Crowley's *Ordo Templi Orientis*.

The sole aim of this Lodge was to make further researches into the origins of the Aryan Race and the manner in which magical capacities slumbering in the Aryan blood could be re-activated to become the vehicle of superhuman powers. Surprisingly enough, one of the works which proved an endless source of inspiration to the leading members of this Lodge had been written by an Englishman. Bulwer-Lytton, a speculative Freemason and a member of the English Rosicrucian Society, wrote many other lesser-known works besides the celebrated novel *The Last Days of Pompeii* for which he became famous. In one of these little-known books called *The Coming Race* he veiled many of the truths he had learned through personal initiation into the Secret Doctrine. Lytton, a man of integrity and a scholar of some merit, was deeply interested in the prophecies concerning good and evil mentioned in the *Apocalypse* of Saint John The Divine. He had no idea that this book, in which he described the emergence of a new race with lofty spiritual faculties and superhuman powers, would become the evil inspiration of a small group of Nazis intent on breeding a Master-Race in order to enslave the world.

The first news of the Vril leaked out to the Western world through Willi Ley, the rocket scientist, when he fled from Nazi Germany in 1933. According to Ley the disciples of Haushofer believed that they were unveiling a secret knowledge through which they would be able to create a mutation in the Aryan Race. Amongst other items of information, he mentioned stories he had heard about their strange meditations and the kind of exercises they undertook in order to develop superhuman powers of concentration and clairvoyant vision.

A dedicated natural scientist and engineer, Ley regarded the whole affair as quite harmless and more than slightly ridiculous. He was unable to foresee that the Luminous Lodge would one day be taken over by Reichsführer SS, Heinrich Himmler and incorporated into the Ahnenerbe, the Nazi Occult Bureau; or indeed that it would provide a blueprint for the foundation of the new Order in the Burgs, and ultimately lead to experiments with the bone marrow and the decapitated heads of Jewish-Marxist Commissars!

The Vril is the ancient Indian name for the enormous resources of energy which can be made available as the result of the expansion of the Etheric Body or Time Organism in man. Ley's reports were quite correct that the Initiates of the Vril spent untold hours in silent contemplation of seeds, leaves, blossoms and fruits, even apples cut in half! In fact, the members of this Lodge were studying the laws of metamorphosis in plants which had first been worked out in Europe by Goethe. Goethe was the first European to achieve through such contemplation a partial extension of the etheric organism, which explains both the source of his genius and his remarkable extra-sensory powers.

It has been fully documented how Goethe was able to predict many future events, and how he was aware of great storms, eruptions, and earthquakes taking place thousands of miles away. Karl Haushofer's startling and somewhat similar ability to foretell the future is also comparatively well known. As a General on the Western front in World War I, he was able to predict the dates and the exact times of enemy attacks, the extent of casualties in coming battles, and he even moved his own headquarters on a number of occasions because he could correctly anticipate the patterns of enemy bombardment, and even where individual shells would fall.

Haushofer gained these extraordinary gifts through membership of the Green Dragon Society in Japan in which the mastery of the Time Organism and the control of the life-forces in the human body is the central aim of ascending degrees of initiation. One of the highest tests of this type of initiation in the Green Dragon Society demands the capacity to control and direct the life forces in plants in a somewhat similar manner to the former powers of the Atlantean people. The initiate must activate the germination process in a seed and bring about magically its growth into a mature plant so that the blossom appears in a matter of minutes. Such powers are not only connected with the control of elemental spirits but also with the full development and activation of the ten-armed Chakra situated in the astral body and interpenetrating the abdomen around the physical navel. Only two other Europeans have been permitted to join this Japanese Order, which demands oaths of secrecy and obedience of a far more strict and uncompromising nature than similar secret societies in the Western world.

The initiates of the Vril realised only too well that their aim to create a mutation in the Aryan Race was totally impossible in terms of the materialistic science of the twentieth century, which concludes that all differences of race have come about solely through long-term influences of environment. But contemporary science in their eyes was a Jewish-Marxist-Liberal Science, a conspiracy of mediocre minds and worthy of nothing but contempt. They had replaced it with a Nordic-nationalistic science, a magical world conception based on the cosmology of *The Secret Doctrine*. Only the chosen initiates were permitted to know the realities of this cosmology. For popular consumption it was exteriorised as the twin of Geo-Politics and circulated in a propaganda wrapping known as the *Welteislehre*.*

* The prophet of *Welteislehre*, the Doctrine of Eternal Ice, was Hans Hörbiger, who was already 70 years of age when Adolf Hitler came to power. Looking like a figure out of the Old Testament—he had flowing white hair and a long white beard—he provided the Nazis with a Cosmology in complete contradiction to western mathematics and astronomy. The Wel assumed proportions of a vast popular movement. Hörbiger claimed to have reached his new conception of science and of the evolution of the world in states of higher consciousness. Hitler called him 'the German Copernicus'. His theory was based on the perpetual struggle between ice and fire and between the forces of repulsion and attraction in the evolution of the Cosmos. The Nazis accepted Hörbiger's ideas because they appeared to confirm the writings of Friedrich Nietzsche and the visions of Wagner regarding the origins of the Aryan Race. The theories of Hörbiger still claimed some half a million followers after the defeat of Nazism.

247

The cosmology veiled behind the popular fiction of the *Welteislehre* had its origins nine millennia ago in ancient Tibet, an echo of the hidden knowledge of the great initiates which first appeared in written form thousands of years later in the *Vedas, Upanishads* and Sankhya philosophy.

The Universe was conceived to be one vast organism embracing within itself both Macrocosm and Microcosm, the succession of events on earth having their origin and stimulus in the spiritually directed movements of the sun and planets against a background of the cosmic emanations from the Fixed Stars.

This same theme of spiritual astronomy, in which recurring rhythms of the heavenly bodies activated changing conditions of life on earth, is also to be found in many other Eastern and Western systems. Perhaps it found its most sophisticated expression in the works of Dionysius the Areopagite and the Enneads of Plotinus, and indeed in the thinking of the whole Neo-Platonic School, one of the most spiritually and intellectually profound systems of philosophy the world has ever known.

An integral part of this cosmology was the idea that the Earth itself was also a conscious living organism, a kind of giant reflection in every way of man himself, every aspect of the physical and psycho-spiritual constitution of man finding its exact counterpart in the Earth Organism.

In the same way that man was seen to have an etheric body, a similar but gigantic etheric organism was attributed to our planet. And the whole process of spiritual and physical evolution of mankind was related to the one great central rhythm of the inbreathing and outbreathing of the Time Organism of the Earth, resulting at the same time in a corresponding contraction and expansion in the life body of evolving man.

The members of the Vril believed that the critical point in the contraction of the Time Organism of the Earth coincided exactly with the appearance of the Aryan Race and the eclipse of all magical powers on the Atlantean continent. And they saw the vital counterpoint in the expansion of the etheric organism of the planet to be taking place in the twentieth century. It was for this reason that they anticipated a great new dawn of magic.

Horst Wessel, a member of the Vril and one of the chief exponents of the *Welteislehre*, gave the actual date of this critical point as 1909, exactly thirty years after the end of the Kali-Yuga, or Dark Age. This was the year in which Adolf Hitler first stood before the Spear of Longinus in the Hofburg in Vienna!*

The theories and conclusions of the Vril were made available to Adolf Hitler who took a lively interest in any details which might contribute to the personal brand of biological mystique now taking shape in his own crude and demented mind.†

Adolf Hitler believed that the twentieth century would turn out to be "a critical turning point in Time" in the whole evolution of mankind. He imagined that the re-emergence of magical powers would take place with astonishing suddenness. And he even compared the anticipated transition with the appearance of puberty in adolescence, when forces lying dormant come to birth with alarming speed to mark the significant change from childhood to manhood.

* Horst Wessel, a great favourite with Hitler, was shot by the Communists while campaigning for the Nazis in Berlin. His death was commemorated by a hymn which was to become the sacred hymn of the Nazi Party. Horst Wessel openly prophesied in his public speeches the emergence of superhuman magical powers in the Aryan peoples in the twentieth century.

† We know from several sources of his fascination with the whole concept of the etheric formative forces in cosmos, earth and man. The most sensational revelation to this effect came to light when Hitler called a halt to the tests on the V2 rockets at Peenemunde.

General Walter Dornberger, who was in charge of these tests on the early type guided missiles, tells in his 'Memoirs' how Hitler believed that the rockets would interfere with layers of etheric forces around the earth. Hitler had apparently dreamt, and later intuited in trance, that a dreadful vengeance would be called down on humanity if the workings of these formative layers originating from the cosmos were disturbed.

Although it was believed at that time that the V2 weapons might even save Germany from defeat, the tests were held up for more than two months until Hitler was persuaded that no such reactions would result from unleashing his missiles through the stratosphere en route to the destruction of London.

We have already described how Hitler imagined that he himself was on the very threshold of such magical powers, the faculties which he had attained through initiation being in themselves a sort of foretaste of what was to come in the immediate future when the great unseen forces of the etheric world became ever more available to man.

According to him the new type of man shortly to emerge on earth would be able to travel backwards and forwards through time, recapturing events of the far-distant past and beholding the destiny of man thousands of years to come. "What today is known as history," he said, "we will abolish altogether."

But Hitler did not only anticipate the birth of spiritual faculties, he even went as far as prophesying actual physiological changes in the immediately-coming generations such as the opening of the fontanel and the visible reappearance of the "Cyclops Eye".

"Hitler was always talking about this Cyclops Eye," says Rauschning who several times heard Hitler's views about the coming Superman. "Some men can already activate their pineal glands to give a limited vision into the secrets of time," Hitler told him, obviously referring to his own experiences of former reincarnations. "But the new type of man will be equipped physically for such vision in the same manner as we now see with our physical eyes. It will be a natural and effortless gift."

Adolf Hitler had come a long way since he first read Friedrich Nietzsche's *Superman* back in his impoverished Vienna days. One is tempted to wonder what Nietzsche himself would have thought about Hitler's views on the theme of his most celebrated work. By summing up everything which Hitler had to say about the coming Superman, a fantastic picture emerges.

The New Man would have an intrepid countenance, giant stature, glorious physique, and superhuman strength. His intuitive powers would mightily transcend mere intellectual thinking, a magical faculty of imagination, a kind of superhuman picture consciousness, obviating the need for the sense-bound combination of intellectual and abstract thoughts.

This Superman, who would arise in our midst in so short a

time, would manifest magical faculties including magical powers of speech, which all lesser mortals would be powerless to disobey. All spirits between heaven and earth would obey his commands. Even the weather and the chemical combinations of the elements would be subject to his acoustic powers. Such Supermen would become the élite of the earth, the Lords of all they surveyed. Nothing would be hidden from their spirit-vision and no power on earth would prevail against them. "They will be the Sons of the Gods," said Hitler.

And the key to this staggering potential in man? It would be realised through the nature and quality of the blood! Only the Aryan blood would be sensitive to the newly released resources of creative cosmic power!

Those peoples, arising from the remnants of other races that had survived the destruction of Atlantis, would not be included in the coming mutations. And the Jewish Race, which had arisen at a time when creative etheric power was at its lowest ebb, would be excluded from all such superhuman development.

"They merely imitate men but do not belong to the same species," said Professor Karl Haushofer. "The Jews are as far removed from us as animals are from human," reiterated Heinrich Himmler. "I do not look upon Jews as animals, they are further removed from animals than we are," said Adolf Hitler. "Therefore it is not a crime to exterminate them, since they do not belong to humanity at all."

Adolf Hitler was voicing the conclusions of the Vril when he stated that the only true race was the Aryan Race, and only the Aryan Race could take part in the great heroic adventure of the sudden magical leap in the progress of human evolution.

This was the Nazi creed and Adolf Hitler became its prophet. He spoke on many occasions about his vocation as the herald of the new race of Supermen: "Creation is not yet completed. Man must pass through many further stages of metamorphosis. Post-Atlantean man is already in a state of degeneration and decline, barely able to survive. . . . All creative forces will be concentrated in a new species. The two types of man, the old

251

and the new, will evolve rapidly in different directions. One will disappear from the face of the earth, the other will flourish. . . . This is the real motive behind the National Socialist Movement!"

"I am founding an Order," Adolf Hitler confided to Gaulei- ter Rauschning, shortly before the latter defected to the West. He was speaking on this occasion about his plans to establish the Burgs where the next phase in the breeding of a new race was to take place. "It is from there that the final stage in human mutation will emerge—the MAN–GOD! This splen- did Being will become the object of universal worship!"

Yet Hitler's ultimate aim in biological mutation was not meant to pave the way for the reappearance of the kind of hybrid God-Man mentioned in *Genesis* who once walked the earth in ancient Atlantis. Such Spirit-Beings, who ranked above man but below the celestial hierarchies, were able to assume human form because the greater plasticity of the human con- stitution permitted it at that time. But these divine messengers were only permitted to act as a bridge between two worlds because man himself was not mature enough at that time to undertake the guidance of his own destiny.

The harsh training and pitiless and inhuman disciplines imposed on the unfortunate children in the Burgs was designed to mould their souls into a selfless chalice for the incorporation of demonic spirits of a high order. For Hitler's God-Men would have been none other than the legions of Lucifer, the hosts of the anti-spirit associated with the Spear of Destiny. It is fortu- nate for the world that the German Armies were defeated in battle and the Nazi régime liquidated from the face of the earth. For who is to say that over the next hundred years such experi- ments in human mutation might not have borne some measure of their intended aims!

CHAPTER TWENTY

AGARTHI AND SCHAMBALLAH

The Twin Resonators of Evil

Tracing back the history of the Earth Planet by means of the Cosmic Chronicle, *The Secret Doctrine* describes how the whole evolution of the earth and the being of man developed out of the spiritual Macrocosm as the result of the ceaseless creative activities of Spirit-Beings. According to this Doctrine the inner life of man has been from the earliest times under the guidance of these hierarchies of Spirit-Beings, but some of these hierarchies are inimical to the divine plan of human evolution.

The consciousness of early man should have remained an infallible mirror-image of the world, but this aim was diverted by a hierarchy of opposing powers who sought to evoke in the soul of man a kind of resistance to these conditions. These spirits, the first hierarchy of the trinity of evil, collectively known as Lucifer, sought to divest man's consciousness of the character of a mere mirror. The Luciferic adversaries of the celestial hierarchies wished to bring about prematurely a capacity in man to unfold a free activity within his consciousness so that he would become severed from the guidance of the Macrocosm.

The intervention of Lucifer initiated a process through which man became master of his own cognition and capable of personal resolve. At the same time man was led into the possibility of evil and error. The human "I", or ego, fell into dependence

253

upon certain lower elements in the soul. Higher spiritual influences were no longer able to control and regulate the cravings and passions to which man now became exposed. In this manner he became too involved in the wheel of physical existence and too interfused with the material processes of the earth.

This period in the evolution of mankind, which took place in yet earlier epochs than Atlantis, is described in *The Bible* in the symbolic picture of the "Fall from Paradise" in which man is won over to the aims of evil by the subtle temptations of the Serpent.

Within the forces of the earth itself under whose influence man was now brought, other demonic powers were at work. These spirits, which belong exclusively to the material world in which Lucifer involved mankind, are called Ahrimanic Spirits, and collectively known as "Ahriman". The second hierarchy of the trinity of evil, they seek to cut man off from all vision into the Macrocosm, and to lead him down into a total confinement in the three dimensional world of measure, number and weight. Ahriman wishes to mislead man into regarding the sense-perceptible world of physical existence as the only reality. But for the intervention of Ahriman, the spiritual powers under-lying the forces of nature would never have been veiled from human vision.

Lucifer and Ahriman are the two great adversaries of man-kind's evolution. Lucifer leads man into a spiritual independ-ence of the celestial hierarchies, tempting him, as it were, to set himself up as a God. Ahriman strives to establish a purely material kingdom on earth which is entirely isolated from spiritual realities, and he seeks to draw mankind so deeply into this kingdom that he loses all awareness of his spiritual origin and destiny.

The hierarchies of evil were responsible for the degeneration of the soul life of the masses of mankind in Atlantis which we have already described. Lucifer incited the lust for power, the false pride and the egotism which led to the misuse of magical powers, whilst Ahriman utilised the perverse sexual cravings of the populace to inspire black magic rites which brought about the eventual obliteration of the whole continent.

Even the disciplines and training which accompanied the foundation of the Aryan Race were not sufficient to ward off the harmful influences of the evil powers. Two separate sections of the Aryan peoples, led by defected Initiates from the Oracles, turned to the worship of evil and set up their own separate communities in the mountains which are now submerged below the Atlantic ocean in the proximity of Iceland. It was from their bloodthirsty and gruesome civilisation that the Legend of Thule arose. These initiates of evil also survived the catastrophe which *The Bible* describes as the Great Flood. They too migrated eastwards across Europe to Asia and they settled in Tibet in two vast cave encampments below the mountain sanctuaries of the Sun Oracle where the Great Initiates established themselves to direct the wise guidance of the civilisations of the Post-Atlantean Age.

Whereas the Sun Oracle fell into decline after some five thousand years, the Cave Communities which served the evil hierarchies continued to thrive into the modern age. The sudden and final eclipse of these demonic mystery centres took place when Communist China annexed Tibet in 1959 and the soldiers of Mao massacred all the contemporary adepts.

Many rumours and stories about the demonic activities of these Cave Adepts had reached the West in the first decade of the twentieth century. The literature of the Thule Group spoke of these two secret Orders which followed the "Left-hand Way" and the "Right-hand Way". The Luciferic Oracle was called "Agarthi" and believed to be a centre of meditation which concentrated on giving sustenance to the Powers. The Ahrimanic Oracle was named "Schamballah", a centre where rituals were performed to control elemental powers. The Initiates of Agarthi specialised in astral projection and sought to inspire false leadership in all civilisations in the world. The Adepts of Schamballah sought to foster the illusion of materialism and lead all aspects of human activity into the abyss.

It was largely through the initiative of Professor Karl

Haushofer and other members of the Vril Society in Berlin and Munich that exploratory teams were sent out to Tibet. The succession of German expeditions to Tibet, which took place annually from 1926 to 1942, sought to establish contact with the Cave Communities and persuade them to enlist the aid of Luciferic and Ahrimanic Powers in the furtherance of the Nazi cause and in the projected mutation which would herald the new race of Supermen.

Three years after the first contact had been made with the Adepts of Agarthi and Schamballah, a Tibetan community was established in Germany with branches in Berlin, Munich and Nuremberg. But only the adepts of Agarthi, the servants of Lucifer, were willing to support the Nazi cause. The Initiates of Schamballah who were concerned with the advent of materialism and the furtherance of the machine age, flatly refused to co-operate. Serving Ahriman, they had already made contact with the West and were working in affiliation with certain Lodges in England and America!

The adepts of Agarthi were known in Germany as "The Society of Green Men" and strong measures were taken to keep silence about their real significance. They were joined by seven members of "The Green Dragon Society" of Japan, with whom they had been in astral communication for hundreds of years.

Adolf Hitler held regular discussions with the leader of the Tibetans in the German capital, a man with proven clairvoyance who had mastered the arts of prediction. It was rumoured that he had predicted the exact date upon which Hitler would become Chancellor, and the date of the commencement of the World War.

The teachings of this Tibetan Group, which had been built up on the direct inspiration of Professor Karl Haushofer, attracted the enthusiastic attentions of the Reichsführer SS Heinrich Himmler. Himmler set up a school of occultism in the Berlin Branch and many of the leading ranks of the Totenkopf SS, the *Sicherheitsdienst* and the Gestapo were ordered to attend courses in meditation, transcendentalism and magic.

It was in this establishment that Himmler was persuaded to

found the Ahnenerbe, the Nazi Occult Bureau. The Ahnenerbe incorporated the membership of Crowley's spurious Templar Order, the Vril, and the Thule Gesellschaft into the Black Order of the SS. Its aims: to make researches into the localisation, general characteristics, achievements and inheritance of the Indo-Germanic Race.

The director of research was a close personal friend of Karl Haushofer, a certain Professor Wirrst, an expert in Oriental philosophy who taught Sanskrit and lectured in the sacred texts at Munich University. Many of the leading academic minds in Germany were pressed into the ranks of the Ahnenerbe which had forty-nine branches. Such was the extent of the influence of Agarthi on Nazi Germany.

Against the occult background we have uncovered, it should now be possible to understand how the Geo-Political teachings of Karl Haushofer and his cry for *Lebensraum* were merely an outer façade for exclusively demonic aims. It was not the search for the real source of the Aryan Race which interested him. His sole intent was the conquest of the world in the service of Luciferic powers. The defeat of the German Armies at Stalingrad put an end to his dreams. It also brought an eclipse in the Nazi confidence in the magic of Agarthi.

During the final months of the war the lamas from Tibet were utterly neglected by the Nazis. They had failed in their mission to harness the powers of Lucifer to the Nazi cause. To show his personal disfavour Hitler ordered that they should live on the same reduced rations as the inmates of the Concentration Camps. When the Russians reached their quarters in the suburbs of Berlin, they discovered their naked bodies lying in orderly rows, each with a ceremonial knife piercing the abdomen. They had chosen the Oriental form of suicide rather than surrender to the Communists and further disgrace.

The earliest association of the Nazis with the Tibetan Cave Oracles did not go unnoticed by shrewd and observant men in the Western world. Men of the stature of Lord Tweedsmuir, better known as John Buchan the novelist, warned contemporary politicians of the advent of a satanic religion in Germany and of the sort of civilisation which might develop out of a fusion of German technology and Oriental mysticism and magic. Needless to say, all such warnings went unheeded. Even at the Nuremberg Trials at the conclusion of a world war costing 25,000,000 lives and exposing the horrors of the Concentration Camps, there were only embarrassed titters of laughter when former members of the Ahnenerbe stood in the dock and gave evidence which included a mention of Agarthi and Schamballah.

The representatives of the Western world simply refused to admit what their defeated enemies were really like. Their strange beliefs, inhuman practices and horrible crimes could only be explained in psycho-analytical terms as mental aberrations. Western science, which had produced an Atom Bomb, denied the very existence of evil and spoke in terms of behaviourism and a relativity of morals. The religion of the West, which had reduced its God to a simple carpenter from Nazareth, could make no sense of men who worshipped the cosmic Anti-Christ and gained initiation into supersensible worlds through rites of ritual sacrifice. Those who knew kept silent. The leaders of the Occult Lodges and Secret Societies linked with power politics in the Western hemisphere had nothing to gain by exposing the satanic nature of the Nazi Party. Such a serious public investigation into occult rites and initiation knowledge might have unveiled spiritual realities which they themselves sought at all costs to keep hidden from the mass of mankind.

Such was the blindness and ignorance of the Allied Security Officers in charge of the Nuremberg prisoners, they did not even recognise the demonic nature of the 'last rites' which were given to some of the convicted men awaiting the hangman's rope.

SS Colonel von Sievers, the general manager of the Ahnenerbe, who was rightly convicted for his part in monstrous crimes against humanity, went unrepentent to the gallows. The last visitor to his death's cell was a certain Friedrich Heilscher, one of the most mysterious figures of the twentieth century and the man responsible for the original conception of "The Society for the Study of Ancestral Heritages".

Heilscher, an initiate of a yet higher degree than Haushofer and vastly his superior in the knowledge of *The Secret Doctrine*, never joined the Nazi Party. A member of a world cult of a higher order, many of the leading Nazis regarded him as their spiritual teacher and father-confessor. Von Sievers, Heydrich and Kaltenbrunner were devoted to him. Heinrich Himmler spoke about him in reverent whispers and considered him to be the most important single figure in Germany after Adolf Hitler himself.

When Haushofer fell into disfavour at the Nazi Court, it was Freidrich Heilscher's advice which the Führer sought in all occult matters, especially regarding the environment, training and pan-religious rites in the Burgs from which the Luciferic Race was to emerge. Heilscher was also responsible for creating the "Ritual of the Stifling Air" in which select members of the SS took oaths of irreversible allegiance to satanic powers. Had the Nazis won the war, Heilscher may well have become the High Priest of a new world religion that would have replaced the Cross with the Swastika.

In full view of the guards of the condemned cells, who were watchful mainly for the passing of poisons through which their charges might evade the gallows, Wolfram von Sievers knelt in reverence whilst Heilscher incanted the words of a Black Mass, a final hymn of worship to the powers of evil awaiting his soul on the other side of the grave. It is to the origin of the Black Mass that we must now turn our attention.

CHAPTER TWENTY-ONE

THE SPEAR AS THE SYMBOL OF THE COSMIC CHRIST

Hitler's greatest Adversary

Destroyed is my badness; annihilated is my evil.
Put away is the sin which was my own.
I wander on the path that I know, in the direction of
the island of justification.
I arrive in the land of the heavenly horizon; I pass
through the holy portal.
O Gods who come to meet me!
Stretch out your hands toward me!
I have become a God, one among you.
I have restored the eye of the Sun.
After it had been injured
On the day of battle by the two adversaries.

The Egyptian Book of the Dead.

It is a common error to believe that the powers of evil do not themselves recognise the divinity of Christ. The very reverse is the truth. Goethe, well aware that this is so, illustrated the true relationship between Good and Evil in the Prologue to *Faust*, in which he stages a dramatic meeting and discussion between the Lord and the Devil.

Goethe's Mephistopheles, an admixture of both Lucifer and Ahriman because the poet was unable to distinguish between these two different types of evil, grudgingly admits himself to be a subservient member of God's retinue with a special task within it to tempt man to oppose the divine order in the world.

MEPHISTOPHELES: Since Thou, O Lord, deignst to approach
        again
     and ask us how we do, in manner kindest,
     and heretofore to meet myself wert fain,
     Me, too, among Thy Retinue Thou findest.
              (*Faust*: Bayard Taylor translation)

It is in this sense that the innermost circle of Nazidom were self-confessed satanists. These men, who were dedicated to the service of evil, were very far removed from the lukewarm congregations of the Christian churches who are barely able to convince themselves of the reality of anything other than a material existence

Adolf Hitler recognised the divinity of Christ with the same inner certainty characteristic of medieval saints like Francis of Assisi. But Hitler hated Christ and felt only scorn and contempt for all Christian aims and ideals. And such dedication to the service of evil explains his singular fascination with the Spear of Longinus. In his eyes the Spear was an apocalyptic symbol of a Manichaean war of worlds, a mighty cosmic battle waged between hierarchies of Light and Darkness, which reflected itself on earth in the struggle between good and evil powers to guide the destiny of mankind.

The Nazi Party rightly scorned the Christian Churches—both Roman Catholic and Reform Churches—for their insistence that Christianity is superior to all other religions because it was entirely free from all Mythology. They correctly assessed that the strictured and unimaginative theology of contemporary Churchmen, dominated by a pathetic mixture of cartesian intellect and superstitious faith in dogma, was totally incapable of comprehending how the Christianity of the Grail and the Revelation is the very climax and fulfilment of all mythology.

The Cosmic Christianity of the Grail and the *Revelation of St. John The Divine*, have one thing in common with the Nazi worship of the Anti-Christ. Both enter mythological realms— like a divine and a demonic Romanticism come of age—under the same 'open heaven' of the Apocalypse from which the veil has been rent, and in which closed intellectual speculation has neither power nor validity.

For the aspirant to the Holy Grail, who has devoutly and patiently prepared his soul for the moment of Grace, the veil is legitimately rent from 'top to bottom' by the Christian Time Spirit. Black adepts like Eckart, Haushofer and Heilscher had to tear away the veil from below upwards by means of drugs, mantras, rituals and other satanic arts. Yet both the good and the evil adepts must pass through the same curtain of the sense world into the same higher dimensions of time and consciousness, read from the same 'Cosmic Chronicle', and share a vision and participation in the same supersensible worlds.

Without such a background knowledge of occultism it is impossible to understand why the leading Nazis considered their real adversaries to be among the hidden groups of people who had achieved initiation into the mysteries of the Holy Grail. And this explains why the SS and the Gestapo went to such extreme lengths to search out, persecute and torture men who appeared to have no political significance and outwardly represented no threat to Nazidom.

Without some measure of such occult insight it appears incredible that Adolf Hitler, who rose to supreme power in Germany and all-but conquered the world, should have regarded an unknown Austrian philosopher called Rudolf Steiner as his greatest enemy.

Yet when the history of our century is seen in its true perspective in the evolution of human consciousness, it will be fully realised that the Luciferic Principality inhabiting the soul of Hitler sought by means of racist doctrines to lead mankind away from an inward recognition of the Individual Human Spirit. It will also be appreciated that Dr. Steiner was the prophet of the Cosmic Christ in our time and the solitary herald of the eternal significance of the Spiritual Self, which seeks to come to birth in the souls of men in our age.

Adolf Hitler ranted against Dr. Steiner at political meetings in the early days of the Nazi Party, naming him as the war criminal directly responsible for the failure of the Schlieffen Plan and the consequent loss of the World War. Rudolf Steiner had been a personal friend of General Helmuth von Moltke, and Hitler accused him of using black magic powers to disturb the balance of mind of the Supreme Commander in the critical period of the German invasion of Belgium and France in 1914.

Hitler's personal reasons for wanting to put Steiner out of the way were of a more sinister nature. Dietrich Eckart had identified Rudolf Steiner as the leading figure of an extensive circle of Grail Initiates who had discovered the satanic nature of the Thule Group and watched over all their meetings and initiation rituals from the astral plane. Eckart was convinced that nothing could be hidden from Steiner's penetrating occult faculties. And because Steiner was openly engaged in warning Germany of the secret aims of the Nazi Party, he had been put at the top of the list of victims for immediate liquidation by Thule assassins.

It was planned to murder Steiner inside a railway carriage on Munich Station where both barrels of a sawn-off shotgun were to be emptied at short range into his face.*

Rudolf Steiner arrived promptly at the railway station to take the midday train to Basel. He admitted later that he was aware that an attempt would be made on his life that morning but he refused to cancel his travel arrangements because he had been pre-warned of the murder plan only through his own occult faculties. According to his ethical standards it was black

---

* During the first four years following the foundation of the Nazi Party no less than 397 political murders took place in Germany and the majority of them were committed by the inner circle of the Thule Gesellschaft. The Thulists followed the customs of the ancient medieval societies in plotting and carrying out their killings. After the manner of the Fehme, lots were drawn among a number of eager candidates to decide who should put the victim to death. None of these killings perpetrated by the Thule Group led to anything more than a short term of imprisonment for the culprits. Ernst Pohner, the Police President of Munich, and Wilhelm Frick, his assistant, both dedicated Thulists, warned Hitler and Eckart to stay clear of the scenes of Thule inspired assassinations carried out in public.

magic to attempt to avoid coming events by occult means. For this reason, too, he took no precautions to protect himself.

He would certainly have met a swift and bloody end that spring morning in 1922 had it not been for the timely arrival of Walter Johannes Stein and some associates. Stein had infiltrated the Thule Gesellschaft and unearthed the details of the murder plot. Rudolf Steiner now felt morally justified in quitting the scene as quickly as possible, and his friends surrounded him on all sides as he hurried from the station. The same evening he was driven across the Border into Switzerland and he never set foot in Munich again.

During this period Dr. Steiner was fully occupied in completing the Goetheanum, a building which was to represent, both in its architecture and the artistic forms of its inner construction, the principles of the Goethean world conception expressing the manifold relationships between Macrocosm and Microcosm. Steiner conceived it as the central building of a kind of 'Free University' for the teaching of Occult Science, where students could undergo the moral, artistic, scientific and spiritual preparation for Initiation into the deepest mysteries of esoteric Christianity.

Walter Johannes Stein had seen the Goetheanum in the spring of 1919 when he looked out across the mountains from the entrance to the Grail Hermitage at Arlesheim, near Basel. In the distance, crowning a foothill of the Jura, a strange but singularly impressive double-domed building glistened in the soft sunlight. In the small village of Dornach, which nestled below this twentieth-century Temple of the Grail, he discovered an international community which had gathered to study Rudolf Steiner's startling teachings on the spiritual origin and future destiny of mankind. These people, a cross-section from seventeen different nations, included leading men and women in all walks of life, academic, professional and industrial. He was delighted to find a small nucleus among them who, like himself, had also progressed far on the path to the Grail. But it

264

did not take him long to discern that his own maturing occult insight, including as it did a memory of former incarnations and a direct vision into the supersensible, was utterly dwarfed by Rudolf Steiner's immeasurable grasp of spiritual realities.

Rudolf Steiner was an 18-year-old science student at Vienna University when in 1879 he first beheld the Spear of Longinus in the Treasure House at the Hofburg. His researches into its history and the significance of its legend anticipated Adolf Hitler's interest in this talisman of power by exactly thirty years.

The sight of the Spear led Rudolf Steiner to take exactly the opposite course from every other personality through the centuries who had ever looked upon it with some knowledge of its legendary powers. Whereas the Spear had always inspired others to search out some means of attaining a vision into the supersensible, it influenced him to try and rid himself altogether of his own inherited clairvoyant powers.

The association of the Spear with a whole chain of claimants, who had served or opposed the Time Spirit through two thousand years of history, evoked in young Steiner a direct vision of this mighty celestial Being who inspires the constantly changing tasks of mankind through the passing epochs.

His immediate experience in the face of this vision of the *Zeitgeist* was one of reverence, humility and painful self-knowledge. He apparently became aware with a singular clarity of the dual nature of his own soul. He saw how on the one side his personality was dominated by intellect which weaved thoughts like dead shadows of reality and confined him to sense-derived knowledge; whilst the other half of his soul looked directly into the supersensible with a type of spirit-vision which did not unveil how the world of spirit passed over into the natural kingdoms of the earth.

He perceived how this division of soul was reflected universally in the tragic duality between science and religion, causing such havoc in the contemporary scene. Natural Science regarded the material world as the only reality, conceiving the whole process of creation and evolution in purely physical terms. Religion, secretly considering itself wholly discredited by science, had fallen back on unquestioning faith in dogma, hitching a hypothetical three-dimensional heaven on to the end of life to house the faithful after death. In neither case was there any recognition of the existence of a Macrocosm from which creative powers fashioned, informed and sustained the world of Nature.

On his first visit to see the Spear in the Schatzkammer, Rudolf Steiner sensed that it was his personal destiny to find a bridge between the world of the spirit and the world of nature.

Although he had already commenced to interpret the historical process in terms of the evolution of consciousness, he now became aware just how swift and radical the changes in the character of human awareness had been in the last three thousand years. And he discovered that the very history of Western philosophy traced the gradual steps in the contraction of consciousness and the way in which all knowledge of the Macrocosm had been lost.

He found the key to this evolution in human consciousness in man's slowly changing attitude to the nature and validity of thought, and in the increasing value he began to place in the evidence of the senses.

It appeared to Steiner as deeply significant that the Greek philosophers had considered that Ideas grasped by thinking were more real than the phenomenal world itself. And he traced how this belief in the intrinsic ability of thinking to reach truth gradually faded in the Middle Ages.

He also saw the critical deed which brought about man's scepticism regarding the spiritual validity of thinking to have taken place in the Grail Age in the ninth century when the Roman Church erased the Individual Human Spirit from the former trichotomy of man. From thence forward, because Spirit had been relegated to a mere shadowy intellectual quality in the soul, thinking was no longer trusted as a means to truth. It was inevitable that mankind should turn to the evidence of the senses as the only reality.

For this reason he saw it as a natural consequence that the real nature of the thought and art of the ancient world should have been totally misunderstood on the advent of the classical renaissance in the fifteenth century. The reappearance of Greek learning did not revive a longing for the knowledge of the spirit but, instead, only quickened man's thirst to unveil the secrets of the physical world. And in this battle to gain mastery over nature the despiritualised intellect reigned supreme with its effective inductive method based entirely on the evidence of the senses. The seed of a materialistic age had been planted and with it came an ever-widening gap between spirit and matter. Indeed, the very gap which Rudolf Steiner himself felt so acutely in his own soul.

Yet he felt that it was part of the divine plan of evolution that men should be utterly cut off from the spiritual (Macrocosm) and dwell completely within the isolation of three-dimensional experience in an apparently God-forsaken world. He realised that only in such isolation from the divine could men develop the necessary *self-consciousness* and *freedom* which are the pre-requisites for the appearance of *Love* on the Earth.

Faced with these conclusions, Steiner began to consider his own clairvoyant powers as more a hindrance than a help. In certain ways such faculties actually retarded the possibility to gain the fullest self-consciousness in the sense world. By this time he had come to the point of discriminating that his own spirit-vision, which he had enjoyed since earliest childhood, had arisen by some freak of blood heredity. He identified this kind of faculty as the very last vestige of the atavism of the ancient Germanic tribes, which had once been symbolised by the four-armed Swastika!

Standing in front of the Spear of Destiny in the Hofburg, he became aware that he had one foot in modern times and the other in the world of the old Germanic heroes like Baldur and Siegfried! He determined to find a way of ridding himself of his spiritual vision so that he could share in the blindness of his fellow men. And thus it came about that Steiner stripped himself of the very faculties which later became the most cherished possession of Adolf Hitler!

Many years passed before Steiner's atavistic powers dwindled

267

completely so that he could look upon the Spear of Destiny without it evoking the least trace of atavistic vision. The most potent resonator of spiritual faculty known to man no longer had any effect upon him. At last he had entered fully into the arena of what he called "the wrought works of the Gods", the total confinement within the material existence which the medieval alchemists had labelled "the dustbin of consciousness."

Though he could no longer look into a world of spirit-beings, his constant companions since childhood, Rudolf Steiner knew his own ego was in itself a Spirit living in the now invisible world of Spirits. And this knowledge acted like a sheet anchor against the contemporary tide of materialism as he turned his full attention to building a bridge between the world of the Spirit and the world of Nature.

It appeared to him that the bridge existed in man himself and could only be crossed by the attainment of some form of higher consciousness. He felt an inner certainty too that the same path of scientific knowledge that had brought man down into the seeming impasse of materialism, also held the key to a re-ascent into a far more penetrating vision of the Macrocosm. He set about finding a way through which thinking as an instrument of scientific investigation could itself be raised to such a level of higher consciousness that it would pass the bounds of sense existence and arrive at an objective and rational understanding of the spirit-background of the physical world.

Although it was our task to illustrate how the Spear of Longinus brought about a critical turning point in the life of Rudolf Steiner, our context will not permit a detailed description about how he built this bridge between spirit and nature. It must suffice to say that he followed two apparently contradictory paths which later fused into what he called Spiritual Science. One path was of a philosophical nature and led him into a deep study of the activity of thinking itself, the fruits of this labour appearing in *The Philosophy of Spiritual Activity*.* The

* *The Philosophy of Spiritual Activity* has now been published in paper-back edition by The Anthroposophical Publishing Company, New York.

other path led him into a lifetime study of the scientific writings of Goethe, and to developing the theory of knowledge implicit in Goethe's world conception.

At the age of 23 Rudolf Steiner contracted to edit and write a commentary on Goethe's scientific writings for an edition of the German classics. The quality of his scholarship earned him a place at the Goethe Archives in Weimar where he was able to study the personal diaries and unpublished manuscripts of the poet in order to contribute to a new edition of his works. And thus it came about through personal destiny that Steiner could earn his living for a period of fourteen years and establish his academic reputation at the very work which was itself demanded by his path of inner spiritual development.

Goethe conceived that Nature had two separate and distinct boundaries; one leading into a sub-material world in which the intelligent design in the universe could never be found; the other in which Nature herself became a chalice for the Spirit which designed, informed and upheld it. Steiner's interest was first aroused in Goethe through his theory of 'metamorphosis', that is, the transformation of a lower physical form into a higher one, as the result of the working into it of supersensible forces. By following the laws of metamorphosis at work in the life cycle of plants, Goethe conceived the idea of the Archetype Plant. And he hoped that by finding the same laws of metamorphosis at work in the higher kingdoms of nature he would be able to conceive the spiritual Archetypes of all living things.

Goethe did not achieve very much towards these lofty aims, nor did he get further in this direction than regarding the Ur-Plant as an idea. But Rudolf Steiner, following in the poet's footsteps in the development of "extra-sensorial-fantasy", not only conceived the Idea of the Ur-Plant but also directly perceived it with a quite new form of spirit vision; Imaginative Cognition.

Steiner had often wondered in his youth whether thoughts— universal ideas—were the means by which realities of the spirit-world clothed themselves in ordinary consciousness. He now received confirmation of this theory of knowledge. For him the

Archetype Plant was no longer just an Idea but a Spirit-Being, the active egohood of the whole plant kingdom on earth.

In this manner Steiner began to re-enter the Macrocosm with a heightened consciousness in which scientific disciplines and rational thinking were also included. The spiritual realities were not only unveiled behind the world of plants but also behind the world of minerals, animals and man.*

During the period in which Rudolf Steiner was employed in editing Goethe's scientific writings, he was developing in secret his own spiritual faculties to an ever-higher degree. By this means he gained a profound knowledge of the spiritual background of the Universe, Earth and Man. It was not until he reached the age of forty-four that he began to make public his new path to spiritual knowledge. During the following twenty-five years he delivered 6,000 public lectures and wrote some fifty books elaborating a path which guided the Spirit in man towards the Spirit in the Universe. He claimed that he always approached supersensible realities as a scientist and he called his method of investigating such realities by the name of "Spiritual Science".†

---

* Dr. Steiner has described the process through which he achieved clairvoyant perception of the Archetypes in his autobiography, *The Story of My Life*. Further details are to be found in his books, *Goethe's World Conception* and *The Theory of Knowledge applicable to Goethe's World Conception*.

† "He maintained that it was not sufficient today to reveal the facts of spirit-reality by recounting the great spiritual teachings of the past, but that the time had come when man should begin to advance to a direct knowledge of the supersensible world, by developing his latent faculties, in full rational consciousness.

"He declared that the development, in the last three centuries, of logical thinking and of the scientific spirit of observation, had been a necessary step in human evolution, towards man's discovery, at a higher level, of the spirit-background of the Universe. His only quarrel with science was that it accepted the limitation of scientific observation to the phenomena of sense existence, and that, in forming its concepts, it regarded the atomistic basis of matter, rather than the forms of physical objects, seen in relationship to their environment and their particular metamorphoses, as the key to ultimate knowledge, and took refuge in theoretical concepts, unverifiable by direct observation. He regarded it as fundamental that spiritual knowledge should be justified before the scientific way of thought." (*Scientist of the Invisible*: A. P. Shepherd. Hodder and Stoughton.)

The unique aspect of Rudolf Steiner's way to knowledge of spiritual realities rests in the fact that he reversed the traditional initiation procedures hitherto practised by all Eastern and Western occult systems.

For instance, the path of Eastern and Western initiation cults insisted on the development of the Chakras in the astral organism from below upwards—that is, by commencing the whole process with the opening of the four-armed Lotus Flower associated with the gonad glands. For this reason, such traditional paths demanded a complete withdrawal from life into an Ashram or a monastery, or the like, where a novice was protected from all temptations of the world, especially from sexual desire.

Steiner, basing his path on the initiation of thinking, grasped the Serpent by the head, as it were, developing these centres from the cerebral hemisphere downwards. His specific path can best be described as a wholesome 'way of living', which is in fullest accord with Christian ideals and responsibilities. Indeed, Steiner himself was able to tread such a path while fully involved in all the hundred and one activities which were an integral part of his contemporary scene. He claimed that anybody could follow the path to the attainment of the Holy Grail, if he was able to give as little as ten minutes a day to 'sense-free' meditation. At the same time he warned that it was necessary to take five steps in the strengthening of moral character for every step towards the attainment of supersensible vision.

Rudolf Steiner's way of initiation falls into three stages: Probation, Illumination and Initiation. It also ascends in three phases of spirit-perception: Imagination, Inspiration and Intuition. Imaginative Cognition opens up the vision of the spirit-background of the physical world; Inspiration unveils the Macrocosm, giving an understanding of its conditions and of the spiritual hierarchies who inhabit it. Intuition enables man himself to become a full citizen of the Macrocosm and gives him the means both to act within it and to communicate with all grades of spiritual beings. The unfolding of these faculties was described in an earlier chapter, "The Name inscribed on the Stone."

It is the third level of spirit-perception which also yields that category of intuitive knowledge gained through reading the "Cosmic Chronicle" in which the whole past of mankind can be recovered.

We have told how Adolf Hitler first attained a partial vision into this unfolding ribbon of time by means of drugs, and how Haushofer was able to unravel from it the history of Atlantis as a result of his initiation into the Green Dragon Society. This is how Rudolf Steiner describes the Akashic Record in one of his basic works, *An Outline of Occult Science.**

"The facts concerning the primeval past have not passed beyond reach of occult research. If a being comes into corporeal existence, his material part perishes after physical death. But the spirit-forces, which from out of their own depth, gave existence to the body, do not disappear in this way. They leave their traces, their exact images, behind them, impressed upon the spiritual groundwork of the world. Anyone who is able to raise his perceptive faculty through the visible to the invisible world, attains at length a level, on which he may see before him what may be compared to a vast spiritual panorama, in which are recorded all the past events of the world's history. These imperishable traces of everything immaterial are called in *Occult Science* the Akashic Record."

Our context requires a very brief consideration of what Rudolf Steiner had to say from this imperishable source about the Incarnation of Christ, which he saw as the central turning point in the evolution of human consciousness.

The origin of Steiner's Christology and the source of all his Christo-centric teachings was a direct result of standing before the Cross on Golgotha within the spiritual experience of the Cosmic Chronicle—a reality which remains eternally as living

* Now published in a paperback edition by The Anthroposophical Publishing Company of New York.

and as vivid as the actual event of the Crucifixion on the scene of earthly history.

"The evolution of my soul," wrote Steiner in his auto-biography, "rested upon the fact that I stood before the mystery of Golgotha in a most inward and most solemn festival of knowledge."

Throughout his life he had not been willing to accept any-thing out of 'faith in revelation', and for this reason he had been openly hostile to the orthodox Christianity of the Churches. When he reached the level of intuitive-perception in his path of self-initiation, he was utterly astounded to discover that the Akashic Record confirmed the authenticity of the New Testament.

He delivered a whole series of lecture cycles on the Gospels, reading directly from the "Cosmic Chronicle" as he spoke in a quiet, dignified and impersonal way about the scenes and hap-penings in the life of Christ which were there and then re-enacted before the eye of his soul.* Because he had no tradi-tional allegiance to overcome, for he favoured no church denomination and had never before studied the Gospels in detail, he entered this field of sense-invisible reality without prejudice and with the scientific detachment of a trained observer.

Among these lecture cycles given by Rudolf Steiner on the Gospels, which are perhaps the most important contribution to the understanding of Christianity in modern times, there is a set of lectures published under the title *The Fifth Gospel*. This specific title was chosen to denote that the Akashic Record itself will one day become the new Gospel for the whole of mankind.

In these particular lectures Steiner fills a gap, which somewhat

---

* When Rudolf Steiner was describing the scenes and realities of the spirit-world, he seemed to be absolutely at home with them. He was not describing, he was actually seeing the objects and scenes of these unknown regions, and he made them so visible to others that cosmic phenomena appeared actual. Listening to him, one could not doubt the reality of his spiritual vision, which appeared as clear as visible sight, but with a far more extended range. (Extracts from conversations with Edouard Schuré, the French dramatist and authority on the Ancient Mysteries, after attend-ing a lecture cycle by Steiner given in Paris in 1906.)

mysteriously exists in all four Gospels, by giving certain details of the life of Jesus between the ages of twelve and thirty, that is, from the time of the Temple scene, when the youth was found in earnest discussion of the Hebrew Scriptures, to the moment of the baptism by John in the Jordan when the Cosmic Christ descended into Incarnation.

We hear from the lips of Steiner the details of the world travels of Jesus, which have been the source of so many unconfirmed legends, and we see the young Nazarene voyaging to many foreign lands to study the religions and the initiation cults of the various peoples.

It appears that Jesus of Nazareth with penetrating clairvoyant perception traced how the evil hierarchies of Lucifer and Ahriman had brought about the slow decline in spirit faculties and the gradual contraction of consciousness towards total confinement in the sense-world, which occurred during the succession of great civilisations following upon the migrations of the peoples from Atlantis.

Everywhere he journeyed—India, Persia, Egypt, Babylonia, Chaldea, Greece—he discovered that the mystery cults of these ancient civilisations, through which Brahmins, Priest-Kings, Pharaohs, Prophets, and Sibyls had once received the guidance of the celestial hierarchies, had fallen into decadence.

The twin corrupting influences of Lucifer and Ahriman had stripped man of those faculties through which he had formerly experienced himself as a Spiritual Being in a Spiritual Universe. Lucifer had established himself in the blood of mankind to create a boundless egoism and an overall feeling of self-sufficiency, whilst Ahriman had severed man's connection with the Macrocosm, blinding him even to the working of the spiritual powers behind nature. Lost to the world of the spirit, man saw the physical world as his only existence and, in consequence, he entered the Macrocosm after death in a state of spiritual blindness. And since a human soul which finds itself in the clutches of Ahriman in the spirit-world can only be born again on earth as an even greater egotist, a chain reaction had been set up which left mankind without any hope of salvation.

The gradual continuation of the tragic process of the Fall did not affect man alone. The whole earth organism and all its kingdoms were equally entrapped in this descent into isolation from the spirit, entering too deeply into the condition of matter and of death. It appeared to Jesus of Nazareth that the whole planetary existence had passed into the hands of evil powers and that mankind together with nature would be plunged into the eternal darkness of the abyss.

Rudolf Steiner describes how Jesus of Nazareth heard the triumphant hymn of the powers of evil wheresoever he journeyed across the earth, and this hymn of darkness rang loudest in those very Temples and Sanctuaries where the mysteries of the Spirit had once been nurtured and cherished:

> Aum, Amen!
> The Evils hold sway,
> Witness of Egoity becoming free,
> Selfhood-Guilt through others incurred,
> Experienced in the Daily Bread,
> Wherein the Will of the Heavens does not rule,
> In that Man severed himself from Your Kingdom,
> And forgot Your Names,
> Ye Fathers in the Heavens.*

> Aum, Amen!
> Es walten die Ubel,
> Zeugen sich lösender Ichheit,
> Von andern erschulte Selbstheitschuld,
> Erlebet im täglichen Brote,
> In dem nicht waltet der Himmel's Wille,
> Da der Mensch sich schied von Eurem Reich
> Und vergass Eure Namen,
> Ihr Väter in den Himmeln.

---

* German original from *Fifth Gospel*. Published by the Rudolf Steiner Press, London. Originally published by Nachlassverwaltung, Dornach, Switzerland.

Perhaps the immediate meaning of this hymn of triumph of the evil powers will become more clear when it is stated in a less poetical way. It was as though the hierarchies of Lucifer and Ahriman mocked man saying: Evil holds sway. Man is led into temptation by false pride and insatiable desire. A boundless egoism involves him in enmity and debt with his neighbour in a bitter struggle for power and material gain (Daily Bread). The Will of the Father goes unheeded, the Kingdom of Heaven is cut off from the earth, and the very name of the Spirit is no longer hallowed.

In such form it is easier to recognize this hymn of evil as the reverse of the Lord's Prayer, which Christ gave unto man in the assurance of his salvation from the abyss and the restoration of his true spiritual identity.

For many centuries there has existed a superstitious belief that the saying of the Lord's Prayer backwards constitutes a form of Black Mass. Yet nobody knew the real meaning of such a strange ritual. The Nazis were the exception. The hymn of evil was offered up as an act of worship both at the Ceremonies of the Stifling Air, at which the inner core of the SS took irreversible vows in service of Lucifer, and at the Black Mass which was celebrated with the potentised blood of Adolf Hitler.

Steiner reveals in Jesus the union of two human streams, the fusion of the sinless nature of the soul before the Fall with the fullest earthly wisdom gained by millennia of reincarnating development after it. And he conceived this mystical union between heavenly innocence and earthly wisdom to constitute the Vessel of the Holy Grail.

For Steiner, the entry of Christ into the physical-historical process took place at the baptism by John The Baptist. At this moment the sacred Being of the God of Love was poured forth into the vessel of the Grail, the first inter-penetration between "the glory of eternity and the masterpiece of time".

The Cosmic Chronicle reveals that the union of the divine

and human natures took place in progressive stages throughout the three years of Christ's earthly life, the succession of miraculous deeds and events described in the Gospels indicating the ever-deepening extent to which Christ had united Himself with the elements of the Earth and penetrated the psyche and body of Jesus.

The final stage in this progressive passion took place when the Christ emptied Himself into the death-ridden processes of the physical body, the ultimate phase of the Incarnation being achieved only on the Cross itself with the words: "My God, my God, why hast Thou forsaken me?"

The Spirit of the Universe had contracted in sacrificial deed into a total identification with the body of fallen man, experiencing the confines of human consciousness fettered to a mortal brain. The God of Love had entered the utter isolation of three-dimensional consciousness to conquer death, and reanimate the dying earth existence, in order to lead mankind back to a full citizenship in the Macrocosm and the fulfilment of a Cosmic Destiny.

The limits of this book only permit us to follow up one single aspect of the life of Christ: the way in which Christianity became the fulfilment on the scene of world history of the *secret* Initiation Cults of all previous civilisations. By following this specific theme we shall be able to illuminate to a certain extent the significance of the shedding of the Blood on Golgotha, and the manner in which the Spear of Longinus became a magical talisman of destiny.

The many and various rituals of pre-Christian initiation had one goal in common. Their purpose was to create a temporary dissociation from physical awareness in order to enter higher dimensions of time and consciousness in which the fullness of the spirit-worlds was made manifest.

By the observance of ascetic rules of living and self-discipline, and by following various differing systems of meditation, the centres in the astral body were brought to fruition, and the etheric body was partially raised from the physical, so that the projected journey into the spiritual Cosmos should be imprinted on the memory of the candidate.

During the actual process of initiation, when the astral body of the candidate was expanded and guided through a world of spirit-beings, his ego, or 'I', took no part whatsoever in the proceedings. That is to say, the ancient forms of initiation were concerned with the astral body only, and the candidate himself was totally unaware of what was going on. His self-consciousness was extinguished by means of hypnosis so that he passed into a condition of deep trance before the real spiritual initiation began. Only when the ritual was over did the candidate awaken to a self-conscious awareness in which he *remembered* the spiritual experiences through which his astral body had passed in the Macrocosm.

The techniques of Initiation gradually became more sophisticated and perilous until reaching their most highly evolved state in the "Temple Sleep" of the Ancient Egyptians. Here the candidate went through a form of ritual death. Wrapped in graveclothes and enclosed in a tomb, his ego was put into a condition in which it hovered on a razor's edge between life and death in the physical processes of the body.

At the conclusion of the whole perilous procedure, the Hierophant came forward to call forth the candidate in what virtually amounted to a ritual resurrection from a tomb. The newly-initiated soul had undergone a form of mystical death in the physical processes of the body metabolism, and now he was awakened to life with the *memory-knowledge* of his Eternal Self, which had been astrally perceived beyond the veil of sense. It appeared to him that he had been born anew. Indeed, the Initiates of Egypt were often called the "Twice Born".

The moment in man's evolution finally arrived when the etheric body was too deeply immersed in the physical body to permit such methods of Initiation with any measure of safety. And it was at this period that drugs were used, including the so-called Sacred Mushroom, to attain a kind of synthetic form of Initiation. In the states of higher consciousness evoked by drugs the seeker after spiritual realities could even enter the sphere of the Akashic Record, and behold the past and the future in one continuous undivided ribbon of time. The *Dead Sea Scrolls* bear testimony of the drug-induced visions of the Essene Initiates, who, like the Theraputae of Egypt, followed such practices. In a world forever darkening to the light of the spirit any means of attaining a vision into spiritual realities was morally justified.*

The last crude ritual of Initiation, which was both highly dangerous and, often as not, only partially successful, was total immersion in water until the candidate was all but drowned. This method brought about a partial raising of the etheric body from the physical and led to a kind of experience of the Higher Self. The candidate saw his life before him in one vast panorama and for a few brief moments experienced the existence of the Individual Human Spirit. It was at such a ritual of spiritual baptism in the masterful hands of John The Baptist, that Christ descended into Incarnation.

The descent of Christ down the Jacob's Ladder of the Nine Hierarchies of the spirit-world was witnessed by the leading Initiates of all the ancient Mystery Temples. The advent of the Sun-God had been foretold by Prophets and Sibyls alike, by the mythologies of all races, and by the sages of all peoples. But when Christ clothed Himself in an earthly body and walked among men, He was not recognised as the long-anticipated

---

* John Allegro has described in his work *The Sacred Mushroom and the Cross* how the Essenes attained higher levels of consciousness by means of Amanita muscaria. He insists that the events described in the Gospels never took place on earth at all but were perceived only in transcendent states evoked by the powerful influence of the sacred mushroom. A similar erroneous point of view was held by a heretical sect called the Docetists in the Third Century A.D. John Allegro's misconception arises as a result of a complete lack of understanding of higher dimensions of Time. The fact that the events of Christ's life were perceived in pre-christian times by Essenes in drug-induced consciousness is certainly no indication that Jesus Christ never lived on earth. On the contrary the fact that such events were clair-voyantly perceived in the 'Cosmic Chronicle', a dimension embracing past, present and future in one unbroken ribbon of time, should be regarded as an indication that the earthly Incarnation later took place.

Messiah. The greatest spiritual event in the evolution of mankind happened almost unnoticed.

"Who think ye that I am?" Christ asked His disciples after two eventful years in their midst. The reply came that some people believed He was the reappearance of Elijah, evidence that they believed in reincarnation. Other people, they said, had suggested that He was John The Baptist, returned from the dead. An indication that the possibility of 'incorporation' was also conceived at this time. Only Peter in a moment of heightened intuition recognised Him as the Son of God, begotten in eternity.

The teachings and the miraculous healings of Christ were in themselves both a giving out and public enactment of the doctrines and the practices which had hitherto stemmed only from the secret Mystery Centres. But the fact that the whole life of Jesus Christ was the public fulfilment of the Initiation Cults of antiquity first becomes visibly apparent at the raising of Lazarus from the dead.

Lazarus, the brother of Mary Magdalene and Martha, had undergone the ancient form of initiation, which had been practised for hundreds of years by the Hebrew Prophets under the Sign of Jonah.

The process of initiation had gone badly wrong. While the astral body of Lazarus winged in the spirit-worlds, his ego had passed through actual physical death. When the moment came to raise him from the tomb, it was found that he was not only dead but that his body was in the process of decomposition.

The St. John Gospel makes it abundantly clear that Lazarus was undergoing the Temple Sleep of Initiation. Jesus Christ says: "Our friend Lazarus sleepeth; but I go, that I may wake him out of his sleep."

"Then said the disciples, Lord, if he sleep, he shall do well.

"How be it Jesus spake of his death, but they thought he had spoken of taking rest in sleep.

"Then said Jesus plainly, Lazarus is dead.

"And I am glad for your sakes that I was not there, to the

intent that ye may believe; nevertheless let us go unto him. . . .

"And some of them (the Jews looking on) said: Could not this man, which opened the eyes of the blind, have caused that even this man should not have died?

"Jesus therefore again groaning in himself cometh to the grave. It was a cave, and a stone lay upon it.

"Jesus said, Take ye away the stone. Martha, the sister of him who was dead, saith unto him, Lord, by this time he stinketh: for he hath been dead four days.

"Jesus saith unto her, said I not unto thee, that, if thou wouldst believe, thou shouldest see the glory of God?

"Then they took away the stone from the place where the dead was laid. And Jesus lifted up his eyes, and said, Father, I thank thee that thou hast heard me.

"And I knew that thou hearest me always: but because of the people which stand by I said it, that they may believe thou hast sent me.

"And when he had thus spoken, he cried with a loud voice, Lazarus, come forth.

"And he that was dead came forth, bound hand and foot with graveclothes: and his face was bound with a napkin. Jesus saith unto them, Loose him, and let him go.

Lazarus was the very last person to undergo the traditional form of Initiation of the Old Testament Prophets. He was also the first human soul to experience the new form of Initiation which Christ brought to mankind: The Initiation of the Ego. As far as rational understanding will permit it, let us try to understand how this momentous transition came about.

The "I" of Lazarus, his earthly mortal ego, had been put to sleep in the physical body while his fructified astral organism was expanded into the Cosmos. Had the initiation proceeded normally, Lazarus would have awakened to remember these astral visions of spirit-beings in the celestial spheres of the Macrocosm. He would also have felt himself to have been united in memory with the Folk-Spirit which lived in the blood of the Jewish Race. That is, Lazarus would have reached a degree of initiation in which he would have won the right to call himself by the name "The Israelite", the rank through which he would have been accepted as a genuine witness and prophet of Jehovah.

One thing that this ancient form of Initiation could not achieve was the permanent union between the soul of man and his Higher Ego. That is, such initiation could evoke only a kind of memory of the existence of the Eternal Self; it could not so transform the soul that it became the living and continuous vehicle of the Individual Human Spirit. The intervention of Lucifer and Ahriman in human evolution had precluded the possibility for the human Spirit to find a permanent home within the soul of man while he lived upon the earth. Only after death itself were the soul and the spirit so united.

And this is exactly what happened in the case of Lazarus when his initiation failed and he passed across the threshold of death. At that moment he was united with his Higher Ego, and from this sacred spiritual vantage point he beheld the tapestry of his earthly life unfolding before him.

But it was precisely the Higher Ego, the Individual Human Spirit, to which Christ made reference in this context as the "Father". Indeed the whole meaning of the Incarnation of Christ can be expressed in His words: "I am the Way, the Truth, the Life. No one cometh to the Father but by Me." And again in the words: "I and the Father are One".

The voice that called forth Lazarus from the grave was the voice of his own Higher Ego. The power that gave him back his life, and re-animated and made whole his body, was the same power which emanated from his Eternal Being. For the intuitive experience of the Christ Being was one and the same as that of his own Individual Spirit.

When Jesus Christ took the place of the Hierophant, or Master Initiate, at the ritual of raising from the tomb, He stood there as the Saviour of mankind, the Representative on earth of the Eternal Self which had sought in vain to come to birth in the soul of each and every man.

In full accordance with the traditions of the mysteries of antiquity, the self-consciousness of Lazarus had been ex-tinguished through hypnosis. But the original hierophant had failed to call him back to life. Instead, Lazarus was called forth by the power of Infinite Love, the Macrocosmic Ego of Christ. For Lazarus the fulfilment of this ancient tradition had a new meaning. He had been born anew in the intuitive knowledge that in Christ the human soul could become a living vessel of the Spirit.

Lazarus was the very first human being to experience through Christ the recovery within himself of his own Higher Ego. An experience which St. Paul later put into words after Christ had consummated a similar deed for all mankind by His Death and Resurrection on Golgotha: "I live; yet not I, but Christ liveth in me."

Rudolf Steiner reveals in his lectures on the Gospel of St. John that it was not only Lazarus who returned to the body when Christ raised him from the dead. His investigations into the Akashic Chronicle in this regard brought to light an astonishing fact: John The Baptist, who had been beheaded on the orders of Herod Antipas some nineteen months earlier, also returned to embodiment at this moment. And Steiner describes how Lazarus and John lived together in one and the same body, united in motive but working on different levels of soul activity.

And Steiner elucidates this sublime mystery yet further by revealing that the individuality of John The Baptist, returned from the grave, is one and the same person as John The Divine, the writer of the John Gospel and the Revelation. This truth is actually indicated in the Gospel itself when John is named as "He whom the Lord loved". Of course, the God of Love gave his love equally to all mankind. The expression is used only in the sense in which it fulfils the ancient tradition of initiation in which the Hierophant named the candidate whom he called forth from the tomb: "The Loved One".

The Incarnation of Christ into the body and blood of the human Jesus was the descent of the Sun Spirit into the Moon Chalice, the configuration which became the symbol of the Holy Grail in the Middle Ages.

283

Christ came to lead the ego-consciousness of the Jews, and thereafter of all mankind, beyond the limited and prejudiced loyalties of family, tribe and race. But in order to transform human egoism and bring a Universal Love to all men, it was necessary to change the very nature of the blood itself, for blood is the vessel of tribal and racial identity. And Christ could only accomplish this deed for mankind by ensouling the elements to become the Spirit of the Earth. Indeed, Jesus Christ told Peter (whose name Cephas means a stone) that it was upon this rock —the Earth—that He would build His Church.

Moses, who led the Jews out of captivity in Egypt, had been the first to perceive the reflection of the descending Christ, who appeared to him indirectly in the thunder and lightning and in the 'burning bush'. This gradual sacrificial process of penetration and ensoulment of the elements continued throughout the life of Christ on Earth.

A further stage in this mighty invisible process in which the Sun Spirit united with the Kingdoms of Nature came at the Last Supper when Christ gave to His disciples the Sacraments of Bread and Wine, saying: "Take, eat; this is my body. Drink ye all of it; for this is the blood of the new covenant." The final deed, through which the Divine-Human Christ Jesus passed over into Incarnation in the body of our planet, took place at the shedding of the Holy Blood on Golgotha when the Roman centurion pierced His side with a Spear.*

---

* When Earth evolution began, the human Ego was connected physically with the blood. The blood is the outer expression of the human Ego. Men would have made the Ego stronger and stronger, and if the Christ had not appeared they would have been entirely engrossed in the development of egoism. They were protected from this by the Event of Golgotha. What was it that had to flow? The blood that is the surplus substantiality of the Ego! The process that began on the Mount of Olives when the drops of sweat fell from the Redeemer like drops of blood, was carried further when the blood flowed from the wounds of Christ Jesus on Golgotha. The blood flowing from the Cross was the sign of the surplus egoism in man's nature which had to be sacrificed. The spiritual significance of the sacrifice in Golgotha requires deep and penetrating study. The result of what happened there would not be apparent to a chemist—that is to say to one with the power of intellectual perception only. If the blood that flowed on Golgotha had been

The Death on the Cross and the Resurrection of the Phantom from the Tomb was the public fulfilment of the old form of Initiation on the arena of world history; the secret Initiation Ritual transferred to the visible plane of the historical process.

The defeat of Lucifer and Ahriman on the Cross rescued the earthly life of man from the abyss, and hallowed it into a daily path back towards the spirit worlds; a deed of Infinite Love which guaranteed the gradual recovery of the Eternal Ego and the fulfilment of a spiritual destiny for all mankind. The God of Love had sacrificed Himself to the level of the human soul so that it might become the living vessel for the Individual Human Spirit: Father, into Thy hands I commend My Spirit.

The accoutrements which were used in this singular mighty ritual on Golgotha became the treasured reliquaries of the Middle Ages. Yet the religious devotion with which these reliquaries were held was not the result of either false sentiment or misplaced materialism.

The various articles and vestments which were used in the ancient Initiation Rites were rightly considered to have been 'charged' with spiritual powers and were regarded as talismans of white magic. And it was for this same reason, though in a far more sacred sense, that the Spear, the Nails, the Cup, the Crown of Thorns, the Robe, the Shroud, and the like, were held in such high regard by all Christians until the dawn of rationalism at the time of the Renaissance in the fifteenth century.

Each reliquary became associated with unique powers. The Cross was revered for its powers to ward off the evil. The Crown of Thorns evoked the deepest humility in all those who beheld

chemically analysed it would have been found to contain the same substances as the blood of other human beings; but occult investigation would discover it to have been quite different blood. Through the surplus blood in humanity men would have been engulfed in egoism if infinite Love had not enabled this blood to flow. As occult investigation finds, infinite Love is intermingled with the blood that flowed on Golgotha. The writer of the Gospel of Saint Luke adhered to his purpose, which was to describe how, through Christ, there came into the world the infinite Love that would gradually drive out egoism. (R. Steiner: *Lectures on Luke Gospel*. 1909.)

it. The Robe bestowed health and life anew to the sick and inspired spiritual vision of the life of Christ on Earth to those who followed the contemplative path of monasticism. The Jasper Vessel,* out of which the Christ Being gave the Sacraments of Bread and Wine, and in which Joseph of Arimathea collected a portion of the Holy Blood, became known as the Holy Chalice; it symbolised a Christian path to the death of egoism and rebirth of the Spirit in Christ. And in a like manner, too, the Spear of Longinus was to take on a unique significance for the evolution of human consciousness within the historical process; a significance which moulded the belief in its powers to inspire a world historic destiny.

We have already described in the Prologue of this book how the Roman Centurion Gaius Cassius, the representative of Pontius Pilate at the Crucifixion, protected the body of Jesus Christ from mutilation at the hands of the soldiers of the Pharisees. And how, in piercing the body of Jesus with a Spear to prove that death had taken place, he also fulfilled the prophecy of Isaiah: "A bone of Him shall not be broken", and the prophecy of Ezekiel: "They shall look upon Him whom they have pierced."

Yet the deed of Longinus has an even greater significance. And in order to understand the full implication of his deed on Golgotha we must consider what actually happened at the moment when he thrust the Spear into the right side of Jesus between the fourth and the fifth rib, piercing the body of the very heart.†

* The Jasper Vessel was contained within the bowl of a large Silver Chalice, which was reputed to have been handed by the mysterious figure of Melchizedek to Abraham, the Founder of the Jewish Race. It later came into the hands of Joseph of Arimathea in whose Upper Room the Last Supper took place.

† According to the mythology of the Old Testament the body of woman had been created out of the Fifth Rib of man. In the development of the human embryo, the sexual organs do not take form until after the formation of the fourth rib and before the formation of the fifth rib. The symbolism here was also fulfilled at the Crucifixion, the Blood flowing from the wound of the Spear emerging from between the fourth and fifth rib as an indication that Christ transcended the division of the sexes.

The Blood streaming to the Earth from the wound was the vehicle through which the Spirit of the Sun passed into Incarnation within the body of the Earth itself. It was the Spear-thrust of Longinus which brought about the birth of the Cosmic Christ as the Earth Spirit.

The Spirit-Essence within the Holy Blood streamed into the Earth from this wound in the manner of a sacred trace-element, a kind of circulating homeopathic balsam, through which the Macrocosmic Ego of the Christ Being could rekindle the astral sphere and permeate the etheric realm of the Earth Organism.

The Christ Light which blinded the spiritual eye of St. Paul on the road to Damascus was the new Sun-Aether-Aura of the Earth, the initial shining forth of the Earth in promise of the reanimation of the whole dying earth existence and its re-integration into the Solar dominion of the Macrocosm.

If Longinus had not been inspired by the Time Spirit to thrust the Spear into the body of the Saviour at this moment, the Holy Blood would never have flowed forth. The great miracle according to the *Gospel of St. John* was that the Blood came forth from a lifeless body: "But one of the soldiers with a Spear pierced his side, and forthwith came there out blood and water. And he that saw it bare record, and his record is true: and he knoweth that he saith true, that ye might believe."

Gaius Cassius Longinus accomplished the rightful deed in the correct manner at the exact place and at the decisive moment in time. And in that moment the whole future evolution of the Earth and Humanity rested solely in his hands.

And thus the shape of a legend arose around the Spear of Longinus that whoever claimed it held the destiny of the world in his hands. For any claimant to the Spear in the passing centuries of the history of Christendom could carve out for himself a world-historic destiny by carrying out in the correct manner the rightful aims of the Time Spirit according to the specific tasks demanded by the age within the evolution of human consciousness. Or, he could become the vessel of the Anti-Spirit of the Time and obstruct and divert such aims in

287

order to lead humanity into the worship of false gods or into the abyss of materialism.

The Spear of Phineas, symbol throughout the Old Testament of the unique powers inherent in the blood of the Jewish race, also played its definitive part in the outer ritual of the Crucifixion. It was this Spear upon which the sponge of vinegar was lifted to the mouth of the dying Christ, a symbol that the Jewish blood had become gall and would be no further significance in the evolution of humanity, for it had been replaced with the Blood of the New Covenant for all mankind. For this is indeed the principle involved in the evolution of human consciousness: that which was once the greatest vehicle of good becomes when outdated and taken beyond its appointed time a vehicle of tragedy and evil. To maintain tribal customs and rituals and a rigorous racial prejudice in the face of a new and universal impulse which sought to embrace the whole of mankind could only bring down upon the Jewish race the most terrible suffering a single people have ever experienced on Earth.

Rudolf Steiner incorporated his conception of Cosmic Christianity into the architectural forms of the Goetheanum at Dornach, Switzerland. The interior of the double-domed building was a masterpiece of woodcarving. Dynamic means of shaping and forming integrated every aspect of the work into the central theme of the Apocalypse, huge wooden pillars carved in sequence illustrating Goethe's conception of the law of metamorphosis through the Seven Seals of the Revelation. The first psychedelic paintings of the century appeared as frescoes on the domes and on the vividly coloured windows.

It was Dietrich Eckart's dying wish that this building, which was originally to have been built in Munich and called 'Johannesbau', should be burned to the ground and that Dr. Steiner and his immediate circle of adepts should die in the flames. The Goetheanum was set on fire on New Year's Eve, 1923, whilst Dr. Steiner was giving an evening lecture to some 800 people inside it. The arson was committed by a German-Swiss watch-maker who was both a fanatical Nazi and a zealous member of an established Church. His payment for the deed in gold coins was found on his charred corpse beside the ashes of the building the following morning. Dr. Steiner and his associates only escaped death by fire because the incendiary failed to work as quickly as planned.

The prime reason for burning down the Goetheanum was to destroy a huge woodcarving of the Trinity of Evil. Dr. Steiner had taken several years to complete the 30-foot high carving in elmwood which depicted Jesus Christ as the Representative of Humanity in the act of overcoming Lucifer and Ahriman. In both public and private lectures he had indicated the nature of the demonic spirit which inhabited the soul of Adolf Hitler and inspired the Nazi *Weltanschauung*. The woodcarving depicted Lucifer in characteristic gesture. Hitler was infuriated by it and Eckart persuaded him to try to destroy it. This carving, not yet fully finished at the time of the fire, was still housed in Steiner's studio in the grounds of the Goetheanum and escaped the flames. It is now the central piece in the new Goetheanum which Steiner designed in concrete before he died in March, 1925. More than a million people, including a high proportion of Germans, have since travelled to Dornach to see it.

CHAPTER TWENTY-TWO

THE *DOPPELGÄNGER*

Heinrich Himmler: The Anti-Man

"Himmler has been compared with a length of wire whose electric current is supplied from outside—that current being Hitler. He himself could not supply any current.

"Almost every member of his staff relieved his own conscience by unloading the official and moral responsibility for his SS practices on Heinrich Himmler. His staff served him faithfully, they needed him as a leader because without him as a potential whipping-boy of God, of history and Germany's enemies, they could not have gone through with what they did. . . .

"Even in death Heinrich Himmler still fulfils a similar function. . . . The German conscience is clear because the blame for everything sinister, contemptible, criminal and horrible that happened in Germany and the occupied countries between 1933 and 1945 rests on Himmler."

Himmler: The Evil Genius of the Third Reich: Willi Frischauer
(Odhams Press)

There exists in every human being a kind of 'anti-man' which the dictionary defines as a 'counterpart, or wraith'. Many philosophers and poets have described their personal experiences of this wraith which occultism calls the 'Double'.

Goethe, for instance, has spoken of the time when he entered the study at his home in Weimar and saw what appeared to be an exact counterpart of himself sitting in the chair behind his desk and looking brazenly back at him.

Suppressing an immediate feeling of alarm at this unusual experience, he stood and gazed for several seconds into the eyes and leering face of this momentarily visible counterpart of himself which he named the *Doppelgänger*. It was the first of several such experiences through which the poet came to understand the reason for the existence of this merciless and inhuman shadow element in the human soul.

The confrontation with the Double is a common experience to people who tread an occult path. It is one of the many experiences in the search for the Holy Grail which call forth both an inward moral power and the ability to achieve that balance of mind which is needed to face up to spirit-realities which are hidden to the mass of mankind.

Like Mephistopheles himself, the *Doppelgänger* also has its rightful place in the Lord's retinue. The task assigned to the Double is to provide in the human soul an opposition in the life of feeling towards the Good, the Beautiful and the True. Only by opposing the Double, as it were, by pressing against it with firm resolve, are we capable of finding the right moral path as human beings. The constant tension throughout life between the human soul and the Double gives a hidden stimulus to obey the dictates of conscience.

Though the actual conscious experience of the inner working of the Double is still hidden from the majority of people, it is simple enough to recognise its effects *en masse* in every sphere of human life in contemporary times. The whole aim of the *Doppelgänger* is to dehumanise every human activity, that is, it seeks to drag the human being down into an inhuman sphere. The *Doppelgänger* is anti-human, the anti-man.

The Double does not exist only as an Ahrimanic shadow in individual men. There are members in this *Doppelgänger* sub-hierarchy of far greater power who act as the anti-spirits of peoples, nations and races. And finally there is the World *Doppelgänger*, the Anti-Spirit of Humanity, which plays its historic role as a servant of Lucifer in opposing the rightful evolution of human consciousness.

We have depicted at some length how it came about that the

soul of Adolf Hitler became possessed by the Principality of the Luciferic hierarchy. We must now add to this picture the presence of the World *Doppelgänger*, the global Anti-Man, in the egoless body of the Reichsführer SS Heinrich Himmler, the most dreaded instrument of terror and inquisition in the entire history of mankind.

It has been pointed out by many eminent authorities how Heinrich Himmler time and again mysteriously anticipated the later policies of Adolf Hitler. Yet there is no real substance in the apparently endless controversy as to whether it was Hitler or Himmler who was the real evil genius of the Third Reich. For the Luciferic Intelligence possessing the soul of Adolf Hitler was in constant unspoken communion with the *Doppelgänger* which occupied the body of Heinrich Himmler. Occult insight reveals that behind the separate earthly personalities of these two deluded men, Lucifer and the Spirit of the Anti-Man worked as a single united intelligence, the Luciferic Principal galvanising the *Doppelgänger* like an unseen electric current from outside in order to administrate the arm of terror which would break all internal resistance to Nazism.

This hidden inner relationship between Hitler and Himmler was in itself a kind of anti-picture of the right relationship between the Ego and the Ahrimanic Double in every human soul.

The Double does not become effective in our lives until we begin to pass from childhood into adolescence. It is normally in the twelfth year that the first effects of the Double appear and we unconsciously press against the presence of inhuman feelings to reach personal moral decisions.

This inhuman onslaught of the Double on the soul intensifies as we get older, and the conscious experience of resisting evil in order to achieve moral aims continues throughout our lives. But the *Doppelgänger*, a shadow Being of fear and darkness, is afraid of death, for it cannot face a confrontation with the Light of Spirit-existence beyond the grave. For this reason the Double quits the human soul exactly three days before death. Sensitive souls are aware of this moment when the Double departs and leaves them with an inner sense of peace and harmony during the last three days of their lives on earth. Thousands of instances could be quoted from both World Wars in which men of pronounced conscience and aesthetic sense intuited the imminent approach of death when the Double departed from them.

The whole progressive relationship throughout a life span in which the human Ego holds the Double at bay, and overcomes its merciless and inhuman influences, was played out as a demonic mirror-image on the scene of history in the ever-deepening relationship between Adolf Hitler and Heinrich Himmler. For while Hitler surrendered his soul step by step to become the vessel of Lucifer, the World *Doppelgänger* at work in Himmler sought to smother the moral awareness of the German people, the dreadful pogrom of terror and inquisition finally liquidating the national conscience altogether.

It is deeply significant in this respect that Heinrich Himmler was born in October, 1900, when Adolf Hitler reached his twelfth year. And equally significant that Heinrich Himmler was himself exactly twelve years old when his future Führer underwent the first experience of demonic possession by Lucifer before the Spear of Destiny in the Treasure House at the Hofburg in Vienna. But this relationship between Lucifer and the World *Doppelgänger* became most marked three days before Adolf Hitler died.

When the moment finally arrived in the Underground Bunker in Berlin (April, 1945) for Adolf Hitler to face the spiritual consequences of his deeds, Heinrich Himmler was afraid to accompany his Führer through the gates of death.

For some weeks before the final crumbling of German resistance in Berlin, Himmler had been full of grandiose talk about sacrificing his life at the head of his SS Escort Division in one final full-blooded attack on the Russian Armies enclosing the capital. Yet secretly Himmler had been contemplating negotiations for a separate peace with the British and Americans through the medium of the Swedish arbitrator, Count Folke Bernadotte.

According to Walther Schellenberg, who accompanied Himmler throughout this period, the only obstacle which had prevented the Reichsführer from initiating such negotiations was his personal oath of allegiance to Adolf Hitler.

Exactly *three days* before Hitler shot himself in the Bunker, Himmler suddenly decided to go ahead with peace negotiations behind his Führer's back. Within hours his offer for a separate peace with the Western Allies was broadcast on the Swedish radio. It was an act of treachery which Adolf Hitler was unable to forgive, and his last deed was to dictate a political testament in which he expelled Heinrich Himmler from the Party and condemned him to death. "Before my death, I expel from the Party and from all his Offices the former Reichsführer SS and the Minister of the Interior, Heinrich Himmler."

At the very moment in which he decided to betray the doomed Hitler, Himmler suddenly reverted back into an ineffective nonentity. The electric current had been switched off. The World *Doppelgänger*, the source of all his power, had departed from him. From that time forward Himmler did not even have the initiative to muster his still loyal and fully equipped SS units to consolidate his position of power against other contenders to the leadership through force of arms; or even to use the vast resources of the secret police organisations to flee the country with false identity papers and money.

Instead, Himmler allowed himself to be apprehended by a couple of English soldiers at an insignificant road checkpoint near Bremervörde. Dressed in a plausible disguise and accompanied by two staunch SS Adjutants, who could easily have disarmed the bored and unsuspicious sentries, Himmler panicked and blurted out his real identity. Stripped naked during a personal search of his clothes and belongings in Field Marshal Montgomery's Intelligence H.Q. at Lüneburg, he crunched a capsule of cyanide between his teeth and died within minutes. He was buried by an English sergeant whose pre-war employment had been that of a dustman. Wrapped in camouflage nets and trussed up with barbed wire, his body was put beneath the soil somewhere in the forest outside Lüneburg.

Nobody except the ex-dustman knows where. The vessel of the *Doppelgänger*, the man who never was, had been dumped like any old rubbish in an unknown grave.

It was the deep-seated and widespread myth of 'the stab in the back' which gave the possibility for the World *Doppelgänger* to appear on the scene of German history in the twentieth century. The dissemination of this myth, so loudly proclaimed by Adolf Hitler, persuaded the masses that the German Armies were both unconquered and invincible, and that the Armistice which ended World War I was forced upon Germany by internal treachery.

Within the shadow of this widely-held and dangerous illusion the global Anti-Man arose almost invisibly to power until it was too late to stop it. For the monster who occupied Heinrich Himmler, the world's most unlikely tyrant, achieved the pinnacle of personal power of life and death over the people of Germany under the guise of safeguarding their interests and protecting the Nation from non-existent enemies!

The vessel for this role of mass enslavement and mass extermination of millions of innocent people had to be a man without an Ego, a soulless zombie totally incapable of the experience of love or of any human motive. And this is exactly what Heinrich Himmler was, an anti-human in a human body. One cannot even call Himmler a soul imprisoned and possessed by evil as was the case of Adolf Hitler. For in Himmler there was no self-conscious soul to be possessed, only a body and brain to be occupied and bent to inhuman purposes.

Himmler's father, Professor Gebhard Himmler, had spent several years as a personal tutor to Prince Heinrich of Bavaria, whom he instructed in the august family history of the Wittelsbach monarchy. And the young Heinrich, named after this Roman Catholic prince who became his God-father, grew up in a cultural atmosphere in which he too was nurtured from childhood on the same princely diet of German mythology and stories of the great heroes and kings of Germanic history.

295

Later at Landshut High School, where his father became headmaster, Heinrich Himmler astonished his teachers with the extent of his colourless card index memory of events and dates in European history. This talent to store away information and spill it out like a computer bank when needed was to become the very talent which took Himmler to power. His capacity for memorising history was also a preparation through which the World *Doppelgänger* could anticipate the *Weltanschauung* of Adolf Hitler, which in itself developed out of a pronounced historical cast of mind.

Entirely lacking in human warmth and personality and devoid of any sense of fun, Himmler appeared to his school fellows as a complete nonentity. Their attitude towards him was a mixture of contempt and fear, for he quickly gained a reputation as a sulky spoilsport and a notorious informer.

Family connections in service of the Bavarian Royal Household assured the right social background for officer training during World War I, but hostilities were over a few weeks before Ensign Himmler was considered old enough for battle service on the Western Front. Still determined to become a professional soldier, he applied for a permanent place in the post-war Reichswehr, a highly efficient force limited to one hundred thousand picked men. He was astonished to find himself refused on the grounds that he was both physically and psychologically unsuitable. He entered Munich Technical College to take a diploma in agriculture and later found a lowly place as a representative of a firm concerned in the manufacture of artificial fertilisers. A morose and disappointed youth he seemed to face a future which offered no hope of success.

While still a student in Munich, Himmler began to take an interest in the contemporary political scene. The race ideology of Nazism with its brutality towards the Jews excited him immensely and he attempted to join the ranks of Adolf Hitler's S.A., the Brown Shirts who appeared *en masse* at Party meetings to terrorise hecklers or to break up the local Communist groups. The tough Non-Coms who recruited for the S.A., all hardened veterans of trench warfare, spurned his repeated applications to join up. The weedy young man with the high-pitched voice and the strangely staring eyes magnified behind the lenses of rimless glasses was the very type of man they did not want. Finally he found a place in one of the many insignificant patriotic front organisations called the *Reichskriegsflagge*.

It was an exciting day for him when he put on his military uniform once more as a member of the *Reichskriegsflagge* who were called out by Captain Ernst Röhm in support of Adolf Hitler's pocket revolution in Munich in 1923.

After the farcical *Putsch* was broken up and dispersed by a couple of well-aimed volleys from the armed police, Himmler stayed on grimly as a member of a revolutionary picket posted outside the War Ministry. Soon the police arrived to break up this picket and arrest its members. But nobody considered the awkward looking ex-Ensign worth arresting, nor did they even bother to relieve him of his pistol! And finally the pale and puffy-faced young man walked back unmolested through the streets of Munich to catch a train home.

Yet fate was plotting secretly for a meteoric rise to power for the egoless zombie who had not been able to secure attention even with a loaded gun. The very failure of the Munich *Putsch* was to bring about the banning and temporary disbandment of the S.A. which had so haughtily spurned his services. And he was to find a backdoor right into the heart of the new and infamous formation which was created to circumvent the ban. When Hitler emerged from the Landsberg Fortress his very first act was to form the SS, the *Schutzstaffeln* or Protective Guards. This new formation of men who wore black breeches, jackets and shirts provided the bodyguard for Adolf Hitler and other Party Leaders when they held political meetings in areas hostile to Nazism.

Meanwhile Himmler had been sacked from the chemical firm which had been employing him, and in seeking for a new job he applied for the position of Secretary to Gregor Strasser, the local Nazi Party Chief in Landshut. Himmler secured the job for one reason only. Strasser overlooked the obvious lack of personality, hesitant manner and stuttering voice of Heinrich Himmler when he discovered that he had graduated in chemistry. For Strasser himself had been a chemist before turning his hand to full-time political activities. Hitching his career to Strasser's star, Himmler's position became more important when his boss was promoted to assume control of the overall propaganda and publicity of the Party.

The next link in the unlikely chain of events which would lead Himmler along the path to a position of power took place when Adolf Hitler found a remunerative way of employment for the volunteer members of the newly formed SS. Adolf Hitler had a large financial stake in the Party newspaper, *Der Völkischer Beobachter*, and the members of the SS were given jobs as space-sellers.

And so it came about that the first members of the most dreaded Order in Nazi Germany earned their living selling advertising space, acting as both extra reporters gathering news and as spies collecting information about the activities of local Communists and other enemies of the Party. Himmler, in his capacity as Secretary to Gregor Strasser, collated and indexed the information which the SS men brought back to the newspaper office. Very quickly Himmler was promoted to the imposing post of Assistant Propaganda Chief of the Nazi Party.

Willi Frischauer, the author of a work on Heinrich Himmler, spent many months researching the details of Himmler's life at this period. His description of the events leading up to the meeting between Hitler and Himmler and the manner in which their later relationship developed gives a staggering picture of the hidden communion between Lucifer and the World Double. Of course, Frischauer is not an occultist and he had no intention of illustrating such an occult relationship. It is simply that his work is so faithfully researched that the very sequence of events in this biographical study contains within itself all the clues to the presence of the Anti-Man behind the outer façade of Himmler's life.

"The young Party official (Himmler) occupied a small desk in a room crammed with newspaper files and shelves stacked with Party records and correspondence. A framed picture of Adolf Hitler adorned the wall facing Heinrich Himmler: 'I look up to you, mein Führer, look up to you literally!' Himmler ingratiatingly used to say in an attempt to make a deferential joke after his fashion. Hans Erhard, one of the people who knew Himmler at this time, told me he had secretly observed Himmler not only looking up to Hitler, but addressing the picture as a sort of rehearsal for the first time he would meet the Führer.

"When that day came, not much later, Himmler had no opportunity to speak to Hitler. The Führer looked through him, never even asking his name. It is characteristic of Himmler's nebulous insignificance at the time that I have failed to discover any definite date or occasion on which these two men established personal contact. Himmler was around—that was all. Imperceptibly he grew into the group of Nazi leaders who at first disregarded him, later accepted him as someone to whose presence they had become accustomed. His most prominent trait at that time was a dog-like subservience to his superiors, a determined reluctance to express any views of his own, an untiring diligence in keeping records and notes of any sort. Himmler has later often been described as a walking card index. . . ."*

There can be no doubt that Hitler himself was totally unaware at this time of the secret communion between the Spirit which possessed him and the World *Doppelgänger* in Himmler, or even that Himmler was occupied by such a Being. Yet it is equally beyond doubt to occult insight that the Luciferic Principal, which utilised the Führer's subconscious mind like a pawn, not only recognised the Cosmic Anti-Man in Himmler but also sparked it into life, directing its inhuman purposes towards the fulfilment of the demonic aims of Nazism.

It is deeply significant in this light that Hitler regarded Himmler at this period in 1925 with every sign of outward contempt. Assessing Himmler's longing for further promotion and his fascination with titles of office, however meaningless, he rewarded him for his services with a title which was regarded

* Willi Frischauer: *Heinrich Himmler* (Odhams Press).

by all the leading Nazis as the greatest joke in the history of the Party. Even the doleful Rudolf Hess is said to have slapped his thighs with laughter when he heard about it.

The time had arrived for the removal of the Government ban on the S.A. and a fresh and vigorous recruiting campaign was bringing in tens of thousands of new recruits to join the old core of veteran Brown Shirts who now reappeared in the streets in their pre-*Putsch* uniforms.

The very existence of the SS no longer appeared to have any meaning, and Adolf Hitler was convinced that this tiny force of two hundred men in black uniforms would soon disappear altogether from the contemporary Nazi scene.

Accordingly with mock pomp and ceremony he promoted the ambitious filing clerk to the rank of Deputy Leader of the SS. And he gave into Heinrich Himmler's personal keeping the so-called 'blood-flag' of the abortive November *Putsch*, the symbol of the greatest fiasco in the history of the Party.

The only person who did not regard this appointment as uproarously funny was Himmler himself, who did not even sense that he was the butt of the greatest leg-pull in years. He regarded his new post as a personal triumph, a generous recognition of his ability, and a stepping-stone to even greater things. Unfortunately for millions of innocent people, besides the leaders of the S.A., history itself was to prove Himmler correct in his apparently crazy assessment of the importance of his new promotion, title and appointment.

What Adolf Hitler himself was unable to see, but what the evil genius possessing his soul anticipated with startling exactness, was that the day would come when the S.A. would prove a terrible embarrassment to his personal ambition to become the undisputed Führer of a Third Reich. And that there would be an urgent need for an alternative force of determined and dedicated men to liquidate the leaders of the Brown Shirts.

It is true that Adolf Hitler was astonished at the sudden change which had inexplicably come about in the goofy filing clerk, and equally amazed and delighted with the manner in which Himmler had moulded his SS formation, and with the innovations and strict disciplines he had introduced, which conformed with the highest Nazi racist ideals. And for this reason Hitler maintained his SS bodyguard, the *Liebstandarte Adolf Hitler*, and permitted Himmler to increase the establishment of the SS to a strength of some 30,000 men.

Yet it was not a further application of Hitler's time-worn tactics of divide and rule which permitted the growth of the SS as a kind of counter balance against the increasing power of the S.A. After all, on the face of it, what were a paltry 30,000 SS compared with the might of the *Sturmabteilung* which numbered approximately three million men.

As late as 1933, when Hitler came to power by means of political cunning, he did not yet foresee that he would be forced to murder off Captain Röhm and the entire Staff Command of the S.A. in order to eliminate the Brown Shirts as a potential danger to his own position as leader of the Nazi Party. Even when he became Chancellor and handed out titles and offices to all the Nazi hierarchy, Himmler received only a minimal recognition for his services with the promotion to Police President of Munich, and his SS formations still remained a nominal part of the overall command of the S.A.

It was the High Command of the German Army, the originators of the myth of 'the stab in the back', who finally forced Hitler to turn against his oldest comrades among the 'Alte Kämpfer' of the S.A. And in demanding the elimination of the *Sturmabteilung* the High Command were unwittingly responsible for bringing Himmler suddenly and almost miraculously to a zenith of power, an unchallengeable position in the land, and second only to Hitler himself.

Watching the emergence of the Nazi régime the German General Staff had dealt shrewdly with Hitler, gaining many vital concessions for their promise not to intervene with force of arms in the internal political scene. The Generals had even induced Hitler to pass a law (Army Law 20) through the House of Representatives which removed all Reichswehr personnel—officers and other ranks—outside the jurisdiction of the

Civil Courts. And they had persuaded the senile President von Hindenburg that he should retain the right to appoint a Minister of Defence of his own choice to any Government in power. In this manner the German Army had gained a position of total independence outside the control of the Nazi Party when Hitler became Chancellor.

Captain Ernst Röhm, the Chief of Staff of the S.A., and one of Adolf Hitler's closest personal friends, had scant respect for the Generals or for the rigid traditions of the Officer Corps. He pointed out that his own armed volunteers outnumbered the Reichswehr by thirty to one. He was sure he could persuade his Führer to overthrow and disband the German Army and to make the three million strong *Sturmabteilung* the nucleus of the new military arm of the nation.

In such hopes Röhm was greatly deluded, for Adolf Hitler now believed his own constantly-repeated lie about the complete invincibility of the German Army. He considered the Reichswehr to be indispensable for the fulfilment of his dreams of world conquest. He believed that he could not do without their traditional disciplines and fighting spirit, their training courses, military skills, and technical expertise. If it came to a choice between the Reichswehr and the *Sturmabteilung*, it was his old comrades who had helped him in his struggle to power who would have to go to the wall.

For a period Hitler sought a form of compromise in which the cream of the S.A. could be incorporated into the German Army. But such a compromise the German generals would under no circumstances accept.

The Officer Corps rightly regarded the *Sturmabteilung* as a pack of uncouth and undisciplined bums who had been responsible for a reign of violence on the streets unprecedented in the history of the nation, a period of crude brutality and terror in which even innocent people had been murdered in settlement of personal grudges under the guise of justified political activity.

And beyond this the generals pointed to the complete lack of moral qualities in Captain Röhm and his colleagues on the

Staff of the S.A., men such as Heines who had gained a nation-wide reputation for the disorder and luxury of their living and for indulging in homosexual practices. Yet it was not such criticisms of his own former henchmen which influenced Adolf Hitler in his final decision.

What finally convinced Adolf Hitler of the potential danger of Röhm and his *Sturmabteilung* was an open threat of a counter-revolution. The rank and file of the S.A. felt they had been shamefully left out in the scramble for titles and jobs when Hitler came to power. And now they could not wait to take over the ranks, prestige, pay and perks of the professional army, and were prepared for any amount of blood-letting to attain their aims.

Captain Röhm facing a state of mutiny within his own organisation was forced to voice publicly his understanding of their needs. "Anyone who thinks that the tasks of the *Sturmabteilung* have been accomplished," he told thousands of S.A. men assembled on the Tempelhofer Feld outside Berlin, "will have to get used to the idea that we are here and intend to stay here come what may." In another speech in which he complained that Hitler's revolution had not gone far enough, he shouted out: "We must begin to clear out the pig-sty and drive some of the dirty swine from their troughs."

This was the sign for Adolf Hitler to promote Heinrich Himmler to a position in which he could become the official state butcher in order to carry out the blood bath which would involve the murder of 4,000 leading members of the *Sturmabteilung*, the legacy of Hitler's years of struggle. And where in German history is there to be found such a spectacular series of promotions and extensions of power as those given to Heinrich Himmler at this time? The World *Doppelgänger* was on his way to that pinnacle of personal power from which he could hold the lives of every man, woman and child in Germany, and later in all Europe, in the palm of his hand.

"From October, 1933, onwards the German Press began to announce the stepping-stones of Himmler's rise with monotonous regularity: 27th October, Himmler Chief of Political Police in Mecklenburg and Lübeck; 20 December, Himmler Chief of Political Police in Baden; 21 December, Himmler Chief of Political Police in Hesse and Anhalt; 24 December, Himmler Chief of Political Police in Bremen. The headlines screamed: the German people who were beginning to get acquainted with Himmler's methods, trembled. Ernst Röhm and the S.A. recognised the writing on the wall. Other appointments soon followed: Thuringia, Saxonia, Hamburg, Württemberg. Within a few months Himmler had become Chief of Political Police in every province in Germany except Prussia, where Göring clung to his job." (*Heinrich Himmler:* Willi Frischauer.)

While Himmler took over the running of the Gestapo from Göring and organised it on a national scale, and spies from the *Sicherheitsdienst* (SS Political Intelligence Dept.) kept a close watch on the day-to-day activities of Captain Röhm and his colleagues, Adolf Hitler continued to waver in a state of indecision over the prospect of killing off the men who had brought him to power.

It was at this moment that a significant thing happened which was to precipitate events. Fourteen years earlier, a certain General McClean, a Freemason of a high degree, had suggested to General Eric Ludendorff that the German Army had been stabbed in the back. The two Generals were dining together after the 1918 Armistice and Ludendorff was putting forward his belief that the German Army could never have been beaten on the field of battle. "You mean you were stabbed in the back," said the English General. "Yes, that's it. That is exactly what I do mean. We were stabbed in the back!" said Ludendorff, excited to have heard so apt an expression for the myth he sought to spread.

And now, in the moment of crisis in 1934, Anthony Eden, the British Foreign Secretary, a man who followed in the Tory tradition of mixing Freemasonry with power politics, arrived in Berlin for consultations with Adolf Hitler. He had come to Germany with the specific task of demanding that the strength of the *Sturmabteilung* should be reduced by two-thirds. There is

no intention here to suggest any form of Freemason conspiracy, simply an attempt to illustrate how the Law of Karma
worked on an international level in bringing the World *Doppelgänger* in Heinrich Himmler to power.

By conceding to Eden's demand to scrap the S.A., Hitler saw
an opportunity to gain an aura of international confidence
under the screen of which he could re-arm and expand the
Reichswehr. General Blomberg, Army Chief of Staff, mysteriously chose the moment of Eden's visit to force Hitler's hand.
"Relax the tension in the nation or President Hindenburg will
declare martial law and hand power over to the Army," he
told Hitler. The die was cast.

When an unknown assailant aimed a shot at Hitler in the
grounds of Göring's home at Schorfheide outside Berlin, it was
immediately assumed to be part of an S.A. plot to murder
him.

Himmler, standing between Hitler and the unseen gunman,
was wounded in the arm. "How grateful I am to destiny," cried
the jubilant Himmler. "It has permitted me to save the life of
my Führer!" From that time forward Himmler was to refer to
himself as Adolf Hitler's "blood brother". The Röhm purge
followed almost immediately.

The *Liebstandarte Adolf Hitler*, under the command of Sepp
Dietrich, accompanied the Führer to Bavaria to despatch Ernst
Röhm and his immediate henchmen. Himmler remained in
Berlin to set up an execution H.Q. at the Lichterfelde Barracks
where he could personally supervise the killings of the mass of
arrested S.A. leaders and other revolutionaries.

The man without a conscience walked up and down behind
his firing squads. Among those shot in cold blood was Gregor
Strasser, his former boss of Munich days. While the dead piled
high and gun barrels became almost too hot to hold, the Anti-
Man made note of the names of the waverers and weaklings
among his own Blackshirts who showed no stomach for cold-
blooded murder.

Every shot fired paved the way for Himmler to assume total
power, the blood bath inaugurating what was to become the

short and gruesome history of the Black Order. The era of the *Doppelgänger* had begun.*

By means of a *Schutzhaftbefehl*—an Order of Protective Custody—Reichsführer SS Heinrich Himmler, his plain-clothes agents in the Gestapo and his minions in the dreaded black uniforms could arrest whosoever they chose. All that was required was the entry of the prisoner's name on a readily available printed form—"In accordance with Paragraph I of the Order for Protection of Nation and Folk, to be taken forthwith into protective custody." This was the road of no-return along which millions were to tread to the brutality, torture and mass extermination of the Concentration Camps.

In the light of all that happened later it is simple enough to identify in retrospect the dissembling of the *Ur-Doppelgänger* in all Himmler's blatant and audacious falsifications regarding the moral justification for the use of 'Protective Custody' and in the manner in which he veiled the real conditions existing in the Concentration Camps.

"Protective Custody is an act of care," said Himmler in a public speech in Munich in the year in which he personally founded Dachau Concentration Camp. On this occasion he was attempting to silence the atrocity stories which were spreading abroad. "If I have taken such measures in rather an extensive

---

* The most prominent feature in the working of the *Doppelgänger* is an endless capacity to counterfeit and dissemble, to make something look what it is not, and to feign benign reasons and moral justification to cover up evil motives.

The whole Nazi regime was built up on such practices. For instance, Adolf Hitler achieved personal power through such a counterfeit law, the so-called 'Enabling Law', by which the Führer gained complete independence from both President and Reichstag. The actual title of this law, which Hitler secured by burning down the Reichstag to prove the existence of dangerous enemies of the state, was 'Law for Removing the Distress of People and Nation'. In this manner the power of all other political parties, state institutions and the Trades Unions was eliminated overnight. The application of the same law on an individual level extinguished the personal liberty of every single German in the Reich.

manner, I have been misunderstood in many places! You must understand there was justifiable excitement, annoyance and hostility against those who opposed us. Only by taking them under Protective Custody was I able to save these personalities who have caused this annoyance. Only in this way was I able to guarantee their security of health and life."

"May I say right here," he told assembled foreign newspaper men on another occasion in his characteristic high-pitched voice, "for us the Jews are as much citizens as those of non-Jewish faith. Their lives and property are equally respected. Protective Custody where it concerns Jews must be understood in this spirit."*

Under what Heinrich Himmler called 'an act of care' millions of men, women and children were mercilessly enslaved, starved and worked to death in what became a state industry with by-products. The Planetary *Doppelgänger* or Anti-Man inhabiting the body and brain of the Reichsführer SS demonstrated the mastery of this counterfeit technique, culminating with such items as innocent-looking bathhouses for use as disguised extermination chambers and hidden radium-ray machines to sterilise unsuspecting slave workers as they stood at counters to fill in complicated but meaningless forms.

The archetypal instance of this counterfeit working of the *Ur-Doppelgänger* in the evolution of mankind† took place at the Crucifixion itself when Caiaphas, the Jewish High Priest and Chief of the Sanhedrin, ordered the Captain of the Temple Guard to break the bones of Jesus Christ. The moral justification feigned behind this order was that by Jewish Law no man could be put to death on the Sabbath Day. The real motive behind this subterfuge, as we have already described in the

---

* Extracts from German newspapers 1933–4, translation from *Heinrich Himmler*: Willi Frischauer.

† The *Doppelgänger* has been active throughout two thousand years of Christendom. And, of course, the working of the *Doppelgänger* sub-hierarchy in the twentieth century has not been confined to the machinations of the Nazis. In the current newspapers and TV news bulletins one can see endless instances of the working of the Anti-Man in all parts of the globe.

Prologue of this book, was to mutilate the body of Christ so that the masses should not believe in Him as the Messiah; for it was written in the Scriptures that "a bone of Him shall not be broken." It was the presence on Golgotha of the Roman Centurion Gaius Cassius and his martial but compassionate deed with the Spear which defeated this diabolical plan.

In the light of the spiritual background we have uncovered regarding the first unleashing of the *Ur-Doppelgänger* against Jesus Christ and the obstruction of its inhuman aims by the timely, decisive and world historic deed of the Roman Centurion, it is not surprising that the same monstrous Anti-Man inhabiting Himmler had some association with the Spear of Longinus in the twentieth century. Heinrich Himmler was fascinated by the Spear of Destiny and involved himself compulsively in a deep study of its history through the ages. In fact, the two great central themes of interest in the life of the Reichsführer SS were the Spear of Longinus and the occult significance of the blood!

Whereas Adolf Hitler waited patiently for thirty years between his first sight of the Spear in the Hofburg and the day he claimed it as his own possession, Heinrich Himmler anticipated the event by having an exact replica of the Spear made for himself in 1935, three years before his Führer annexed Austria and plundered the treasures of the Hapsburg Dynasty.

It was the threat contained within a Germanic prophecy made a thousand years ago which spurred Heinrich Himmler to order a replica to be made of the Spear associated with a legend of world destiny. This prophecy, from the lips of a Saxon soothsayer in the tenth century reign of King Henry The Fowler, was to come true to the letter. It spoke of "a gigantic storm which would appear out of the East to overwhelm the German peoples if it was not confronted and turned back in the region of the Birkenwald in Westphalia."

Himmler, the man with the card-index mind that registered every facet of German history and legend, interpreted this prophecy to mean that Germany would be vanquished and overrun by Slavonic and yellow hordes from Russia and

Siberia unless they were met by a disciplined and dedicated Order similar to the Order of the ancient Teutonic Knights.

Every German schoolboy is familiar to this day with the heroic deeds of the Teutonic Knights. They came from many lands and had proved their knightly spirit in battle under many different sovereigns and flags. But when they entered the austere precincts of the Marienberg they abandoned their personal shields engraved with the heraldry and arms of at least four knightly and aristocratic ancestors. Their single emblem then became the Cross. They sought no other identity but as selfless Members of the Order and no other honour but to die in battle in order that they might gain eternal life.

For some years Himmler had considered transforming the SS into such a knightly Order. Though a crusade in service of the Cross was very far from his mind. He conceived an Order based on Aryan Blood in which each member should prove the blood in his veins to be unblemished by 'race-shame', *Rassenschande*, or indeed any admixture of non-Aryan blood for at least five generations. And now he envisaged a burg in Westphalia which should become the sacred assembly point and retreat for the leaders of the SS formations and other senior and totally dedicated members of the *Schutzstaffeln*. From this burg would go forth that dedicated Order of the new SS Warriors who would defeat and turn back the prophesied storm from the East. And in this burg would be kept the replica of the Spear to which was attributed powers of world conquest.

On the site of the ruins of an ancient but unidentified medieval burg near Paderborn, Heinrich Himmler ceremoniously laid the foundation stone of what was to become the infamous Wewelsburg. The project, which cost some 13 million marks was built in less than a year, the heaviest labour being carried out by slave workers from a nearby concentration camp under the whips of their SS guards.

"When it was completed it was a unique reconstruction of a medieval castle, yet built to realise the image in Himmler's mind. Every room was furnished in a different style—not even a single desk was duplicated. Only leading craftsmen of every branch had been employed to produce fine tapestries, solid oak furniture, wrought-iron door handles, candlesticks. Priceless carpets were acquired, curtains of heavy brocade flanked the high windows. Doors were carved and embellished with precious metals and stones. Built in the old Germanic style on a triangular foundation, the burg's towers rose high over the surrounding forest.''*

Though Bartels carried out the major architectural work in the construction of the Wewelsburg, Himmler added his own personal masterstroke in the way that he made the Spear of Destiny the progressive theme of the interior design and symbolic decoration of the whole castle. For Himmler conceived that each room should be designed, laid out and decorated in every detail to personify the life-style, traditions, beliefs and achievements of every individual claimant of the legendary Spear from the ninth century to the nineteenth century—that is, from Charles The Great until the collapse of the Old German Empire in 1806 when the ancient and historic weapon was secreted out of Nuremberg and taken to Vienna where it was out of the ambitious clutches of Napoleon Bonaparte.

There was a room for Frederick Barbarossa which was always kept locked and reserved for Adolf Hitler should he ever wish to visit the sacred sanctuary of his SS elite. There were rooms for Otto The Great, Henry The Lion, Frederick Hohenstauffen, Philip of Swabia, Conrad IV—just to mention a few of the illustrious Kings and Emperors who had staked their claims to the Spear of Longinus and associated the fulfilment of a world-historic destiny to its powers.

Each room contained genuine period pieces and such items as swords, shields, armour, even personal garments and jewels which had belonged to each heroic figure in the succession of claimants to the Spear. Paintings and tapestries hung from the walls along with the regalia of their courts. Himmler sent his minions all over Germany and Europe to search museums and private collections and to bring back their finds whatever the cost.

* *Heinrich Himmler*: Willi Frischauer.

When the leaders of the SS formations and members of the senior ranks came together several times a year at the Wewelsburg to attend conferences and the like, each officer was allocated a different room on each occasion so that gradually all became thoroughly acquainted with the history of this ancient weapon upon the powers of which the Reichsführer set such store.

Heinrich Himmler never exchanged his own room in which nobody else was permitted to sleep in his absence. This was the room created as a shrine to the memory of the celebrated Henry I, sometimes called the 'Bird Catcher', the first of the great Saxon Kings of whom the ghoulish *Reichsheini* believed himself to be the reincarnation! And it was in this room, the memorial of the Warrior King who turned back the marauding hordes of Magyars from the East, that the replica of the Spear of Destiny was kept. There it stood on Himmler's desk, resting on a faded red velvet cushion in an ancient-looking leather case. A temporary talisman of power until the day the Führer grabbed Austria and brought back to the Fatherland the genuine article, which Himmler wrongly assumed would be handed over to the SS as a symbol of the new Holy Order.

It is not possible to consider the personality of Himmler in connection with reincarnation, for there was no real 'Ego' within him. The question arises here as to what was the real nature of his personal experience of identity. It is a baffling question. He must have experienced several levels of synthetic self-consciousness. For instance, a family identity was very strong in him and he wept like a small child when his mother died, apparently for a time quite unconsolable. There were also elements of an Officer Class identity onto which he clung in the aftermath of World War I. And there was a Race Identity, a totally unrealistic castle in the air upon which much of his personality as Reichsführer SS was based, and under the spell of which he was to commit endless crimes against humanity.

One thing is quite certain, and that is that there was never at any time a human 'I' in Himmler which could be over-shadowed by an Individual Human Spirit containing within itself the spiritual biography of former lives on earth—what we called earlier "the spiritual lineage of Reincarnation".

Had Himmler ever any idea, however inarticulate, of the real nature of the Spirit which worked in him and through him? Did he for one moment sense that he was the vehicle of the *Doppelgänger* of Mankind, the Planetary Anti-Man? Of course, the answer must be that he did not, for there was no Ego within him to become aware of it.

However there is evidence that Himmler knew of the exist-ence of such a Being and even knew what it looked like to spirit-vision, because a painting of it was discovered among his treasured books and belongings in the study of his home after he went into hiding at the end of hostilities and before he committed suicide.

It was a print of a painting which Rudolf Steiner had worked into the design of one of the windows of the Goetheanum which the Nazis burned down. The painting depicts a serpent-like body with a horned head and gigantic flapping ears. The face has a moronic and vacuous expression rather similar to Himm-ler's own inhuman countenance, a kind of mongoloid look.

What was in Himmler's mind when he looked at this paint-ing it is impossible to tell. According to some sources Himmler considered it to be the 'Spirit of Race-Shame'. It is certain that he never recognised it as a portrait of himself. Those Adjutants, who were close to Himmler and knew some of the answers to these riddles, are either dead or remain silent.

What finally made Himmler settle for Henry The Bird Catcher, as his supposed former incarnation is not known. The people in history whose thinking Himmler implemented in his everyday administration of the Gestapo and *Sicherheitsdienst*, were all sinister personalities. Such men as Ignatius Loyola, the founder of the Jesuits, Torquemada, the Ur-Inquisitor, and Fouché, a master-builder in the historical development of the Police State. But Henry I fitted in conveniently with the idea of a thousand-year gap between incarnations, the wish to associate

312

himself with one of the historic claimants to the Spear, and the illusion that he was destined to obstruct the fulfilment of the ancient prophecy concerning the destruction of Germany by hordes from the East.

CHAPTER TWENTY-THREE

HITLER CLAIMS THE SPEAR OF LONGINUS

The bell of the Royal Chapel of the Hapsburg Emperors rang out to celebrate the German annexation of Austria and its incorporation in the Third Reich. Crowds filled the Ring and lined both sides of the entire length of the Ringstrasse to welcome the German Führer to Vienna, the capital city of his homeland.

The picked troops of Keitel's 8th Army Group and the tanks of Guderian's vaunted Panzer Division, which had crossed the border into Austria two days previously, were now assembled before the huge reviewing stand immediately in front of the ancient Hofburg. All now awaited the arrival of the man who had once tramped the pavements of the ancient Imperial City "as a vagabond, unwashed and empty-bellied". The same man "who but four years before had assumed in Germany the powers of the Hohenzollern Kings and had now taken upon himself those of the Hapsburg Emperors."*

Adolf Hitler crossed the frontier to drive through decorated villages on his way to Linz where he had once lived and attended school. In Linz he awaited the arrival from Vienna of Reichsführer SS Heinrich Himmler to confirm that his well-laid plans to secure the Spear of Longinus had been successful

---

* *The Rise and Fall of the Third Reich:* William L. Shirer.

314

and that a guard of picked Stormtroopers were standing guard over it in the Treasure House of the Hofburg.

His fears that this talisman of world-historic destiny might evade his grasp at the last moment, in the same manner as it had eluded the clutches of Napoleon, were now abated. Yet fearing an assassination attempt, like that of Friedrich Staps on the person of the French Emperor in the grounds of the Hapsburg summer palace, Hitler delayed his entry into Vienna for a further day so that additional security measures could be taken to protect him. While excitement reached fever pitch at Hitler's unexpected announcement of a total Anschluss, and the SS rounded up thousands of known and potential anti-Nazis, Adolf Hitler visited Leonding to place a wreath on his mother's grave.

It is not difficult to imagine the feelings of resentment and bitterness which arose in Hitler's heart at the recollection of the poverty and isolation in which his widowed mother had died in Linz, and his own terrible years of starvation and loneliness as an outcast in Vienna which followed immediately upon her death.

Adolf Hitler was to tell the Bürgermeister of Vienna: "Be assured that this City is in my eyes a pearl—I will bring it into a setting which is worthy of it." Yet nothing could have been further from the truth.* He was determined to reduce the ancient Imperial City to the status of a Provincial town and Austria itself to the position of the most insignificant German satellite. The people who "had rejected him and condemned him in his youth to a starved and miserable gutter life" must now pay the price for their mistake.

When Hitler was driven down the Ringstrasse to the Ring and onto the Heldenplatz to the reviewing stand in front of the Hofburg, the tumultuous jubilation of the crowds reached near

---

* Hitler spoke with incredible and endless venom to rant against the people of Vienna. "Vienna should never have been admitted into the Union with greater Germany," Hitler said. He never felt any love for Vienna. He loathed its people. *Testimony at Nuremberg of Baldur von Shirach, Gauleiter of Vienna.*

delirium. How could the citizens of Vienna have known that the ecstasy on the face of Adolf Hitler was the twisted ecstasy of revenge!

The blasphemous spirit of Friedrich Nietzsche must have choked with glee as Adolf Hitler broadcast the greatest deception of his life to his new and unsuspecting subjects: "I felt the call of Providence had come to me. In three days the Lord has smitten them (Miklas, Schuschnigg and those others who had dared to resist him). And to me the grace was given on the day of the betrayal to be able to unite my homeland to the Reich. I would give thanks to Him who let me return to my homeland in order that I might now lead it into the German Reich. To-morrow may every German recognise the hour and measure its import and bow in humility before the Almighty, who in a few weeks has wrought such a miracle upon us!"*

After reviewing the assembled ranks of the Austrian SS, and granting permission for the founding of a new SS Regiment *Der Führer*, Adolf Hitler refused an invitation to make a grand tour of the City in which he had once frequented the flophouse. He left the Ring to drive directly to the Imperial Hotel where the most luxurious suite in the city awaited him. Arrangements for a civic dinner and reception were cancelled while Hitler, still terrified that an attempt would be made to kill him, remained in his closely-guarded suite.

It was long after midnight when he left the Imperial Hotel in the company of Heinrich Himmler to make the long-awaited visit to the Weltliche Schatzkammer to claim the Spear of Destiny as his own personal possession.

Awaiting him at the Hofburg were Wolfram von Sievers,

---

* "The ubiquitous Papen, rushing by plane from Berlin to Vienna to get in on the festivities, found Hitler in the reviewing stand opposite the Hofburg, the ancient Palace of the Hapsburgs. 'I can only describe him,' Papen wrote later, 'as being in a state of ecstasy.'

"Yet underneath the ecstasy, and unnoticed by the shallow Papen, there may have burned in Hitler a feeling of revenge for a city and a people which had not appreciated him as a young man and which at heart he despised. This in part may have accounted for his brief stay." *The Rise and Fall of the Third Reich*: William L. Shirer.

head of the Nazi Occult Bureau, Major Walter Buch, Nazi legal expert and chief of the USCHLA, and Ernst Kaltenbrunner, SS Führer, Austria. All three, along with Reinhardt Heydrich's *Sicherheitspolizei*, had played a separate role in helping to secure the Spear for him.

Von Sievers, responsible to Himmler for organising academic research into the history of the Heilige Lance, had arrived in Vienna several days before the Anschluss to ensure that the talisman of power was not removed from the city. Confidential dossiers had been made on all personnel connected with the Hofburg, from the Director and his archivists down to the most humble attendants.

When German troops first crossed the border into Austria, President Miklas had given orders that special reinforcements of police should be set to cordon off the inner city and that protection should be given to all government buildings, including the Hofburg. When the police arrived outside the Hofburg, they were met by determined ranks of black uniformed SS, fully armed and determined to brook no interference. The keys of the Treasure House, the equivalent of the chamber in the Tower of London where the Crown Jewels are guarded, had been handed over to the Nazis by defected officials. Ernst Kaltenbrunner himself had appeared on the scene with orders that the SS should open fire rather than concede to the directions of the police. As was the case in every city, town and village throughout Austria that night, the police gave in to the Nazis, so obviously on the brink of total power.

Major Walter Buch, father-in-law to Martin Bormann and Head of the *Oberstes Parteigericht*, was present to arrange the legal take-over of the Reichskleinodien, the precious symbols of the ancient German Empire which included the Heilige Lance. His task was to organise the return of the Spear of Longinus across the German border to Nuremberg. But Walter Buch, an occultist who was responsible for the liquidation of Freemasonry in Nazi Germany, had more than a legal interest in the Spear of Destiny and had been allowed to share Hitler's secret concerning his visions before this talisman of world destiny.

317

Hitler entered the Treasure House with Heinrich Himmler while Kaltenbrunner, von Sievers and Walter Buch waited outside with Hitler's aides and members of his personal body-guard. Shortly afterwards Heinrich Himmler came back down the narrow staircase of the Schatzkammer leaving the German Führer quite alone. There is no evidence of any kind of what took place during the hour or more in which Hitler remained in solitude with the talisman of world-historic destiny he had now come to make into his own personal possession.

Although, as we have amply illustrated, the Spear of Longi-nus had been the inspiration of his whole life and the key to his meteoric rise to power, it was more than a quarter of a century since he had last seen it, and nearly thirty years since he first beheld it and heard of its unique legend.

Whatever Hitler's visions on this occasion, the scene of the German Führer standing there before the ancient weapon must be regarded as the most critical moment of the twentieth century until the Americans claimed the Spear in Nuremberg in 1945, and, while holding it in their possession, inaugurated the Atomic Age by dropping their atom bombs on Hiroshima and Nagasaki.

The British, French, Russian and Czechoslovak Governments had not lifted a finger to stop Adolf Hitler's annexation of Austria, which they regarded as no more than the inevitable union between two German peoples who shared the same heritage, language and culture.

Only the solitary voice of Winston Churchill warned the world that Hitler's entry into Vienna constituted such a decisive change in the balance of European power that world war was now inevitable. In possession, through Dr. Walter Stein, of all the facts regarding Adolf Hitler's fascination with the legend of world destiny associated with the Reich's Lance in the Hofburg, Winston Churchill could see with an even greater transparency the Nazi Führer's plans for world con-quest.

In Churchill's eyes, "the acquisition of Vienna, for centuries regarded as the gateway to south-eastern Europe, placed the

German Army on the edge of the Hungarian plain and at the threshold of the Balkans."*

Hitler had also added some seven or eight million German subjects to the Third Reich. He had gained a common frontier with Italy to bolster up the Berlin–Rome Axis. His armies now outflanked Czechoslovakia on three sides and Churchill maintained rightly that his next step would be the liquidation of the Czech State. And beyond this, Adolf Hitler had learned through his nerve-shattering political opportunism that Britain, France and Russia were so afraid of armed conflict that all their apparently measured plans to curb his territorial ambitions were no more than empty threats.

This same night would be known in Vienna as 'the night of the terror' or 'the night of revenge'. On Hitler's personal orders from the Imperial Hotel, the most dreadful pogrom was initiated against the large, rich and influential Jewish population, and in the coming days 70,000 Jews would be arrested. Such were the scenes of sadism and brutality in the streets that many Jews fled into Germany itself to find refuge. A new Concentration Camp was set up on the north bank of the Danube which was to earn an infamous reputation—Mauthausen. Here the official execution list was to be longer than in any other camp within the confines of the Reich. Reinhardt Heydrich was quickly doing a brisk trade with a new department named 'the Office for Jewish Emigration'. Later, under the direction of Karl Eichmann it would switch its role. Instead of selling exit permits to rich Jews in exchange for their worldly wealth, the department would organise mass deportations to the Gas Ovens of the death camps. It was admitted at the Nuremberg Trials that the decision to go ahead with the plans for the 'final solution' dated from the night of Hitler's triumphant entry into Vienna.

This was the night of decision. The time had come to cast away the instruments of guile and political cunning. From this moment forward Adolf Hitler would strike out openly to achieve his ultimate aim—the conquest of the world.

* *Hitler: Study in Tyranny*: Alan Bullock.

On this occasion, unlike his previous visits to the Treasure House, there were no guards, petty officials and attendants to keep a suspicious and wary eye on an unkempt outcast. The successor to the Hapsburg Emperors was free to remove the ancient weapon from its faded red velvet dais behind the protecting glass case. One can presume that he held the talisman of power in his hands, feeling the cold blackened metal of the tapering point which had pierced the side of Jesus Christ at the Crucifixion.

It was surely a scene which that genius of the bizarre, Charlie Chaplin himself, would never have dared to stage!

A happening outwardly so comical and so unlikely that it is hardly credible! And yet a happening so potent with evil that it would cause an eruption more violent and destructive than the world had ever before known. A happening which concealed the first incendiary flicker of a merciless 'Will to Power' which would soon spread in blazing desolation across the rubble of a continent. An unseen communing with 'Principalities and Powers' which would inspire a satanic reign of terror and cold-blooded butchery outstripping in primitive savagery and bestial cruelty all previous ages of tyranny and oppression in the entire history of mankind.

CHAPTER TWENTY-FOUR

THE ASHES

Astrological Pest Control: Rabbits, Rats, and 'Sub-Humans'.

The rabbits on Count Keyserlingk's estates in Silesia had become a menace. Formerly kept in check with guns, the shortage of manpower and the absence of organised shooting parties throughout World War I had allowed their numbers to grow to serious proportions and the rabbits were overrunning the farm lands in the region of Koberwitz.

The situation became yet more chaotic after the war when Count Keyserlingk announced that he would no longer countenance the shooting of any form of wild life on his own estates or the lands of his tenant farmers. He also refused to permit the use of poisons. "I am searching for some alternative method to get rid of the pests," he told his angry neighbours.

In the spring of 1924 Count Keyserlingk invited interested landowners, farmers and market-gardeners from all over Europe to attend an Agricultural conference at his Koberwitz home in order to promote "an attitude to farming in which the earth and nature were no longer regarded as objects of short-sighted financial exploitation." The conference would also consider a new bio-dynamic method of farming to produce healthier crops, prevent soil erosion, combat pollution, and curtail the multiplication of plant and animal diseases arising from the use of industrial poisons and synthetic fertilisers. The

321

highlight of the conference would be a demonstration of a new form of 'Pest Control' which would rid the estate and neighbouring lands of the whole rabbit population in three days.

A rumour circulated amongst the local peasantry and smallholders that Count Keyserlingk was bringing to Koberwitz a celebrated 'Wizard' who, like the legendary Pied Piper, would spirit the rabbits away. They waited with a mixture of apprehension, superstition and curiosity for the appearance of this magician who would wave his wand and conjure away the teeming rabbit population without recourse to guns or poisons.

The man about to perform this apparent miracle was Dr. Rudolf Steiner who was to deliver a series of lectures at the conference. On arrival at Koberwitz he requested that a male rabbit should be shot and brought to the room temporarily set up as a laboratory. He removed the spleen, testes and a portion of the rabbit skin. These items were burned to ashes. The ashes were then mixed with a neutral powder, sugar of milk, and homeopathically 'potentised' beyond the boundary of ponderable existence. There was nothing new in itself with homeopathic potentisation. It is a process used regularly at such institutions as the Royal Homeopathic Hospital in London and by several thousand fully qualified medical practitioners throughout the world. It was the purpose for which Dr. Steiner intended to use this particular potentisation that was of startling significance.*

---

* Dr. Ernst Lehrs, one of Steiner's closest pupils, has given a short description of Homeopathy and the process of potentising which may help the reader who is unfamiliar with these concepts:

"The method in question is associated with the school of medicine known as Homeopathy, founded by the German doctor, Hahnemann. The word 'Homeopathy' means healing through like'; the basic principle is to treat disease symptoms with highly diluted substances which produce similar symptoms if ingested in normal quantity. Experience has in fact shown that the physiological effect of a substance taken from external nature is reversed when the substance is highly diluted.

"The method of diluting, or 'potentising', is as follows: A given volume of the material to be diluted is dissolved in nine times its volume of distilled water. The degree of dilution thus arrived at is 1 : 10, usually symbolised 1x. A tenth part of this solution is again mixed with nine times its bulk in

His intention was to induce a condition of such total insecurity in relation to their present habitat that the whole rabbit population would quit the area in panic. To achieve this end he was utilising those organs from the buck rabbit which in his opinion were the physiological basis for the instinct of survival within the species. The homeopathic potency would transform this instinct into its very opposite. Spread on the wind and absorbed through respiration, he conceived that the concoction would have a functional effect on the rabbits similar to that condition which nature herself induces in Lemmings when, their numbers greater than their environment can withstand, they gather in their thousands bent on self-destruction.

Dr. Steiner carried his concoction in a bucket to the paddock near the house. He held in his other hand the type of brush normally used to sweep crumbs into a dustpan. He dipped the brush into the liquid and flicked it like fine rain into the wind. Young assistants carried similar buckets up wind to the borders of the estate and also spread the homeopathic potency like fine spray.

water. The degree of dilution is now 1 : 100, or 2x. This process is continued as far as it is necessary for a given purpose. Insoluble substances can be dealt with in the same manner by first grinding them together with corresponding quantities of a neutral powder, generally sugar of milk. After a certain number of stages the powder can be dissolved in water; the solution may then be diluted further in the manner already described.

"We can carry the dilutions as far as we please without destroying the capacity of the substance to produce physiological reactions. On the contrary, as soon as its original capacity is reduced to a minimum by dilution, further dilution gives it the power to cause even stronger reactions, of a different and usually opposite kind. The second capacity rises through stages to a variable maximum as dilution proceeds.

"A simple calculation shows that not a single molecule of the original substance will remain in solution after a certain degree of dilution is reached. Yet the biological and other reactions continue long after this, and are even enhanced.

"What this potentising process shows is that, by repeated expansion in space, a substance can be carried beyond the ponderable conditions of matter into the realm of pure functional effect. The potentisation of physical substances thus gains a significance far wider than that of its medical use."

Dr. Ernst Lehrs: *Man or Matter*. Faber and Faber.

During the following two days nothing happened. The rabbit population were still very much in evidence guzzling the spring vegetables and apparently quite oblivious of their fate. The peasants and farm labourers breathed a sigh of relief. The 'Wizard' was apparently an ordinary mortal after all. Count Keyserlingk would have to permit shooting once more!

Dr. Steiner pointed out to the members of the conference that homeopathic treatments were unlike their allopathic counterparts which induced an immediate physical reaction. His homeopathic concoction would take three days to penetrate the life organism of the rabbits. By dusk the following night there would not be a single rabbit in the whole area. He described how vermin throughout the world would slowly build up a resistance to the allopathic poisons at present in use. And he predicted correctly that science would be hard put to it in the second half of the century to devise poisons which had any effect on vermin. The type of pest control which he was now demonstrating would, by necessity, be recognised by future generations as the only possible answer to the problem.

When dawn broke the following morning thousands of rabbits were to be seen in a huge cluster round an old ash tree in the paddock. They appeared to be in a state of intense excitement, restless, quivering, running up and down and sniffing the air with obvious perturbation. From all directions they were joined by more and more rabbits that came dashing across the fields, running across farmyards and stables, and even scampering down garden paths, apparently oblivious of the dangers of human contact.

Reports came in from all parts of the vast estate and neighbouring farm lands. Throughout the entire area rabbits were quitting their burrows and warrens as though their natural habitat was now a threat to their very survival, forming other huge clusters in a condition of frantic agitation. By late afternoon the separate clusters had joined together in a single mass in a far corner of the estate. Shortly before dusk the entire rabbit population disappeared in one enormous panic-stricken swarm heading in a north-easterly direction towards the distant wastelands and marshes. No rabbit would be seen nor rabbit spoor discovered on the Keyserlingk lands for many years to come.

There was to be a sinister sequel to this astonishing demonstration of pest control at Koberwitz. The Nazis repeated the experiment with the 'potentised' ashes of the testicles, spleens and portions of the skin of virile young Jews in an attempt to drive the remnant of the Jewish population out of Germany for ever. It was the last horrific act in the final solution when the Third Reich was collapsing before the onslaught of the Allied Armies. The order to carry out this diabolical plan came from Hitler himself, but the evil genius who conceived it was Reichsführer SS Heinrich Himmler.

Born in an apartment directly above the famous Liebig Apothecary in Liebigstrasse, Munich, Himmler became fascinated by the whole realm of chemistry at an early age. At eighteen, he enrolled at Munich High School for a diploma in Agriculture in which he specialised in farm chemistry. His single job before joining the Nazi Party was with a firm* concerned with the production of agricultural fertilisers. He worked as a laboratory assistant in a department engaged on field tests.

It was through Adolf Hitler, who loudly proclaimed his confidence in Homeopathy and was attended by homeopathic physicians, that Himmler was first introduced to the idea of potentising. It was not long before he came into possession by illicit means of Dr. Steiner's Koberwitz lectures on Bio-Dynamic farming and realised the immense possibilities in homeopathic treatments to the soil and the application of potentising in the elimination of plant and animal diseases. A branch of the Ahnenerbe was later set up to carry out experiments in this aspect of farming. Himmler also learned all the details of the homeopathic techniques of pest control but was too involved at this time (1929) in building up the SS to undertake experiments in this direction.

* Stickstoff GmbH (Nitrogen), Ltd.

The possible application of such pest control in the human sphere did not arise in Himmler's mind until 1943 when the Final Solution was fully under way and he was involved in an attempt to liquidate some thirty million people, including the total destruction of European Jewry, the Polish intelligentsia and a large slice of the Slavonic Race.

After the fall of Stalingrad and the retreat of the German Armies on the Russian Front, it became gradually apparent to Himmler that the Germans might eventually lose the war and become overrun by their enemies. The urgent call for all available manpower to serve the expansion of the war economy put an end to the mass killings of Jews, Poles and Slavs. Himmler was faced with a new problem: how to sterilise these 'subhumans' so that they could no longer reproduce their species.

The first attempts to achieve an efficient and practical method of sterilisation were conducted on Jewish males at Auschwitz with *Caladium Seguinum*, a drug recommended for the purpose by Dr. Alfred Pokorny. Its failure to achieve the desired effect initiated further attempts by Dr. Karl Clauberg to sterilise thousands of Jewesses at Ravensbrück. For a while Himmler placed the utmost confidence on Professor Gebhardt's rapid techniques of sterilisation surgery but the procedure was found to be too slow and cumbersome to achieve the sterilisation of the entire Jewish race. Dr. Victor Brack's plan to castrate Jewish males by means of powerful X-rays held far more promise and met with Himmler's immediate approval until it was found that a single costly installation could only effectively castrate 200 Jewish males per day. What possible use were such techniques to a man who had been incarcerating on average some 50,000 Jews a week in Gas Ovens?

After the Allied invasion of Europe in 1944 and further disastrous reversals on the Eastern Front, Himmler was confronted with yet another problem: how to ensure that the remnant of European Jewry would quit the Continent for all time after the final defeat of the Third Reich. It was to achieve this aim that he conceived the idea of the application of pest control to humans.

Before moving to live beside the lake at Lindenfycht, Heinrich Himmler had himself run a small poultry farm at Munich-Trudering where he had been faced with the problem of liquidating rats with poisons which did not infect his own fowls. As a result of this experience, he ordered that the first experiments in pest control should be carried out with the potentised ashes of rats.

A branch of the Ahnenerbe under the direction of Wolfram von Sievers were ordered to undertake the experiments in all haste, but only one out of five potency samples was effective in a rat-infested area neighbouring on Auschwitz. There was one vital factor which the Nazis had overlooked, and that was the time factor. For some reason the potentised ashes only achieved their maximum functional effect at particular times of the year, for apparently such potencies were sensitive to extra-terrestrial influences in the manner that the phases of the moon effect plant germination and growth. In short, the technique involved astrological aspects the key to which they did not have.

In a long and exhaustive investigation after the War Dr. Walter Stein discovered that the first potentised ashes of male Jews were injected into Jewish inmates at Buchenwald. These experiments were carried out in Block 46 by Wolfram von Sievers and Dr. Eugen Haagen, both later executed for crimes against humanity. At this time the Camp inmates were also forced to submit themselves to other vaccines such as typhus, diphtheria, cholera, small pox, etc., and the results of the pest control injections were destroyed along with the records of the other inhuman experiments in which thousands are known to have died horrible deaths. Nor could these particular victims be identified by the nature of their reaction to the injections of the potentised ashes, for all the human guinea pigs in this block attempted to escape from it only to be kept inside by the prison foreman Arthur Dietzsche with a cat-of-nine-tails.

Himmler appears to have believed that a successful potentisation in this respect depended on discovering the physiological basis of the racial characteristics of the Jewish people. Wolfram von Sievers decided to make a special collection of Jewish skulls and corpses so that researches could be made on the blood and bone marrow and the organs of reproduction. The Wehrmacht were ordered to capture alive Jewish-Bolshevik Commissars whom Himmler considered to be the prototypes of this 'sub-human race'. Instructions were relayed as to how the heads should be severed from the shoulders and forwarded separately in hermetically sealed containers. For the sake of secrecy Himmler countermanded this order to the Army on the Eastern Front and decreed that the required specimens should be selected from the living inmates of Auschwitz. These pseudo-scientific researches were still under way when the Allied Armies crossed the Rhine and penetrated into the heart of Germany.

Many rumours, later the subject of a number of black books, circulated in post-war Germany that the SS had scattered the ashes from the gas ovens in the concentration camps across the length and breadth of the Reich. Yet no satisfactory explanation could be given for such an action except in such superstitious terms as 'the final act of sacrifice to the powers of darkness'. These rumours only reflected a half-truth. It was not the ashes which were scattered but the potentised ashes which whisked into the wind like a fine spray.

Immediately following the defeat of the Third Reich in April 1945 there was an exodus of a high proportion of the remnant of the Jewish race from the Continent. Was it the result of this diabolical form of pest control? Or was it because the Jews believed that man's inhumanity to man would always be the rule rather than the exception on this blood-soaked continent?

EPILOGUE

After the Anschluss, when Adolf Hitler claimed the Spear of Longinus as his own personal possession, the ancient weapon remained in Vienna, where it was guarded in the Weltliche Schatzkammer by a posse of picked SS under the direct command of Dr. Ernst Kaltenbrunner, SS Führer, Austria.

Hitler was determined to proceed with an aura of legality concerning the transfer of his talisman of power, together with the Reichskleinodien, back to Germany. In a long drawn-out procedure, which bordered on farce, a special law was enacted proclaiming the historical right of Germany to the treasures and reliquaries which had rested in the Hapsburg Treasure House for more than a hundred years.

Adolf Hitler spoke publicly about the special decree of the Emperor Sigismund who had stated in the fifteenth century that it was 'the Will of God' that the Heilige Lance and the Crown, Sceptre and Orb of the Germanic Dynasty should never leave the soil of the Fatherland. Official historians joined in the debates to trace the history of the Reichskleinodien from the moment Napoleon's armies approached Nuremberg in 1796 when the treasures were removed via Regensburg to Vienna. A certain Baron von Hugel, the Imperial envoy with the Reich-Diet at Regensburg, was named the traitorous villain of the piece. German newspapers described how the Regalia of the Holy Roman Empire had been passed into his care and how he had betrayed his promise to return the treasures to Nuremberg at the earliest possible date. And how on the dissolution of the Holy Roman Empire in 1806, the wily Baron had passed the cherished Germanic symbols to the Hapsburgs at a price; a theft which was not disclosed until three years after Napoleon's final defeat at Waterloo. The Hapsburg Emperors had scornfully refused to return the Spear and the Crown Jewels to the City of Nuremberg, "maintaining this breach of right solely by their superior power."

The Goebbels Propaganda Ministry prepared the Austrian people for the daylight robbery of their historic heirlooms with a calculated and sustained campaign to project the historical justice of their removal to Nuremberg; even publishing a series of pictures illustrating how the German Kings were crowned in Aachen before visiting Rome to be touched on both shoulders with the Spear of Longinus to signify their right to the title of Holy Roman Emperors. Only Heinrich Himmler, normally fascinated by such aspects of Germanic history, failed to understand why his Führer bothered with such trifles. In his opinion the Spear should have been despatched on the instant to the shrine of Henry The Fowler, in the SS Sanctuary in the Wewelsburg.

Meanwhile Hitler himself had personally selected the exact place where the Spear of Destiny should rest on its arrival in Germany. Thirty years earlier when the youthful Hitler had first seen the historic talisman of power, he had been inexplicably reminded of the mystical lines in Wagner's opera, *The Meistersingers*:

> And still I don't succeed.
> I feel it yet I cannot grasp it.
> I can't retain it, nor forget it,
> And if I grasp it, I cannot measure it.

And now he claimed that it had been revealed to him in trance that the Spear of Destiny, the very inspiration of his meteoric rise to power, should rest in the ancient Hall of St. Katherine's Church in Nuremberg where once the famous 'Battles of Song' of the Meistersingers had taken place in the Middle Ages in the presence of this legendary talisman of revelation. St. Katherine's, originally built as a convent in the

330

thirteenth century, was now prepared to become a Nazi War Museum where the loot accumulated in each victorious stride towards world conquest would be put on view.

Besides the inspired choice of the Meistersinger's Hall, Nuremberg itself, universally accepted as the 'Mecca' of the Nazi movement, was the ideal City to house this symbol of world power. Not only the historic fortress city where the Spear had been kept for almost five hundred years, Nuremberg was also the centre where the Nazi Party rallies took place each year. It was at these stupendous propaganda spectacles, which Hitler called 'Feasts of the Blood', that he had always given his most inspired speeches to the German people. Like a demonic meistersinger his magical Klingsor powers of oratory elated the assembled Nazis in the torchlit arena into paroxysms of fanaticism and hysteria.

Oberbürgermeister Willi Liebel, the man who master-minded the rallies, was selected as the new guardian of the Spear On 13th October, exactly six months after the Anschluss, the Spear, together with the other items of the so-called Haps-burg Regalia, were loaded on an armoured train guarded by SS and brought from Vienna across the German border to Nuremberg. Ernst Kaltenbrunner, later to replace the mur-dered Reinhardt Heydrich as Chief of the Political Intelligence Department, travelled in the compartment with the Spear. A national holiday was proclaimed throughout Germany to celebrate the momentous return of the precious Insignia of the ancient German Emperors to the Fatherland.

Crowds from all over Germany massed in the ancient city, now emblazoned with Nazi flags and swastikas and garlanded with flowers, to watch the arrival of the SS train bringing the treasures back to the homeland. Troops lined the route between the Bahnhof and St. Katherine's Church while armoured cars took the Imperial Regalia on the last stage of its journey to the Meistersinger's Hall. Willi Liebel, surrounded by Nazi hierar-chies, waited at the entrance of the Church to receive the official presentation from Kaltenbrunner on behalf of every loyal German in the Austrian Gau. And according to the plebiscite which followed ten days after the Anschluss that meant 99.8 per cent of the total population.

All was prepared for the instant display of the Germanic Insignia within St. Katherine's. Day by day for several weeks to come there would be long queues outside the Church awaiting their turn to get a glimpse of the treasures—the tenth-century Crown which had once been worn by such heroes as Otto The Great, Frederick Hohenstauffen and Barbarossa. Imperial Globe, sceptres, swords and jewelled ornaments. And there were other items, too, to delight the Bavarian population who had somehow managed to become fanatical Nazis and yet remain devout Roman Catholics. Such items as "a monstrance with part of the cloth of the 'Last Supper' "; "Part of the apron of our Lord"; a splinter from the true Cross; "a golden box with three links from the chains of the Apostles Peter, Paul and John"; "the Purse of St. Steven". Even "a tooth of John The Baptist."

Among the first batch of visitors allowed into the Meister-singer's Hall were many of the original members of the inner core of the Thule Gesellschaft, now incorporated into Heinrich Himmler's Occult Bureau. They were among the very few who knew that the Heilige Lance was the only significant item among the strange assortment of Germanic antiquities and religious reliquaries. For Professor Karl Haushofer, one of the honoured guests at the official review of the treasures in their new abode, it was a day of triumph. The architect of Adolf Hitler's plan to conquer the world, he knew that the arrival of the Spear of Destiny on German soil was the signal for hostilities to begin. Less than a year later the world was at war.

The Spear of Destiny stood at the central piece of the Reichs-kleinodien and Reichsheiligtümer in St. Katherine's Church throughout the lightning and victorious Polish campaign and the shattering and totally unexpected *Blitzkrieg* defeat of the French Armies when the British escaped by the skin of their teeth via Dunkirk. But Adolf Hitler's confidence that there was no need to find a permanent wartime shelter for his Talisman of Power proved sadly misplaced as RAF bombers penetrated further and further into the Third Reich and began reducing its great cities to rubble.

The industrialisation of Nuremberg had been initiated after the Nazis came to power and now the historic city offered a whole number of genuine military targets including the M.A.N. factories manufacturing engine parts for Panzer tanks and German U-Boats and the large complex of the Siemens-Schuckert electrical works adjoining the vast railway shunting yards. The first RAF raid did extensive damage to the area around St. Katherine's, blowing off a part of the roof of the Church itself. No time was lost in removing the Lance and the other treasures into the deep vault of Kohn's Bank on the corner of the Königstrasse.

After the fall of Stalingrad when the whole of Germany went into mourning and the Nazi hierarchy first tasted the possibility of defeat, Adolf Hitler ordered that a permanent hiding place should be found for his Talisman of Power somewhere in the vicinity of Nuremberg. Heinrich Himmler and Ernst Kaltenbrunner made a special visit to the city to discuss the various alternatives suggested by Willi Liebel.

The historical cast of mind of the Reichsführer SS inevitably settled for the idea of opening up one of a whole warren of tunnels which had been built several hundred feet below Nuremberg Fortress in medieval times. It was within one such tunnel 900 feet below the Castle that the Reichskleinodien had been temporarily hidden away in 1796 before the historic Lance had been smuggled to Regensburg out of Napoleon's grasp. And now Heinrich Himmler ordered that no expense should be spared in opening up and widening this tunnel and in building an air-conditioned vault in which the Spear and the ancient Germanic Regalia could be hidden.

Only trusted Nazis who could be depended upon to maintain absolute secrecy regarding the project were employed in the work. The entrance to the ancient tunnel lay behind one of the seventeenth-century gabled houses in the Oberen Schmied

333

Gasse (Upper Blacksmith's Alley). The Schmied Allee, a narrow lane of picturesque buildings, backs on one side onto the towering escarpment above which the historic Fortress stands. The tunnel was cleared and widened and extended some 90 feet into the rock where at its furthest end an air-conditioned bunker was erected. Massive steel doors embedded in concrete guarded the entrance to the vault where the treasures were to be deposited.

Oberbürgermeister Willi Liebel selected two trusted men to direct the work, Stadtrat Heinz Schmeissner, a building expert on the city council, and Dr. Konrad Freis, who was in charge of the air raid precautions for the area. The presence of these men in the Oberen Schmied Gasse was likely to cause little suspicion. When the work was completed, Dr. Freis was given the key to the lock on the vault doors and Heinz Schmeissner held the secret of the five numerals on its intricate coding device. Neither man could open the vault alone. Only Willi Liebel held both the key and the code.

The Reichskleinodien together with the Reichsheiligtümer (Holy Reich Relics) were removed by night from the deep vault of Kohn's Bank at 26 Königstrasse in the heart of the city and loaded onto a truck. Willi Liebel ordered the driver to take a long and devious route to the Oberen Schmied Gasse so that even the Bank authorities should believe that the ancient treasures had been driven out of the area. The truck was driven through the innocent-looking garage doors of the gabled house which now disguised the tunnel entrance. A false back wall of the garage noiselessly slid sideways and the vehicle moved down the secret passage to the huge iron doors of the vault 900 feet below the eleventh-century Fortress. The Heilige Lance had found a hiding place where the enemies of Germany would never find it!

It was now the turn of fate to take a hand in the fulfilment of the age-old legend of the Spear of Longinus. A massive air raid on the 13th October, 1944, RAF bombers by night and wings of US Flying Fortresses throughout the day, wrought a terrible destruction on the Mecca of Nazism. Nuremberg became a heap of smouldering ruins. Bombs overshooting their targets turned the Oberen Schmied Gasse into a chaos of burning wreckage and rubble. The disguised entrance to Adolf Hitler's secret vault was exposed nakedly to the light of day. The outer garage doors were blown away and the sliding false wall reduced to twisted metal. Soon the news of a secret passage leading to a bunker with huge iron doors leaked through the town, even reaching the ears of slave workers and British and American prisoners of war. Willi Liebel ordered that work should commence immediately to camouflage the gaping entrance to the tunnel. Though the work was both quickly and efficiently carried out, orders came from Heinrich Himmler that an alternative hiding place must be found.

And now it happened that the most extraordinary and comical misunderstanding took place which was so mysteriously to fulfil the legend of the changing ownership of the Spear of Destiny.

Neither Heinz Schmeissner nor Konrad Freis, though both trusted executives on the Council of Germany's most fanatically Nazi city, had any knowledge of the real significance of the Spear of Longinus; nor indeed of its legend or the vital role it had played in the very inception of Nazism and Hitler's rise to power. And when Willi Liebel enumerated the items to be hidden in an alternative hiding place, he called the Holy Lance by its official title, "The Maurice Lance". It so happened that one of the six central pieces of the Reichskleinodien was a sword known as "The Maurice Sword". And it was the Sword of St. Maurice which was hidden instead of the Lance of St. Maurice, the central piece of the Reichsheiligtümer.

A plumber named Baum was ordered to prepare in secret a number of copper containers in which to place the Imperial Crown, the Sceptre, Reichsapfel and the Sword of St. Maurice. These items of the Imperial Regalia were wrapped in glass wool, sealed in the containers, and carried by night into the basement of a school on the Panier Platz (Panier's Square is at the entrance of the Oberen Schmied Gasse). The Infants' School, also built into the hill below the Fortress, was used as an air-raid shelter, its deep basement offering excellent protection. From the corner of the basement a trap door opened into a large cavern in the rock. The containers were placed in a niche in the roof of this cave. The niche was walled up by specially selected workmen in the presence of Schmeissner, Freis and Julius Lincke, another Building Department executive. Willi Liebel appeared for a few minutes. According to Heinz Schmeissner the Bürgermeister was in a state of great distress. News had just come through that American tanks and motorised infantry had reached Gemunden and Hammelburg. Nuremberg would soon be in the very centre of the battle area. Such was Liebel's state of mind—he was on the brink of suicide—that the error over the Spear of Longinus was not noticed. The date was 30th March, 1945.

An elaborate decoy was set up to give the impression that the Imperial Regalia had been removed from Nuremberg and taken out of Franconia to a hiding place in another part of Germany.

In the presence of Willi Liebel, still unaware of the dreadful error which had been made regarding his Führer's cherished talisman, a convoy of vehicles with both a Gestapo and SS escort drove into the Oberen Schmied Gasse in broad daylight. No attempt was made to hide the apparent reason for the visit. A large number of wooden boxes were brought out of the tunnel entrance and loaded onto the trucks. With a blaring of sirens the convoy drove off. A rumour was circulated throughout the City that all the ancient Germanic treasures had been dropped to the bottom of Lake Zell near Salzburg.

After the defeat of Germany confirmation was found that the orders to carry out this counterfeit operation had come directly from Heinrich Himmler, who shared the real secret of the temporary hiding place under the Panier Platz with Ernst Kaltenbrunner and Muller, head of the Gestapo.

According to the files of the American Army Intelligence Service: "The information so far obtained suggests that the order to bring the Imperial Insignia to a place of safe-keeping came from

Himmler. Apart from Himmler and the Nürnberg city officials
who were charged with their removal (to the Panier Platz), only
Kaltenbrunner, the chief of the German Security Service, and
Muller, the head of the Gestapo, may have been informed of the
true location of the Crown Insignia. At a meeting of the department heads of the Reichssicherheitshauptamt, which took place
in Berlin on 1st April, e.g., one day after the actual removal of the
insignia, Muller reported to Kaltenbrunner 'The Imperial
Insignia have been sunk in a lake by reliable agents of mine.'
Kaltenbrunner's only reply was: 'Good!' The source of this
information is Oberführer Spacil, who as head of AmtII of the
Reichssicherheitshaupt, had to attend the meeting. Spacil inferred from this exchange that Kaltenbrunner must have details
of the operation, since otherwise he would have asked questions
about it. From the remark of Muller, however, it may also be
inferred that the idea of covering up the tracks of the removal by
the fictitious story that the insignia had been sunk to the bottom
of a lake, must also have originated in the highest circles of the
German Security Service, and that the orders to stage a fake
removal of the insignia in Nürnberg came from Berlin. The fact
that not even the heads of the Reichssicherheitshauptamt were
considered worthy of being initiated into the secret illustrates the
political importance attached to it.

"On the ground of these facts and conversations between captured SS officials, which were reported by Third Army Intelligence Center, it would appear that the Imperial Insignia were
slated by the chiefs of the German Security Service to become the
symbols of the future German resistance movement. Oberbürgermeister Liebel of Nürnberg may have been aware of this role
of the Insignia. The other city officials who participated in their
removal, this investigator believes, were not.

> quoted from "Report on Recovery of Imperial German In-
> signia of Holy Roman Empire", MGO, Detachment E–203,
> Company C, 3rd Military Government Regiment, AP403.
> USA.

When, three months before the defeat of Germany, Dr.
Walter Stein had advised Sir Winston Churchill that the Holy
Lance and the Imperial Regalia might become symbols of an

underground German resistance after the war, his advice was not acted upon. Only later in March, 1945, when Allied intelligence reports brought news of the intended Werewolf underground movement and plans for a last-ditch resistance in the Hartz mountains, was his suggestion to form a special Section to trace the Imperial Insignia taken seriously. This Section, under the command of Captain Walter Thompson was attached to the American 7th Army preparing the final onslaught on Nuremberg.

"Defend Nuremberg to your last drop of blood," the Führer of the collapsing Third Reich signalled to Gauleiter Karl Holz and the 20,000 SS troops defending the spiritual home of Nazism.

The battle for Nuremberg began on the 16th April. It was one of the fiercest engagements of the war. Elsewhere in Germany the armies were in total rout. General Model had been defeated in the Ruhr with heavy casualties, and 300,000 men under his command had surrendered to the advancing British and American troops. The German 1st Army Group in Franconia alone remained intact and was engaged in fighting a rearguard action preparatory to a last all-out stand in the Hartz mountains and the Austrian Alps.

The US 7th Army sought to annihilate this last line of German resistance in the West with a pincer movement to surround the enemy in Nuremberg after a terrifying bombardment from the air and a creeping artillery barrage, which put a wall of steel around the city. The fighting was by no means one-sided. The Germans defending Nuremberg had mustered a hundred Panzer tanks and twenty-two regiments of artillery.

German civilians, men, women and youths, armed themselves to stand alongside the SS in bitter street fighting in which the veteran American 45th 'Thunderbird' Division suffered heavy casualties. The fanatical SS detachments defending the infamous Nazi Congress Hall, which Adolf Hitler once called the heart of Nazism, flung back nine bloody US assaults before dying to a man. No mercy was shown on either side.

Nuremberg became a smouldering inferno. When fighting ended on 20th April, there was hardly a building standing in the once beautiful Gothic city. While Adolf Hitler was celebrating his 56th birthday with champagne in Berlin, the Stars and Stripes were hoisted in the Adolf Hitler Platz in Nuremberg and the band of the US Third Division marched across the rubble-ridden square playing the 'Star Spangled Banner'.

Meanwhile the Section concerned with tracing the Imperial Regalia was searching Nuremberg for Bürgermeister Willi Liebel who had officially taken charge of the treasures when they were moved from Vienna to St. Katherine's Church in 1938. But the burly black-haired Nazi to whom Adolf Hitler had entrusted the original copy of the infamous "Nuremberg Laws", which glorified Aryan blood and relegated Jews to the status of sub-humans, was nowhere to be found. Apparently genuine informants insisted that he had not been seen in the streets of the city during the fighting. In fact, Liebel had committed suicide on the eve of the fall of the city, but his body was not discovered until the afternoon of 25th April. A party of German civilians, rounded up to bury the dead strewn around the ruins of Nuremberg, discovered his corpse in the basement of the Palmenhof, the local Gestapo and SS headquarters. One of these civilians has described the scene:

"On the 25th April in the cellar of the Palmenhof there was still one corpse. We went down into the basement accompanied by an American soldier. The passages and rooms were in wild disorder. The place had been looted. Suitcases, trunks and cupboards lay open and the belongings of the Police Praesidium were scattered everywhere. The floors were covered in blood. We waded through piles of silk underwear, stockings, dresses, boxes of cigars and packets of cigarettes. In some rooms there were carefully stored crates of expensive wines. Everywhere there were leather cases, handbags, uniforms and other items. In the room belonging to the SS Führer there was a body on an Ottoman. The figure was still sitting but sunk into itself. It was the corpse of a man in the uniform of a *folksturmann*. The smell was so strong that one member of the party had to leave the room in revulsion. I had

339

brought a gas mask and was able to approach nearer. The dead man's face was unrecognisable because it was completely covered in dry blood. We pulled the heavy corpse up the stairs and out into the open air where we dumped it down on the Jacobsplatz We hosed it all over. I removed the blood from the face with cotton wool. It was Willi Liebel. All we found on him was a handkerchief with the initials WL and a ring on his finger. All other means of identification were missing. The cause of his death was a bullet in his head. We took him to the cemetery and buried him near the south-west entrance."

The following day SS Colonel Karl Wolf, garrison commander, gave information under interrogation about Willi Liebel's suicide. He had shot himself on the 19th April. "When I told Liebel that the Gauleiter Karl Holz was in action against the Americans, he was unhappy because he was not out there fighting too. He feared that the Gauleiter would not come back and he would be left alone. Liebel then talked about Nuremberg, of its proud history and its fall which was about to take place. He assured me that if he did not die in battle, he was determined never to allow himself to be captured. He did not want to appear before the world as a defendant in a show trial. At about 12.30 Liebel left me. He appeared very depressed. He was hardly gone when I heard a sharp report. I hurried outside and found him in the Gauleiter's room of the bunker. He lay dead on a plank bed, shot in the head. The revolver had fallen from his hand." The discrepancy between Wolf's statement and the position in which Liebel had been found raised questions as to why his body had been moved and searched. Had he some evidence upon his person which would have led the Americans to the discovery of the Imperial Regalia?

The next day—28th April—the American Intelligence found and interrogated Willi Liebel's secretary, Dreykorn. All they got was an absolute denial of any knowledge of the whereabouts of the ancient Germanic treasures, except for a repetition of the rumour that they had been dropped to the bottom of Lake Zell. Dreykorn insisted that all the secret folders concerning the Reichskleinodien and the Reichsheiligtümer **had** been destroyed by fire during an air raid on the city.*

Ten days after the fall of Nuremberg the American military intelligence agents had utterly failed to discover the hiding place in the Oberen Schmied Gasse. It was not until 30th April, the day that Adolf Hitler committed suicide in Berlin, that the secret passage in the Blacksmith's Alley was unearthed. And then only by accident!

The entrance to the tunnel had once more been exposed to the daylight in the pounding air raid which had preceded the assault on the city but had been bricked up again immediately and covered over with a huge pile of rubble. On the 19th April the US heavy artillery had opened up on Nuremberg and shells had pulverised the street and blasted away a corner of the brickwork leaving an aperture some two feet wide above the rubble.

At around 2 o clock on that brilliantly sunny morning of 30th April a party of G.I.s began searching the ruins of the Oberen Schmied Gasse below the towering Fortress which had now become the American 7th Army Headquarters. It is not recorded whether these troops were on official duty flushing out SS still in hiding in basements throughout the city, or whether on their own account they were after loot, food and liquor often found hidden away in the cellars of demolished houses.

One of these men found himself peering down from a pile of rubble into a wide tunnel which apparently stretched far into the murky darkness beneath the escarpment. Calling his companions who unslung their weapons, he led them down by

* "Lt. Horn (the officer who interrogated Dreykorn) had not been successful in his endeavours at securing the secret folders of Oberbürgermeister Liebel which contained the records of the transfer of the Regalia from Vienna to Nürnberg after the annexation of Austria in 1938. Some of the documents according to the testimony of Liebel's secretary, Dreykorn, were destroyed by fire in the Nürnberg air raid of 2 January 1945. A folder which survived this attack, Dreykorn claims, was burned on Liebel's order in March." "Report on Recovery of Imperial Insignia of Holy Roman Empire", Headquarters Military Government, Nuremberg.

torchlight to the far end of the secret passage which terminated with two immense steel doors with a lock and dialling device somewhat similar to an American bank vault. Whatever was behind those doors must be of paramount importance, they decided. While two of the party stood guard at the entrance to the hidden bunker, the others ran out to report their astonishing find to their Army H.Q.

The United States of America had become the new claimants to the Spear of Destiny. The time was 2.10 p.m., 30th April, 1945.

In another bunker fifty feet below the smouldering ruins which had once been the Reich's Chancellery in Berlin, Adolf Hitler was preparing his ritual suicide and Viking funeral.

The once magnificent Chancellery, a mighty Mausoleum with huge rooms, ponderous doors and massed candelabra, had been blasted into a heap of fragmented marble and porphyry slabs into which enemy shells now fell with deadly accuracy. The bright sunshine was hidden by the smoke of battle while the Führer remained skulking below in the Wagnerian twilight of the bunker, reached through a passage in the butler's pantry.

The capital was a blazing inferno. The moment of the Götterdämmerung had come. The Russians, who three days earlier had encircled Berlin, were now street by street closing the ring around it. The east part of the Tiergarten had been evacuated. Scenes of savage hand-to-hand fighting were to be seen at the Invaliden Station, in the Kant Strasse and Bismarck Strasse and across to Charlottenburg. Russian tanks had reached the East-West Axis only a few hundred yards away. The final siege of the Führer Bunker itself had begun. The man to whom the end of life meant the end of Germany itself was about to perish in the cataclysm of his own making.

The previous afternoon—29th April—one of the last items of news to reach the besieged bunker from the outside world concerned the humiliating end of Mussolini, Hitler's personal friend and fellow dictator. Mussolini and his mistress, Clara

Petacci had been apprehended at Como in an attempt to cross the border into Switzerland. They had been executed instantly by partisans and their bodies had been driven to Milan where they were strung up by the heels from lamp-posts on the Piazza. Later, the corpses were cut down to fall into the gutter where crowds had reviled them in a most obscene way.

Adolf Hitler, the man who had a terrible indulgence for blood-letting and had once even strung up a German Field Marshal on a meat hook, could expect an even worse fate from his enemies. For this reason he had decided upon suicide with Eva Braun, whom he had just married in a bizarre wedding ceremony in the bunker. Their bodies were then to be burned beyond recognition in the Chancellery Garden.

The last night of his life, while the remainder of the inmates of the bunker, with intense relief that the end was nigh, held a wild and drunken party in the canteen, Adolf Hitler dictated his last will and testament:

"After six years of war, which in spite of all setbacks will one day go down in history as the most glorious and heroic manifestation of the struggle for existence of a nation, I cannot forsake the city that is the capital of this State. . . . I wish to share my fate with that which millions of others have also taken upon themselves by staying in this town. Further, I shall not fall into the hands of the enemy, who require a new spectacle, presented by the Jews, to divert their hysterical masses.

"I have therefore decided to remain in Berlin and there to choose death voluntarily at the moment when I believe that the position of the Führer and the Chancellery itself can no longer be maintained. I will die with a joyful heart in the knowledge of the immeasurable deeds and achievements of our peasants and workers and of a contribution unique in history of our youth which bears my name. . . ."

And then there followed his parting message to the German people, the last recorded words of the mad genius who had attempted to conquer the world and failed:

"The efforts and sacrifices of the German people in this war have been so great that I cannot believe them to have been in vain. The aim must still be to win territory in the East for the German people."

"It was always understood that Hitler would remain true to his original programme, Weltmacht oder Niedergang—world power or ruin," says Professor Trevor-Roper in his superlative book, *The Last Days of Adolf Hitler*.

"If world-power was unattainable, then (it was agreed by all who knew him) he would make the ruin as great as he could, and himself, like Samson of Gaza, perish in the cataclysm of his own making. For Hitler was not a figure of Western Europe, however he sought to pose as its champion against Asiatic Bolshevism; nor did his melodramatic character respond to the Confucian ideal of a tidy, unobtrusive death. When he envisaged himself against an historical background, when his imagination was heated, and his vanity intoxicated, with flattery and success, and he rose from his modest vegetable pie and distilled water to prance upon the table and identify himself with the great conquerors of the past, it was not an Alexander or Caesar, or Napoleon that he wished to celebrate, but as the re-embodiment of those angels of destruction —of Alaric, the sacker of Rome, of Attila, 'the scourge of God', of Genghis Khan, the leader of the Golden Horde. 'I have not come into the world', he declared, in one of those messianic moods, 'to make men better, but to make use of their weaknesses'; and in conformity with this nihilistic ideal, this absolute love of destruction, he would destroy, if not his enemies, then Germany and himself and all else that might be involved in the ruins. 'Even if we could not conquer,' he had said in 1934, 'we should drag the world into destruction with us, and leave no one to triumph over Germany.' . . . And again, 'We shall never capitulate, no, never! We may be destroyed, but if we are, we shall drag a world with us—a world in flames'."

And now the end had come. The Russians had broken into the Wilhelmstrasse and debouched from the Tiergarten into the Potzdamerplatz. They were only one block away from the Führer Bunker. The moment had come to shoot himself.

His secretary, Frau Gertrud Jurge, has described the look in Hitler's eyes when he said farewell to her. "His eyes seemed to be looking far away, far beyond the walls of the Bunker."

Bormann and Goebbels and a party of officers from Hitler's personal staff waited in the passage outside their Führer's personal suite.

"A single shot was heard. After an interval they entered the suite. Hitler was lying dead on the sofa, which was soaked with blood. He had shot himself through the mouth. Eva Braun was also on the sofa, also dead. A revolver was by her side but she had not used it; she had swallowed poison. The time was half-past three."*

The Viking funeral followed. Hitler's personal valet, Heinz Linge, carried out his Führer's body wrapped in a field grey blanket which concealed the shattered head. Bormann brought out the body of Eva Braun dressed in a black gown. The corpses were carried out into the Chancellery garden during a lull in the bombardment, placed in a shell-hole and ignited with petrol. Goebbels, about to take his own life along with his wife and six children, made a resolute Nazi salute. And then the sudden opening up of the Red Army guns which sent shells spattering into the garden brought a quick end to the ceremony as the mourners scampered for cover. Adolf Hitler had passed into history. The Spear of Destiny had passed to the United States of America.

Meanwhile, back in Nuremberg, the chance discovery of the secret passage in the Oberen Schmied Gasse and the massive steel doors to the bunker had caused considerable excitement and speculation among the staff officers of the American 7th Army H.Q. who were now billeted in the chambers of the medieval castle some 900 feet directly above the vault.

Many officers were in favour of dynamiting the steel doors or

* *The Last Days of Adolf Hitler*: Hugh Trevor-Roper.

cutting them through with gas burners in order to discover immediately what could lay behind them. But Army Commander General Patches refused permission for either of these alternatives in case damage should be done to the unknown contents of the vault. He preferred to put the intelligence sleuths to work to find the key and the code.

The successful operator was a certain Lieutenant Walter William Horn (Service number 01326328), who was a member of the original Intelligence Section detailed to trace and recover the Imperial Regalia. Walter Horn, today a senior Lecturer at the Department of Sociology at the University of Berkeley, California, already had a shrewd idea of what had been hidden away in Hitler's secret bunker. He managed to round up both Heinz Schmeissner and Dr. Konrad Freis. Dr. Freis broke down under a rigorous interrogation, or, at least so Walter Horn thought. In reality Dr. Freis was not too concerned if the Americans should open the vault, for, as far as he knew, the most important items were safely bricked up in the second and still unknown hiding place under the Panier Platz. Freis handed over the key and admitted that his friend Heinz Schmeissner knew the code. Confronted with Freis's confession, Schmeissner offered his co-operation in opening the doors to the bunker.

The two Germans accompanied Lieutenant Horn down the ten-foot-high passage to the vault where Dr. Freis turned the large key and Schmeissner operated the five-figure code. Also present when the doors were opened were: Charles H. Andrews, Colonel, Infantry, Military Governor of Nuremberg; Captain Thompson, American Army Intelligence; Captain Rae, 'Arts Officer', Nuremberg Military Government. A host of other officers unnamed in the official report were also present.

The lights were switched on, the vault having its own separate generator besides the air-conditioning system. Lieutenant Horn was first inside the vault. The whole chamber was crammed full with Nazi loot brought from countless European nations.

Resting on top of an intricately carved ten-foot-high altar, which had been looted from the historic Church of St. Mary in

Krakow, Poland, stood an ancient leather case. Within the case, still resting on its faded red velvet dais, was the Spear of Longinus. The ancient weapon associated with the legend of world-historic destiny had seen many scenes in its passage through 2,000 years of history, but perhaps never so strange a setting as this secret underground vault which contained priceless antiquities, reliquaries, paintings, jewels and art treasures stolen from the peoples whom the Nazis had subjugated during their short and brutal reign of power.

While fellow officers gaped in astonishment at this vast array of precious loot, Lieutenant Horn and Captain Thompson quickly discovered that the Imperial Crown, the Sceptre, Reichsapfel, the Sword of St. Maurice and the Imperial Sword—indeed, the five items of the Reichskleinodien proper—were missing. An embarrassed Dr. Freis and Heinz Schmeissner, who were by this time backing discreetly out of the vault, were about to face another bout of interrogation.

The two men both told the identical story of how an unknown SS Colonel had taken delivery of these treasures from Willi Liebel at the entrance to the tunnel in the Schmied Gasse on 2nd April. Their story was accepted, and after making written statements, they were allowed to go free. Their evidence seemed to corroborate the general rumour circulating among captured SS that the treasures had been dumped on the bottom of Lake Zell in Austria.

Yet Lieutenant Horn was only half persuaded that the Reichskleinodien were at the bottom of the lake. He was not convinced. Instead, he decided to follow up the slight discrepancies in the statements of Freis and Schmeissner. His persistence led to the discovery of the second hiding place below the Panier Platz and the whole of the Imperial Regalia was recovered.*

* "The investigation in Nürnburg having come to a deadlock, Lt. Horn decided to confront Stadtrat Freis with Oberführer Spacil (Chief of the Sicherheitshauptamt) then suspected of being the SS officer to whom the Insignia had presumably been handed by Oberbürgermeister Willi Liebel and Freis.

None of the American Senators, who came to post-war Europe in droves, or the senior US Generals who travelled to Nuremberg to see the vast display of Nazi loot in the underground bunker in the Oberen Schmied Gasse, showed the least interest in the age-old legend of the Spear of Longinus. The

"Arrangements for Freis's arrest and transfer to Theatre Interrogation Center (Third Army) were made on July 28, 1945. The transfer took place on 3 August 1945. Under the effects of a night of solitary confinement and the pressure of a short interrogation which preceded the scheduled confrontation, Freis broke down. He confessed

a) that many of his previous statements concerning the removal of the Crown Insignia had been misleading and false;

b) that the Insignia had never been handed out to any SS men, but had been encased in masonry of the underground corridor system of the Panier Platz bunker in Nürnberg, by Freis himself, Oberbürgermeister Liebel, and Oberbaurat Linke;

c) that this event took place on the 31 March 1945;

d) that in order to cover the tracks of this removal a fictitious removal had been staged on 2nd or 3rd April 1945 with the assistance of local SS men;

e) that he was willing to reveal the location of the Insignia and to assist in their recovery.

"On 6 August 1945 Freis was taken back to Nürnberg. On the evening of the same day, and after he had been confronted with Freis's confession, Schmeissner also confessed. In the morning of 7 August 1945 Captain Thompson and Lt. Horn met with Freis and Schmeissner at the entrance of the Panier Platz bunker. Present also were: Dr. Gunter Iroche, Tech 5 LOHUIS, and Pfe. Dollar, and a mason. Freis and Schmeissner directed the party to the hiding place, a small room of the subterranean corridor system of the Panier Platz bunker, approximately 80 feet below the surface of the Panier Platz. After a hole had been chiseled through the brick wall of one of the small ends of this room, the four copper containers, with the Insignia were recovered. In the presence of all the persons who witnessed the recovery, the copper containers were transferred to their original place, the art cache underneath the Nürnberg Castle, where they are kept behind steel doors."

Recovery of Insignia. Nürnberg Military Government.
Report by: Walter W. Horn, 1st Lt. Inf.
HQ. US GP CC, RD&R Div.
MPA&A Branch, APO 742.

Freis and Schmeissner were subsequently taken before a General Court by the Americans on charges of making false statements and secreting artistic works. They were both sentenced to five years imprisonment and fined 25,000 Reich Marks. They were released after serving two years. The fines were quashed.

only exception was General 'Blood and Guts' Patton, one of the most colourful characters (and possibly one of the best Allied Commanders) of World War II.

General Patton, who had a historically orientated cast of mind, believed in reincarnation and had made a study of the search for the Holy Grail, appears to have been totally fascinated at the sight of the Spear of Destiny. He took the ancient talisman of power from its leather case and removed the golden sleeve which holds the two separate parts of the Spearhead together.

This enigmatic soul, who stopped off at the height of the battle in Sicily to visit Klingsor's castle at Kalot Enbolot in the heights above Monte Castello, demanded the presence of local German historians to fill him in on the entire history of the ancient weapon which was associated with the legend of world power.

Patton demanded to know the exact date on which the Nail had been inserted and was furious to hear that it was not known. He was insufferably rude to the fawning officials who showed such ignorance regarding the passage of the Spear through the centuries. "Were the winged flanges at the base taken from the metal removed to make room for the insertion of the nail?" he asked. "What Kings or Emperors had embossed the golden crosses both on the base of the head and on the nail itself?" Aides scampered round to find the answers to his countless queries.

General Patton was the only American General who realised the true significance of the fact that the USA were now the official possessors of the Spear of Destiny. And he knew, too, the terrible significance of the imminent fulfilment of its legend once again. For the United States had discovered the secret of the manufacture of the atom bomb and the dropping of these fearsome weapons upon Japan was expected to bring an immediate end to the war in the East.

To the veteran General, who still believed in the chivalry of war and would have preferred to have fought alongside Hannibal at Cannae than against Kesselring in the Ardennes, the atomic age meant the final ending of an era in which the individual still had some significance. And while holding the talisman of power in his hands he told his Aides that mankind was standing on the brink of the most evil epoch in the entire history of the planet. His young subordinates did not know about the Atom Bomb which was a most closely guarded secret at this time. They asked themselves what could be more evil than the Concentration Camps of Adolf Hitler's defeated regime, and they wondered if their General had finally gone off his head. General Patton left the bunker beneath Nuremberg Fortress in a sombre mood. Doom was written across the future of humanity unless human beings could live at peace with one another, and Patton could see in all clarity the danger of the new confrontation between America and Russia.

Soldiers from the Third Division were standing guard outside the massive steel doors of the bunker in the Oberen Schmied Gasse when American aircraft unleashed the first atom bombs on Hiroshima and Nagasaki. The atomic age had begun.

A controversy began as to where the Reichskleinodien and Reichsheiligtümer should rest when taken from the bunker. The US Army was not prepared to provide for ever a 24-hour guard on these priceless treasures. The newly-established Austrian Government demanded the return of what they called the Hapsburg Regalia to Vienna. The Germans protested that the ancient Germanic Insignia belonged to them.

"The Austrian Government having asked of the American Military Government of Germany the delivery of the Regalia of the Holy Roman Empire, guarded at present in Nuremberg, I beg to make the following statement, referring for fuller evidence to the folders and the historical and legal statements already in existence and in the possession of the Allied Military Government.

"Neither the Hapsburg family nor the Austrian-Hungarian Monarchy, nor indeed the Austrian Republic since 1919 have ever claimed ownership of the Regalia. These were kept in the

'Weltliche Schatzkammer' (Secular Treasury) in the Hofburg at Vienna as 'deposited', and were catalogued in a 'separates einiges Inventar' (separate own inventory).

"The regalia had got into the hands of the Hapsburgs, and consequently those of the Austrian Republic, by an illegal act of power. The claim to have them re-transferred into Germany has never rested, and at various occasions a solution negotiated with Austria seemed near at hand. The German people have a common interest and right for such asolution.

"The re-transfer of the Regalia to Nuremberg, in August 1938, was effected by an administrative ordinance of the Reich, made feasible by the union of Germany and Austria in March, 1938. It is true that, on this opportunity, stress was also laid on Nuremberg as the city of the Party Rallies, Nazi propaganda methods being what they were. The proper weight of the argument, however, derived from the fact that the city of Nuremberg has to claim the historical right to be the trustee of the Regalia, a right which still holds and which should not be left out of consideration.

"The present legal situation makes it clear that the Regalia are to be regarded as a foundation with a personality in their own right, and that nobody can claim them as property. The acting State authority is in a position to arrange at any time for a new trusteeship of this foundation. If any right can be mentioned, it would have to be merely a historical right, this speaking doubtlessly for Nuremberg rather than any other place.

"The case of the Regalia has nothing in common with the complex of the works of art looted or illegally confiscated by the Nazi Government or its officials in foreign countries. It should be exempted from this complex and be treated in a way entirely separate from such works of art.

"The Allied Military Government is therefore requested not to decide on the matter of the Regalia without a thorough examination of the legal and historical problems involved, and without a hearing of all parties concerned, and to consult the highest governmental and legal authorities who may be trusted to find a just solution."

On behalf of the City of Nuremberg:

Dr. Ernst Gunter Troche

First Director of the Germanic National Museum.

Nuremberg, 1 January 1946

The final decision came from General Dwight Eisenhower, the Commander of the Allied Armies in Europe. He said bluntly: Return the Hapsburg Regalia to Austria.

General Muller, US Military Governor of Bavaria, sent a cable to this effect to Lieut.-Colonel Charles Andrews, Military Governor of Nuremberg:

mg for bavaria
mg for Nuernberg

from omg for bavaria
to co mg det f 211   03 1620 jan 46
                                                         mag no 60
   you are directed to release to mister andrew charlie ritchie cma authorised representative for united states forces austria cma the holy roman jewels and regalia now in a repository under your jurisdiction pd transfer of custody will take place at nuernberg in the presence of mike fox able and able officer this headquarters pd you are directed to take all measures necessary to ensure safe expeditious removal of these objects from nurnberg pd paren cite george nan mike charlie uncle dash eight paren zero three one seven zero baker january.

signed Muller

pla rec
no 60 ok mg nuernberg/hr.

The doors of the vault in the Oberen Schmied Gasse were re-opened on 4th January, 1946, and the Imperial treasures were loaded aboard a convoy of jeeps. Under the wary eye of First Lieutenant Albright, Arts Officer attached to the Military Government of Nuremberg, the Imperial Regalia were loaded aboard a Dakota at Furth Airport and flown direct to Vienna.

Two days later—January 6th—General Mark Clark handed over the Reichskleinodien and the Reichsheiligtümer to the Burgomeister of Vienna. It was a short, informal ceremony with no official speeches. As a temporary expedient the Bürgermeister deposited the Hapsburg Regalia in the vault of the Austrian Postal Savings Bank.

Today the Spear of Longinus is back in the Weltliche Schatzkammer of the Hofburg. The talisman of world historic destiny stands on a faded red velvet dais within an open leather case in exactly the same spot in the Treasure House where Adolf Hitler first beheld it in 1909. It is on view to the public from Monday to Saturday from 9 a.m. to 6 p.m. Admission is free.

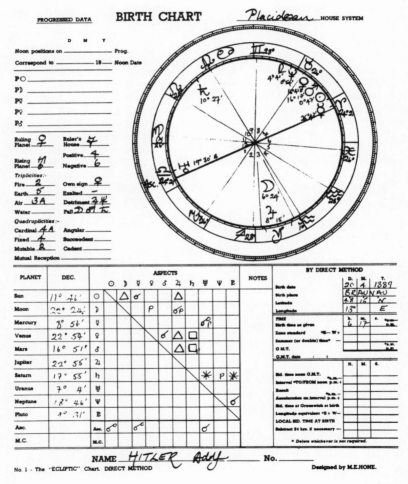

353

The Birth Chart of Adolf Hitler by P. I. H. Naylor with commentary by Jane Dunn

The most outstanding feature is unbounded, ruthless ambition. Being born on the Aries/Taurus cusp he is in good company with Stalin and Mussolini and a bevy of dictators. It is probably the strongest, most tyrannical time to be born.

Emotionally he is an odd mixture. Sun in Taurus and Libra ascending means he is fond of the Arts and should be well endowed with Venusian characteristics. *But* Venus conjunct Mars coarsens his sensuality and Venus square is *very inhibiting*. Definite sacrifice of happiness to an ideal, a material ambition or to a duty. Tends towards an exacting and selfish character with some very *cold* element in him somewhere. Marriage likely to be delayed or prevented altogether by this aspect. "Unhealthy expression of the sex urge." Self-torment and jealousy. Altogether very nasty.

Very interesting that Sun trine Jupiter = social climber, religiosity and *lust* for possessions and power; "the will to expand" in more ways than one.

Pluto in 8th house: suggestive influence upon other people. Fanaticism. Record achievements through tenacity and endurance.

Moon in 3rd: vivid powers of expression particularly emotive. Much changes of mood.

Mars square Saturn: again selfishness and egoism. Some text books say this indicates brutality, cruelty and blood lust, but not invariably the case, thank heavens. It can be directed and externalised so that the life is one of hardships and suffering, with likelihood of physical violence. Danger of strain and excess. Just finally a resumé of his good qualities to mitigate the gloom. Sun trine Jupiter: abundant wealth and success. Mental powers above the ordinary.

Venus trine Jupiter: feelings capricious and restless. Promotes popularity and affection, of great benefit to anyone who has to deal with the public—particularly if he has to amuse or please them, less good if he has to instruct or correct.

Mars trine Jupiter: "the native is often a propagandist or publicist and enjoys nothing more than acting the evangelist proclaiming the truth that sets men free".

These are only the obvious bits of his horoscope and not picked because they coincide to some extent with what I know of the man. It is a pretty powerful mixture whether it belongs to Adolf Bloggs or Hitler.

BIBLIOGRAPHY

Aron, R.: *Introduction to the Philosophy of History*. London, 1961
Assman, Kurt: *Deutsche Schicksalsjahre*. Wiesbaden, 1950
Bartz, Karl, *Als der Himmel brannte*. Hanover, 1956
Belgium, Ministry of Foreign Affairs. Events leading up to German invasion of Belgium in 1940.
Blavatsky, H. P.: *Isis Unveiled*
Bormann, Martin: *The Bormann Correspondence*
Bullock, Alan: *Hitler—A Study in Tyranny*. London, 1952
Butler, C. Dom: *Western Mysticism*. London, 1947.
Clausewitz, Karl von: *Principles of War*. London, 1944
Cohn, N.: *The Pursuit of the Millennium*. London, 1968
Collingwood, R. G.: *The Idea of History*. London, 1946
Croce, Benedetto: *Mit Hitler in die Macht*. Munich, 1935
Diels, Rudolf: *Lucifer ante Portas*. Stuttgart, 1950
Dietrich, Otto: *Mit Hitler in die Macht*. Munich, 1935
Egyptian Book of the Dead, The
Eisenhower, Dwight D.: *Crusade in Europe*. London. New York 1949
Eliade, M.: *Cosmos and History (The Myth of the Eternal Return)*. London 1955
Faithful Thinker, The: Anthology. Hodder & Stoughton
Fingarette, H.: *The Self in Transformation*. London, 1961
Fishman, Jack: *The Seven Men of Spandau*. London, 1954
Friedman, F.: *This was Auschwitz*. London, 1946
Frischauer, Willi: *Himmler*. Odhams, 1966
Gisevius, B.: *To the Bitter End*. London, 1948
Goerlitz, W.: *History of the German General Staff*. USA, 1953
Greiher, H.: *The End of the Hitler Myth*. Vienna, 1947
Goethe, J. W. von: *Faust*. Bayard Taylor translation
Halder, Franz: *Hitler as Tactician*. London, 1951
Halifax, Lord: *Fullness of Days*. London, 1957
Hanfstangel, Ernst: *Adolf Hitler—The Missing Years*. London, 1957
Hegel: Lectures on the Philosophy of History. London, 1902
Heiden, Konrad: *Der Führer*. London, 1945
Henderson, Sir Neville: *Failure of a Mission*. London, 1940
Hindenburg, Field Marshal Paul von Beneckendorff und von: *Aus Meinen Leben*. Germany, 1934

355

Hitler, Adolf: *Mein Kampf*. Munich, 1925
Howe, Ellic: *Urania's Children*. William Kimber, 1970
Jaspers, Karl: *The Question of German Guilt*. New York, 1947
Jung, C. G.: Kerenyi, C: *Essays on the Science of Mythology*. London, 1956
Kant, Immanuel: *The Philosophy of History*. London, 1902
Kaufman, Adams: *Non-Euclidian Mathematics*. Rudolf Steiner Press
Kelly, D. M.: *Twenty-Two Cells in Nuremberg*. London, 1947
King, Francis: *Ritual Magic in England*. Spearman 1970
  Sexuality, Magic & Perversion. Spearman, 1971
Kogon, E.: *The Theory and Practice of Hell*. England, 1950
Kubizek, August: *Young Hitler—Friend of my youth*. London, 1954
Laing, R. D.: *The Divided Self*. London, 1966
Lehrs, Dr Ernst: *Man or Matter*. Faber & Faber
Liddel Hart, B.: *The German Generals Talk*. London, 1949
Lilge, E.: *Abuse of Learning*. London, 1948
Ludecke, K.: *I Knew Hitler*. London, 1938
Ludendorff, General Erich: *Auf dem Weg zur Feldherrnhalle*. Munich, 1935
Mannstein, Field-Marshal Erich von: *Verlorene Siege*. Berlin, 1955
Marcuse, H.: *One Dimensional Man*. London, 1964
Michelet, J.: *Satanism and Witchcraft*. London, 1928
Morizot: *The Templars*. Rudolf Steiner Press
Nadell, G. H.: *Studies in the Philosophy of History*. Harper & Row, 1965
Olden, Rudolf: *Hitler, the Pawn*. London, 1936
Owen, Wilfred: *With Goebbels to the End*. Buenos Aires, 1949
Pauwels, Louis and Jacques Bergier: *The Dawn of Magic*. Gibbs & Phillips, 1963
Rauschning, Hermann: *Time of Delerium*. New York, 1946
  The Revolution of Nihilism
Reed, D.: *The Burning of the Reichstag*. USA, 1934
Reitlinger, G.: *The Final Solution*. London, 1953
  The SS—Alibi of a Nation. London, 1956
Shepherd, E.: *Scientist of the Invisible*. Hodder & Stoughton
Schellenberg, Walter: *The Labyrinth*. London, 1956
Schlabrendorff, Fabian von: *They Almost Killed Hitler*. New York, 1957
Schmidt, Paul: *Hitler's Interpreter*. London, 1951
Schroeter, H.: *Stalingrad*. London, 1958
Schultz, W.: *The Last 30 Days*. London, 1953
Schuschnigg, Kurt von: *Ein Requiem in Rot- Weiss-Rot*. Zurich, 1946
Shirer, William: *The Decline and Fall of the Third Reich*. London, 1960
Skorzeny, Otto: *Secret Memoirs*. New York, 1950
Spengler, Oswald: *The Decline of the West*. 2 vols. Heidelberg, 1918, 1922
  Jahre der Entscheidung. Munich, 1935
Steed, Wickam: *The Hapsburg Monarchy*. London, 1919

Stein, Leo: *I was in Hell with Niemoeller*. London, 1942

Stein, Walter Johannes: *The Ninth Century, World History in the Light of the Holy Grail*. Orient-Occident Verlag, Stuttgart, 1928

Steiner, Dr. Rudolf.: *The Philosophy of Spiritual Activity*
   Goethe's World Conception
   Theory of Knowledge according to Goethe's World Conception
   Macrocosm and Microcosm
   The Story of My Life
   Man as Symphony of the Creative World
   Knowledge of the Higher Worlds
   The Aetherisation of the Blood
   Das Goetheanum
   From Jesus to Christ
   Lectures on the Gospel of St John
   The Riddles of Philosophy

Summers, M.: *Witchcraft and Black Magic*. 1946

Taylor, Telford: *Sword and Swastika*. London, 1953

Thyssen, Fritz: *I paid Hitler*. London, 1954

Toynbee, Arnold: *Hitler's Europe*. London, 1954

Trevor-Roper, H. R.: *The Last Days of Adolf Hitler*, London, 1947

Tudor-Pole, Wellsley: *The Silent Road*. Spearman, 1960

Wachsmuth, Gunter: *Etheric Formative Forces in Cosmos Earth and Man Reincarnation*. Anthroposophical Publishing Co.

Whinkler, Frans E.: *Man the Bridge of Two Worlds*. Hodder & Stoughton

Widgery, A.: *The Meanings in History*. London, 1967

Zen Avesta

Zoller, A.: *Hitler Privat*. Dusseldorff, 1949

INDEX